ALEXANDER SMYTH

SMYTH COUNTY

HISTORY AND TRADITIONS
VIRGINIA

Goodridge Wilson

HERITAGE BOOKS
2013

HERITAGE BOOKS
AN IMPRINT OF HERITAGE BOOKS, INC.

Books, CDs, and more—Worldwide

For our listing of thousands of titles see our website
at
www.HeritageBooks.com

A Facsimile Reprint
Published 2013 by
HERITAGE BOOKS, INC.
Publishing Division
5810 Ruatan Street
Berwyn Heights, Md. 20740

Copyright © 1932 Goodridge Wilson

— Publisher's Notice —

In reprints such as this, it is often not possible to remove blemishes from the original. We feel the contents of this book warrant its reissue despite these blemishes and hope you will agree and read it with pleasure.

International Standard Book Numbers
Paperbound: 978-0-7884-0929-5
Clothbound: 978-0-7884-6829-2

DEDICATED
TO THE MEMORY OF
B. FRANK BUCHANAN
WHOSE LOVE FOR SMYTH COUNTY
and
KEEN INTEREST IN ITS HISTORY WAS
LARGELY RESPONSIBLE FOR THE
WRITING OF THIS BOOK

PREFACE

This book, written in commemoration of the one hundredth anniversary of the organization of Smyth as a county, is an attempt to preserve some of its history and traditions and show in readable form the development of its life, industries, and institutions.

In treating the period prior to the formation of the county the aim has been to show how occupation of the territory was effected and to record interesting incidents and major historic events occurring within the county limits, and to indicate at least to some extent the names and character of the earlier settlers. For this last purpose the list of early surveys culled from Summer's *Annals of Southwest Virginia* is given, which is a fair but incomplete index of landowners before 1800. Col. John Buchanan's journal is included because it is an interesting original document believed never to have been published before which gives an account of the nearest settlement to Smyth at the time of first explorations and shows what manner of business led this first of the surveyors to come into Smyth territory. Other documents copied directly from the originals and supposed to be published for the first time are Capt. John Buchanan's letter from Gwyn's Island, William Campbell's letter to his wife, and the Tory warning to Campbell. For other documents and much information concerning this period acknowledgment is due the publications of the Wisconsin Historical Society, and Pilcher's Historical Sketches of the Campbell and Kindred Families. It will be noticed that after leaving this preliminary period the aim has been to make each chapter a complete survey of the phase indicated in the chapter heading from the beginning to the present time.

While this work is not intended to be in any sense a reference book for genealogy, much family history is recorded in one way or another. Such family data as was supplied the author has been worked into the narrative. This sort of data was repeatedly requested through the county papers. Those who supplied it thereby rendered a distinct service in compiling the history. Those who failed to respond to these requests for family data will please remember their failure if it should seem that their families have not been accorded due recognition.

Grateful acknowledgment is made to Mr. L. P. Summers and Col. W. C. Pendleton for information derived from their books and given in person; to Mr. Herbert Kent, the efficient Clerk of Smyth County Courts, for invaluable help in searching out information from the court records; to Mr. J. P. Sheffey for searching and copying extracts from the court records; to Mr. John P. Buchanan for photostatic copies of original documents; to Miss Nellie C. Preston for access to official records of the War between the States and to original family documents; to Hon. J. W. Flannagan and Hon. J. Tyler Frazier for securing data from government files in Washington and in Richmond; to very many interested persons within and without the county too numerous to mention for supplying information verbally or by letter; to Dr. S. W. Dickinson, Rev. J. W. Cassell, Rev. Elridge Copenhaver, and Miss Miriam Sheffey for the sections written by them; to "Alkalite," a publication of the Mathieson Alkali Co., from which the greater part of the material about that company is taken; and to Miss Eleanor White, the very efficient stenographer who copied the entire manuscript.

The author also desires to record that the cost of publication has been subscribed by the following persons: B. F.

Buchanan, H. P. Copenhaver, R. T. Greer, J. D. Buchanan, George A. Wright, W. H. McCarty, Walter S. Johnston, J. A. Eller, Q. A. Eller, R. L. Anderson, W. F. Culbert and Sons, Mrs. C. C. Lincoln, W. H. Copenhaver, J. L. C. Anderson, H. L. Kent, Beattie Gwyn, Crockett Gwyn, I. W. Hutton, John D. Lincoln, C. C. Lincoln, Jr., Miss Nellie Preston, James D. Tate, J. Tyler Frazier, W. N. Neff, M. M. Seaver, Frank Sanders, C. S. Wassum, T. E. King, E. A. Holmes, B. E. Copenhaver.

CONTENTS

CHAPTER		PAGE
I	HEAD OF HOLSTON SURVEYS	1
II	COL. JOHN BUCHANAN'S JOURNAL	10
III	PERMANENT SETTLEMENT	16
IV	DUNMORE'S WAR	45
V	THE REVOLUTION	56
VI	COUNTY ORGANIZATION	73
VII	POLITICAL NOTATIONS	101
VIII	CHURCHES	120
IX	SCHOOLS	151
X	NEWSPAPERS	164
XI	INDUSTRIES	170
XII	BANKS	211
XIII	TRANSPORTATION	219
XIV	THE WAR BETWEEN THE STATES	235
XV	NEGROES OF SMYTH	261
XVI	WORLD WAR	266
XVII	SOUTHWESTERN STATE HOSPITAL	275
XVIII	TOWNS	282
XIX	BENJAMIN FRANKLIN BUCHANAN	340
XX	VILLAGES AND COMMUNITIES	350
XXI	LAUREL FARM	380
	INDEX	391

LIST OF ILLUSTRATIONS

	FACING PAGE
Alexander Smyth	*Frontispiece*
Old Smyth County Courthouse	72
Present Smyth County Courthouse	82
Aërial View of Mathieson Alkali Plant	196
Memorial Bridge at Seven Mile Ford	218
Covered Bridge on Marion Battlefield	252
Marion	296
Overflow from Marion Town Spring	304
Aërial View of Saltville	332
Benjamin Franklin Buchanan	340

CHAPTER I

HEAD OF HOLSTON SURVEYS

GEOGRAPHICALLY and historically Smyth County is on the head of the Holston. Geographically because the triple forks of the Holston take their rise within its bounds; historically because in its territory were made the beginnings of the famous Holston settlements of potent influence in making the nation that was to cross the western seas. Furthermore, some of the most influential leaders of that settlement in its critical, early stages dwelt in this territory. At an unknown date prior to 1747 an adventurous free-lance pioneer with the lure of the wild woods in his soul came alone into the western wilderness and made a corn right claim, pitching his camp within thirty feet of the head spring of the Middle Fork. He cleared and planted in corn thirteen acres of land for which, under Colonial law, he acquired title to thirteen hundred acres. As he thought upon the waters flowing westward, he just had to find out where those waters went. So he sold his corn right title, made him canoes, and voyaged down the present Tennessee, Ohio, and Mississippi Rivers to Natchez returning thence by land to his old home in Culpepper County, Virgina, and eventually settling farther down the Holston in Eastern Tennessee. His name was Stephen Holston. In the earliest records of this country the river is called the Indian River. The French called it the Cherokee River. The Indians called it Hogoheegee. After this wild adventurous voyage its name has been Holston River. So that the Holston takes its name from one who dwelt by its head spring in Smyth and who from Smyth began the first white man's voyage exploring its course to the "Father of Waters."

Mountain ranges divide the county into three great valleys, each of which gives birth to and is drained by its own fork of Holston. The North Fork, with one spring across the line of Bland and another in Tazewell, springs from the hollows and hills of the great Rich Valley and throughout Smyth and Washington counties carries off the surplus waters of all that rugged and splendid region. The Middle Fork with head springs near the Smyth-Wythe line drains the Middle Valley, broadest and most populous of the three. The Southern or Rye Valley is drained in its lower portions by the South Fork, which starts from the great springs at and above Sugar Grove and is fed by bold and beautiful mountain torrents that rush in from either side. In the upper end of Rye Valley Cripple Creek, a beautiful, picturesque stream rises from Smyth's mountains and flows across this corner of the county eastward through Wythe to New River.

Documentary history of this head of Holston country may be said to begin with a grant of land to Colonel James Patton of Augusta County in the year 1745. Under this grant, issued in the name of King George II by the Governor and Council of Virginia, he was allowed to take up one hundred and twenty thousand acres of unoccupied land west of the mountains. He and his son-in-law, Col. John Buchanan, Deputy Surveyor of Augusta County, became immediately and greatly busy locating and surveying lands under this grant. They entered choice tracts along the upper James and on opposite sides of that stream laid out the town sites of Buchanan and Pattonsburg; located boundaries in the valleys of Roanoke and of New River; and Buchanan, perhaps alone, perhaps accompanied by Patton or others, made preliminary explorations that carried him through Smyth County. He entered in the records of Augusta two surveys of land lying in the present Smyth and Washington counties dated March 14, 1746, and, therefore, must have passed through this county ascertaining desirable locations in the winter of 1746. In October of 1745 he made a trip to New River which he records in a journal that survives, but apart from the entries in the surveyor's book in the archives of the Augusta County Court there seems to be no written record of the first visits to Holston. The early surveyors came in winter because Indians would roam these unoccupied hunting grounds in summer and in the winter would be in their villages hundreds of miles away.

The surveys dated in March of 1746 are recorded in the name of James Patton and are the Crab Apple Orchard tract of seven hundred and seventy acres lying on waters of the South Fork of Indian River near the present Thomas' Bridge, and the Kilmackronan tract of twenty-six hundred acres, now the Huff lands near the Smyth-Washington line, lying on the Middle Fork of Indian River. These are the earliest surveys made on the waters of Holston. Other trips were made in 1746 and 1747. On one of these, while in camp near the present Seven Mile Ford, whose beautiful river bottoms were then a vast dense canebrake where bear, buffalo, elk, and deer fed, the surveyors were visited by a man of mystery whose name was Charles Sinclair. Sinclair it seems was an Englishman who had for quite a while been living alone in the deep woods, attracted by the magnificent solitude, the abundant game, and the mystery of this undiscovered country. There were many of these lonely hermits of the woods who in the early days of American life loved to live apart from their fellows in the deep wild stillness of the forest. Sinclair may have been simply a hermit hunter or he may have been looking for land on which to found his fortunes. At any rate, he had hunted far and wide over all these mountains and valleys, knew the country well and was on friendly terms with the

Indians. He advised Buchanan that should he meet any wandering bands of Indians he would probably have no trouble if he could pass simply as a hunter, but warned him that should they glimpse his surveying instruments he would be in deadly peril of his life. To the forest Indian a chain and compass meant but one thing—the beginning of the end of his hunting grounds. Therefore his law of self-preservation decreed death to the man who carried the chain and compass. Sinclair agreed to act as a guide for the land hunters and in payment of his services they agreed to survey and enter in his name any one thousand acres which he might choose. He chose a boundary on the South Fork which was duly surveyed and recorded in his name under date of March 14, 1748, and still bears the name of Sinclair's Bottom.

One James Davis had purchased Stephen Holston's corn right title to thirteen hundred acres about the head spring of the Middle Fork. John Buchanan surveyed this land for Davis. The survey bears the date March 19, 1748. Other surveys entered at Staunton prior to Patton's notable exploring expedition were: dated Nov. 16, 1746, in James Patton's name a survey of 640 acres on the northwest side of Indian River at the mouth of Cedar Run; Oct. 14, 1747, the Royal Oak survey, seven hundred and forty acres, on the Middle Fork of Indian River in John Buchanan's name; Nov. 21, 1747, in John Buchanan's name, a tract of land on Indian River of five hundred and fifty acres called Richland; and on Nov. 24, 1747, in Buchanan's name on Indian River the Wasp Bottom of one thousand acres; and on March 15, 1748, two tracts on Indian River one without name assigned to John Shelton containing nine hundred and ninety-five acres, the other containing one hundred and thirty acres and called Gooseberry Garden, assigned to Charles Campbell. This last is the land upon which Mr. J. R. Shanklin now lives.

HEAD OF HOLSTON SURVEYS

In the spring of 1748 Col. James Patton organized and equipped a strong force which he led in person to the Holston country for the double purpose of surveying land under his one hundred and twenty thousand acre grant and of making extended explorations with the view of securing a larger grant and embarking on yet more extensive land speculations. This expeditionary force of 1748 was composed of James Patton, his son-in-law, John Buchanan, Buchanan's brother-in-law, Charles Campbell, all of Augusta County, James Wood, associated with the founding of Winchester, and Dr. Thomas Walker of Albemarle. With these gentlemen were an unknown but considerable number of chainmen, axemen, hunters, and servants, and quite a cavalcade of riding horses, pack horses, and hunting dogs.

This expedition of 1748 is of primary historical importance. It penetrated to Cumberland Gap and it was at this time that this famous pass was discovered and named. An immediate result of the expedition was the taking up of choice lands within Smyth County that were to be occupied by men and women, relatives of Campbell, Buchanan, and Patton, who with their descendants have profoundly influenced the life and character of Smyth County and its people. It led to the formation of the Loyal Land Company with a grant of eight hundred thousand acres under which a large part of Southwest Virginia lands were patented and made easily available for settlers. It was largely instrumental in bringing at this critical time in America's history that peculiar type of capable, high-toned immigration so signally adapted to life on an Indian infested wilderness frontier into Southwest Virginia and turning this tide of immigration on westward to the mastery of the continent. It and its offspring, the Loyal Land Company, were responsible for bringing to Smyth County and Southwest Virginia much of that masterful leadership which guided the West into the patriot side of the Revolution and contributed both to the winning of the War of Independence and to the moulding of American life and institutions.

A notable monument of this expedition of 1748 still remains in Smyth County. Colonel Patton was a dreamer of dreams and a see-er of visions, an empire builder with the practical energy and ability to make his dreams come true. He saw his wilderness transformed into a thickly settled country of prosperous farms and thriving towns. He chose a site for a town that might become the metropolis of a future great country. The site he chose is now occupied by the town of Chilhowie. On a hill commanding a beautiful prospect of river bottom and of uplands rolling back to mountains, he built a log house as the beginning of his town and called it the Town House. This original log house, subsequently weatherboarded and enlarged, still remains on a hill in the center of Chilhowie and is still known as the Town House. Prior to the coming of these hunters of land on a princely scale there were free-lance adventurers who visited the head of Holston, woods roamers like Charles Sinclair and Stephen Holston, attracted by the alluring mysteries of the lonely untrodden ways, by the passion for hunting, and by the hope of gain. Practically no record remains of these early wanderers other than the two already named. It is known that Samuel Stalnaker traded with the Indians of the south and west, but probably not until after Buchanan's visit. There is mention of one Vaughn who lived in Amelia County, Virginia, and traveled through Smyth as early as 1740 to trade with the Cherokee Indians. Traders would travel the old Buffalo Trail, a well-trod trace, worn out by the buffalo of untold generations, and which is followed in the main today by the Lee Highway.

Buchanan and Campbell made surveys in 1749 and in December of 1748 they entered in Campbell's name the Buffalo

Lick survey which is now Saltville and Campbell's Choice which includes the beautiful lands above Broadford.

In the spring of 1750 Dr. Thomas Walker, in behalf of the Loyal Land Company, led an exploring expedition through Southwest Virginia into Kentucky. He entered Smyth County March 22, 1750, and left it on March 26 or 27 as shown by this extract from his daily journal:

March 22nd. We got to a large Spring about five miles below Davises Bottom on Holstons River and Camped.

March 23rd. We kept down the Holston River about four miles and camped; and then Mr. Powell and I went to look for Samuel Stalnaker who I had been informed was just moved out to settle. We found his camp, and returned to our own in the evening.

March 24th. We went to Stalnaker's, helped him raise his house and camped about a quarter of a mile below him. In April, 1748, I met the above mentioned Stalnaker between Reedy Creek Settlement and Holstons River, on his way to the Cherokee Indians and expected him to pilot me as far as he knew but his affairs would not permit him to go with me.

March 25th. The Sabbath. Grass is plenty in the low grounds.

March 26th. We left the inhabitants, and kept nigh West to a large Spring on a Branch of the North Fork of the Holston. Thunder, Lightning, and Rain before Day.

27th. It began to snow in the morning and continued till Noon. The Land is very Hilly from West to North. Some snow lies on the tops of the mountains N. W. from us.

This house of Stalnaker's was the fourth recorded as built on Smyth County soil. The cabins of Sinclair and Holston and Patton's Town House having preceded it. Walker's expression "left the inhabitants" indicates that this was the farthest habitation in March, 1750, and it is so indicated on the Frye and Jefferson map of 1751. For this reason much unsuccessful effort has been made to fix its exact location. The mileage given by Walker and other inconclusive evidence indicates that it was probably along the river about two miles below Marion. From it Dr. Walker probably proceeded through Cleghorn Valley and Lyons Gap to the North Fork. It was destroyed by Indians in 1755 and Stalnaker himself was captured, but escaped, and his wife and son were murdered and scalped. Either Stalnaker or another of the name later lived at the Town House. He appears in earlier records among the New River settlers. Later he figures in the defense of the New River settlements. From 1750 to 1755 Patton and associates continued to acquire land and dispose of it to settlers. In these years quite a few people came to live on the waters of the upper Holston. A survey in Rye Valley is dated Jan. 15, 1751, and recorded in the names of Joseph and Esther Crockett. It contained four hundred and fifty acres lying "about the head of the South Fork" at the present Sugar Grove. Joseph and Esther Crockett probably lived there until Indians induced them to move back to near the Crockett Springs of Montgomery County. Their descendant, Robert Ward, now owns and lives upon this land.

At the beginning of the French and Indian War, the Shawnee and other northwestern Indians struck suddenly and terribly on the Virginia frontier. Colonel Patton was killed July 8, 1755, in the Draper's Meadow Massacre. About the same time all the settlers on the Holston were either killed, captured, or driven back to the more populous settlements. An old list of those killed, wounded, or captured during the years 1754 and 1755 names the following who may have dwelt and probably did on Smyth County land:

1754, October—Stephen Lyon, Holston River, killed. John Godman, Holston River, killed. Benjamin Harrison, Holston River, killed.

1755, May 3— —— Burk, Holston River, Prisoner; escaped. Mary Baker, Holston River, wounded.

June 18—Samuel Stalnaker, Holston River; Prisoner; escaped. Samuel Hydon, Holston River, Prisoner. Adam Stalnaker, Holston River, killed. Mrs. Stalnaker, Holston River, killed. A servant man, Holston River, killed, Mathias Counie, Holston River, killed.

June 19—Michael Houck, Holston River, killed.

This list is not accepted as complete. There can be little doubt that others were killed whose names are now lost and it is certain that others were captured, for reference is made to the route taken by the Indians with Stalnaker and other captives. Stalnaker in some way effected his escape and made his way back to New River where he assisted in the building of a fort. How many families were here at that time it is impossible to say, but all of them fled the country in terror of their lives and the permanent settlement of the Holston was postponed until after the close of hostilities.

On his expedition against the Cherokees, about 1760, Col. William Byrd led his troops through Smyth. He spent much time improving the Buffalo Trail into a wagon road. This, the first road building in the county, was done at government expense.

Chapter II*

COL. JOHN BUCHANAN'S JOURNAL

Friday, the 4th to October 1745
This day I took my journey. went to Adam Taylors and lodged that night.
Saturday the 5th. This day I went to Peter Salleys.
Sunday the 6th. I remained at Peter Salleys.
Monday ye 7th. This day I spent in writing parts of Salley's journal.
Tuesday ye 8th. This day I finished Peter Salleys journal and prepared for my journey next day.
Wednesday ye 9th. This day it rained very hard so that I could not set out.
Thursday ye 10th. This day I set out in company with Peter Salley, and about twelve of ye clock we came to "Cedar" creek over which is a natural Bridge of a solid rock 203 feet high ye creek seems to cut through ye side of a very high hill making a very deep and narrow trench in each side of ye bridge as far as I could view.

Ye bridge is about two polls broad. and hath ye gradual (apex?) of ye hill.

Ye arch is I suppose one hundred and fifty feet high and is very near regular ye side is smooth and plain. Neither can ye discover any creek or stream in this part of ye wood.

After having satisfied my curiosity in viewing this surprising production of nature I proceeded on my journey. Come to Looneys and give ye old woman one———

---

*Throughout this chapter, 2-em dashes indicate parts of Col. John Buchanan's Journal which were illegible.

Friday ye 11th. This morning I left with mother Looney six shillings cash for Andrew Jones, sete out and come to John Millers here I stayed all night.

Sat. ye 12th. This day I rode to Captn. Robinson's sent part of ye day with him returned in ye evening to Millers where I stayed till Monday ye 14th day.

Monday ye 14th day. This morning I sete out early (?) with Vance and Cahagan in ye fore noon it rained very hard. About two of ye clock it cleared up and blew a very hard gale of wind, in so much that we were in great danger of trees falling very near us in severall places as we road along. We lay on ye head of Cotapa it was a cold and winday night.

Tuesday ye 15th. This morning we set off to Israel Larkins lodged there——

Wednesday ye 16th. This morning I confirmed to Larkin his Ld. by taking memorandum in writing.

Sete off from thence, came to Chas. Harts and staied all night.

Thursday ye 17th. This morning Charles Hart, asked me after what maner I would late him have his land. I answered him for three pounds per 100, he paying ye charges of surveying and writing. He then told me he had bought it from Capt. Robinson—clear of charges—and I said that Robinson had not ye selling of the Ld, for I was invested with ye power. Hart said he wanted 600 acres which Ld. he would have surveyed half a mile wide on ye creek and turn as ye creik did.

I answered that it should be laid off as ye Ld. would beare and that if ye running it out in ye manner did not hurt or prefent ye sale of other Land I would agree to it, at ye same time I would not consent there to untill I had a view of ye Ld. And here I am to remember that before Hart had talked five minutes I discovered that he was in a great passion which he did not perceive—I observed after we had discoursed considerable time. I took horse and road to Markes cabin where I arrived in the evening. Here I met with one of ye brethren of Ephratapha, whom ye vulgar call Dunkers. I found ye man very affable —— in conversation. I asked him concerning their way of living all which he answered with freedom. I then discoursed with concerning —— and of sundry of ye fundamentals —— I asked him what advantages there was in celebacy more than in a married state for as God who was goodness had ordained and instituted marriage for ye benefit and comfort of man neither did the wisdom and goodness of God intend ye aneything in this life should mar or hinder man in his progress toward heaven, but on ye contrary were all ordained and designed as so many helps to further him therein why then did he deprive himself of so great a blessing as the enjoyment of a good wife is.

To this he answered in the words of paul that he who married did well but he who did not did better allso ye married man studied to please his wife and ye unmarried to please God.

I then asked him whether he acknowledged ye fall of adam and the corruption of mans nature thereby—he said he Did —ye scriptures held it forth and he could not deny it—I then replayed—that as god made all things very good —— made man perfict capable of ye—enjoyment of his work and made him governor of all ye creation—yet as he was alone with respect to an agreeable companion it was ye sentence of god himself that it was not good for man to be allone, therefore ye power and wisdom of ye trinity was consulted as it were to make him an helpmeet which in the original signified a second self one that is capable to assist man in all ye stations and various scenes of life both with regard to soul and body —and then if it was not good or expedient for man to be allone in a steate of perfict bliss and happiness is it not much more so in a deprayed state and as St. paul says ye believing husband sanctified ye unbelieving wife.

He answered all I said was very good But with respect to ye fall I had passed it over too lightly—here our Conversation was interrupted by other company for sometime which I again resumed by asking him what it was in ye fall of Adam that I had not taken notice of.

His reply was that when god said it was not good for man to be allone man was not then in ye state he was created in at first but was fallen from ye love of his maker by his being conversient with ye creatures and I asked him if woman was not first in ye fall—he said that woman was not to blame but so much as ye man for he was already depraved and had degenerated from ye love of his maker by pleasing his delight too much in ye inferior creatures—therefore god thought proper to make him a companion of ye same substance with himself.

I then asked him if it was not nesecery for mankind to be of difrent sex in order to propogat his own species. he answered it was not nesecery for when god created man he made him male and female with a natural power of multiplying owen species. without ye help of difrent sex having the seed within himself as ye trees of the woods in a comparative way of speaking—here he noted ye dissent our Saviour had with ye Saducees that in ye ressurection ye shall be as ye angels, alleging that man was so in ye beginning that ye difrance of sexes was not untill after ye corruption of man's nature and even after ye creation or formation of woman man's ability of propagating his own species was continued for some time without the help of woman for said he Cain went out because a great nation ye —— we hear nothing of his haveing a wife and here I asked him if he was of opinion that ye angels multiply and he said ye scriptures seem to hold it forth—but here he complained of his want of good English to make me rightly understand him but said he these ar my opinions.

I suppose then said I that you look upon these opinions as no essential part of a saving faith or nesecery to be believed in order to obtain salvation. he answered yes that was all ye use he made there of and that each man had liberty to serch and judge for him self—here our discourse ended company interrupting.

here I am to take nottice that after I had this conference with this man I met another of his brethren with whom I discoursed upon ye foregoing articles and enlarged very much further but as his opinions was ye same in substance with what I have related I forbear inserting any part there of as being too tedious.

Friday 18th. This morning I had ye esteate of William Marks apprised by Adam and Jacob Harmon—No other person could be had after I had agreed with ye afore mentioned Longbeard to gather and take care of ye crops and comiting ye rest of ye things to ——— Griffeth, who engaged to be forth coming—for which I returned to Chas. in company with Adam Harmon staid all night.

Saturday ye 19th. This morning before day Adam Harmon and Hart had a long confrence in Dutch about ye Land as I understood and when Hart talked with me I found he was in ——— from his former notion of ye surveying his land, but that he had before discovered himself so base and continued to do so still that I told him I would be cautious of him and that I proposed to use him well if he deserved it—he used many stubborn arguments to prevail with me which put him still further from his purpose he once said that unless he got his land in such and such a maner he would burn all and go off. I answered him that very expression would compell me to take particular nottice of him above all ye men I had seen within ye settlement and neither would any ye property of my land to him but upon his good behavior.

It rained very hard this day so that I could not start out of ye house we had many froutles arguments during ye day but to no purpose for as I found ye man so unreasonable and unjust I did not complay in ye least aney furder than I intended to do him justice.

Sunday ye 20th. I staid at hart's.

Monday ye 21st. This morning I went out to ye woods with jeremiah glane —— him apeace of land on ye head a Rocky Creek. Returned to hart's staid all night.

Tuesday ye 22nd. Sete out and came to Jacob Harmon mete with sundry of people told Chas. hart he should have his land as his neighbors got theirs if he desired so desired ye company to take nottice of what I said. Left harmon's eving. went to Stornakers lodged that night.

Wednesday ye 23rd. I went to ye light Bottom ordered John Strand to look for apeace of Ld. for himself.

Sold a mear that Belonged to Marks esteat to Stornaker for a guinea and a buckskin—agreed with Stornaker for his Land. Returned to Jacob harmons &c.

Thursday ye 24th. This morning I agreed with sundry men about Ld. —— several warrents. Sete off towards home. Lay on ye head of Roanoke all night.

Friday ye 25th. I came to John Miller's and staid till Monday, being detained and my horse joded.

Monday ye 28th. I left Millers came to J. Collins &c.

Tuesday ye 29th. I came home &c.

Chapter III

PERMANENT SETTLEMENT

The Coming of the Campbells

The dread of Indian barbarities and proclamations of the British Government forbidding settlements on Indian land effectually checked the tide of emigration to the Holston until the country was legally opened to settlement by the Treaty of Fort Stanwix in 1768. After that the preliminary work of Patton and his associates began to bear fruit and permanent settlement of the country was rapidly accomplished. Family connections and in some instances whole neighborhoods moved out from the Valley of Virginia to settle upon these lands. Settlers came also from eastern Virginia, from Maryland, Pennsylvania, and other colonies and a few direct from Ireland, England, and Scotland.

Of the pioneer families the Campbells have a double claim for especial notice from a historian of Smyth County. First, because they founded at Royal Oak the first permanent settlement on Holston waters, and, second, because of their position of leadership in early affairs.

The Campbells emigrated from Pennsylvania to the present Augusta County from whence they came to Smyth. David Campbell, known as "White David" to distinguish him from a cousin with the same name and of darker complexion, is thus described by his grandson: "A large man with silken yellow hair, fair skin, and blue eyes. He was as remarkable for the evenness of his temper as his wife, Mary Hamilton, was for the excitability and pride of hers." He lived in

Augusta and "was a farmer in moderate circumstances, living well, but having at his command but small pecuniary means, and without ambition to make his sons more than farmers like himself. Not so, however, with his wife, Mary Hamilton Campbell, whom I well recollect when eighty years of age, sitting on her horse and side-saddle as straight as a girl of eighteen, and riding miles into the country among her neighbors. She was a very intelligent and ambitious little black-eyed Scotch-Irish woman, and would have her sons educated, and what her husband lacked of means she supplied from the savings of her dairy."

"White David" Campbell and Mary Hamilton, his wife, had thirteen children. Five sons were in the Colonial and Continental service; four were distinguished men: Colonels Arthur and Robert, Captain John, and Judge David Campbell. Their names are as follows: Catherine, Mary, Martha, John, Arthur, James, William, Margaret, David, Sarah, Robert, Patrick, and Anne Campbell.

In 1765 John, the eldest son, accompanied Dr. Thomas Walker on an exploring trip through Southwest Virginia at which time he purchased for his father the Royal Oak survey which John Buchanan had made in 1747 and named because there stood upon it the most gigantic oak tree seen anywhere in the country. This tree is said to have stood near the log church which was built in the northwest corner of the old Royal Oak graveyard. The fact that it stood in an open space is one of many indications that all this country was not densely wooded but had from the beginning open spaces in which native grass grew when first the settlers came, this spreading oak showing that there was such a glade in the Royal Oak neighborhood. The next year, 1766, John and his brother, Arthur, and their eighteen-year-old sister, Margaret, moved out to the Royal Oak to begin making improvements and for over two years these three young people dwelt there alone in the wilderness, during which time Margaret did not see a single white female face. About the year 1768 or 1769 the remainder of the family began to move out. Mary had married a Lockhart and her husband and children came with her, also certain Goodpastures and Hamiltons, relatives of the Campbells, came along. All of the children of David and Mary Hamilton excepting Catherine and William came to live at Royal Oak.

John Campbell while living in Augusta at the age of eighteen did some brilliant Indian fighting under Gilbert Christian's command. He was a man of keen intellect, well beloved, of fine judgment and equitable temper, genial and likable; a strong man, capable of leading the strong pioneers and gifted in winning their confidence and affection. He was captain of militia and rendered great service in Indian wars before, during, and after the Revolutionary War. He commanded a company in the battle of Long Island Flats and throughout the Revolution was almost constantly afield with his rangers patrolling the frontier against Indians. He married Elizabeth McDonald, of Hall's Bottom, between Abingdon and Bristol. They lived until 1789 at Royal Oak, where their son, David, future governor of Virginia and authority for most of this data on the Campbell family, was born. In 1789, he sold his Royal Oak farm to Abraham Goodpasture and moved to his wife's farm in Hall's Bottom, where for many years he entertained in old Virginia style, sought out for counsel by public men from far and near, and keeping open house for wayfarers, particularly for wayfaring preachers. For two score years he was clerk of Washington County court but conducted the business of the office through deputies.

Arthur Campbell was captured by Wyandot Indians while gathering wild plums outside the stockade of Fort Dickenson in the present Bath County when a lad of fourteen. He was carried to the country around the Great Lakes and held in captivity as the adopted son of an Indian Chief for three years. At Detroit he came in contact with Jesuit priests who gave him some schooling. When General Johnson made his campaign against the Northern Indians about 1759, Arthur Campbell made his escape, reached the army, and rendered important service in piloting it through the country.

Col. Arthur Campbell was above middle stature, not quite six feet high, his person was good, his gait erect and lofty, his manners very graceful. His fine eyes, long chin and nose, and general outline of his face would strike the observer in a moment, and impress upon him that he was looking upon no ordinary man. He was easy and pleasant in his manners when he chose to be so, but these traits were not natural to him. In conversation he was remarkably fluent and interesting. His reading had been extensive so that he seemed familiar with all subjects, without having a really scientific knowledge of them. And among the most intelligent gentlemen he was capable of taking the lead in conversation. His hobby, both in letter writing and in conversation was politics, and I suppose no man in the country carried on a more extensive correspondence. With the man of society he was not personally popular, although much respected, owing principally to the circumstance that he would not relax in his manners to suit it. In his temper, he was hasty and excitable and disposed to be overbearing; and was often engaged in violent personal quarrels. He was a most zealous Whig taking an active part in favor of the Revolution from its first dawn, and never at any period entertaining the smallest doubt about the success of the people in their struggle for independence. I knew him intimately for twelve or fifteen years of his life, commencing about his sixtieth or sixty-fifth years. He then resided on the farm he first settled after going to Holston. A few years before his death he moved to Kentucky and died there, on Yellow Creek in that state, of cancer in the face, about the seventy-fourth year of his age. His wife survived him a short time, and died there also about the age of seventy. They had twelve children, six sons and six daughters, all of whom grew to manhood and womanhood, and I believe were all alive when their parents died.

Arthur Campbell married Margaret, daughter of Charles and sister of William Campbell, some time about 1772 or 1773. His nephew, David, says: "This young wife encouraged her husband and urged him forward in all his plans by which he might acquire distinction and reputation as a public man. Her whole mind seemed to be devoted to this one object, to which she made every other bend. No privation, however great, in the smallest degree annoyed her if she believed it was in consequence of her husband's efforts to acquire either military or civil distinction. Her extreme solicitude and promptings to push her husband up the ladder of fame, caused him sometimes to make false steps and involved him in unnecessary altercations with his brother-in-law and others. Except in this, and it was always done in a mode and manner to gratify her husband, she was the most exemplary of women, in her deportment towards him never having a thought in opposition to his upon any subject, and believing him to be the greatest man in the country, not excepting her brother, of whose qualities she entertained a very exalted opinion.

When forty-five years of age I saw her, and then she was very beautiful, although she had become rather corpulent, and was afflicted with rheumatism.

Arthur Campbell after his marriage lived in a log house that stood above Staley's Mill race just west of the present home of D. D. Staley, a house which by virtue of the character and reputation of its master and the beauty, intelligence, and gracious charm of its mistress was for many years the most noted residence on Upper Holston. John Campbell lived in a house that stood a little west of the present home of Mrs. R. C. Gwyn and owned the land comprised in the Royal Oak and Staley additions east of Marion.

David, the fourth brother of those who came to Holston, was educated for the bar, and practiced law a few years in Washington County after it was established. He then married, and removed to what afterwards became the state of Tennessee—was first Federal Judge in the Territory and when the State was formed he was made one of the judges of their Supreme Court, and held office for many years. A year or two before his death, which took place in 1812, he was appointed Federal Judge in the Territory, which afterwards formed the State of Alabama, but died of fever, before he removed his family to the country, in the sixty-second year of his age.

Their father occupied a house whose exact location is not known, but it is supposed to have been somewhere on Staley's Creek.

Margaret, who came out with her brothers, John and Arthur, to break the ground of the Royal Oak home, married her cousin David Campbell. She was a great woman. Her nephew, Gov. David Campbell, writes of her as follows:

Margaret, when a girl of eighteen, accompanied, as I have before stated, her brothers, John and Arthur to Holston, and managed their household affairs for two or three years without a murmur, and without, in that time, seeing a single female friend. In two or three years after the removal of her father and mother, she married David Campbell, and in 1781, removed to the country, afterwards Campbell's Station, Tenn. She was a most intelligent, mild, and placid woman; always thoughtful, and always calm and prepared for every emergency. So conspicuous were these traits in her character, whenever any difficulty occurred, or any alarm took place, she was first looked to and consulted, not only by the women in the blockhouse and station, but even by men.

This excellent lady died, with cancer in the breast, in 1799, at the age of fifty-one, universally beloved and regretted, and lies buried in the Presbyterian Church burying ground near Campbell's Station.

Tradition ascribes to her credit for founding the Royal Oak Presbyterian Church, asserting that in agreeing to come out to the wilderness and live alone with her brothers she exacted the promise that when the number of settlers should warrant it they would build her a church, and that she had the promise fulfilled by the erection on her brother John's land in 1776 of the first log church in Smyth County.

The youngest daughter, Anne, married Archibald Roane, a young lawyer from Pennsylvania who lived for a time in the Royal Oak settlement and then removed to Tennessee. He was one of the first Judges of the Supreme Court of that State and was Governor from 1801 to 1803.

Martha died in 1801 unmarried. Sarah also appears to have lived a spinster. James contracted smallpox which left him blinded.

Robert when nineteen years of age made his first military campaign, as a volunteer against the Shawnee Indians in 1774, as is supposed, in the company of Capt. William Campbell. In the summer of 1776, he again volunteered, joined Capt. John Campbell's company, and acted with distinguished bravery and presence of mind in the battle of the Island Flats. He was also in Christian's campaign in October 1776—and in 1780, he was an ensign under Colonel Campbell at the battle of King's Mountain, and distinguished himself in that battle. In December of the same year, he performed another campaign against the Cherokee Indians, under Col. Arthur Campbell. His education was not equal to that of his older brothers, nor was his capacity—but he was a brave, active, and patriotic Whig, and a man of much energy through life. He acted as a magistrate in Washington County for upwards of thirty years, and until he removed to the vicinity of Knoxville, Tenn., where he died in 1831, in the seventy-seventh year of his age.

Patrick, the youngest brother, performed less military service than the others, and had less capacity. He was a volunteer in the battle of King's Mountain, and performed his duty well. He remained with his father on the farm and inherited it after his death—married, had a large family of children—and in his old age removed to Williamson County, Tennessee, where he died in about the eightieth year of his age. He was a good man through life, with indolent habits and very little energy of character.

Col. Robert Campbell lived in Abingdon and he once accused Mr. Robert Preston of cowardice in connection with the King's Mountain campaign. Preston challenged him to a duel which was fought under some trees near Bristol. Campbell was wounded in the hip and was lame for the rest of his life.

Charles Campbell came to the Holston with Col. James Patton and Col. John Buchanan and took up choice tracts of land in Rich Valley. He acquired the beautiful lands up and down the Middle Fork from Seven Mile Ford which were patented to Col. John Buchanan in 1753. He died in 1767 and perhaps two years later his widow, Margaret Buchanan Campbell, sister of Col. John Buchanan, removed with her son, William, and her four daughters, Elizabeth, Jane, Margaret, and Anne, to the Seven Mile Ford lands, building a home called Aspenvale, just south of the old Preston burying ground. William became the most noted military leader that Southwest Virginia has ever produced, and is immortal as the patriot commander at King's Mountain. Elizabeth married John Taylor and went to live on the tract of land above Broadford now known as the Cobb place and the Taylor lands. Jane married Thomas Tate and falling heir to the lands above the Taylor place, they lived in the neighborhood of the present McCarty's mill; Margaret married Col. Arthur Campbell and lived at Royal Oak, and Anne married Richard Poston. Her lands included the site of North Holston and they lived in a house that stood exactly where the home of Mr. Ed Clark now stands.

Capt. John Campbell of another line settled in Rich Valley and rendered distinguished service in the Revolutionary War. Also Campbells of still another line settled in the South Fork Valley.

Among the earliest settlers "about the Royal Oak" were Lockharts and Goodpastures, relatives of the Campbells, and Abram Staley for whom Staley's Creek is supposed to have been named, and the Crows who first took up lands on Hunger's Mother.

The Valleys Occupied

Among the earliest settlers in the Middle Fork Valley were the Davises, on Davis Fancy about the head springs of the stream and Robert Buchanan in the same section. On June 28, 1777, nine hundred and ninety-five acres "on Holston River between Davis' and the Royal Oak, commonly called the Magazine Spring" were deeded to James McCorkle, and on Aug. 6, 1782, deeded by him to James Culton and William Patterson. The large spring just below the Lee Highway on the old Cassell place between Atkins and Mt. Carmel is still called the Magazine Spring, and a tradition handed down in the family declares that early settlers living near there fled because of an Indian alarm and having a large quantity of powder and lead which they could not take with them wanted to put it where the Indians could not get it. It was a time of drought and the spring spreading over a much larger expanse of ground than now had almost dried up, leaving the sandy bottom exposed. They decided to hide their ammunition in that sand, loaded it on a cart drawn by a little

PERMANENT SETTLEMENT 25

mule, and backed the outfit into the sand. It proved to be quicksand. Cart and mule began to sink and despite strenuous efforts to extricate them continued to sink until completely buried. The Cassells for generations have told their children about the mule, cart, and ammunition buried in the quicksand that used to lie under the spring. Another version of the story says that the fleeing settlers put their powder into waterproof containers, buried it in the sands of the spring bottom, and, returning after the scare was over found it safe and dry. Whatever the truth of the incident may be this court entry shows that it was commonly called the Magazine Spring in 1777.

John, Robert, Edward, James, and William Crow were early settlers on the Middle Fork, some of them above Marion, some apparently on Hunger's Mother. Surveys of 1774 by Robert and John Crow show that this stream had its unusual name that early, so if the story be true concerning a lost child found after several days' search on its banks and greeting its rescuers with the words "Hungry Mother," it occurred prior to 1774.

John Groseclose, progenitor of the Smyth County family of that name, settled at an early date along the Lee Highway just west of Mt. Pleasant Lutheran Church site.

Cullops, Henderlites, and Wassums settled near the mouth of Nicks Creek during or just after the Revolution, when the German element began to come. The old stone house there was built by a Cullop and is perhaps the oldest stone house now standing in the county.

Below Marion the Dungans and Ferrises were among the first to come. They settled first on what proved to be parts of Charles Campbell's patents at Seven Mile Ford and then moved nearer to the mountains, taking up lands some of which are still owned by their descendants. The Gooseberry Bottom tract, now the Shanklin farms, was patented to Jacob

Anderson in 1753, and his son Isaac lived there prior to and during the Revolution. The Carlocks settled where Tyler Frazier, Jr., now lives and gave their name to that branch. Joseph Drake also settled on this creek. William and Joseph Bates were somewhere in that neighborhood. Arthur Bowen lived on what is now called the Haller place. Henry Bowen had land on the Middle and South Forks. Charles Bowen lived on the old Crab Orchard patent, the first survey made in Smyth County which ran towards Laurel Spring Church from the river near Thomas' Bridge. His place was the appointed rendezvous for militia marching against Tories in June, 1780, as appears from this extract of a letter that Col. Arthur Campbell wrote on June 24, 1780, to Maj. William Edmondson.

Goodwood, June 24, 1780

Dear Sir:

A Letter just received from the Commanding Officer at the Lead-Mines, I am informed that the Tories have embodied themselves up New River, and intend to take that place also that they have killed nine Men, and are committing various outrages. I am also call'd upon in a most pressing manner to send assistance as the Mines is in great danger.

You are therefore desired to Order four full Divisions out of the Companies commanded by the Captains Montgomery, Beattie, Dysart, Edmondson, Lewis, Neil, and John Campbell R(oyal) Oak, to go under the Command of Captains Dysart, and Beattie, and such Subalterns as you may think proper, and the whole to be headed by yourself. I think the Men ought at farthest to set out Tuesday Morning, taking with them provision to Serve them some days, as they cannot be supply'd until they get to the Mines. Such as chooses had better take Horses. Let both of the Companies rendezvous at Charles Bowens one time where I will met them on giving me notice as it may be proper to take different routs from thence. I judge it improper to leave home, therefore cannot see you as I intended.

PERMANENT SETTLEMENT

The next day Colonel Campbell again wrote Major Edmondson telling him that two hundred Tories were embodied in the Glades, which is the country crossed by the present county line west of Rural Retreat. Charles Bowen, born in Rockbridge County in 1747, was in Capt. William Edmondson's company at King's Mountain. In 1832 he was living in Blount County, Tennessee.

The Blessings located on the Middle Fork, and when the county was formed one of that name lived where the road from Adwolfe joined the main stage road. Mary Blessing was born Feb. 24, 1832, one day after the birth of Smith County, and on Feb. 24, 1932, celebrated her one hundredth birthday at her home in Marion. Friends presented her with a bouquet of one hundred rosebuds. In full possession of her faculties she received the many visitors who called that day and graciously acknowledged their courtesy. She is the widow of the late Vincent L. Morgan, and mother of the late Haynes L. Morgan, Mrs. George W. Miles, and Mrs. Mamie Painter.

Philip Greever started the Greever family in 1780 in a log house still standing on the James Greever farm. He came from Pennsylvania, bringing two indentured servants with him. They were German, and he overheard them plotting in that language to murder him. He handled the situation in such a way that he not only turned their purpose, but won their respect and affection, so that they gave him loyal service until their terms expired. They then acquired land of their own and became substantial citizens. A Stalnaker family was at Chilhowie in 1769. Hennegars, Humphrey, Smith, Fuller, and Galbraith are names of other first settlers on the lower Middle Fork in Smyth.

There were others who were here prior to or during the Revolution. These are some whose names happen to appear in records available at the moment of this writing. In the decades 1780–1800 a great many people came, among them the Hulls and Dentons, Cullops, Wassums, Wolfes, Foxes, and Goodmans. A lot of people who had no money squatted on unoccupied land to which in many cases they later acquired title.

Capt. John Buchanan and his brother, Archibald, seem to have been the first settlers in Rich Valley, though it is impossible to say who was actually the first. Capt. John Buchanan had married the youngest sister of Colonel John, the first surveyor of the Holston, who gave to his sister the lands he had taken up on the Cove. Capt. John Buchanan settled the land up the Cove on the lands of his wife and he is the progenitor of most of the Buchanans in the Valley. He was wounded at the battle of Guilford Court House, brought home and died of the wound.

There was a family of Lammies who came with the Buchanans prior to the Revolution; Spratts, three brothers; the Davises, and William Richardson, ancestor of the Rich Valley Richardsons, who was called Buckeye Billy, from a buckeye forest, on Buckeye Bottom.

As to who were the first permanent settlers in Rich Valley, it is impossible to say with certainty. Col. John Buchanan and Charles Campbell made entries of surveys in the Valley before 1750 and took up some of the choicest land. Campbell's daughters and their husbands, as has been noted, settled along the river at North Holston and above Broadford. Colonel Buchanan gave the Locust Cove to his youngest sister who married a cousin, Capt. John Buchanan, and they came to live on this land among the first comers. Capt. John Buchanan and his wife lived in a large double log house at the head of the Cove, where they reared a large family from whom most of the Rich Valley Buchanans descend. Archibald Buchanan, a brother of Captain John, settled near the mouth of the Cove, lived there until after the Revolution, moved to Kentucky and thence to Nashville where he died.

PERMANENT SETTLEMENT

William Richardson was permanently settled in Rich Valley in the early seventies. One of his descendants says he was there in 1751, which is worthy of note. It is known that there were no permanent settlers in Smyth territory prior to the coming of the Campbells in 1766. But from 1750 to 1754 there were quite a few settlers scattered about in all three of these valleys. All who were not killed or captured by the Indians lit out in 1754-1755 and permanent settlement in volume was not resumed until several years after the coming of the Campbells. It is possible that William Richardson came to the Valley in 1751, left, and came back when it was safe to stay. He came from North Carolina and was the progenitor of all the numerous and distinguished Richardson family of Smyth. He settled on the land now owned by his descendant, Robert M. Richardson, which land has never been sold out of the family. There was a forest of buckeye trees on it, and one of the first patches cleared is still called Buckeye Bottom. William Richardson, himself, was known as Buckeye Billy.

Robert Davis, of the Davis-Fancy family, was settled in 1769, as was one Starns, both mentioned in the first records of Botetourt County Court. Robert Davis was a Revolutionary captain.

Three Spratt brothers were among the first settlers of the upper Valley. At least one, possibly all three of the Spratts, were Loyalists during the Revolution. By a Loyalist is meant a Tory who was a man of honor. William Campbell in zealous discharge of his duty in suppressing Tories led a patrol to Spratt's house on Spratts Creek with the intention of hanging him. Spratt and his sons barricaded the house and prepared to sell their lives as dearly as possibly.

Archibald Buchanan and other neighbors prevented bloodshed by finally persuading the fiery red-haired colonel that Mr. Spratt was a valuable citizen and excellent gentleman who should not be molested if he would give his word not to engage in plotting or fighting against the Colonial cause, which he did.

The Harmons, scions of a famous Indian fighting family, a Burk, several Hayses, and Hubbles were others among the first settlers in the upper Valley.

Around Saltville the Crabtrees, Hennegars, Lees, Archers, Scotts, Hatfields, and others had taken up lands among the very first settlers of the county.

On the South Fork, the Coles, Isaac and Joseph, bought lands in Sinclair's Bottom and were living there as early as 1770.

In the Rye Valley, a name noted in the old Fincastle County records and derived from the wild rye growing abundantly along the creeks and in the glades, the first permanent settler seems to have been Jenkins Williams who cleared a corn right and built a cabin on the north side of the river below Sugar Grove prior to 1774, possibly as early as 1769 or 1770. The Nelsons, and three families of the James name, and the Griffitts followed as the next known settlers of Rye Valley, the two former purchasing land about Sugar Grove from the children of Joseph and Esther Crockett, and John Griffitts building a cabin in 1776 where a Griffitts home now stands. The Allisons and Kincannons and Duttons were settled on the Cripple Creek waters in the Fincastle County days, and John Scott was the original pioneer of the Blue Spring neighborhood, locating on the land where Maurice Hale, his descendant, lives. He was the ancestor of the Scotts in the Middle Fork Valley.

Old Parson Woolsey was in the Holston Mills vicinity in the early seventies and the Houstons, Bonhams, Pierces, and Gollehons were pioneers further down the South Fork. John Gross, ancestor of most of that name in the county, settled about the headspring of the creek that bears his name and his spring now supplies water to the town of Chilhowie.

The following list of early surveys culled from Sumner's Annals of Southwest Virginia indicates most of the Smyth County inhabitants prior to 1800. Frederick Copenhaver, ancestor of the Smyth Copenhavers, and Frederick Slemp, forbearer of all the Slemps, came in 1804, and numerous other old families started in the county after 1800. Some of the surveys here listed may have been in Washington County, but effort was made to confine the list to those that now lie in Smyth.

EARLY SURVEYS AND DEEDS
Botetourt County Deeds

Grantor	Grantee	Date	Acres	Location
Davis, Jas. & Agnes, his wife.........	Henry Davis	Feb. 20, 1771	200	Head of Holston River.
Davis, James & Agnes, his wife...	Henry Davis	Mar. 1, 1771	140	Branches of Holston River.
Davis, Samuel & Hannah, his wife.	Robert Davis	Feb. 2, 1771	350	Headwaters of Holston River.
Campbell, John....	Campbell, David	Aug. 7, 1771	300	Royal Oak on Holston Indian River

Fincastle County Deeds

Grantor	Grantee	Date	Acres	Location
Preston, Wm. & Wm. Campbell, acting exors. of last will of John Buchanan, late of Augusta County.........	Bowin, Lillie, of Fincastle County	Jan. 5, 1773	880	Waters Indian or Holston River.
Preston, Wm. & Wm. Campbell, acting exors. of last will of John Buchanan, late of Augusta County.........	Anderson, Jacob	Jan. 5, 1773	130	Waters of Mississippi, on br. called Indian River.
Crockett, Walter & Margaret his wife of Bedford County	Allison, John & Charles Campbell, Robt., Alexander, & Wm.	Mar. 2, 1773	450	On. hd S. Fork Holston.
Christian, Wm.....	Keewood, John of Berkley	May 2, 1775	940	Holley Bottom on Holston R.

SMYTH COUNTY HISTORY

FINCASTLE COUNTY SURVEYS

Grantee	Date	Acres	Location
Allison, Wm.........	May 12, 1775	224	Headwaters South Fork Holston.
Allison, Robt.........	May 12, 1775	340	Headwaters South Fork Holston.
Anderson, Peter......	Dec. 2, 1774	80	Fork of Holston River.
Bishop, Jos..........	Mar. 12, 1774	157	Branch of South Fork Holston
Border, Mitchel......	Mar. 12, 1774	282	South Fork Holston.
Bowen, Henry.......	Mar. 9, 1774	426	South Fork Holston.
Bishop, Mathew......	Mar. 12, 1774	77	South Fork Holston.
Baker, Thos..........	Mar. 12, 1774	324	At Reedy Hill, Branch of South Fork Holston River.
Bledsoe, Isaac........	Feb. 15, 1774	300	Rich Valley, North Fork Holston.
Bright, Thos..........	Feb. 16, 1774	96	North Fork Holston River Rich Valley.
Buchanan, Moses.....	Mar. 15, 1774	170	South Fork Holston
Brindley, Richard....	Dec. 8, 1774	80	In the Valley on branch of North Fork Holston.
Barnet, Jeremiah.....	June 7, 1774	256	Joining James Thompson's tract on which he now lives on the Middle Fork Holston R.
Buchanan, Samuel....	Mar. 15, 1774	87	North side of South Holston.
Bates, Wm...........	Jan. 15, 1774	130	Branches of Middle Fork Holston.
Burk, Thos..........	Feb. 22, 1775	210	In Locust Cove, waters of North Fork of Holston River.
Bryan, John.........	Mar. 2, 1775	180	Both sides South Fork of Lick Creek, waters of North Holston R.
Blackly, Charles......	Feb. 28, 1775	180	Both sides of Lick Creek.
Campbell, John......	Apr. 16, 1774	200	Rich Valley, North Fork of Holston.
Crow, Robt..........	Jan. 21, 1774	241	Hungers Mother, branch of Middle Fork of Holston.
Crow, Thos..........	Jan. 13, 1774	226	Middle Fork Holston River.
Crow, Edward.......	Jan. 21, 1774	299	Branch Middle Fork Holston River.
Cole, Jos., Jr.........	Mar. 10, 1774	221	Branch of South Fork Holston.
Cole, Jos.............	Mar. 8, 1774	278	South Fork Holston.
Cox, Wm............	Feb. 11, 1774	220	Reedy Creek, Branch of Holston.
Crabtree, Abraham...	May 31, 1774	104	Both sides North Fork Holston River, joining and between tracts known as Pawpaw Bottom and Clay Lick.

PERMANENT SETTLEMENT 33

FINCASTLE COUNTY SURVEYS—(Continued)

Grantee	Date	Acres	Location
Campbell, Charles....	June 9, 1774	285	South Branches Middle Fork Holston.
Crabtree, James......	May 27, 1774	373	Branches of Beaver Creek, waters of North Fork Holston.
Crabtree, Wm........	May 26, 1774	98	South side North Fork Holston, Lick Valley.
Crabtree, John.......	May 27, 1774	129	Including head spring of Elk Horn Branch, waters of North Fork Holston River.
Crabtree, Isaac.......	May 7, 1774	50	Head of Cedar Branch waters of North Fork Holston.
Carlock, Hunchrist...	June 8, 1774	126	South Branch of Lick Run, waters of Middle Fork Holston.
Carlock, Conrod......	June 1, 1774	168	Branch of Lick Run, Middle Fork Holston.
Collier, Aaron........	Dec. 2, 1774	45	Branch of North Fork Holston.
Cockran, Peter (decd.)	Dec. 2, 1774	145	Rich Valley, waters of North Fork Holston River.
Clemons, Zachariah...	Dec. 6, 1774	160	Fork of Holston River.
Carson, Robt........	Dec. 6, 1774	190	Rich Valley, North Fork Holston River.
Campbell, John......	Feb. 25, 1775	260	Rich Valley, North Fork Holston.
Campbell, David.....	Feb. 27, 1775	141	East side Middle Fork Holston.
Crow, John..........	Feb. 25, 1775	210	Both sides Hungers Mother, being the North Branch of Middle Fork Holston.
Campbell, John......	July 8, 1775	156	Both sides Middle Fork Holston.
Campbell, Arthur....	Feb. 8, 1775	279	Both sides Middle Fork Holston.
Campbell, Alexander..	Feb. 28, 1775	173	North side of South Fork of Holston River.
Davies, John.........	Feb. 21, 1774	275	Beaver Creek, North Fork of Holston River.
Doran, Alexander....	———, 1774	105	Head of Cane Brake on spur of Iron Mt., on Holston River.
Drake, Jos...........	June 8, 1774	326	Carlock's Branch, waters of Middle Fork Holston River.
Dungins, Hellens.....	June 11, 1774	354	Head spring of Neils Branch of Middle Fork Holston.
Dean, Jonathan......	June 11, 1774	60	North side So. Fork Holston.
Dougherty, Henry....	Feb. 24, 1775	240	Both sides Big Creek, waters of North Fork of Holston.

SMYTH COUNTY HISTORY

FINCASTLE COUNTY SURVEYS—(*Continued*)

Grantee	Date	Acres	Location
Davies, Wm.	Mar. 4, 1775	573	Both sides Beaver Dam Creek Head waters of Middle Fork Holston River.
Evans, Mathew	Mar. 10, 1774	197	Branch of South Fork Holston.
Ellis, Abraham	Feb. 16, 1774	82	Rich Valley.
Fuller, James	June 8, 1774	126	Carlock's Branch, waters of North Fork Holston River.
Galbreath, Arthur	Jan. 25, 1774	356	Middle Fork Holston River.
Gash, Martin	Mar. 12, 1774	195	Branch of North Fork Holston River.
Gobble, Frederick	Dec. 23, 1774	32	North Fork Holston River.
Gross, John	May 18, 1775	200	South Fork Holston River south side thereof.
Henly, Wm.	Feb. 15, 1774	227	North Fork Holston; Rich Valley.
Henderson, Wm.	Feb. 16, 1774	160	Rich Valley, North Fork Holston.
Hays, John	Mar. 4, 1774	227	Foot of Bushy Mt., both sides of Leatherwood Run, branch of North Fork Holston River
Hennegar, Conrad	June 7, 1774	37	North side Middle Fork Holston.
Hamilton, John	June 9, 1774	165	Higgins Mill Run, Branch of Middle Fork Holston River.
Higgins, Richard	June 9, 1774	119	Mill Creek, Branch of Holston.
Humphreys, Richard	June 7, 1774	404	Neils Branch, waters of Middle Fork Holston River.
Hopton, John	June 5, 1774	279	Head of Neils Branch, Middle Fork of Holston River.
Hoffaker, Michael	Dec. 6, 1774	100	Rich Valley; waters of North Fork Holston River.
Hatfield, Jeremiah	Dec. 6, 1774	140	North Fork Holston River.
Hatfield, Geo	Dec. 6, 1774	120	North Fork Holston River.
Hays, John	Mar. 2, 1775	234	Rich Valley, waters of North Fork Holston River.
Hays, Wm.	Feb. 28, 1775	224	Both sides North Fork Holston.
Henderson, Alexander	May 11, 1775	308	Head waters of Cripple Creek.
Hays, John	Feb. 7, 1775	308	Both sides Spruce Creek branch of Middle Fork Holston R.
Jones, John	Dec. 28, 1774	219	South Fork Holston River.
Jones, Joshua	May 15, 1774	373	Both sides Elk Creek, branch of South Fork Holston River.
Jekes, John	Feb. 24, 1775	249	East Side Middle Fork Holston, opposite Aspin Bottom.
Johnson, Hugh	Feb. 26, 1775	341	North Branches Middle Fork Holston.

PERMANENT SETTLEMENT 35

Montgomery County Deeds

Grantor	Grantee	Date	Acres	Location
Christian, Wm. and Anne his wife of Botetourt County.............	McCorkle, Jas.	June 28, 1777	995	On Holston River betwixt Davis' and the Royal Oak, commonly called the Magazine Spring.
Campbell, Wm. Exor. of Margaret Campbell, decd................	Hays, John, Jr.	Sept. 7, 1779	220	N. Fork Holston or Indian River.
Preston, Wm. Exor. of John Buchanan......	Scaggs, Jas.	Apr. 6, 1778	68	Meadow C. Br. New River.
Campbell, Wm., Robt. Campbell, John Allison, Chas. Allison, Alexander Campbell....	Vaught, David	Aug. 18, 1779	158	So. Fork Holston River.
Campbell, Wm. Robt., Campbell, Alexander, Campbell, Jno. Allison, Chas. Allison........	Smith, Jarvis	Aug. 18, 1779	...	South Fork Holston River.
Campbell, Wm. Robt., Campbell, Alexander, Campbell, John Allison, Chas. Allison....	Wiseman, Jno.	Aug. 18, 1779	104	At head Holston River.
Same as above except Robt. Campbell omitted................	Campbell, Robt.	Aug. 18, 1779	188	So. Fork Holston River.
Allison, Chas., John Allison, Robt. Campbell, Alexander Campbell and Wm. Campbell...	Kincannon, Francis	Aug. 18, 1779	205	So. Fork of Holston.
McCorkle, Jas..........	Culton, Jas. & Wm. Patterson	Aug. 16, 1782	995	On head Holston River.
Davies, Jas............	Davies, Jos.	Aug. 31, 1782	200	Middle Fork of Holston River.
Davies, Henry & Jane his wife................	Davies, Jas.	Aug. 31, 1782	140	Hd. Brs. Holston River.
Davies, Henry & Jane his wife.............	Davies, Wm.	Feb. 22, 1785	230	Holston River.
Ligitt, Wm.............	Elma, Christopher	Oct. 24, 1786	200	Br. Middle Fork Holston River.
Campbell, Jas..........	Griffitts, Jno.	Sept. 6, 1787	188	S. Fork of Holston.
Gooding, Abram & wife Elizabeth............	Kennaday, Philip	Aug. 30, 1788	162	Holston River.

Montgomery County Surveys

Grantee	Date	Acres	Location
Gilbreath, Arthur....	Jan. 28, 1774	255	Middle Fork Holston River.
Groseclose, Peter.....	Nov. 11, 1782	272	So. Fork Lick Creek, water Holston River in Rich Valley
Groseclose, Peter.....	Nov. 6, 1782	400	Rich Valley No. Fork Holston River.
Gooding, Abraham...	May 16, 1783	387	Hd. Waters on So. Fork Holston.
Hays, Andrew.......	Jan. 13, 1784	105	Both sides N. Fork Holston.
Harman, Peter.......	Jan. 17, 1783	140	Br. Middle Fork Holston R.
Johnson, David......	Mar. 19, 1783	290	Hd. Middle Fork Holston.
James, Wm..........	June 27, 1783	59	Near So. Fork Hd. Holston R.
Ligitt, Wm...........	May 29, 1783	80	Br. Middle Fork Holston River.
Lastly, Jno...........	May 15, 1783	250	Head Spring Cripple Creek.
Liggett, Jno. S.......	Sept. 14, 1784	368	Middle Fork Holston.
McMullin, Wm.......	Mar. 10, 1774	350	South Fork Holston River.
McCown, James......	Oct. 16, 1782	200	In Rich Valley North Fork Holston.
Mansaker, Gasper....	Dec. 16, 1774	190	Mockinson C. Br. N. Fork Holston River.
Pirtle, Geo...........	Dec. 8, 1774	190	In Rich Valley N. F. Holston River.
Patterson, Wm.......	Oct. 11, 1782	100	Br. Middle Fork Holston River
Richardson, Wm......	Oct. 19, 1782	200	Rich Valley waters N. F. Holston.
Sharp, John.........	Jan. 20, 1775	100	Beaver Creek Br. Holston R.
Spangler, Geo........	Nov. 12, 1782	270	Brs. Middle Fork Holston River.
Spangler, Peter.......	Nov. 6, 1782	350	Rich Valley N. Fork Holston River.
Spangler, Jacob......	Nov. 12, 1782	200	Rich Valley N. Fork Holston.
Buchanan, Robt......	June 16, 1774	722	Hd. waters Holston River.
Butler, Wm..........	Feb. 27, 1783	80	Br. Middle Fork Holston River
Buchanan, Robt......	Mar. 18, 1783	900	Hd. waters Middle Fork Holston.
Busterd, Wm.........	Mar. 22, 1782	200	Hd. springs Cripple Creek.
Cole, Jos., Jr.........	Mar. 20, 1774	215	Br. So. F. Holston River.
Campbell, Wm.......	Feb. 21, 1775	1345	Inc. 100 A. part of a tract grtd. to Chas. Campbell by letters patent date (omitted) and since became vested in sd. Wm. Campbell remaining 345 A. being a part of the Loyal Co's. grnt. lying on both sides Holston River & called Sophian Vale. (Middle F. Holston).

PERMANENT SETTLEMENT

Montgomery County Surveys—(Continued)

Grantee	Date	Acres	Location
Campbell, Arthur....	Feb. 8, 1775	1215	Lying on both sides of Middle Fork Holston R. and called the Royal Oak.
Calhoun, Wm........	Oct. 10, 1782	300	On a Br. Middle F. Holston.
Creager, Peter.......	Oct. 9, 1783	210	Hd. Waters Cripple Creek.
Davies, Henry.......	April 18, 1783	52	Middle Fork Holston.
Davies, Jos..........	Mar. 15, 1783	84	Lymrick Br. waters Middle Fork Holston.
Erwin, Geo..........	Aug. 4, 1784	170	Hd. Br. N. Fork Holston River.
Foster, Wm..........	Oct. 17, 1782	200	Lick C. Br. So. Fork Holston.
Foster, Wm..........	Oct. 16, 1782	200	Rich Valley waters of N. Fork Holston R. inc. place called Paulings Camp.
Fulton, Hugh........	Feb. 28, 1784	157	Hd. North Fork Holston River.

Washington County Surveys

Grantee	Date	Acres	Location
Allison, John.........	Sept. 1, 1781	400	Beaver Creek.
Anderson, John......	Aug. 15, 1782	400	Middle Fork Holston R.
Anderson, John......	Aug. 15, 1782	300	Middle Fork Holston R.
Anderson, Isaac......	July 15, 1782	50	South Fork Holston R.
Anderson, Barnabas ..	Jan. 30, 1783	205	South side Middle Fork Holston.
Bermum, John.......	Aug. 10, 1781	150	South Fork Holston.
Bright, Thomas......	Oct. 16, 1782	150	Rich Valley.
Bowen, Charles......	Mar. 31, 1784	100	South Side Patent Tract.
Bates, Thomas.......	Sept. 5, 1784	500	Middle Fork Holston R.
Brown, Robert.......	Aug. 24, 1781	100	Cedar Creek.
Buchanan, Moses.....	Aug. 25, 1781	200	South Fork Holston R.
Bunton, Andrew.....	Aug. 18, 1781	200	South Fork Holston R.
Bishop, Matthew.....	Aug. 30, 1781	100	South Fork Holston R.
Burk, Benjamin......	May 5, 1785	180	Both sides North Fork Holston River.
Barnes, Cornelius.....	Aug. 15, 1786	5000	North Fork Holston.
Buchanan, Mathew...	May 26, 1786	220	Both Sides South Fork Holston River.
Brooks, Henry.......	Aug. 17, 1781	200	North Fork Holston.
Bredan, Samuel & James	Mar. 22, 1790	330	Rich Valley.
Bluebaugh, Jacob....	Feb. 9, 1786	150	Both Sides North Fork Holston River.
Byrd, Francis & Chas.	Jan. 20, 1787	200	North Fork Holston R.
Bennet, Wm.........	Sept. 8, 1792	400	Rich Valley.
Bishop, Levi, & Peleg, Tilson & Lemuel Tilson	Aug. 12, 1796	330	Adjoining Elisha Dungan's Land.
Callahan, Edward....	Aug. 25, 1782	400	Mill Creek, North Fork Holston R.

WASHINGTON COUNTY SURVEYS—(Continued)

Grantee	Date	Acres	Location
Cochran, Jas..........	Sept. 1, 1781	300	Rich Valley.
Cole, Joseph..........	Aug. 18, 1781	400	South Fork Holston R.
Crabtree, John........	Aug. 27, 1781	150	Poor Valley.
Crabtree, Jas..........	Aug. 27, 1781	400	Rich Valley.
Craven, John.........	May 8, 1783	100	Rich Hill, South Side Short Mt.
Campbell, Robert & Joseph Sinclair.....	Sept. 1, 1781	150	South Fork Holston.
Cole, Joseph & Hugh..	Aug. 31, 1781	400	South Fork Holston.
Campbell, James......	Aug. 31, 1781	400	South Fork Holston.
Carmack, Cornelius...	June 6, 1783	370	Rich Valley.
Cole, Sampson........	Sept. 8, 1781	400	South Fork Holston.
Cole, Zachariah & Nathaniel McClure.	Mar. 11, 1783	382	South Side South Fork Holston.
Cole, Lankens & Nathan McClure...	Aug. 28, 1781	400	South Fork Holston.
Colley, Wm...........	Nov. 25, 1781	152	Middle Fork Holston.
Campbell, Patrick....	Sept. 1, 1781	400	Middle Fork Holston.
Cole, Israel...........	Sept. 8, 1781	400	South Fork Holston.
Cooley, John..........	Aug. 22, 1786	70	On Laurel Fork Holston River.
Cerbrours, John......	Aug. 31, 1781	200½	South Fork
Couts, John..........	Apr. 7, 1795	150	South side South Fork Holston River.
Cox, Jacob...........	May 29, 1796	59	North Side North Fork Holston River.
Campbell, John.......	Aug. 24, 1781	100	Washington Co., adjoining Jno. Campbell & Wm. Bennet.
Crow, Robert.........	Feb. 11, 1796	49	South Side Middle Fork Holston River.
Campbell, John, Jr....	Aug. 29, 1796	100	Rich Valley.
Davison, Andrew.....	Aug. 15, 1781	250	Rich Valley.
Dean, Jonathan, Jr....	May 28, 1782	241	Middle & South Forks Holston River.
Dougherty, Jas........	Aug. 29, 1781	400	Lick Run.
Denniston, Robt......	Aug. 30, 1781	252	North Fork Holston.
Dean, Jonathan......	Aug. 31, 1781	200	North Side of South Fork Holston River.
Dougherty, Geo......	Aug. 29, 1781	300	Middle Fork Holston.
Debusk, Elijah.......	June 7, 1792	200	South Side South Fork Holston River.
Doyle, John..........	Sept. 11, 1795	100	Near Salt Lick on South side North Fork Holston River.
Deck, Adam..........	May 2, 1796	30	Cove Creek in Rich Valley.
Dungan, Helius......	Aug. 28, 1781	400	Neil's Branch.
Dungan, Elisha......	Nov. 14, 1781	404	Neil's Branch.
Evans, Andrew.......	Aug. 25, 1781	300	Hungers Mother.
Edgar, Geo...........	Aug. 17, 1781	400	Rich Valley.

PERMANENT SETTLEMENT 39

Washington County Surveys—(Continued)

Grantee	Date	Acres	Location
Elder, Mathew	Aug. 18, 1781	400	Middle Fork Holston.
Fleenor, Gasper	Aug. 17, 1781	250	Rich Valley.
Fowler, John	Aug. 8, 1781	400	North Fork Holston.
Faris, Gideon	Aug. 17, 1781	250	South Fork Holston R.
Faris, Robert	Aug. 29, 1781	400	South Fork Holston R.
Faris, Edward	Aug. 31, 1781	400	Middle Fork Holston.
Frost, John	Aug. 29, 1781	200	North Fork Holston.
Glen, James	Aug. 20, 1781	250	North Fork Holston.
Gwyn, John; Wm. Goforth & Hugh Bryson	Aug. 25, 1781	400	North Fork Holston.
Goff, Andrew	Aug. 21, 1781	400	North Fork Holston.
Gobble, Frederick	Aug. 25, 1781	100	North Fork Holston.
Gobble, George	Apr. 20, 1782	100	North Fork Holston.
Greenway, John	Mar. 25, 1784	241	Between Middle & S. Fork Holston River.
Gillilan, James	Aug. 16, 1781	200	North Side Holston River.
Gibson, Samuel	Aug. 29, 1781	400	Washington Co., Adjoining Gen. Wm. Campbell's Patent Line.
Gallougher, Joel	Mar. 17, 1785	121	Middle Fork Holston.
Gestineau, Joab	Feb. 17, 1790	316	South side Middle Fork Holston River.
Gillenwaters, Elijah	Mar. 10, 1797	700	Both Sides North Fork Holston River.
Henderson, Robt	May 2, 1782	250	Rich Valley.
Henderson, Wm	Aug. 17, 1781	100	Rich Valley.
Halfaker, Michael	Jan. 15, 1783	100	Rich Valley.
Halfaker, Michael	Sept. 1, 1781	100	North Fork Holston.
Hensley, Samuel	Aug. 25, 1782	400	Rich Valley.
Hawley, Jos	Oct. 19, 1782	126	Rich Valley.
Hobbs, Vincent	Aug. 16, 1781	300	North Fork Holston R.
Humphreys, Wm	Aug. 31, 1781	400	Holston River.
Houston, James	Sept. 2, 1781	400	South Fork Holston River.
Houston, Christopher	Sept. 2, 1781	400	South Fork Holston R.
Houston, Samuel	Aug. 21, 1781	400	Holston River.
Houston, Robt	Sept. 2, 1781	400	South Side South Fork Holston River.
Henry, Samuel	Aug. 30, 1781	400	Middle Fork Holston R.
Hubble, Justis	Aug. 31, 1781	282	South Fork Holston R.
Hennegar, Conrad	Aug. 18, 1781	250	Middle Fork.
Higgins, Richard	Nov. 24, 1784	136	Washington County, Adjoining Seven Mile Ford.
Henderson, Andrew	Aug. 30, 1781	400	South Side Middle Fork Holston River.
Holliett, Richard & John Woolsey	Aug. 1, 1781	400	North Side Middle Fork Holston.

SMYTH COUNTY HISTORY

WASHINGTON COUNTY SURVEYS—(*Continued*)

Grantee	Date	Acres	Location
Hammon, Wm.......	June 6, 1786	130	South Side Holston R.
Heton, Jno...........	Nov. 8, 1785	100	On Hungers Mother.
Hays, Jno...........	Apr. 5, 1790	84	On Hungers Mother.
Head, Wm...........	Aug. 25, 1781	400	Rich Valley.
Hortenstine, Jacob....	June 8, 1793	109	On Branch South Fork Holston.
Hoofacon, Michael....	Oct. 20, 1794	140	North Side Chestnut Ridge & South Branches North Fork Holston.
Heron, Jas...........	Feb. 17, 1795	10430	Middle & North Forks Holston.
Heron, Jas...........	Feb. 16, 1795	16058	North & Middle Forks Holston.
Heron, Jas...........	Feb. 25, 1795	62800	Waters of New River & South Fork Holston.
Harvey, Matthew....	Mar. 6, 1795	36345	Waters Laurel & N. Fork Holston & Waters of Clinch River.
Harvey, Matthew....	Mar. 2, 1795	13655	Laurel Fork & Beaver Dam Fork.
Hovemaster, Goodlove	Apr. 22, 1795	100	Walker's Mtn. & Waters North Fork Holston.
Heart, Elijah........	May 30, 1795	45	South Side North Fork.
Hogart, Jas..........	Apr. 13, 1795	100	Both Sides North Fork Holston.
Holt, Henry.........	June 7, 1797	70	North Side North Fork Holston.
Ickis, John..........	Apr. 11, 1784	400	East Side Middle Fork Holston River.
Ickis, John..........	Aug. 31, 1781	400	East Side Middle Fork Holston River.
Johnson, Hugh & Margaret Buchanan	Jan. 26, 1785	400	Middle Fork Holston R.
John, Benjamine.....	Sept. 23, 1790	10	Oar Bank on Branch of South Fork Holston.
Johnson, Hugh & Margaret Buchanan	Aug. 25, 1781	400	Holston River.
Johnston, Thomas....	Apr. 9, 1789	100	North Fork Holston.
Jeans, Henry........	Oct. 18, 1793	50	North Side Middle Fork Holston River.
Jones, Elizabeth......	Aug. 29, 1781	100	Branch Middle Fork Holston River.
Jamison, Edward & John..............	Mar. 26, 1785	414	Middle Fork Holston River.
Kincade, John........	Oct. 30, 1783	182	Middle Fork Holston River.
Kinkanan, Jas........	Jan. 14, 1783	50	Rich Valley.
Keywood, Moses.....	Aug. 25, 1781	400	Rich Valley.
Karlock, Conrad.....	Aug. 29, 1781	300	Lick Run.
Kirk, John..........	Sept. 1, 1781	300	Middle Fork Holston.

PERMANENT SETTLEMENT

WASHINGTON COUNTY SURVEYS—(*Continued*)

Grantee	Date	Acres	Location
Kerr, Adam	Aug. 17, 1781	300	Holston River.
Kindrick, John	Aug. 13, 1781	400	North Fork Holston.
Kounts, Henry	June 10, 1786	330	Both sides Middle Fork Holston.
Keeywood, Berry	Feb. 14, 1794	400	Rich Valley.
Kincade, Robt	Feb. 26, 1795	150	On Young's Creek.
Lee, Peter	Aug. 27, 1781	400	Rich Valley.
Lyon, Humberson	Apr. 24, 1783	370	North Fork Holston.
Lutspike, Christopher	Apr. 22, 1782	156	Carlock's Crk.
Linder, Anthony	Aug. 25, 1781	400	North Fork Holston.
Long, Wm	Sept. 1, 1781	400	Middle Fork Holston R.
Lerberber, Adam	Aug. 30, 1781	150	South Fork Holston.
Lefever, Abraham	May 3, 1784	200	South Fork Holston R.
Logan, James	Nov. 3, 1784	240	Rich Valley on North Fork Holston R.
Lewis, Aaron	Dec. 13, 1784	300	South Side Middle Fork Holston R.
Lloyd, Thos. A	Aug. 31, 1781	200	South Fork Holston R.
Lewis, Andrew	Aug. 25, 1781	300	Both Sides Hungers Mother.
Long, Wm	Oct. 8, 1788	400	Middle Fork Holston R.
Lockhart, Wm	Feb. 13, 1794	60	Rich Valley.
Lee, John, Sr	Feb. 13, 1794	48	South Side North Fork Holston.
Lee, John, Sr	Feb. 13, 1794	90	Both Sides North Fork Holston.
Lonard, Griffin	Jan. 23, 1796	50	North Fork Holston R.
Lammie, Jas	Dec. 12, 1795	50	Cove Creek.
Lee, Thos	June 22, 1797	25	North Side North Fork Holston.
McCormack, Joshua	Apr. 18, 1782	400	Middle Fork Holston.
McReynolds, Samuel	Feb. 4, 1783	70	Rich Valley.
McLung, Francis	Aug. 17, 1781	400	Middle Fork Holston River.
McCutcheon, Jno	Aug. 17, 1781	300	South Fork Holston R.
McNutt, Alexander	Aug. 25, 1781	400	South Fork Holston R.
McClure, Halbert	Aug. 16, 1782	400	Rich Valley.
McAll, Peter	Sept. 1, 1781	400	North Fork Holston R.
McCarthy, Enoch	Oct. 2, 1782	116	Rich Valley.
McKenny, Colin	Aug. 27, 1781	200	Cedar Creek.
McReynolds, John	Feb. 4, 1783	126	Rich Valley.
McGinnis, Edward	June 2, 1782	400	South Fork Holston.
McCauley, John	Aug. 28, 1781	280	Holston River.
McCulloch, Robt	June 3, 1781	250	Both Sides North Fork Holston River.
McCulloch, Jno	June 3, 1785	175	Both Sides North Fork Holston River; Canoe Bottom.
McNutt, Alexander	Aug. 25, 1781	300	South Fork Holston R.

SMYTH COUNTY HISTORY

WASHINGTON COUNTY SURVEYS—(Continued)

Grantee	Date	Acres	Location
McHenry, John	Apr. 28, 1785	190	North Fork Holston in Rich Valley.
McCord, Benjamin	Aug. 29, 1781	100	Laurel Creek.
McMackin, Thomas, & James Rogers	Aug. 29, 1781	400	North Branches Middle Fork Holston River above Seven Mile Ford.
McNew, Geo.	Apr. 10, 1795	120	Halfacre's Crk.
McClure, Halbert	Mar. 16, 1793	109	South Side Middle Fork Holston.
McDonald, Columbia.	Mar. 4, 1793	148	North Side Middle Fork Holston River.
McNew, Elisha	Apr. 26, 1793	95	North Fork Holston.
McCall, John	Nov. 13, 1794	100	South Side Walker's Mtn.
McNeal, Neal	June 25, 1795	50	Rich Valley.
McKee, Andrew	Oct. 5, 1789	228	Branch Middle Fork Holston River.
McClure, Nathaniel	Aug. 8, 1785	400	Branch South Fork Holston River.
Moffet, John	Aug. 22, 1781	400	North Fork Holston.
Morrow, Adam	Aug. 29, 1781	400	South Fork Holston.
Morgan, Edward	Aug. 28, 1781	150	Washington County.
Mattingly, Walter	Apr. 13, 1785	134	Rich Valley, North Side Laurel Fork.
Magee, Samuel	Aug. 29, 1786	217	South Side Holston.
Markland, Wm.	Aug. 30, 1781	300	Both Sides Lick Run.
Murdock, Jno.	Mar. 20, 1790	300	Both Sides Chestnut Ridge & North Fork Holston.
Miller, Hugh	Sept. 11, 1792	150	Middle Fork Holston.
Main, Sibeus	Apr. —, 1795	280	On Cove Creek and Red Stone on North Side Iron Mtn.
Marshall, Andrew	Dec. 9, 1795	425	Rich Valley.
Napier, Wm.	Feb. 6, 1783	164	Carlock's Creek.
Nunn, Isley	Sept. 18, 1782	120	North Fork Holston.
Nelson, John	Aug. 29, 1781	250	Lick Run.
Nicholas, Matthias	Mar. 3, 1785	276	Rich Valley.
Norton, Thos.	Mar. 28, 1794	42	On Branch South Fork Holston River.
Nickels, Mathias	Oct. 17, 1794	100	North Fork Holston.
Niel, Francis	Nov. 1, 1783	200	North Fork Holston R.
Outlaw, Alexander	June 26, 1782	247	Rich Valley.
Phillips, David	Aug. 30, 1781	400	South Fork Holston R.
Patterson, Jno.	Aug. 28, 1781	372	Middle Fork Holston.
Posey, Jos.	Aug. 17, 1781	400	Middle Fork Holston.
Piki, Wm.	Aug. 27, 1781	400	Rich Valley on Cedar Crk.
Purkle, Henry	Sept. 11, 1781	200	North Fork Holston.
Poston, Richard	Jan. 7, 1786	450	North Fork Holston.
Phips, Jno.	Sept. 1, 1781	400	North Fork Holston.

PERMANENT SETTLEMENT

Washington County Surveys—(Continued)

Grantee	Date	Acres	Location
Parkey, Christopher	Nov. 21, 1791	272	Holston River.
Peters, Jno	Oct. 27, 1795	104	Both Sides North Fork Holston River.
Porterfield, Robert	Sept. 1, 1781	400	Rich Valley.
Richardson, Nathan	Mar. 13, 1783	74	Rich Valley.
Robinson, Jno	Aug. 16, 1781	250	Rich Valley.
Russell, Andrew	Aug. 30, 1781	400	South Side Middle Fork Holston River.
Robinson, Jas	Aug. 17, 1781	300	South Side Middle Fork Holston River.
Redshaw, Jos	Sept. 1, 1781	400	Middle Fork Holston.
Robinson, Jas	Aug. 17, 1781	300	South Side Middle F.
Reamey, Daniel	Aug. 30, 1781	400	Coon's Run.
Roman, Joshua	Mar. 26, 1785	300	Both Sides Hungers Mother Branch of Holston.
Rogers, Jno	Aug. 24, 1781	400	Washington County At Clay Lick.
Ramsay, Robt	Aug. 31, 1781	300	South Fork Holston R.
Russell, Mrs. Elizabeth	Feb. 10, 1794	140	Both Sides Fowler's Mill Creek
Rigs, Wm	June 8, 1795	100	South Side North Fork Holston.
Rouse, Paulser & Jacob Hortenstine	Aug. 30, 1781	300	South Fork Holston.
Ryley, Daniel	Nov. 28, 1795	200	Both Sides North Fork Holston.
Richmond, John	June 11, 1796	50	Rich Valley.
Scott, Jno	Jan. 29, 1783	400	North Side Middle Fork Holston.
Starns, Mary	Aug. 29, 1781	400	South Side Holston.
Smith, Wm	Aug. 17, 1786	1000	South Side South Fork Holston River.
Stephens, Benjamin	Sept. 1, 1786	100	Rich Valley.
Scott, Samuel	Feb. 20, 1786	100	Rich Valley.
Smith, Nathan	Aug. 15, 1781	150	Rich Valley.
Spharr, Henry	Oct. 17, 1782	400	Rich Valley.
Stevenson, Robert	Aug. 17, 1781	400	South Fork Holston R.
Scott, Alex	Aug. 22, 1781	300	Cedar Crk.
Scott, Wm	Aug. 27, 1781	200	Rich Valley.
Scott, Jas	Aug. 21, 1781	300	Cedar Crk.
Sharp, Benjamin	Oct. 24, 1783	200	Cedar Crk.
Tate, Thos	Oct. 16, 1783	200	Cedar Crk.
Smith, Geo	June 27, 1782	400	Rich Valley.
Starns, John	Aug. 31, 1782	200	Middle Fork Holston.
Shanan, Jno	Sept. 21, 1797	46	North Fork Holston & North Side Walker's Mtn.
Tate, Wm	Dec. 14, 1783	146	South Side North Fk. Holston River.

SMYTH COUNTY HISTORY

Washington County Surveys—(Continued)

Grantee	Date	Acres	Location
Trimble, Jas.	Aug. 30, 1781	400	Middle Fork Holston.
Tillotson, Wm.	July 15, 1782	282	South Fork Holston.
Balbert, Bazil, Jr.	Feb. 8, 1794	170	Both Sides Lee's Crk.
Taylor, Jacob	Sept. 1, 1794	103	North Side North Fork Holston River.
Talbot, Bazell	Mar. 28, 1793	100	North Fork Holston.
Thomas, Jno.	Sept. 15, 1795	230	Waters Redstone on South Fork Holston.
Tucker, Jno.	Oct. 29, 1795	100	Waters North Side Fork Holston.
Thurman, Chas.	Mar. 4, 1796	50	North Side North Fork Holston.
Vanhook, Thos. & Laurence	Aug. 21, 1781	400	Lyons Crk.
Wylie, Alexander	Oct. 1, 1782	181	Rich Valley.
Weir, Samuel	Aug. 14, 1781	200	South Fork Holston.
Woolsey, Thos.	Aug. —, 1781	300	South Fork Holston.
Wier, Johnathan	Aug. 17, 1781	400	Between Middle and South Fork Holston R.
Watson, Patrick	Nov. 30, 1783	264	North Fork Holston.
Willis, Henry	June 25, 1782	400	Rich Valley.
White, Wm.	Aug. 28, 1781	150	Middle Fork Holston.
Walker, Jno.	Aug. 31, 1781	400	Middle Fork Holston.
Watson, Gilbert	Sept. 1, 1781	200	North Fork Holston.
Wheeler, Jas.	Aug. 30, 1781	400	South Fork Holston.
Woolsey, Thos.	June 12, 1782	400	South Fork Holston.
Woolsey, Thos.	Aug. 30, 1781	400	South Fork Holston.
Wright, Jacob	May 7, 1782	400	South Fork Holston.
Wolsey, Geo.	Aug. 31, 1781	300	Middle Fork Holston.
Wilkerson, Francis	May 4, 1784	82	Thompson's Crk.
Webb, Wm.	Feb. 25, 1785	91	Rich Valley.
Wilkerson, Francis	Sept. 17, 1785	120	On Hungers Mother, Whitesides Fork, Thompson's Crk.
Watson, Jas.	Aug. 19, 1785	70	On Gross Crk.
Walker, Wm.	Sept. 3, 1786	400	Laurel Fork.
Wheeler, Stephen	Dec. 1, 1786	62	Hungers Mother.
Williams, Jno.	— 31, 1781	400	North Branch Middle Fork Holston.
Wilkerson, Wm.	Jan. 6, 1795	80	Both Sides Middle Fork Holston.
Wilson, Robt.	May 29, 1795	50	North Side Walker's Mtn.
Woodward, Samuel	June 21, 1797	38	Both Sides Young's Mill Crk.
Williams, Robt.	Aug. 14, 1781	150	Walker's Mtn.
Young, Jas.	Aug. 15, 1781	200	Rich Valley.
Young, David	May 3, 1782	400	Rich Valley.

CHAPTER IV

DUNMORE'S WAR

THROUGHOUT 1773 the dread of Indian uprisings lay heavy upon the hearts of the Virginians. The northwest tribes were bitterly restive and southern Indians were in a menacing mood. Reports were reaching the whites of impending hurling of united tribes in fearful force upon them. Daniel Boone had to abandon settlements in Kentucky for the time being because of an unprovoked attack upon his party in Powell's Valley, when his son and William Russell's son were murdered. The news of this disaster sent a thrill of apprehensive horror through the settlements. It was, in fact, the beginning of Dunmore's War. Daniel Boone turned back to Russell's place at Castle's Woods and from that time until the winter of 1775 he was vigorously engaged in the frontier defense of Southwest Virginia. Boone's residence was on the Clinch River in the region where it passes out of Russell into Scott. He was occupied constantly in the defense of the forts on Clinch and in extensive excursions and scouts into the western woods. It is certain that he passed through Smyth once on his way to Col. William Preston's, stopping at Royal Oak to confer with Maj. Arthur Campbell and it is likely that he paid more than one visit to this frontier leader at Royal Oak. One of the Crabtrees who lived in the vicinity of Saltville, a reckless man and bitter Indian hater, killed a friendly Cherokee Indian at a horse race on the Watauga. This incident seemed about to bring the whole Cherokee nation war-whooping and scalping upon the whites, a danger that was averted by the diplomatic skill of James Robertson, leader of the Watauga settlements. Colonel Campbell writes as follows of this crisis:

Cherokee Indian Killed
Letter of Maj. Arthur Campbell to Col. William Preston

Sir—Since the rash action of killing a Cherokee on Wattaugo, the lower settlement on this, and Clynch Rivers, is greatly alarmed. some preparing to move off: and indeed from the behaviour of the Squa & Indian fellow, that was in Company with the one that was killed; we may expect a reprisal will be made shortly, if there is not some Men sent to cover the Inhabitants, until the matter can be made up with the Chiefs. I imagine a Letter from Colo. Lewis (as he is an old acquaintance and it is a relation of old Outassatus that is killed called Billey) would be of service at this time; at least might prolong an invasion until we are better prepared. One Crabtree is generally suspected to be the Principal, in the late dispatching of Cherokee Billey. However let the consequence of the affair be what it will, I am persuaded it would be easier to find 200 Men to screen him from the Law, than ten to bring him to Justice; Crabtrees different robberies, the Murder of Russell, Boons; & Drakes Sons is in every ones mouth.
I am Sir
your mo. Obedient Servt.
Arthur Campbell

Maj. Arthur Campbell to Col. William Preston.

Royal Oak June 22d. 1774

Sir—Yesterday I received your Letter with the two inclosed. This morning I had a favourable oppertunity to send them to Wattago; and from thence I have reason to expect a speedy conveyance to the nation As I had some acquaintance with Mr. Cameron, I took the liberty to write to him, on the same subject: mentioning briefly the late murder on Wattago; and what degree of detestation it is held in, by the sober minded, in this Country; I also enlarged fully on the provocations we received last Fall; taking the liberty at the same time to blame his conduct, for giving Orders, for robberies, on the Indian Lands whereby, perhaps the profligate part of the nation, is both our Judges, and executioners.

Notwithstanding these earnest endeavours, to prevent a calamity, that may be very destructive to us; It appears that Crabtree, and a few mislead followers, will frustrate all we can do. Last Week he returned from an adventure over, at Nola-Chuckee, to one Browns (a Smith that Works for the Cherokees) as he was informed, before he left Holston, that there was 2 or 3 Indians there a hunting However our Hero, was disappointed in his expectations; for instead of finding two, or three, defenceless wretches he was informed of 37 Warriors being in the Neighbourhood, were apprized of his intentions; and would not fail to examine Strangers, strictly; upon this intelligence, he departed the place, with precipitation; and came up to his Fathers at the Big Lick. Yet still restless he went down the River a few days ago to make another attempt.

Since the alarm on Copper Creek, I think, the most of the people seem to disapprove Crabtree's conduct: They were ready enough then; to ascribe that supposed Murder, to his doings; however inconsistant they were before in avowing, they would screen him from Justice.

I shall esteem it my Duty to transmit to you an account of any true alarm, that may happen; and please favour me with the like account, if the War has actually broke out to the Northward.

I am very uneasy about by Friend Floyd, as my night tho't of him seems to presage his fate; I hope he is only in Danger
            I am Sir Your Obedient Humble Servt.
                              Arthur Campbell

    Maj. Arthur Campbell to Col. William Preston.

Sir—I Received yours of the 20th Inst., and immediately afterwards got my Brother John, to set out down the River, to the settlement adjoining the Indian Line, that he might see to sending out the Spy, and your Orders in other respects more effectually executed, than could be done by Letter.

I have recommended it to the Spy, that he goes from Holston, to go as far as the Ford on Broad River: and to be particularly attentive, to observe the path, as they go along, at least, twice a Day, and to travel some distance, up, and down, the River, after they arrive at the Ford. If this piece of Duty is well executed, I have reason to expect we will have timeous (timely) notice, to be prepared to met a large Body, if an Enemy approaches.

From the expressions of the Little Carpenter, when last on Wattogo; and the behaviour of some Indians, that has since been on Nola-Chuckee; I think the Cherokees would willingly avoid a War with us; except some repeated affront from Crabtree, provokes them to it; and rather so, as I am informed their Magazine of Powder is chiefly damaged, by being Stored up in Bags, in a Cave, or some such place, under Ground. However, it may be prudent for us, to be on our guard, as it may be the Seventy that was to meet at the Grand-Council, may return with some Shawanese in Company, who may choose to take some Scalps with them, by way of a Declaration of War.

I have wrote to Capt. Shelby to send me notice immediately of any alarm that may happen; and I will then, without delay, transmit the same to you by Express.

I expect a few weeks will clear up our Doubts, by whom we are to be attacked; I shall be very uneasy until the Ammunition arrives from Rocky Ridge.

I am Sir Your most Obedient Servt.

Arthur Campbell

June 23d. 1774

Throughout Dunmore's War Smyth County was a part of Fincastle County and as such fought its full share. Arthur Campbell, Major of Fincastle Militia, had his hands full in defending the settlements from Indians and equipping and maintaining rangers and in recruiting and equipping men for the Point Pleasant campaign. He was required to remain at home during that famous campaign in charge of directing the settlements against the murderous raids of savages. One of his brothers and his cousin, William Campbell, and others from the Smyth County settlement marched with the troops to Point Pleasant. Arthur Campbell's correspondence gives a vivid picture of conditions in that time.

In his letters to Colonel Preston and others he speaks of Captain Harrod's being at Royal Oak, having led his men from the settlement he was just starting in Kentucky because of the folly of remaining in that isolated place with all the tribes on the warpath; of Boone and his services; of the various officers of militia; of shortage of powder, having to send men out to range with Indians with only two, three or four "shoots" apiece. On one occasion he had to send some out without any "shoots." When they had as much as six "shoots" they seemed to feel well supplied.

He records his disgust and mortification at seeing a "family flying by" his home, in flight to safer regions. When one considers the prevailing shortage of ammunition and of food the wonder is that many more were not "flying by," putting distance between them and the bloodthirsty red devils that were apt at any moment to come raging through the settlements. He voices his contempt and disgust at certain slackers and wants to know what to do with them to make them take their part of the load. He had quite a time of it getting his quota of men for the Point Pleasant campaign as men were not enthusiastic about going on that long march to distant regions while their women and children must be left exposed to savage fury. That he succeeded speaks both for his qualities of leadership and for the heroic fortitude of these frontiersmen of Holston and Clinch. In both Dunmore's and the Revolutionary War it was Arthur Campbell's big job to recruit and send out men on the distant campaigns that issued in notable battles and led to glory, while he himself attended to the harder, more important and equally perilous but obscure task of keeping up morale at home and defending the hundreds of miles of far-flung frontier, with scattered cabins, from deadly attack. His difficulties were not confined to raising and equipping men for the expedition but also in composing their jealousies and differences when they had agreed to go.

Through August of 1774 militia were being mustered at the Town House. The plan was to march them under Capt. John Floyd and Capt. William Campbell, but Capt. Joseph Drake, a bold fearless fighter and a man of ability and popularity who had seen considerable service, thought that he ought to lead. He had a following who refused to go under any other leader. The wrangling went once to the point of open mutiny by Drake and his supporters in a muster at the Town House. Floyd and Arthur Campbell write harshly and bitterly of Drake. Joseph Drake lived on Carlocks Creek near Chilhowie. He was killed in the Indian fight at Blue Lick in Kentucky.

While the men were gone on the Point Pleasant campaign Arthur Campbell with the help of some mighty good men, such as James Thompson and Daniel Boone defended the frontier with reasonable success, but Logan, the outraged Mingo Chief seized this opportunity to slake his thirst for vengeance on the blood of Fincastle people.

In September of 1774 the Indians raided Rich Valley, but the settlers were forewarned by one Bradshaw who had seen the ravages they had committed across the mountain in Tazewell, ran ahead of them and got the people out just in time. Then some of the inhabitants congregated at the fortified house of a Mr. Harrison in the lower Valley; most of them crossed the mountain to Arthur Campbell's fort at Royal Oak, arriving in panic-stricken and pitiable condition.

September 8 is the anniversary of this drama of terror enacted in Thompson Valley, Tazewell County, and Rich Valley, Smyth County. John Henry, his wife and three small children had been living in Thompson's Valley only a few months. Early in the morning of Sept. 8, 1774, he was standing in his cabin door, looking out into the still morning beauty of the wild woods. A musket shot; an Indian yell; John Henry running into the woods, mortally wounded. His wife and children carried off. In the woods Henry accidentally met with old John Hamilton, who concealed him in a thicket until he should alarm the fort and bring him assistance. Hamilton had the courage to go by Henry's house, but saw nothing either of the Indians or of the women and children. Hamilton, hurrying to the fort, met with one Bradshaw, who had found Indian signs in his cornfield and was likewise hurrying to the fort. About three miles from Henry's place they happened on the spot where some twelve or fifteen Indians had breakfasted. The trail showed them headed for upper Holston country and Bradshaw lit out for Rich Valley, getting there in time to warn most of the settlers. The next morning the families of the Rich Valley settlement were across the mountain at Royal Oak "in a distressed condition." Bradshaw's run across Clinch Mountain had brought warning just in time for them to get out ahead of a general massacre. The Indians came on into Rich Valley on the eighth. Samuel Lemmey was taken captive and John and Archibald Buchanan's families barely escaped. We would like to know just how.

There are almost as many Buchanans living in and around Rich Valley today as there were Indians in the whole Shawnee tribe, among them Johns and Archibalds. There are quite a few Lammies there, too, although the spelling of their name is somewhat different from Arthur Campbell's chirography.

Things like this were happening all around through Southwest Virginia and all through that fateful September. They happened, too, in August and October, but mostly in September. Not the least of it was that nobody knew when or where they might happen. Nobody anywhere in all the widely scattered settlements along Holston, Clinch, Powell, or New Rivers knew when they might hear the crash of musket, the blood-chilling yell, the sickening crash of tomahawks into skull. The corn crop was ripening. The wild animals had to be kept out of it and it had to be harvested. How to save and harvest the crops was a ticklish and serious problem when no man knew when he went into his cornfield whether he would come out with a scalp on his head. It was especially serious because without that corn there would be no bread that winter. With the families of Rich Valley forted at Royal Oak, from ten to twenty miles across a mountain, they still managed somehow to save most of the crops.

The superabundance of foodstuffs indicated by the rich displays at our county fairs bring out by vivid contrast the hard bitter scarcity of that time. The officers' letters reveal their frantic, sometimes almost despairing, search for flour to supply the forts and the rangers scouting for Indians. The powder burned in a single night's brilliant pyrotechnic display at one of our fairs would have been a generous supply for whole companies of rangers throughout the whole of this critical period of strenuous warfare. Colonel Preston, conserving carefully his meagre supply, doles it out in half pound and pound lots. Major Campbell sends out companies to range supplied with enough powder to give the men three "shoots" apiece. In one letter to the colonel he is jubilant over being able to send out a company supplied with "half dozen shoots apiece." Colonel Preston once expressed the hope that he may be able to get two pounds at a certain place. Major Campbell writing one of his letters is "mortified at the sight of a family flying by." The surprising thing is that all of the families were not "flying by," back to the valley of Virginia where there was at least something to eat and powder enough for all the "shoots" that might have to be shot.

Late in the evening of the twenty-fourth of September Logan and his band murdered and scalped the Roberts family in Tennessee just over the line from Scott County. Here on the body of one of his victims, or in the house, Logan left his famous note explaining why he had turned from the friend into the deadly foe of the white man. The note was turned over to Arthur Campbell and he forwarded it to Colonel Preston.

The situation in October is described in this letter from Col. Arthur Campbell to Col. William Preston:

Maj. Arthur Campbell to Col. William Preston.

Royal-Oak, Octo. 6, 1774

Sir—The after Mr. Cummins left this, I Received your Letter of ye 1st. Inst. sent out by Paddy Brown; who tho't proper, to carry the Letter past, and it was returned me this day open. I wish it was in my power to humour every Inhabitant, consistant with Justice to the Service; but there is many of them so unreasonably selfish I dispair of succeeding in every case.

Paddy Brown is an Old Weaver Body, that lives with one of the Doughertys, he came here one day and applied for to get in for a Spy. I very flatly refused him; he then went off in dudgeon.

Upon the alarm of Lammey being taken, Vances & Fowlers Wives with several other Families convened at Mr. Harrisons which lyes upon the Main path to Clinch, in the Rich Valley opposit to the Town-House, upon the request of several Inhabitants in both sides, I ordered Six men to be Stationed there for ten Days; two of which was always to be out ranging. Heny. & Joso. Dougherty moved their Families to this side the mountain, disagreeing with ye. Majority of ye. Inhabitants, as to the place to build a Fort. Mr. John Campbells Wife has been in this side the mountain this two months past, and himself has acted as Ensign to Capt. Smith, on Clynch ever since that Gent. was Ordered on Duty. Archibald & John Buchanans Familys, and Andw. Lammeys came here; who has continued in this side yet; Capt. Wilson went

Immediately with 15 Men, and ranged near a Week in the Neighbourhood where Lammey was taken, and he left four of his best Woodsmen with the Neighbours, for several days longer. I also ordered two of the most trusty persons I could get., for to act as Spys along Clynch Mountain for 10 days which they performed I am satisfyed faithfully; besides they Six Men, at Harrisons, I ordered Mrs. Vance & Fowlers Wife 3 Men a Week particularly to assist about saving their fodder, which they got removed with safety.

All the Men stationed in this side Clynch, I give particular directions that they should if possible, be Young Men; and be ready to march to other places if called upon; Indeed when I first Ordered these men I had a Scheme in it, to send such good hands as could be best Spared out of them over to fill up Capt. Looneys and Smiths Companys on Clynch when the fears of the people in this side was a little abated. It had fell out extremely unlucky, that both them Gentlemens ranging Stations, was very thin when ye. Indians came. Capt. Smith having to wait until he was reinforced from this side before he could pursue. And at Blackmores the other Day the Indians coursd one of the Negroes they took, near a quarter of an Hour, several times a view of the Fort.

In short the most of the people in this Country, seem to have a private plan of their own, for their own particular defence.

The people in the Wold-Hill Settlement, will have the Indians to come up the Valley & North fork, opposite to them, and then make a Right-Angle to their habitations, they people on ye. South fork will have the Enemy, to steal Slyly, up the Iron Mountain, and make one Grand attack, on the Head of Holston, and Sweep the River before them; the Head of New River will have it, that the Cherokees will fetch a Compass, round Wattago Settlement, and come down New River on a particular Search for their Scalps. The Rich-Valley and North fork people will have Sandy the dangerous pass. for proof of which the(y) quot(e) former and recent Instances; to wit Stalnaker & Henrys Family being carried out the same road. You may thus see what a task one would have to remove every ones wears; I wish I could be instrumental in defending from real ones, imaginary dangers would give me less anxiety.

I am Sir Your most Obedient
Arthur Campbell

Note the term "wears." It was pronounced "weer"—and is still in colloquial use. Just the other day I heard a mountain woman saying: "Now, honey, don't you be wearying," meaning "worrying," of which Arthur Campbell and all the Smyth County inhabitants had plenty during Dunmore's War.

A postscript to a letter dated, Royal Oak, October 12, 1774, from Arthur Campbell to William Preston says:

P. S. I have sent you inclosed Logins Original Letter which came to hand this Day.

A. C.

(The words of the original Letter.)

To Captain Cressap—What did you kill my people on Yellow Creek for. The white People killed my kin at Coneestoga a great while ago, & I though(t nothing of that.) But you killed my kin again on Yellow Creek, and took m(y cousin Prisoner) then I thought I must kill too; and I have been three time(s to war since but) the Indians is not Angry only myself.

CAPTAIN JOH(N LOGAN)

July 21st. Day.

CHAPTER V

THE REVOLUTION

WHILE the battle of Point Pleasant was being fought, the Continental Congress was sitting in Philadelphia working out resolutions that were to lead to separation from England. The Congress called upon every county to have a Committee of Safety empowered to make its recommendations effective. In January, 1775, the free holders of Fincastle responded by a mass meeting which selected the Committee of Safety consisting of the following: The Rev. Charles Cummings, Col. William Preston, Col. William Christian, Capt. Stephen Trigg, Maj. Arthur Campbell, Maj. William Inglis, Capt. Walter Crockett, Capt. John Montgomery, Capt. James McGavock, Capt. William Campbell, Capt. Thomas Madison, Capt. Daniel Smith, Capt. William Russell, Capt. Evan Shelby, and Lieut. William Edmondson. Of these Arthur Campbell lived at Marion, William Campbell, at Seven Mile Ford, William Russell later lived at Seven Mile Ford and at Saltville, and Thomas Madison later lived at Saltville. David Campbell of Royal Oak, brother of Arthur, was appointed clerk of the Committee.

This Committee sitting at the Lead Mines on Jan. 20, 1775, drafted a set of resolutions which has been styled the first Declaration of Independence, although it did not declare for independence; but it did declare the intention of the free holders of Fincastle to defend their liberty at the cost of their lives. It seems to have been the first formal paper written by a representative body in support of the action of the Continental Congress as against the British Government. It is remarkable that the first of these should have come from the hunting-shirted pioneers of the remote southwest wilderness, and that these western woodsmen should have gone at that time as far as they did in declaration of purpose to resist with arms encroachments on their liberties.

Far more significant than the accident of priority is the meaning of the paper itself whose significance, strangely enough, seems to have escaped the notice both of students of national history and of local eulogists of this section's patriotic glories. It was in effect the declaration of western allegiance to the Colonial cause and it meant that the great Mississippi Valley was to be aligned with the United States instead of Canada, for Fincastle County was at that time the West. Tennessee and Kentucky as well as Southwest Virginia spoke through its Committee of Safety. It was the formative base of the Great West that was to be, and was then the only region on western waters sufficiently settled to have a county government or any other organization through which to express the sentiments and direct the action of its people. In the Greenbrier country there were a few scattered cabins. Along the upper Ohio and the Great Lakes military posts at Pittsburgh, Detroit and other points had been occupied since the French and Indian War, but the country about them was still Indian country save for the traders and a few settlers. It would be more than a year before the rapidly increasing influx of immigrants would really occupy even regions east of the Ohio. The Susquehanna Valley was still the true Pennsylvania frontier. The free holders of Fincastle, and the Watauga settlers acting with them, represented the organized West and constituted the only body through whom the West could take corporate action. Had they declared for the British Government instead of for the Continental Congress, the subsequent history of America would be totally different.

The inhabitants of Smyth County's territory having contributed to committing the West in this Declaration of Liberty contributed largely to the winning of liberty on the field of battle. Their own immediate and most pressing responsibility in that war was the holding of the western frontier, a duty which they discharged in repelling raids in constant Indian ranging, and participating in repeated elaborate campaigns into the Indian country. They suppressed Tory uprisings at home. Smyth County's leader led the Southwest Virginia troops and commanded the patriots at King's Mountain and residents of this territory were fighting in the Continental army from the beginning to the end of the Revolution.

Space allows only a bare summary of the intensely interesting Revolutionary period.

July 15, 1775—requisition upon Fincastle County for sixty-eight expert riflemen for the regular service, of whom some lived in Smythe territory.

1776. Cherokees defeated in Battle of Long Island, above Kingsport. Smythe men under command of Capt. John Campbell of Royal Oak and Capt. James Thompson in this fight.

Capt. William Campbell and Lieutenant John Buchanan with other Smyth County men in Campaign against Dunmore ending in battle of Gwyn's Island.

Capt. William Campbell in command of a regiment at Williamsburg.

Major Arthur Campbell and Capt. William Russell, delegates from Fincastle County in Virgina House of Representatives, first representatives from Mississippi waters to sit in an American legislative body after independence was declared.

Indian incursions into Smyth. Fort built at Aspenvale.

Col. William Christian led an army of seventeen hundred men, many from Smyth, on successful invasion of Cherokee country.

THE REVOLUTION

1777. Fincastle County dissolved and Washington, Montgomery, and Kentucky Counties formed.
Major Arthur Campbell, with rank of Colonel, made County Lieutenant or chief commander in Washington County.
Capt. William Campbell, with rank of colonel, made lieutenant-colonel, or second in command.
Tories, spies and British agents begin making trouble, and are vigorously suppressed in Washington County by Colonels Arthur and William Campbell. Horse thieving and murdering gangs hunted down and hung. Others brought to trial in regular courts.

1778–1779—Tory fighting. William Russell, Capt. John Campbell of Rich Valley and others in Continental line.

1779–1780—Arthur Campbell recalls expedition planned for Kentucky to disperse Tories gathered in force against lead mines. William Campbell suppresses Tories by expedition up New River.
Col. Evan Shelby leads expedition against Chicamaugua Indians.
Colonels William and Arthur Campbell raise recruits for King's Mountain campaign. Col. William Campbell commands at Battle of King's Mountain. Col. Arthur Campbell leads expedition against Cherokees.

1781. Col. William Campbell leads his men to Greene's Army and Battle of Guilford Court House. Capt. John Buchanan wounded at Guilford, brought home and died.
William Campbell promoted to brigadier general. Dies below Richmond from pneumonia.
Smyth men at Yorktown.
Throughout the whole of the war ranging companies under Capt. John Campbell of Royal Oak, John Campbell of Rich Valley, John Buchanan, Robert Davis, Arthur Bowen, and other leaders in those parts of Montgomery and Washington that were to become Smyth were actively engaged in the arduous and dangerous duties of ranging the woods against Indians and renegades. It is a pity that the exploits and even the names in most cases of these rangers from Smyth are unknown. Around the big family fire-places of winter

evenings they must have told many a thrilling tale of lying out in the woods, of endurance, of personal combats with Indians, of defense of frontier forts, of rescuing women and children, of savage massacre around lonely cabins. Much about them that may eventually be brought to light is no doubt told here and there in old letters and papers filed away in archives at Richmond, Washington, New York, Nashville, Madison and other places.

With the following letters from Lieut., later Capt., John Buchanan, and Capt., later Gen., William Campbell, and some account of Tory warfare we must leave the Revolutionary period.

Dear Sir:
I make no doubt you have rec'd a more full account than I am able to give you of Dunmore's being forsed to abandon Gwyn's Island, but perhaps not more true.

On the 28th of June we pitched our camp before the Island and begun to dig trenches and erect batteries during which time the vidglance of the officers and soldiers was not wanting as we mounted fatigue once in two nights, thow repeatedly fired on by the enemy from nine pounders and downward. We rec'd but little damage—two men wounded, one of which is dead. On the 8th of July Genrell Lewis came down and found all things in good order and on the 9th in the morning we reopened our ambezours and begun a cannonading by the Genrell firing the first gun. Dunmore returned but three shot, how he had sworn by his God which I presume to be Belzebub that if we begun with our damned batres he would play us such a tune as we never heard! But insted of that we made him lead of such a dance as he never before was taught, to the tune of Yanke Dodle and the rogues march. At every fire we could hear our eighteen pounders strik like if one was throwing stones against an old frame tobaco house, it being almost a perfect calm he could get off no other way but by towing numbers of the vessels, cut their cables and their ankours.

Capt. Arandale of our artilery was kiled by a project of his own, in working of a wooden mourtour that busted when he put a match to it. Next morning we took two tenders that lay in the heavin about 12 o'clock we landed on this island with four companies under the command of Capt. McClanahan. The enemy perceved our landing, left their camps and went to the fleet that lay in the bay. We not with a man lost. We thought they was preparing to give us battle at Cherry Point which is the fair side of the island. But when we got leave reconniter the island we took 33 neagros fore white men and a woman prisoners and got about 3 or 4 thousand pounds worth of plunder. We found numbers of the bodes of dead neagros lying on the surface of the ground that died of the smalpox and goil fevour. There is three of our company dead since we left home the rest are in good spirits. Capt. Crockett with Lieut. Sayer desires to be remembered to you.

These with my compliments to Madam Preston, Miss Betsy and the rest of the Children, and sister Janey and remain your loving cuson,

John Buchanan

Camp near Gwynn's Island, Aug. 3 '76.

P. S. We have heard of a batle our people had with the Indians on Holston's River. We hear they kiled 13 and we lost none. Dear Sr. If opertunnity offers fail not in wrighting to me. J. B.

(Letter from William Campbell to his wife—addressed to Hanover)

Williamsburg, Aug 18 1776

My Dearest Betsy:

When I wrote you last it was in the greatest hurry and had only time to inform you that I was permitted to continue at this place untill the time for which I engaged expires. I thought to have wrote to you by John Henry, but he went off unknown to me; since I have had no opportunity only by post and I now write without knowing of a conveyance.

Last Tuesday a Man (Samuel Newell) arrived here Express in five Days from my house; by whom I was informed that a fort is built there about 400 people cons—— (illegible line) has removed much of my anxiety, as I hope my mother and Sisters will be prudent enough not to expose themselves to danger and the men gathered there will be a means of preserving the crops at least. Eighteen of our Men, two or three women and some children have been killed: Our People have scalped 27 Indians and it is thought that many more have been killed from the large quantities of blood that flowed from those who were wounded and ran away— These Indians were seen about a half mile from my house and several small parties have been discovered a considerable way on this side—I have now the scalp of one who was killed eight or nine miles from my house about three weeks ago—The first time I go up I shall take it along to let you see it—From the success our people have hitherto had in every encounter with the Indians I flatter myself that the savages are now much intimidated and that they are now convinced they cannot make such an easy conquest as they at first imagined.

19th inst. by Col. Meredith. The fears you impressed about my going to the Northward or against the Cherokees you may entirely lay aside— My fate has done you this favor I must confess over against my inclinations. I last week applied to the General for leave to go home, and was peremptorily refused. He ordered me to stay here and take command of the soldiers belonging to the first regiment who continue at this place. I do not know how long I will have to stay, but I make no doubt it will be above a month yet. If the horse you mention pleases you well by all means buy him. (Instructions about buying Horse) (fragments torn) I most heartily thank you my dear for your attention in providing me such necessaries as I stood in need of. I fear you are too sollicitous cause yourself too much trouble. You fling to my remembrance Soloman's excellent description of a good wife. She searcheth wool and flax and worketh willingly with her hands—she layeth her hands to the spindle and her hands hold the distaff—— She maketh to herself covering of tapestry—her clothing is silk and purple—Her husband is known in the gates when he sitteth among the Elders of the land—such is my dearest Betsy—her worth I esteem above rubies.

I have now lived above a week in the house where I was first blessed with a sight of My dear Betsy.

Little did I at that time think such superlative happiness was destined for me. From that happy moment (blurred by folding) ——* I have the charge of about 200 men—(about one-third sick no other officer to help him—2 ensigns then on duty at Jamestown).

I have got the needles and pins for you which you wrote for. I wish they may serve the purpose as I believe both are the manufacture of Philadelphia and the first attempts in things of that line do not in common succeed very well. No such thing as a card to be secured here. Had you not better get several pairs of the clothiers cards I heard you talk of. They would be better than none at all (blurred) price is trifling——

By Sam Newell I wrote to Col. Christian and hinted to him that I was desirous to have some soldiers stationed at my place if he thought there was any necessity for them there. It will be a means of preventing the people from flying farther off if they could think themselves safer there. Newell could not inform me whether the Col. would accept of the Command upon the Expedition as the Letters from the Council had not come to his hands when Newell came along.

I have been tolerably well since I came down but do not recover my health near so fast as while I was with you. I most heartily wish —— this country. It does not at all agree with our highland constitution—see you as soon as I properly can. May you be peculiarly——

Wm. Campbell.

P. S. Our friend Mr. Trigg is recovering fast. He is now able to take an airing in a Chair, and has walked this day from Captain Anderson's to pay me a visit. He thanks you for the apples you sent him and acknowledges them as a very grateful present.

W. C.

Not long after the writing of this letter Colonel Campbell returned to his home at Aspenvale, bringing his "dearest Betsy" with him. She had been Elizabeth Henry, sister of Patrick. Soon after her arrival at Aspenvale she attended a

* Illegible.

camp meeting, the first, by the way, mentioned in Southwest Virginia records. When the people heard of her relationship to their idolized Patrick Henry, they cheered and crowded about her so that she had to climb up on a stump to avoid being injured by the crush. Of her more anon.

An illegible sentence in the above letter seems to have been to the effect that about four hundred people were in the neighborhood to be served by this fort. In that year of 1776, the year parties of Indians were roaming all about to a considerable distance east of Seven Mile Ford, killing these eighteen men, two or three women and some children, the year that the fort was built, that Campbell and Trigg and others were off with the Continentals hoping that their mothers and sisters would not unduly expose themselves to danger, the year in which Colonel Christian mobilized an army of seventeen hundred men near Kingsport to crush the Cherokees in the battle of Long Island Flats, in that year a log church was built at Royal Oak, the first meeting house to be erected in the bounds of Smyth County.

John Broady was a slave and the body servant of General Campbell, and attended on many of his military expeditions. John was present when the notorious renegade, Hopkins, was captured and hung and his account of the incident given from memory in his old age and written down by Gov. James McDowell is the most authoritative account extant.

Colonel Campbell with his lady and infant daughter was returning from Church at the Ebbing Spring in Washington County on the Middle Fork of Holston when a man was seen coming towards them when at the distance of a hundred or more yards from them suddenly turned off from the highway road and roade into the woods. As soon as Colonel Campbell perceived this he said to his wife that the man was some scoundrel or he would not have so behaved. He then determined to pursue him and for this purpose placed his child that he was carrying in the arms of his servant John Broady and made instant pursuit, Mrs. Campbell fearing a conflict took her child and directed him to follow his master which he did and overtook him just as he was entering the Holston River in time to see the encounter between him and the man he was pursuing. This occurred in the river. When John came up Colonel Campbell was just plunging into the river which the man was endeavoring to ford but could not do so from his horse taking fright and refusing to go onward. In this situation Colonel Campbell seized him, plucked his pistols from their holsters and threw them into the river and then drew the man's own sword from its scabbord and used it to enforce his submission but without striking him with it. He then took the man to the bank of the river leading him on his horse. Here he found three of his neighbors, James Fulton, Edward Farris, and William Bates, who being a little behind him only as he came from church and seeing him quit the road as he did followed after him and got up whilest he was engaged with his antagonist. But whether they aided Colonel Campbell to seize him in the river or not he does not now recollect. As soon, however, as the man was brought out they all aided in preparing to hang him which was done with little delay and with the halter taken from his own horse. The halter was fastened to the limb of a tree projecting over the river, the man then placed upon his horse, when the other end was tied around his neck and the horse led off. John Broady states that a paper or papers were found on this man containing the names of many persons who had agreed to enlist under him or some other person to fight with the Tories against the country but whether these papers were examined before or after this execution he is not sure. The man's name was Hopkins—had once labored as a hireling for Col. Campbell—was notorious as a tory and horse thief throughout the country—was understood to have gone amongst the Indians and incited these to plunder and murder the settlers—that on this accusation hue and cry had been made after him, and he had fled the country and had not been seen or heard of for some 12 or 15 months until met as above said by Col. Campbell, returning from church. Hopkins was a young man of twenty odd, had no family—was large, strong and active, but made no vigorous resistance when seized by

Col. Campbell, appearing to be panic stricken and self condemned.

The three men mentioned as assisting Col. Campbell were amongst the most respectable in the neighborhood, all land holders with families and one of them—Wm. Bates—an elder in the church.

John Broady further states that several men whose names were on the list of Hopkins' were apprehended by Col. Campbell and tried but most of them were discharged. His main accomplices were ascertained to have staid in a cave on the banks of the Holston from which they fled as soon as they learned his fate leaving behind them quantities of blankets and other bed clothing. (Note: This was probably the McMullin Cave, between Marion and Seven Mile Ford.

The horse that Hopkins was riding when taken was a stolen one and was afterwards restored to the owner. Hopkins was dressed in a fine gold laced cocked hat and John says had just come from Canada where he had gone after he left Washington and where he had laid the plans of raising and arming tories in western Virginia. Hopkins had a brother in Washington who was a Whig. He was in the jail just before he fled the country, but escaped by breaking off the door which he carried far as Wolf Creek where he left it with a label upon it. John states that he quit the country with threats of violence—that Col. Campbell was constantly threatened with hanging and house burning by the tories— that he often laid out all night with his arms in his hands to protect his family and property and further adds that it was owing to the habitual and great terror with which the tories regarded him that "people said that they were kept down and over awed in Washington." John Broady also says that he never heard of anyone condemning Col. Campbell for this act but always praising him for it as Hopkins was so dangerous a man. "I never heard anyone mour his hanging, but all were glad."

The above statement was taken and recorded by James McDowell, in 1839.

Among those old documents in the Preston home are two

originals of the anonymous threats written by Tories against William Campbell.

One of them is a rather lengthy communication defending the Tories as the true and loyal patriots and worthy citizens, and branding as lies the charges that they were involved in inciting the Indians to murder and outrage, although admitting that Cameron and Stuart and other British agents among the savages were doing it. Then come copious quotations from Scripture designed to show the perilous condition of Campbell's soul and exhorting him to repent and turn from his bloody and wicked ways, and calling down just retribution upon him from the widows and orphans that he had made. He did make quite a few. Mr. B. F. Buchanan told me of riding on the train from Christiansburg to Marion with Col. Thomas L. Preston, a grandson of General Campbell, who pointed out to him several sycamore trees from which his grandfather hung Tories. And the above-mentioned pious Tory's assertions to the contrary notwithstanding he found on the person of more than one of those he hung written instructions, letters to the Indians, and other unmistakable evidence that they were commissioned to incite the savages to murder and rapine. The other warning, originally posted somewhere about Campbell's premises, is shorter:

To Cornl Will the bloody tyrant and murderer of Washington county and Court we desire you to prepare yourself for death. For we hope that vengeance is pursuing you fast and if not by law it must be according to your desarts for the Scripture saith that whosoever spilleth man's blood by man shall his blood be spilt, therefore prepare yourself for deth, for as you rule by arbitrary powere by that power you must expect to be tried.

Such nice little notes as these were not uncommonly found about his place. When at home he often laid out all night fully armed to protect his family and property. When away on military duty or other public business he would leave competent guards on watch, for these were not idle threats. The Tory ascendancy when Cornwallis seemed to be victorious in the Carolinas and about to invade Virginia occasioned dire peril to patriots, and the Tory uprising in Washington County at this time is said to have been repressed only by the terror and awe inspired by Campbell's name.

Tories organized and equipped by trained British officers constituted a serious menace in the years 1779 and 1780, and in Montgomery County were in such force that the militia of Washington was called in for their suppression. Colonel William and Colonel Arthur coöperated during both these years with the Montgomery officers against Tories.

The following letter, undated, probably refers to the campaign of July, 1779.

Upon receiving your letter which you wrote from Fort Chiswell, informing me that the insurgents were embodying up New River, and that their design was to destroy the works at the lead mines, I immediately wrote to Captains Edmiston, Lewis, and Dysart, directing to order fifteen men out of each of their companies, to assemble at my house early next day, equipped to march with me to the lead mines. I also wrote to Captain Campbell of Royal Oak to order ten men out of his company who were directed to join me on my way up. The men met as early as I could expect, and we left this place about twelve or one o'clock. That night we got to Radcliffs marsh where we halted for a small party I had detached the day before to apprehend some persons that were much suspected, and it being late before they joined us, we were obliged to lie at that place all night. We got to the mines next day soon in evening. There I was informed two men had been sent up the river, to discover, if possibel, the designs of the insurgents, and that it was expected they would return that night. About an hour and a half before day next morning they came to the mines, and informed me that they had been as far as Captain Cox's, where they counted

THE REVOLUTION 69

one hundred and five men assembled in arms, beside a considerable number without arms. They also reported that they had been detained as prisoners about twenty-four hours, and that when they were suffered to come away, the people that had assembled were dispersing, apparently with a design to return home. They brought with them a piece of writing signed Cox's and Osborne's Companies, directed to Colonel Preston, of which the enclosed is a copy. I then determined to go up New River with the men who went with me from this county; but some of the Militia officers of Montgomery county being there, they proposed to collect as many men that day as they possibly could, and to be in readiness to march early next day, which we did with about one hundred and forty men. That evening we got about sixteen miles above the lead mines without getting any certain intelligence of the designs of the insurgents. Next day we continued our route up the river, through the most populous part of the settlement, and found no people at home but the women and children, excepting a few very old men. Upon our arrival at Captain Cox's, in the evening, we were informed that about forty of the insurgents, about two hours before, had crossed the river, and taken Captain Cox's son a prisoner. They expected we would have gone up the south side of the river, in which they would have met us, and designed to give us battle. We then followed after them in best order we could, lest they should attempt to surprise us, until it became so dark that we could no longer follow their track, and turned off the path, about a quarter of a mile, and tied up our horses in the most silent manner we could, conjecturing the enemy were not far before us. There was a house about a mile from where we lay, to which I sent a few men, to make what discovery they could, who soon after returned without making any that was satisfactory. I then concluded that they were encamped in the woods, and determined if possible to surprise them and for that purpose set out on foot about two or three hours before day, leaving all our horses tied, where we halted in the evening. In this order we marched about a mile, when we again made a halt, and sent off four or five very trusty men, to find if possible where the enemy lay. I also sent with them a man whom I the day before had caused to come with me. Being informed he had a brother among the insurgents, I imagined he knew something of their schemes and designs, and told him if he did not discover where the insurgents lay, I would put him to death. They returned in about an hour and informed me that they had been within twenty yards of the enemy's camp and was fired upon by one of their sentries; that their encampment was in piece of woods in a large glade made perfectly clear for at least a quarter of a mile all around where they lay. At this place (I then understood) they were that day to be joined by a considerable number more, and concluded that these would in such a place so secure themselves that the lives of a great many good men must be lost in an attempt to dislodge them, which I was unwilling should be the case in subduing such worthless wretches. I then, with the advice of the officers, went back to where we left our horses, it being then about break of day.

As soon as it became so light that we could see a small distance around us, we set out a second time toward the enemy's camp on horse-back. We got to the side of the glade just as the sun was covering the flight of the enemy, nor did we know they had fled until Captain Cox's son came to us, who in their hurry they had suffered to escape. Upon going to their camp, we found they had gone off with the greatest precipitation, having left everything behind them excepting their arms. Before we followed them we had to wait a few minutes to get a horse for Captain Cox's son, who said he could conduct us the way they proposed to go. As soon as he was ready we pursued with all the expedition we could upon the trace; but upon their discovering that we (were) pursuing them, they dispersed and hid themselves among the bushes and weeds. We had not the fortune to find any but one of them, who was immediately shot. The woods were searched upon the way they fled for three or four miles. Some of them ran into the mountains and laurel thickets where it was impossible to pursue them on horseback. You cannot conceive my chagrin when I saw the situation of the enemy's camp. I found that had I known it myself, it was in my power to have destroyed nearly the whole of them, though it may perhaps be better ordered, as I believe the most of them are now well convinced of their folly, and may yet become very good citizens.

After the pursuit was over we all assembled at the enemy's camp and breakfasted upon the provisions they left behind them, having eaten very little from early in the morning the day before. That night we went again to Captain Cox's. I then considered that it was to no purpose to search for those people in that mountainous country, and that there was a probability of their embodying again, if they could not then be prevailed upon to surrender. These considerations induced me to disperse among them copies of the enclosed, signed by Major Crockett and myself. It has had the wished for effect, only a few of the principals having refused to come in.

That night we went again to Captain Cox's where we were next morning met by a party of 130 men under the command of Colonel Cleveland from Wilks County, North Carolina. They had the day before apprehended a certain Zechariah Goss, a fellow who belonged to a party under the command of Samuel Brown and (James) Coyle, two noted murderers, horse-thieves and robbers. Goss was immediately hung, I believe with the joint consent of near three hundred men, and two other villains were very well whip'd. I then detached between sixty and seventy men under the command of Captain Francis, with instructions to collect all the stocks of horses and cattle belonging to the insurgents they possibly could, leaving to each family one horse creature and milch cattle were necessary for its support, having previously sent out by some of the inhabitants of the place copies of the enclosed, signed by Major Crockett and myself. This step I was induced to take from the consideration that it was impossible to find those people in that mountainous country—that there was a probability of their being stimulated to join in the like designe again, and that if I could see them they might be reasoned out of those mad schemes. That evening I went up to Captain Osborne's, where I was informed above forty of the insurgents had been embodied in that neighborhood, and that they were dispersed by Colonel Cleveland's party who left Captain Cox's about two hours before me. There were very few of the insurgents came in next day, they being afraid to venture even to their own houses. Those that came in first I disarmed and sent out in search of the others. I lay there two days in which time the greatest —— the remainder of the document is missing. (See Wisconsin Historical Collection, *Frontier Retreat,* pages 236-240.)

Capt. Henry Francis mentioned in this letter was an officer of Montgomery County.

In 1780 an expedition was planned for Kentucky but was called off because of a powerful Tory threat. In the summer of this year William Campbell led another successful expedition against the Tories up New River and Arthur Campbell assembled Holston troops and marched them to the defense of the Lead Mines. The Tories were again severely handled and dispersed, and after this, followed by the battle of King's Mountain in the fall, they ceased from troubling.

OLD SMYTH COUNTY COURTHOUSE

CHAPTER VI

COUNTY ORGANIZATION

GENERAL ALEXANDER SMYTH died April 17, 1830, while serving his fifth term in the Congress of the United States and while the movement for a new county was taking shape. He was one of the most distinguished and popular of Southwest Virginians in public life in his day so that it was natural the new county should be made a memorial to him. The son of Rev. Adam Smyth, Episcopal Minister and Rector of Botetourt Parish, he was born on the Island of Rathlin, off the coast of Ireland, in 1765 and was brought by his father to live at Fincastle in Virginia when a little chap about seven or eight years old. Fincastle was then a hamlet of log and stone houses just starting around John Miller's mill in Botetourt County. Alexander grew up there in the stirring times of the Revolution. When twenty years old he was Deputy Clerk of Botetourt County and two years later the court makes note of his service with the comment that he was a young gentleman of honest demeanor and unblemished character. At that time he owned a plantation on Craig's Creek. In 1789 he was licensed to practice law in the courts of Virginia by the Botetourt justices and in that year removed to Abingdon to practice his profession. On January 13, 1791, he was married to Miss Nancy Binkley of Wythe County and in 1792 they removed to Wythe to live until his death. They had four children: Alexander; Harold; Melvina, wife of Captain John P. Matthews; and Frances, wife of Colonel James H. Piper, who climbed Natural Bridge when a student at Washington College, and for years taught a noted academy in Wytheville.

Smyth published two books, one a scriptural treatise dealing with the Apocalypse, and the other, by order of the President, a military treatise on regulations for the United States infantry. He served various terms in the state House and Senate and was five times elected to Congress. Jefferson made him Colonel of a Southwest Virginia rifle regiment. In July of 1812 he was appointed Inspector General of the armies of the United States with rank of Brigadier.

In October, 1812, he was given command of a proposed invasion of Canada. After some fruitless campaigning in New York State he put his army in winter quarters and came home on furlough. His failure to enter Canada and winter there led to his retirement by act of Congress, against which he protested in the following memorial:

The petition of Alexander Smyth, a citizen of Virgina, respectfully represents—That having in 1807 written to an honorable member of the house of representatives, that in case of war with Great Britain he was desirous to enter into the regular service, he received in 1808 an appointment as colonel of a regiment of riflemen. That although war had not commenced yet the event being probable, he abandoned his profession, which was then lucrative, left his family, vacated his seat in the senate of Virginia as the representative of thirteen counties, and joined the army of the United States. That your petitioner had the good fortune to give the utmost satisfaction to his superiors, General Wilkinson, General Hampton, General Dearborn, and the late Secretary of War, while acting under their immediate orders; was promoted to the rank of brigadier and inspector in July 1812; given the command of a brigade in September; and of one of the armies of the United States in October in the same year. That at the expiration of five weeks, during which period he made every exertion in his power to serve the nation, he found it necessary to put his troops into winter quarters.

Having determined on that measure, as your petitioner had been absent from his home the last eight winters, much the greater part of the last five years, and the whole of the last fourteen months, and had been refused leave to visit his family in the month of July preceding, and calculating that it was probable the campaign of 1813 might terminate his existence, he, without resigning his command, asked for leave of absence, which was granted until the 1st of March, 1813, at which time your petitioner was ordered to report himself to the Secretary of War. That your petitioner left his troops in cantonments, under the command of an officer of thirty-six years experience, and in February, 1813, reported himself by letter to the Secretary of War, and solicited orders; and as the failure of your petitioner to take Fort George, York, and Kingston, and to winter in Canada as he was instructed, had created some clamor, your petitioner proposed that an enquiry into his conduct should take place, which the honorable secretary, through the medium of the adjutant-general was pleased to promise; since which time your petitioner has not had the honor to hear from the war-office.

Your petitioner would further represent, that he has heard that some members of your honorable body are of the opinion, that by an act of the last session, regulating the staff of the army of the United States, your petitioner has become a private citizen; and with this opinion, his own might, perhaps accord, were it not impossible to believe that the Congress of the United States, at their last session, could have intentionally committed an act of injustice.

Your petitioner affirms that he has not done or omitted anything to the injury of the nation; that his chief, if not his only error, has consisted in expressing too freely his indignation against those who had done injuries, or omitted to perform duties, to the nation. The motives which led astray, he conceives might procure for this error forgiveness. That this affirmation is true, he believes he can satisfy a committee or committees of your honorable body, on short notice.

Your petitioner has essayed to engage again in the pursuits of civil life, but he finds that while the din of war continues, it is impossible for him to give the necessary attention to any peaceful pursuit. He desires to serve, to die, if Heaven wills it, in the defence of his country; a country that has protected his infancy, given him a family, and at times distinguished him with considerable honors; from whose government no act of wrong, personal to himself, will force his esteem, while it maintains, with steady perseverance, that country's rights.

Your petitioner confidently trusts, that in deciding on his prayer you will be mindful of the rule of justice—To others do, the law is not severe, what to thyself thou wishest to be done; and of the rule of policy. "The social body is oppressed, when one of its members is oppressed."

The prayer of your petitioner is, that you will revise the act organizing the staff of the army of the United States, and by a declaratory act preserve the rank of your petitioner, as a brigadier-general in the line, abolishing only his authority as inspector-general, etc.

His worth and popularity are attested by the fact that after this experience he was reëlected to the Virginia Legislature and five times elected to Congress.

The county of Augusta, authorized by act of 1738 and organized in 1745, included the upper Holston and all country beyond to western limits of English claims. Botetourt County, authorized Nov. 28, 1769, and formed in 1770, began at the North Fork of the James River and extended indefinitely westward. Fincastle County authorized 1772 and formed 1773 reached from the Roanoke-New River watershed to the Mississippi. Fincastle was dissolved, 1777, into Montgomery, Washington, and Kentucky, the line between Montgomery and Washington running through the ford of the Middle Fork of Holston just above Captain John Campbell's house at Royal Oak, and passing across Comers Creek, and through Locust Cove. Wythe County, formed in 1790, joined Washington along the old Montgomery line.

In July, 1831, citizens of Wythe and Washington counties presented a petition to the Legislature setting forth that these were two of the largest, most populous, and wealthiest coun-

COUNTY ORGANIZATION

ties of the state; that the distance to court entailed great hardships upon the citizens, particularly upon those residing in the western portion of Washington; that "if about one-third of the territory of Washington County was added to a small portion of Wythe County, it would form a county, as to wealth, population and territory, superior to most of the counties in the Commonwealth, and such as would not, as is too often the case, be an expense to the State, and would leave the present counties in better form, and sufficiently large and respectable, and with their Court-Houses more central. To this arrangement, there is no objection felt in those counties, (except self-interest, in some few individuals), and the interest of your petitioners, would thereby, be greatly promoted, and their present grievances alleviated."

The petitioners asked that the new county be formed and "called Smyth in honor and memory of the name of the late General Alexander Smyth whose name it thus becomes us to immortalize."

The petitioners asked that the western line begin at a white oak, at the head of a large spring, in front of Joseph Meek's dwelling house, forks of the Lee Highway and Glade Spring road.

A memorial was presented to the Legislature from certain citizens in the lower part of Washington County. They raised no objection to the proposed county but disputed certain statements of fact in the petition and protested against locating the line so far to the west.

The act creating Smyth County was passed on Feb. 23, 1832, and began the western line at a point several miles east of Joseph Meek's spring, "on the main stage road, at a bridge in a hollow, at a point where the spring branch of Philip Greever crosses the same." This Philip Greever came from Pennsylvania in the spring of 1780 and built his cabin, which still stands, about one mile up the branch from this point. In the summer of 1780 he followed Col. William Campbell against the Tories on New River, and that fall followed him to King's Mountain and fired the first shot in that battle. From this bridge the line ran direct to the Russell line, passing equidistant between Preston's and King's salt wells, and south twenty-five degrees east to the southern boundary of Washington County. To avoid squabbling over the county seat, the act named a commission composed of five citizens of other counties to select a site and make a report thereof in writing to the county court which should order the buildings erected at the place so chosen. Charles L. Crockett of Wythe, John H. Fulton of Washington, William Price of Russell, Samuel McCamant of Grayson, and Thomas Peery of Tazewell were members of this commission. These gentlemen, or all except Mr. Crockett, whose name is not signed to the report, informed the justices sitting in the May term of court of 1832 that, having viewed several situations pointed out by citizens of Smyth, they had determined to fix the county seat on lands of William Humes west of Staley's Creek and south of the main road, which then crossed Staley's Creek near the Handle Mills, ran straight up the hill by Dr. Dickinson's, through Marion College, and the Look property, or Isaac Collins' land it then was, coming into the present road below the spring in the corner of this property. They reported that they had run off one acre of land on the hill, west of a fence dividing a rye and a wheat field, and north of a straight line running through the said fields, as a public square, which is the courthouse square; and the line through the rye and wheat fields is on the main street of Marion. This commission spent a night with Mr. Thomas Thomas, on the South Fork, where a discussion arose concerning a name for the new county seat. Mrs. Freelove Cole Thomas, their hostess, opined that it would be fitting to name it in honor of Gen. Francis Marion, which was done.

COUNTY ORGANIZATION

The Act of Legislature creating Smyth provided for other things. Among them, that Gov. John Floyd should commission fifteen justices of the peace who should constitute the county court; that these should assemble at the house of John Thomas at Royal Oak on the first Monday of April, 1832, to organize the court, elect a clerk, fix a place for holding court until the permanent site should be decided, and make nominations to his Excellency, the Governor, for sheriff and coronor; also, this act provided that Isaac Leftwich of Wythe, Edward Fulton of Washington, and John Campbell of Smyth should run and mark the county lines which they did at once and with a degree of accuracy, but with sufficient inaccuracy to necessitate, nearly a century later, the naming of a commission consisting of H. P. Copenhaver, John R. George, and Walter Umbarger to determine, with commissioners from Washington, whether the schoolhouse at Konnarock and those at other points were in Washington or Smyth counties, and, with B. L. Dickinson of Smyth and John Blakemore of Washington, to mark the line so determined. This work was finally completed and recorded in 1931. Also uncertainty as to the line south of Saltville occasioned difficulty in enforcing liquor laws against certain makers and sellers of spirits on one side or the other of it in the days when liquor laws varied in different counties. A commission was at one time appointed to run the line between Grayson and Smyth. A dispute arose as to where Smyth ended and Tazewell began which was settled by commissioners B. L. Dickinson, J. P. Sheffey and J. T. Frazier, Jr., with three from Tazewell in 1931. A commission appointed 1923—W. L. Umbarger, John R. George—reported in 1928 the adjustment of the line between Smyth and Russell. Still Messrs. Leftwich, Fulton, and Campbell completed a fair job in short time, reporting to the satisfaction of the justices at the first term of court April 19, 1832, and receiving $100 for their work.

Messrs. Charles Tate, Samuel Williams, Hatch D. Poston, Thompson Atkins, Joseph P. Bonham, James Taylor, George W. Davis, Joseph Atkins, William Porter, Robert Houston, Abram B. Trigg, and Isaac Spratt, having been commissioned by Gov. John Floyd, the first justices of Smyth County, assembled, as directed, at the house of John Thomas to take the oath and organize the court. They proceeded to elect a clerk from four candidates: George T. Lansdown, James C. Spotts, Robert Beattie, Jr., and W. Davis. Robert Beattie, Jr., was elected and declared clerk for a term of seven years from that day. He was living then at Seven Mile Ford and had a store across the river from, and nearly opposite to, where Captain Preston's barn was later built. The next year he removed to the Town House, which he enlarged and made into a tavern in which he at times entertained President Andrew Jackson. Beattie did not assume the duties of clerk. He stood for the office to secure it for his friend, James F. Pendleton, who had had experience as deputy clerk of Tazewell County and, being at the time a legal resident of Tazewell, was not eligible for election to the office. Beattie immediately appointed Pendleton his deputy, turning over to him all the duties and emoluments of the clerkship. The clerk's office was kept in Pendleton's house just west of Marion until the courthouse was built. Mr. Pendleton was elected to the office at the expiration of Beattie's term and reëlected until defeated by William C. Sexton in 1858. In 1870 he came back to Marion to live, dying there Sept. 12, 1878. He came to Smyth from Tazewell in 1830 to teach school at Broadford and in 1831 taught school near the old Mitchell Scott place, one mile west of Marion. He purchased a farm in 1835 from Isaac Collins, building a house on it which was later owned by Nathan Look. Through his apple orchard at the back the railroad was built in 1856, and through his sugar

COUNTY ORGANIZATION 81

orchard in the front the stage road was built when changed from its old location and macadamized.

Mr. William Currant Sexton, born at Chatham Hill May 30, 1828, was elected clerk in 1858 and served until 1869. In that year Mr. James L. Cox, one of the justices of the County Court, served as clerk for two terms of court and R. M. Goodell served until the election of E. L. Roberts of Broadford, a brother-in-law of Mr. Sexton. Mr. Roberts was born at Broadford April 4, 1831, and lived there until his death on Oct. 3, 1909. Mr. Roberts was repeatedly elected to the Legislature and the state Senate. Mr. Sexton was reëlected clerk in 1875 and continued in office until his voluntary retirement in 1905, thus serving as clerk for a total of forty years. He married Miss Rachel Roberts of Broadford in 1852 and for four years thereafter lived there and kept a store. When he removed to Marion he lived at first in the brick house at the foot of Hospital Hill, where Mrs. Dora Stephenson now lives. In 1868 he bought the farm west of Marion which Mr. J. R. Shanklin now owns and resided there until the fall of 1912 when he went to live with his daughter, Mrs. A. T. Lincoln, in Marion. He died at Mrs. Lincoln's home May 19, 1912. Mr. Sexton was a genial, kindly man of strong character and pleasing personality, much loved, and very influential in the county.

Mr. Sexton was succeeded by Samuel W. Kent who had occupied the home and storeroom vacated by Mr. Sexton at Broadford, and, on coming to Marion, had lived in the same brick house that Mr. Sexton first lived in. At Broadford, Mr. Kent married Mrs. Armanda J. Repass, daughter of Capt. R. T. Starritt. He kept store at Broadford sixteen years and was in business at Marion several years before his election as clerk in November, 1906. His son, Herbert L. Kent, went to work in the clerk's office in 1908 as deputy, having previously been a clerk and rural carrier in the Marion post office and clerk of the St. Lawrence Hotel in Bristol. He married Miss Pearl Bunn of Bristol, July 7, 1907. In 1909 he changed places with his father, being elected clerk in that year and again in 1927, his father serving as his deputy.

The county was divided into two districts, north and south of the main stage road for tax purposes, and at the September court, Joseph W. Davis for the first or northern, and Arthur M. Bowen for the second district were elected first commissioners of revenue.

The county was divided by the old Wythe-Washington line into two districts for care of the poor, and the first election in Smyth County was ordered for May 21-22 to choose three overseers of the poor in each district, the voting places to be at Seven Mile Ford on May 21 and at the house of Joseph Atkins on May 22. This election was duly held, and the following were chosen as overseers of the poor: For the western district, James Cole, Theodora G. Pearson, and Mitchell Scott; for the eastern district, Solomon McDonald, William Porter, and Adam Groseclose. On June 21 the sheriff was ordered to collect eighteen and three-fourths cents off every tithable in the county as the poor rate fixed by the overseers of the poor. These overseers secured from Hiram Thompson in 1836 eighty-two acres for a poor farm. In 1874 the Board of Supervisors purchased from John M. Williams two hundred and seventy-four acres in Rye Valley as a poor farm. This was sold in 1914. In 1911 a farm for the poor was purchased from W. G. Lewis on the road between Adwolfe and McMullins Siding. In 1927 Smyth joined with other counties in establishing the district home and farm in Pulaski.

John H. Fulton, Isaac Leftwich, Charles E. Harrison, and George T. Lansdown were appointed to see about building

Present Smyth County Courthouse

COUNTY ORGANIZATION 83

a courthouse and jail. On June 22 they reported bids and plans submitted by James Foncrey of Wythe and by John Dameron and Thomas W. Mercer of Jonesboro. The contract was awarded to Dameron and Mercer, and the courthouse was finished in 1834. A minute of May 8, 1834, reads: "The public buildings and offices for the use of the Courts of this County being now completed, the order of this Court, made at the term in April 1832, permitting Peter C. Johnson, the Clerk of this Court, to reside in Washington County, and the order made at the term in April 1833, directing the Clerk's office at this Court to be kept at the residence of James F. Pendleton, in this County, are rescinded and annulled." This first courthouse was used until 1905 when the present building was erected under the management of the following gentlemen: Building Committee: G. H. Fudge, T. B. Rector, W. W. George, John M. Gwyn, F. G. Davis, J. H. Wisler, F. B. Greever, W. H. Sprinkle, and John B. Whitehead; Executive Committee: R. L. Williams, W. L. Lincoln, H. N. Bell, B. F. Buchanan, J. S. Goetchius, W. F. Culbert, and L. M. Bonham; Board of Supervisors: James F. Scott, D. C. Gollehon, T. B. Ward; and W. C. Sexton, Clerk; Frank P. Milburn, Architect; and Stephenson and Getaz, Builders.

Besides electing a clerk the first or preliminary meeting of the justices fixed upon the house of John Thomas as the place to hold court, and court was held there for two years, until the courthouse was made ready. They nominated to the governor, Messrs. George Byars, and James M. Townsend for coronor. Byars was appointed. They nominated Messrs. Charles Tate, George W. Davis, and Hatch D. Poston for sheriff. The governor declined to act on these nominations because of some irregularity, and at the first term of court they resubmitted these names, and Charles Tate was appointed first sheriff of Smyth.

On April 19, 1832, the Thursday after the third Monday,

as fixed in the Act of Legislature, the first county court of Smyth convened at the house of John Thomas. Charles Taylor was nominated to the governor as county surveyor.

Charles E. Harrison and Andrew Fulton were candidates for commonwealth's attorney, Mr. Harrison being elected. He served in that office until he got himself into some sort of serious trouble and fled the county. A court minute of Oct. 3, 1836, reads: "The office of attorney for the Commonwealth of this Court being vacant by the flight from the county of the former incumbent, James W. Sheffey is appointed to fill that office: and thereupon he took the several oaths prescribed by law."

George W. Jones was elected in 1836 and served until 1852. Up to the latter date there was a commonwealth's attorney for the county court and another for the circuit court. From then on the commonwealth's attorney acted before both courts.

Court at this term divided the county into three magisterial districts which remain unchanged today. They elected constables: John S. Cox, John G. Sexton, John B. Tate, and Chapman A. Spotts for the first or Rich Valley District; Harold Davis, John Killinger, Joseph Newton, and Arthur B. Bowen for the second or Marion District; John Scott, Jr., Rufus K. Williams, George T. Lansdown, and William Pritchet for the third or Rye Valley District. Supervisors with their functions came into being with the change in the court system of 1870.

The first circuit and superior courts of law and chancery in, and for, Smyth County was held at the house of John Thomas, on Monday the thirtieth day of April, 1832, with the Hon. Benjamin Estill, Judge.

The first grand jury was: Thomas M. Tate, foreman, William Porter, Joseph Atkins, Nelson Hopkins, John Steffey, Mitchell Scott, Robert Gollahon, Levi Bishop, Wheelor Jayne,

COUNTY ORGANIZATION

Frederick Copenhaver, Charles Dungan, John Fudge, Nathaniel Harris, Sr., Leonard Hutton, John Goodman, Sr., Robert Houston, William Goodpasture, Jacob Wassum, and Solomon McDonald. They, "having received their charge, withdrew and after some time returned into court, and presented:

An Indictment against Joseph Wolfe, for an assault, a true bill;
An Indictment against John Johnson, for an assault, a true bill;
An Indictment against James Fulkenor, alias Jas. Fortenor, for an assault, a true bill;
An Indictment against John Cullop, for an assault, a true bill;
An Indictment against Israel Wolf, for an assault, a true bill;
An Indictment against Hiram Roark, for an assault, a true bill;
An Indictment against Edward Faris, for an assault, a true bill;

And then the said Grand Jury, having nothing further to present, were discharged."

From this record and many others it appears that fighting was a favorite pastime in the early years of Smyth. In fact, the great majority of indictments brought into court were for assaults, gaming and violation of liquor laws.

Smyth County has passed a hundred years without having had a single legal hanging or electrocution. The death penalty has been twice pronounced, however, by Smyth courts. Both of these cases were tried during the Civil War. The first was tried Feb. 28, 1863, and Beverly, a slave boy, property of William Morgan, was found guilty of attempted rape on a white woman and sentenced to be hanged on Friday the twenty-fourth day of April, 1863. On April 23 he committed suicide in the jail by hanging himself with a rope made by tearing his bed quilt into strips.

The other case is of such unique character that the record is copied in full:

Wednesday, November 23, 1864.

Court sat pursuant to adjournment.
Present P. C. Buchanan, Jr. Presiding Justice, Associated James M. Pruner, John H. Barton, William H. McDonald & Thomas H. Thurman, Gentlemen Justices.

The Court resolved its self into a Court of Oyer and Terminer for the trial of Jim a Slave the property of William Flannagan charged with a felony by him committed, in this: That he did on the 19th day of November 1864 in the night time of that day in the said County did feloniously and burglariously break and enter the dwelling house of the said M. H. Spencer with intent the goods & chattels of the said M. H. Spencer, then and there feloniously and burglariously to steal take and carry away Forty five dollars in Gold, the value of Forty Five Dollars, Two Hundred Dollars in State Bank money of the value of two hundred dollars One Gold Locket & Chain of the value of Two hundred Dollars, one satin vest of the value of Seven Dollars, one & Quarter yards of Broad cloth of the value of Seven Dollars two fine shirts of the value of Seven Dollars, Two Cravats of the value of Four Dollars, Notes & Papers of the value of Five Hundred Dollars, Three gold pens of the value of Twenty one dollars of the goods and chattels of the said M. H. Spencer in the said dwelling house then being feloniously & burglariously did steal take and carry away, and also Five sides Leather the property of A. Thomas & Son of the value of Fifteen Dollars in the same dwelling house then being feloniously and burglariously did steal and carry away. The prisoner was set to the bar in the custody of the jailor of this County, and the Court upon a full and impartial hearing of the testimony & the argument of counsel on both sides doth unanimously decide that said Boy Jim the property of William Flanagan is guilty of the charge alleged, against him; and through its Presiding Justice doth pronounce the following sentence upon him

It becomes my painful duty as Chief Justice of the Court of the County to pronounce sentence upon the Prisoner at the bar, this is a very disagreeable task for me to perform, it would accord with my feelings much more if I was privileged to testify to the innocence of the Prisoner and to set him at liberty, But as painful as this duty is; it is one which the law has imposed upon those who are honored with the position I occupy, After due deliberation of the matter it unanimously considered by the Court that the Prisoner Jim a Slave the property of William Flanagan be hanged by the neck until he be dead, dead, dead, and that execution of this Judgment be made and done upon him the said Jim by the Sheriff of Smyth County on Friday the 30th day of December 1864 between the hours of ten in the forenoon and two in the afternoon of the same day, at the usual place of execution. The Court commends him to the mercy of his maker, and desires to express the hope that he will prepare to meet his end in peace, and the Court doth decide that the value of the said Boy Jim the property of William Flanagan is Thirty five hundred Dollars. And thereupon the said Jim Slave of William Flanagan is remanded to Jail.

P. C. Buchanan Jr. P. J.

Stoneman's raiders released this man from the jail and he went off with the Yankee soldiers.

Prior to 1850, the judges of the county court were nominated by the court and commissioned by the governor. They served without pay and for life or until removed for cause. From 1850 until 1870 they were elected by the people and allowed a small fee for services. By the constitution of 1868, the old justices court was abolished and the county court judge instituted. The county court judge in turn was done away with in 1904, and the present circuit system adopted. Smyth had five county judges. The first of these, Hon. George W. Jones, was for many years commonwealth's attorney for the county and rounded out a useful and honored career with four years on the bench. He built and lived in the frame house, now occupied by Mr. Dixon, on Main Street, adjoining the college campus. Judge A. P. Cole, born at St. Clair's

Bottom, Nov. 27, 1837, and died at New Canton, Va., Oct. 17, 1917, a member of the honored pioneer family of Coles on the South Fork, served a term of six years, having also been commonwealth's attorney. Judge D. C. Miller, while appreciated as a judge, rendered his largest service to the county in the field of education and will be noticed in the chapter on Schools. George W. Richardson, also a commonwealth's attorney, was a native of Rich Valley and for half a century was among the most honored and useful citizens of Marion. Judge Granville H. Fudge, in office at the time that this court was abolished, was later elected commonwealth's attorney. Of the circuit judges, two, John A. Kelly and John P. Sheffey, were residents of Smyth. Judge Kelly was born in Lee County, June 23, 1821. As a lad in his early teens, he carried the mail when carrying the mail meant hard, dangerous riding over roads that were mountain trails. At sixteen he went to work in the clerk's office in Russell, thence he went to Emory and Henry College, and then taught school in Smyth and in Giles, studying law while teaching in Giles. He was admitted to the bar when he was twenty-one years old. He was cashier in the Northwestern Bank of Virginia from 1854 until after the War between the States. Removing to Marion soon after the War, he practiced law in partnership with Robert A. Richardson. In February, 1870, he was elected the first judge of the sixteenth circuit and for twenty-five years rode the mountain roads of this large circuit to preside over the courts of its many counties, discharging the arduous duties of that office so as to set a high standard for all his successors. He died at Marion Nov. 17, 1900. Judge Kelly lived in a large frame house on Railroad Street now owned by Miss Pauline Moody. He reared a large family, among them the late Judge Joseph A. Kelly, Chief Justice of the Supreme Court of Virginia.

Practice of law in the Southwest today may be more re-

COUNTY ORGANIZATION

munerative than in days gone by, but it is a less colorful occupation. Your successful small town lawyer from Southwest Virginia today may, and frequently does, board a through train; engage a lower berth; and ride elegantly anywhere from New York to San Francisco in the transaction of business; his bored seclusion broken with smoking-room comradery. The major portion of business traveling of his predecessor (perhaps, a better lawyer) was done on horseback. With a change of garments, his papers, perhaps a bottle and a pack of cards in his saddle bags, he rode with the other lawyers from one county court to another. Arrived at the county seat they put up for the term at a tavern or in the home of friends, and their nights and daylight hours out of court were taken up with varied forms of entertainment. Prior to 1870 when Marion went dry all the courthouse taverns had bars and they were liberally patronized. Among the lawyers there were few total abstainers, and even fewer excessive drinkers. Those who drank drank like gentlemen, generally, and there were always some among them who had as little use for liquor as Senator Shepherd or Congressman Volstead. There was a great deal of excessive drinking done, however, by throngs of people attending court. While many gay blades among the old-time lawyers were over-fond of social drinking and gambling at cards, these vices were not distinctive characteristics of the profession. As a class they were men of high ideals, temperate for their times, profound students of the theory of law and skillful adepts in its practice. Not a few were men of independent means to whom law practice was a high calling and a fine art rather than a business.

John C. Poston, one of the most brilliant lawyers in Smyth's history, ruined his prospects by excessive drinking; he would build up a practice and lose by dissipation, then make a comeback and lose out again. He was very popular and was several times elected commonwealth's attorney, and used to say that, "if he could get the support of the Buchanans and their tributaries," he felt assured of election.

There have been some great lawyers at the Marion bar who were not addicted to drink, among them: James W. Sheffey; Robert A. Richardson, who served twelve years on the supreme bench of Virginia; J. H. Gilmore, who became professor of law at the University of Virginia; Judge George W. Richardson; and Hon. B. F. Buchanan.

The first day of court was commonly given over to speechmaking. Those were the days of the orator and the forensic powers of the lawyers were displayed in many ways other than in pleading before the court. Many an unrecorded speech of rare, even magnificent eloquence, regaled the mountaineers assembled in the woods-encircled villages.

Classical orations, crude demagogic harangues, elegant discussions, rough-and-tumble debates, impassioned appeals to patriotism and to prejudice, exhaustive expositions of the political questions of the day were all served out on these occasions. People by the hundreds and sometimes thousands would gather for every court, coming for sociability and trade and to learn the news. Newspapers and periodicals were rare and the people depended upon the lawyers as their main source of inspiration and information as to the news and issues of the times. In these degenerate days *The Roanoke Times* and *The Bristol Herald Courier* have taken over many of the most important functions of the old time southwest lawyer.

Court days were formerly great social functions. Crowds thronged the village and participated in social entertainment consisting of the arguing of cases in and out of court, drinking and friendly fighting. This form of pastime was commonly practiced. There were two old codgers in the county who every court day would go to the courthouse town, get tanked

COUNTY ORGANIZATION 91

up on liquor, get in an argument over religion, and fight it out with their fists. One was a Baptist defender and the other championed the Methodists. An interested crowd would gather around them to see and hear the fun. On one occasion the doughty champion of Methodism vanquished his opponent without having to resort to fists. The argument went like this:

"Go to the Bible, go to the Bible. It says nothing about Methodists, but it tells about Baptists. It tells about John the Baptist but it don't tell about John the Methodist. Where is John the Methodist in the Bible? He ain't there, and there ain't no other Methodist there."

"No, you old ignoramus. Of course, there is no John the Methodist there. It was John Wesley that started the Methodists, and there is plenty about him in the Bible. Go to your Bible and see what it says about John Wesley."

"Well, now, I hadn't thought of that. But I guess that is so."

Horse trading was a great feature of the old-time court days. The gathering of the horse traders with their strings of old nags in various stages of dilapidation, and the ingenious tricks that were practiced by slick-tongued, shrewd rascals in their efforts to cheat the other party, formed a colorful feature of life in former days. The passing of the horse-trading gentry and the demise of the horse-trading business is something else to charge to the automobile account.

The old colonial system of a number of justices for each county appointed by the governor and council of state was in vogue in Virginia until 1852. The presiding justice and at least three others designated by him sat at each court, and sometimes more were on the bench. Circuit judges were introduced in 1870 under the constitution of 1868. Judge John A. Kelly, the first judge of the old Sixteenth Circuit which included all the counties west of New River, with his retinue of lawyers, rode this circuit for twenty-four years. His salary was sixteen hundred dollars a year and he paid all his expenses. Today there are six judicial circuits and the city of Bristol in his territory, and they keep seven judges occupied. Judge Kelly was born in Lee County. He was a mail carrier until he reached the ripe age of sixteen when he was employed as assistant to the Rev. James P. Carroll, county clerk of Russell County, who helped him through Emory and Henry College. Then he taught school in Smyth and Giles counties, studied law in the office of Samuel Peck of Giles, and went into partnership with him. After the Civil War he removed to Marion and lived there until he died. In 1895 Hon. John Preston Sheffey of Marion succeeded him as circuit judge. Judge Sheffey, in riding his circuit, sometimes took with him his little grandson, John Preston Buchanan, who can, when he will, talk very entertainingly about those rides.

John Preston Sheffey was born, lived, and died in Marion. He graduated from Emory and Henry in 1857 and studied law at the University of Virginia, beginning practice in 1859 as a partner of his father. He married Miss Josephine Spiller June 19, 1860, and reared a family of two sons and five daughters at his home on the lot where Mr. J. C. Campbell now lives. Succeeding Judge Kelly in the arduous riding of the Sixteenth Circuit Bench, he was an able and upright Judge, held in high and affectionate esteem. Judge Sheffey was a member of the legislature from Smyth County from 1893 to 1894. He died in 1905.

Prior to 1870 Smyth had two clerks, one of the county and the other of the circuit court. After that date one clerk has performed the functions of both. James F. Pendleton held both offices from 1847–1852. E. A. Scott, the next incumbent, was the son of Mitchell Scott and was born and lived

COUNTY ORGANIZATION 93

and died in the old log homestead whose stone chimney still stands about a mile and a half west of Marion beside the ruins of the home. His son, Edward Scott, and daughters, Mrs. Mary Sale and Miss Mattie, lived for a long time in their home on West Main Street. Mr. Charles F. Lincoln functioned as circuit clerk for a few months before the offices were combined. The last regular incumbent was John S. Copenhaver.

Mr. Copenhaver was born Dec. 10, 1831, in the community known as Chilhowie, about five miles west of Marion, and is descended from a family who were among the earliest settlers in that section of the county. He came to Marion in 1856, and became deputy for James F. Pendleton, clerk of the county court. In 1858 he was elected clerk of the circuit court, and as clerk or deputy, from that time practically performed the duties of the office until 1869. He afterwards served as commissioner of accounts. He reached the venerable age of ninety years, dying in December, 1921. His sons, Dr. E. M. and Frank Copenhaver, and his daughters, Mrs. C. C. Whitworth, Mrs. R. G. Baylor and Mrs. W. M. Sclater now live in Marion. Since Mr. Copenhaver's death commissioners of accounts have been E. H. Buchanan and L. Preston Collins.

The court of juvenile and domestic relations was established in the summer of 1922, with L. Preston Collins as the first judge. He resigned after a few months' service and was succeeded by Judge B. L. Dickinson, the present incumbent.

The office of county commissioner of revenue was instituted in 1927 to replace the district commissioners. I. W. Hutton of Atkins, Republican, was elected for the first term over W. B. Echols, Democrat, who had come from Washington to Smyth County in 1907 as bookkeeper for the Marion Foundry and Machine Works, and had served as the last commissioner of revenue for Marion District. In 1932 Mr. Hutton won again over John G. Atkins.

Game wardens have been George H. Miles, G. H. Scott, and Miles Newman. There has been marked increase in dog tags and hunting licenses of late years. For the thirteen years before Newman came into office, there were annually a thousand dog tags and a hundred and fifty hunting licenses; now about three thousand dog tags and fifteen hundred hunting licenses.

First Justices of Smythe County, 1832

Date of Commission	Names of Persons	Date of Qualification
March 1st	Charles Tate	March 26th
March 1st	James Taylor	March 27th
March 1st	Samuel Williams	March 20th
March 1st	Thomas Thomas	March 20th
March 1st	George W. Davis	March 31st
March 1st	Hatch D. Poston	March 20th
March 1st	Joseph Atkins	March 17th
March 1st	Henry B. Thompson	March 20th
March 1st	William Porter	March 20th
March 1st	Thompson Atkins	March 17th
March 1st	Robert Houston	March 14th
March 1st	Joseph P. Bonham	March 17th
March 1st	Abram B. Trigg	Appointed—
March 1st	Robert Beattie	March 24th
April 30th	James Davis	
April 30th	Zachariah Mitchell	May 24th
April 30th	Solomon McDonald	May 24th
April 30th	Arthur Bowen	May 24th
April 30th	John M. Townsend	May 24th
April 30th	John Thomas	May 24th
April 30th	William L. Goodpasture	May 25th
April 30th	James Cole	May 24th
April 30th	Joseph Thomas	May 24th
April 30th	William Scott	June 21st
Nov. 15th	Andrew Cox	Nov. 23rd

COUNTY ORGANIZATION

A List of County Officers of Smyth County from the Foundation, 1832

(Compiled by H. L. Kent, Clerk)

Judges of the Circuit Court

(Prior to 1850 this court was termed the Superior Court of Law and Chancery)

Hon. Benjamin Estill ....1832 to 1851
Hon. Geo. W. Hopkins.................1851 to 1856
Hon. Samuel V. Fulkerson ....1856 to 1861
Hon. Gideon D. Camden ....1861 to 1863
Hon. John A. Campbell ....1863 to 1869
Hon. John W. Johnston ....1869 to 1870
Hon. John A. Kelly ....1870 to 1895
Hon. John P. Sheffey ....1895 to 1904
Hon. Francis B. Hutton ....1904 to 1914
Hon. Preston W. Campbell ....1914 to 1924
Hon. John J. Stuart ....1924 to ——

Clerks of the Circuit Court

(Until 1870, there were two clerks, after that time the two offices were combined)

Peter C. Johnson ....1832 to 1836
Albert B. Moore ....1836 to 1847
J. F. Pendleton ....1847 to 1852
E. A. Scott ....1852 to 1860
John S. Copenhaver ....1860 to 1869
C. F. Lincoln ....1869 to 1870

Judges of the County Court

(Prior to 1870, this Court was formed by the Magistrates)

Hon. George W. Jones.................1870 to 1874
Hon. A. P. Cole ....1874 to 1880
Hon. D. C. Miller....................1880 to 1885
Hon. Geo. W. Richardson..............1886 to 1891
Hon. Granville H. Fudge ....1892 to Jan. 30, 1904, when this Court adjourned Sine Die

County Clerks

Robert Beattie	1832 to 1839	
James F. Pendleton	1839 to 1858	
W. C. Sexton	1859 to 1869	
James Cox (Pro-tem)	1869[1]	
R. M. Goodell	1869 to 1870	
E. L. Roberts	1870 to 1875	
W. C. Sexton	1875 to 1905	
S. W. Kent	1905 to 1919	
H. L. Kent	1920 to ——	

Commonwealth's Attorneys of Smyth County:
County Court

Charles E. Harrison, April 30, 1832

George W. Jones, Aug. 16, 1836, to July 1, 1852, after which period there was only one attorney for the Commonwealth for the County:

Circuit Court

Charles E. Harrison................April 30, 1832
James W. Sheffey, October 3, 1836 (Resigned May 2, 1837)
Andrew S. Fulton, May 2, 1837 (Resigned April 9, 1840)
Peter C. Johnston, May 4, 1840 (Resigned Sept. 29, 1845)
James W. Sheffey............Sept. 29, 1845 to July 1, 1852
John C. Poston.............July 1, 1852 to Sept. 6, 1858
A. G. Pendleton, Jr...........Sept. 6, 1858, to July 1, 1860
John C. Poston.....................July 1, 1860 to 1862
A. P. Cole...................................1863 to 1865
John C. Poston 1866
Wade S. Strother..........June 19, 1866 to April 1, 1869
John S. Slater 1869
John C. Poston 1869
A. P. Cole 1870
N. C. St. John................Jan. 1, 1871 to Jan. 1, 1874
G. H. Fudge..................Jan. 1, 1874 to July 1, 1883
H. C. Jones..................July 1, 1883 to July 1, 1887
A. M. Dickinson..............July 1, 1887 to July 1, 1895

---

[1] James Cox was one of the magistrates composing the County Court and acted as County Clerk for two terms of Court.

COUNTY ORGANIZATION

Geo. W. Richardson..........July 1, 1895 to Jan. 1, 1904
Geo. F. Cook................Jan. 1, 1912 to Jan. 1, 1920
James White Sheffey...........Jan. 1, 1920 to Jan. 1, 1924
Charles F. Funk..............Jan. 1, 1924 to Jan. 1, 1932
R. Crockett Gwyn, Jr..................Jan. 1, 1932 to ——

Treasurers of Smyth County Since 1870

(Prior to this time the taxes were collected by the Sheriff)

H. N. Perkins[2]...............Jan. 1, 1871 to July 25, 1871
James M. Pruner[3]........July 25, 1871 to time of his death
W. C. Seaver[4]...............Nov. 21, 1871 to Dec. 31, 1871
Reese P. Copenhaver..........Jan. 1, 1872 to July 1, 1875
Geo. W. Henderlite ....1875 to 1880
R. T. Copenhaver[5] ....1881 to 1881
John W. Richardson..........................1881 to 1891
A. F. Stone ....1891 to 1899
Geo. W. Wright ....1899 to 1907
J. L. C. Anderson...........................1908 to 1911
Geo. A. Collins ....1911 to 1911
J. L. C. Anderson ....1912 to ——

Sheriffs

Charles Tate ....1832 to 1834
Geo. W. Davis ....1834 to 1835
Hatch D. Poston ....1836 to 1837
Henry B. Thompson ....1838 to 1839
William Porter ....1840 to 1841
Thompson Atkins ....1842 to 1843
Zachariah Mitchell ....1844 to 1845
Robert Houston ....1846 to 1847
Joseph B. Bonham ....1848 to 1849
Isaac H. Spratt ....1850 to 1852
V. S. Morgan ....1852 to 1856
John T. Johnston ....1857 to 1859
V. S. Morgan.........................1859 to 1860

[2] Resigned.
[3] Appointed to fill vacancy occasioned by resignation.
[4] Appointed to fill vacancy occasioned by death.
[5] Appointed to fill vacancy occasioned by death.

SMYTH COUNTY HISTORY

Thomas H. Spratt ....1861 to 1864
E. A. Scott ....1865 to 1866
P. Campbell Buchanan ....1866 to 1868
Geo. W. Henderlite ....1869 to 1871
P. Campbell Buchanan ....1871 to 1874
Robert S. Bonham ....1874 to 1883
Frank W. Leonard ....1883 to 1899
J. V. Richardson ....1899 to 1904
W. N. McGhee ....1904 to 1908
J. H. Rouse ....1908 to 1912
M. D. Cassell ....1912 to 1916
W. N. McGhee ....1916 to 1920
S. F. Dillard ....1920 to ——

MEMBERS OF THE BOARD OF SUPERVISORS OF SMYTH COUNTY

Marion District

D. D. Hull, Chairman.................1870 to 1879
Geo. W. Hubble (Chairman 1881 to 1883) 1879 to 1883
C. F. Lincoln, Chairman ....1883 to 1889
Charles M. Williams ....1889 to 1891
D. D. Hull, Chairman ....1891 to 1901
M. M. Seaver ....1901 to 1904
D. C. Gollehon ....1904 to 1908
Joseph U. Wolfe, Chairman ....1908 to 1912
W. W. Stephenson (Resigned) ....1912 to 1913
Jas. A. Groseclose ....1913 to 1920
J. A. Eller, Chairman ....1920 to ——

Rich Valley District

Wm. L. Richardson ....1870 to 1872
J. B. Whitehead ....1872 to 1873
Wm. L. Richardson....................1873 to 1874
W. W. George ....1874 to 1879
James C. Buchanan (Chm. 1879 to 1881) 1879 to 1883
D. T. Davis ....1883 to 1885
John M. Gwyn (Chm. 1889 to 1891)....1885 to 1893
F. G. Buchanan ....1893 to 1897
John M. Gwyn ....1897 to 1899

COUNTY ORGANIZATION

J. D. Barns ....1899 to 1902
T. B. Ward ....1902 to 1908
W. W. George (Resigned) ....1908 to 1908
J. M. Gass (Chm. 1912 to 1920)........1908 to 1920
S. T. Buchanan ....1920 to 1924
W. W. Buchanan ....1924 to ——

St. Clair District

Robert H. Hubble ....1870 to 1873
James T. Porter ....1873 to 1879
M. L. Umbarger ....1879 to 1883
G. B. Blankenbeckler ....1883 to 1887
Samuel J. James ....1887 to 1889
O. L. James ....1889 to 1891
E. S. Wolfe ....1891 to 1895
Wm. A. Wolfe ....1895 to 1897
James F. Scott (Chm. 1901 to 1908)....1897 to 1908
A. A. Tibbs (Resigned)................1908 to 1910
Martin Houston ....1910 to 1912
Geo. F. Pierce ....1912 to 1920
S. W. Keesling ....1920 to 1928
C. B. Rouse ....1928 to ——

Commissioners of Revenue of Smyth County

Marion District

A. J. Harris..................July 1, 1871 to July 1, 1887
J. L. Gollehon...............July 1, 1887 to Jan. 1, 1904
J. L. C. Anderson............Jan. 1, 1904 to Jan. 1, 1908
T. B. Rector.................Jan. 1, 1908 to Jan. 1, 1912
J. J. Dungan.................Jan. 1, 1912 to Jan. 1, 1916
Jno. A. Greenwood............Jan. 1, 1916 to Jan. 1, 1924
W. B. Echols.................Jan. 1, 1924 to Jan. 1, 1928

Rich Valley District

L. B. Roberts................July 1, 1871 to July 1, 1875
W. P. M. Scott...............July 1, 1875 to July 1, 1879
A. F. Cook...................July 1, 1879 to July 1, 1883
B. F. Call...................July 1, 1883 to July 1, 1895

Chas. M. Shannon............July 1, 1895 to Jan. 1, 1908
B. F. Call ....Jan. 1, 1908 to Jan. 1, 1916
J. A. Campbell...............Jan. 1, 1916 to Jan. 1, 1920
Geo. L. Harmon..............Jan. 1, 1920 to Jan. 1, 1924

St. Clair District

Jno. M. Haulsee.............July 1, 1871 to July 1, 1873
Jno. M. Williams............July 1, 1873 to Mar. 16, 1880
Jos. W. Blankenbeckler......Mar. 16, 1880 to July 1, 1883
Jno. M. Williams............July 1, 1883 to Dec. 30, 1910
D. D. Cole ....Dec. 30, 1910 to Jan. 1, 1912
D. L. Carter................Jan. 1, 1912 to Jan. 1, 1916
W. H. Eads..................Jan. 1, 1916 to Jan. 20, 1919
B. B. Britton...............Jan. 20, 1919 to Jan. 1, 1920
Fred B. Hubble..............Jan. 1, 1920 to Jan. 1, 1928

Smyth County

I. W. Hutton..............Jan. 1, 1928 to ———, ———

CHAPTER VII

POLITICAL NOTATIONS

THE forefathers of Smyth County folk were of those free spirited, independently thinking and acting people whom Governor Dunmore charged with the intention of forming "a Set of Democratical Governments of their own" even before they wrote the notable Fincastle Declaration of Liberty. From then until now they have been intensely interested in affairs political, neither have they been devoid of either politicians or statesmen.

The brilliant and versatile Arthur Campbell was a statesman of ability and a politician with warm friends and bitter enemies. His nephew says he had more and bitterer enemies than any man of his day and he did not hesitate to express his opinion of them in unmeasured terms nor were they backward in saying what they thought of him. He carried on a very extensive political correspondence and his home at Royal Oak was long a sort of unofficial political headquarters for a great part of the western country. In 1776 Arthur Campbell and William Russell were elected to represent this county in the State House of Delegates, the first representatives from the Mississippi Basin to sit in a representative body under constitutional government. He fathered the bill for the division of Fincastle into three counties and has been, not inappropriately, styled the Father of Washington County and Kentucky. In the spring of 1777 the first election in Washington County was held and Campbell was defeated. He protested the election, but did not get the seat. In 1778,

1782, and 1787 he represented Washington County in the Legislature.

Arthur Campbell's eye was on the developing West. He believed in local self-government and was a leader in the movement for forming the State of Franklin, being credited sometimes with originating and fathering that whole scheme. Certainly he had a big part in it and endeavored to align Southwest Virginia with the new state. He drew a map outlining the state he wanted, which would have run from the Kanawha River south into Alabama and from the crest of the Alleghanies to the crest of the Cumberlands.

Sentiment loyal to Virginia was too strong for him to carry his section with him, and his political enemies, headed by William Russell, then brother-in-law of Gov. Patrick Henry, used this to discredit him at Richmond. After the Franklin affair his political influence waned.

Other Smyth inhabitants to represent Washington County before the division were William Campbell, David Campbell, William Russell, William Tate, and William Poston.

William Russell was State Senator of Washington County from 1787 to 1795, while living at Seven Mile Ford and Saltville. Summers gives this sketch of him:

Born in Culpepper County in the year 1748. Settled near the Clinch River, south of Castle's Woods, about 1770. Commanded a company of frontiersmen at the battle of Point Pleasant in the fall of 1774. Member of the House of Burgesses from Fincastle County in 1776. Commissioned captain in the Continental army, and accompanied Colonel Christian upon his expedition against the Cherokee Indians in 1776. Member of the General Assembly of Virginia in 1786, and introduced bill for formation of Russell County, Virginia. Brigadier-General of Virginia militia. Married Mrs. Wm. Campbell, and resided at Saltville. Died in the year 1794 at the home of his son, Robert S. Russell, in Shenandoah County, Virgina.

POLITICAL NOTATIONS

The territory of Smyth was at first embraced in the Third Congressional District and was represented by Andrew Moore of Rockbridge. In 1793 it was in the Fourth District and Francis Preston of Saltville was elected the first Congressman from Southwest Virginia. He was elected as a Federalist, which meant that he was a loyal supporter of George Washington. When the issues between Hamilton's Federalists and Jefferson's Republicans were clarified, he was a staunch Jeffersonian. Summers says of him:

Son of Col. William Preston, of Smithfield. Was born at Greenfield (now Botetourt County) on the 2d day of August, 1765. Graduated at William and Mary College and studied law under Chancellor Wythe. Settled in Abingdon and began the practice of law, and was for many years recognized as one of the ablest lawyers in this section of the State. Married Sarah Buchanan Campbell, daughter of General William Campbell, on the 10th January, 1793. Elected a member of Congress in the same year, and served till the year 1797. After retiring from Congress he settled at the Saltworks. In the year 1810 he removed to Abingdon. Elected to the General Assembly from Washington county. Was commissioned a colonel, and marched with his regiment to Norfolk in 1814. He was elected brigadier-general of militia by the General Assembly of Virginia in 1820. He died at the home of William C. Preston, in South Carolina, on the 26th day of May, 1836, and his remains were interred at Aspinvale, near Seven Mile Ford. He left a family of children, all of whom became distinguished, viz.: United States Senator Wm. C. Preston, of South Carolina; General John S. Preston, of South Carolina; Thomas L. Preston, University of Virginia; Mrs. Wade Hampton, of South Carolina; Mrs. Robert J. Breckenridge, of Kentucky; Mrs. General Carrington, of Albemarle County; Mrs. John B. Floyd, of Washington County; Mrs. James McDowell, of Virginia; Mrs. John M. Preston, of Abingdon.

His son, William C. Preston, went to the United States

Senate from South Carolina and was among the greatest orators that august body has known.

The first congressional election after the formation of the county was between John H. Fulton, Whig, and William Byars, Democrat, held in 1833. The polling place was at the house of John Thomas at Royal Oak, and each voter would step forward and call out the name of the man he was voting for.

The names of the voters in this first election, with the way they voted, are preserved in the clerk's office. Fulton was elected.

The most exciting Presidential campaign before the Civil War was the Polk-Clay affair, at which time the most colorful political gathering ever held in Southwest Virginia was staged at the old Sulphur Springs. An account of it is given in the chapter dealing with Chilhowie.

When James Madison toured this territory during his Presidential campaign and visited Madam Russell, she stopped him on the threshold while she put her hands on his head and prayed for him.

Colonel Pendleton in his *Political History of Appalachian Virginia* says:

In September, 1830, the first National Political Convention that ever assembled in the United States was held in Philadelphia. It was named the United States Anti-Masonic Convention.

The Anti-Masonic party found its origin in the disappearance, or alleged murder, of one William Morgan, an apostate Freemason. Morgan was a Virginian by birth and a very disreputable character; and he was undertaking to publish a book to reveal the secrets of Freemasonry—an Order of which George Washington had been a most devoted member, and of which Governor DeWitt Clinton, of New York, was then an eminent member. On the 11th of September, 1826, at Batavia, New York, a few overzealous Masons seized Morgan, just after he was discharged from jail, and bribed him to go to Canada and never return to the United States. Thereupon, it was alleged by the enemies of Freemasonry that Morgan had been murdered by the Masons. This grave charge produced great excitement in New York and in adjacent states. Certain aspiring politicians availed themselves of this excitement with the expectation of advancing their political interests. The most prominent of these were: William H. Seward, Thurlow Weed, Millard Fillmore, William Wirt, and John Quincy Adams. This party founded upon a single and utterly false principle was very short-lived as it was consigned to oblivion at the Presidential election in 1832.

This William Morgan was probably a Smyth County native; at any rate, he eloped with a sixteen-year-old Smyth County girl, as seen in the chapter on "Schools."

In 1832 Smyth was strong for Jackson and went Democratic rather than Whig in most of the ante-bellum presidential elections. In the Taylor-Cass campaign, however, Smyth cast for old Rough-and-Ready Zachary Taylor, Whig, 326 votes, and for Cass, Democrat, 309. After the War for some time there was no clear-cut division in the national politics in the county, but as between Democrat and Republican the county was overwhelmingly Democratic until the Readjuster days, since which it has consistently gone Republican. In State affairs for the first decade after the War the parties were Radical and Conservative, and Smyth was strongly Conservative. In the readjuster fight the lines were closely drawn and the issues bitterly fought, with the Readjusters mustering majorities in the voting.

In 1855 the State was profoundly stirred by the gubernatorial campaign between John S. Wise, Democrat, and Thomas S. Flourney, candidate of what was called "The Know-Nothing Party." Wise debated the issues of this campaign with Mr. James W. Sheffey before a hugely interested audience at Marion. The county cast 654 votes for Wise and 571 for Flourney.

One of the most interesting of Smyth's political figures was the Hon. LaFayette McMullin.

He was born in Bedford County, Virginia, son of John McMullin and Mary Wysong. His father was of Scotch-Irish and his mother was of French descent. His father was a merchant and ran wagon trains from Bedford to Scott County. LaFayette for a number of years drove a four-horse-wagon team for his father from Lynchburg to Gate City, hauling goods for hire and trading along the way. Then he settled in Marion, in the mercantile business for a while, and became very popular through contacts with his customers. At one time he owned the lot and building now the Jackson Building, which, I am told, he traded for the farm west of Marion now owned by Graham Gardner, and where he spent the last years of his life.

There has been no more popular figure in Southwestern Virginia public life and no more effective canvasser for votes than he in his prime. He is reputed to have personally known every voter in his district and is said to have made more political campaigns, to have delivered more political speeches, and to have kissed more babies than any other Southwestern Virginian.

Innumerable anecdotes are told of him. Senator Vest of Missouri, the same who delivered the immortal eulogy on the dog, tells this one:

Old Fayette McMullin was canvassing his district for a nomination to Congress, years ago, and during the canvass, a man was hanged in that locality for murder. About ten thousand men collected to witness the scene, and among them old Mac, who, by the favor of the sheriff, occupied a place on the platform in the rear of the gallows, his oratorical mouth watering at the sight of the magnificent audience in front of him. When everything was ready, as is usual in such cases, the sheriff asked the culprit if he had anything to say before the sentence of the law should be passed upon him; to which the condemned responded that he would say nothing. Whereupon old Mac stepped forward, rubbing his hands, and remarked: "Mr. Sheriff, if the gentleman will yield his time to me, I will embrace this occasion to make a few remarks on the political situation and to announce myself a candidate for Congress."

A party of horse traders visited Marion. At least one of them was a horse thief. He stole a horse belonging to Mr. James White Sheffey. Mr. Sheffey got McMullin to go with him to their camp four or five miles out in the country. They found the horse, and Sheffey demanded that it be given up. The thief refused. Mr. Sheffey reached for the horse's bridle, and the thief reached for his gun. McMullin pulled a long knife out of the back of his coat collar and with one sweeping thrust cut the fellow's throat and killed him. Many men tell how "Old Mack" would go about canvassing for votes and get them by jollying the men, hugging the ladies, and giving red stick candy to the children. Mr. Phil Francis, of Marion, said: "When I was a little chap going to school in the old schoolhouse above the Baptist church, Fayette McMullin was running for Congress. They marched all of the school children down to the old Continental Hotel to hear him make a speech. He had a big box of red stick candy. I was looking at the candy so that I did not hear what he was saying, but he said one thing that caught my attention and I have never forgotten it. He said: 'Boys, you will have to do what is right, because some of these days you will have to take our places!'" It is said that Parson Brownlow, a noted Methodist preacher and Governor of Tennessee, got into a political row with McMullin and took a shot at him, but missed.

His first marriage seems to have been an unhappy one for while Governor of Washington he secured a divorce by act of the Legislature of that territory.

In July, 1858, Gov. McMullin married Mary Wood, a daughter of Isaac Wood, a pioneer of Thurston County. About the time of his marriage he was removed from office and returned with his new bride to his old home in Virginia.

Mrs. Mary Wood McMullin, a native of Olympia, Washington, won a warm place for herself in the hearts of her Southern neighbors. When she died, in June, 1889, a Virginia newspaper said: "Mrs. McMullin was a kind and very charitable woman, and was a member of the Episcopal church, and gave evidence to her friends that she was fully prepared to meet her God. She was a firm friend of Marion Female College—made donations to it frequently, at one time giving $1,000—and in recognition of her interest in the college, the board of trustees met her body at the depot, and the faculty and students of the college joined the procession and accompanied the remains to Round Hill Cemetery."

In 1838 he was elected to the Senate of Virginia and served in that capacity continuously for ten years. In 1849 he was elected to Congress as a Democrat after being defeated in a previous election by a Whig. Once elected he kept on being elected, being returned to Congress each succeeding election until 1857, when President Buchanan appointed him Governor of the Washington Territory.

Of Governor McMullin's only message to the Legislature of Washington Territory, Edmond S. Meany in a little book called *Governors of Washington,* says:

He outlined ways of protection from Indian troubles, called attention to the beginning of the famous military road from Fort Benton to Walla Walla, and advocated the northern route for the proposed railroad across the continent. He objected to Oregon's attempt to annex a part of the area of Washington territory. The message gives the impression of a governor who saw many needs of the new commonwealth and who was willing to coöperate in every way possible to have those needs supplied. The territorial newspapers published items about the governor's journey home to Virginia, and in many of those items were facts showing that he was a consistent friend of Washington territory. He gave public expression to his belief in its resources and attractiveness for settlers. All of this kindly service was soon silenced by the approach of the Civil War.

Back in Smyth he ran for the first Confederate Congress in 1861 and lost to Walter Preston by nineteen votes. In 1863 he was elected to the second Confederate Congress. After the war he repeatedly ran for Congress as an Independent but was not elected. He was killed by a train at the depot in Wytheville, Nov. 8, 1880.

A Democratic Convention was held in Marion in 1858, and is described by Colonel Pendleton:

In 1858 the Democrats of the Thirteenth District met in convention at Marion, Smyth County, to nominate a candidate for Congress. It was presided over by James F. Pendleton, father of the author. The latter, then a boy of eleven years old, attended the deliberations of the convention and thenceforward became deeply interested in the politics of the Nation, of the State, and especially of Southwest Virginia. There were three candidates seeking the nomination for Congress—George W. Hopkins, Benjamin Rush Floyd, and Fayette McMullin. The latter had resigned as Governor of Washington Territory and returned to Virginia, with an ardent desire to again enter the National House of Representatives. And from that time, until his death in 1880 he was a standing candidate for Congress.

The contest for the nomination at the Marion Convention was spirited and prolonged, but was finally terminated by the nomination of Benjamin Rush Floyd. Mr. Floyd was of distinguished lineage, a man of sterling character, a lawyer of splendid ability; but he was a Roman Catholic. The Whigs and Know Nothings seized upon Mr. Floyd's regilious beliefs as a means to obtain his defeat. They united their forces, as they had done in the gubernatorial election the previous year. And they induced Elbert S. Martin—a Know Nothing —who had been defeated by George W. Hopkins for Congress in 1856—to announce himself an independent candidate in opposition to Mr. Floyd. Martin was a merchant and a man of very ordinary ability; but he made a house-to-house canvass of the mountain sections of the district and inflamed the intolerant spirit of the most bigoted element of the Protestants. He was elected to the Thirty-seventh Congress, receiving 6,382 votes, against 5,779, polled for Mr. Floyd.

On Tuesday, March 20, 1860, a District Democratic Convention was held in Marion for the purpose of electing delegates to the National Convention shortly to convene in Charleston, S. C., the famous convention that split the Democratic party three ways and led to the election of Abraham Lincoln as President of the United States. The District Convention at Marion was called to order at two o'clock in the afternoon by Mr. A. G. Pendleton, and Mr. Robert C. Kent, of Wythe, was elected Temporary Chairman. Mr. Kent was then elected Permanent Chairman, with Messrs. William Porter, of Smyth; John Sanders, of Wythe; and Archibald Peery, of Tazewell, Vice Chairmen. The district was entitled to two delegates in the National Convention, and Dr. Robert Crockett, of Wythe, and Mr. Wm. P. Cecil, of Tazewell, were chosen.

The Readjuster-Funder controversy developed in the seventies and reached an acute stage in Smyth in 1878 when the Funders were supporting Col. James B. Richmond for Congress and Readjusters and Greenbackers had agreed to get behind Fayette McMullin. Then Capt. Samuel H. Newbury became a candidate, dividing the Readjuster vote and electing Richmond.

In January, 1879, the Readjusters held a convention in Marion and from then on through the eighties political fighting was fast and furious. Col. W. C. Pendleton having made his *Patriot-Herald* a strong Readjuster paper, the Funders established the *Conservative Democrat*. Robert A. Richardson, who had come to Marion right after the war from Eastern Virginia and was an able and popular lawyer, stumped the State for the Readjusters. He was elected to the Supreme Bench of Virginia by the Readjuster Legislature. After the political war of the debt question was over, the Readjusters went for the most part into the Republican party.

The successful candidates for the Legislature in Smyth are given below. Some of the unsuccessful candidates were: T. H. Spratt, running against Sheffey in 1875; H. P. Copenhaver against Honaker in 1881; Harmon Newberry against Mustard in 1883; John Barnes against Roberts in 1885; W. H. Sprinkle against Burton in 1889; Maj. A. G. Pendleton against Gwyn in 1897; J. D. Buchanan, George W. Richardson, Maurice Hale, and Frank Miller against Captain Wissler, the popular Pennsylvanian who lived in Rye Valley; Rush C. Gwyn against Anderson in 1919; B. L. Dickenson and E. K. Coyner against Pierce in 1823 and 1825; Pierce lost against Shannon, J. R. George against Lincoln, and Lincoln against Frazier. John M. Gwyn established a reputation while in the Legislature for his business sense, for his originality, and humorous stories.

A. T. Lincoln, Republican, was popular and influential in the Democratic Senate. He was Republican candidate for Lieutenant Governor in 1909.

While B. F. Buchanan was Lieutenant Governor, his son, John Preston, was in the Senate, and R. A. Anderson in the house, all three descendents of old pioneer Jacob Anderson who settled on the place now owned by J. R. Shanklin prior to the Revolution.

Mr. Buchanan had more weight in State affairs than any other Smyth man since the days of Arthur Campbell. He was so popular with Republican voters that only two, R. A. Anderson and L. P. Summers, would ever run against him and they did not run very far.

G. W. Henderlite ran for Congress and was beaten by General William Terry in 1847.

In 1880 G. G. Goodell was an unsuccessful candidate for Congress in a four-corner race, in which the Readjuster candidate Abram Fulkerson won over C. F. Trigg, Funder; G. G. Goodell, Republican; and Fayette McMullin, Independent.

William H. Rouse, a Smyth boy who lives in Bristol, was the Democratic candidate in 1928, losing to Mr. Shaffer of Wytheville.

David Campbell, born at Royal Oak, was governor of Virginia and his brother, John, was treasurer of the United States.

Henry A. Stuart, reared at Saltville, is an ex-governor of Virginia.

Since the Readjuster days, the vote in Smyth has been fairly close between Republicans and Democrats, the Republicans having the edge with a normal majority of around three hundred. The Democrats always put up a stiff fight and have usually succeeded in electing one or more of the county officers, and now and then put over their candidate for the Legislature. The Anderson brothers, Robert A. and John L. Combs, have been powerful factors in the Republican organization for the past quarter of a century. John L. Combs Anderson entered politics in 1903 as a candidate for commissioner of revenue in the Marion District and had to borrow the money to buy a horse from his Democratic cousin, Charles Anderson, in order to ride around in making his canvass. He was elected then and got the habit. He was elected county treasurer in 1908, and has been reëlected ever since, defeating such candidates as George W. Wright, James A.

Groseclose, Thomas G. Sanders, J. E. Thomas, Maurice Hale, and Archie Buchanan.

George W. Henderlite, a treasurer of Smyth, was killed by a fall from a hotel window in Richmond. Within a few months of that time Fayette McMullin was killed by a train at the station in Wytheville.

John W. Richardson, for ten years treasurer of Smyth, was for twenty years register of the State Land Office in Richmond.

Members of the House of Delegates from Smyth County

Henry B. Thompson 1832–33
Joseph W. Clemands 1833–34
William R. Hurley 1834–36
Joseph W. Davis 1836–39
Hiram A. Greever 1839–40
Thomas M. Tate 1840–48
H. B. Thompson 1848–49
John M. Campbell 1849–51
Hiram A. Greever 1852–53
Madison L. Crockett 1853–54
Thomas L. Preston 1855–58
Charles J. Shannon 1859–63
John H. Thompson 1863–65
V. S. Morgan 1865–67
J. A. Kelly (Resigned) and Jas. L. Buchanan.. 1869–71
N. C. St. John 1871–73
Thomas H. Spratt 1874–75
James W. Sheffey[1] & Chas. J. Shannon...... 1875–77
Charles J. Shannon 1877–79

Smyth County and Bland County

Hezekiah Harmon 1879–80
Jas. D. Honaker 1881–82

[1] James W. Sheffey died, and Charles J. Shannon was appointed to fill vacancy.

S. P. Mustard 1883–84
Edward L. Roberts 1885–88
John Burton 1889–90
W. W. Edwards 1891–92
John P. Sheffey 1893–94
Haynes L. Morgan 1895–96
John M. Gwyn 1897–98
J. D. Honaker 1899–1900
W. W. George 1901–04

Smyth County

A. C. Beattie 1904
J. H. Wissler 1906–12
A. T. Lincoln 1914–15
H. L. Bonham 1916
R. A. Anderson 1918–20
A. C. Beattie 1922
Geo. F. Pierce 1924–27
C. M. Shannon 1928
W. L. Lincoln 1930
J. Tyler Frazier 1932

MEMBERS OF THE STATE SENATE REPRESENTING SMYTH COUNTY

David McComas 1832–36
Samuel McCamant 1836–40

Tazewell, Wythe, Grayson, Smyth, and Part of Pulaski

James H. Piper 1840–41

Tazewell, Wythe, Grayson, and Smyth

James H. Piper 1841–42
James H. Piper 1842–43
James H. Piper 1843–46
John W. Johnston 1846–48
Thomas M. Tate 1848–51

Smyth, Wythe, and Washington

Thomas M. Tate 1852–56
Benjamin R. Floyd 1857–58
Hiram A. Greever 1859–61

Smyth, Wythe, Washington, and Part of Bland

Joseph J. Graham and Wm. E. Peters (resigned) 1863–65

Washington and Smyth

Joseph W. Davis 1865–67
James S. Greever 1869–77
Abram Fulkerson 1877–80
David F. Bailey 1881–84
William F. Rhea 1885–88
Edward L. Roberts 1889–92
B. F. Buchanan 1893–96
Charles W. Steele 1897–1900

Washington, Smyth, and City of Bristol

J. Cloyd Byars 1901–04

Washington, Smyth, and City of Bristol, Composing District No. 1

J. Cloyd Byars 1904
A. T. Lincoln 1906–10
D. C. Cummings, Jr.,[2] and B. F. Buchanan....1912
J. P. Buchanan 1916–19
J. H. Hassinger 1920–22

Washington, Smyth, and City of Bristol, Composing District No. 15

B. F. Buchanan 1924–32

[2] Cummings died, and Mr. Buchanan appointed in his stead.

CONSTITUTIONAL CONVENTIONS

CONVENTION OF 1850–51

Smyth, Wythe, and Washington

Benjamin Rush Floyd Thomas M. Tate
George W. Hopkins Connally F. Trigg

CONVENTION OF 1861

Smyth County

James W. Sheffey

CONVENTION OF 1867–68

Smyth and Washington

Joseph T. Campbell John H. Thompson

CONVENTION OF 1901–2

Smyth and Bland

A. T. Lincoln

A list of the citizens who voted in Smyth County's first congressional election, April, 1833:

For John H. Fulton: Elijah Debusk, William Sanders, Charles G. Dungans, Andrew Lealy, Francis Kincannon, William Umphry, James Flemming, Thomas Harris, John Cummingham, Mathias Nickles, Robert Young, Thomas Wheeler, Simon Yanders, Elijah Debord, Rufus K. Williams, Jesse Dungans, John Edmonston, George Snavely, John Roberts, Henry Harmans, John Gauldin, Abijah Debord, Samuel Bernum, John Betts, Davis Winneford, Cornelius Debord, Jesrell Harmon, Peter Totten, Zebulon B. Skates, Hiram Dougherty, Charles Hopkins, Joseph Sexton, Charles Foglesong, John L. Cox, William James, William Riley, Frederick Cullop, Jacob Criger, Jacob Hays, Benjamin McCarty, Patrick Buchanan,

POLITICAL NOTATIONS

James Shepherd, John Shepherd, David Tilson, Robert Graham, Edmond Tibbs, George West, Lewis Jones, Jr., Joseph Brown, Samuel Totten, Joseph Cornwell, James Bryant, Greenberry Patrick, Benjamin Chapman, Robert Buchanan, Alexander Young, John Wolf, Aaron Whited, Harvey Debord, James Gilpin, William Hubble, Joseph Cormny, Samuel Williams, Isaac Wickliff, William S. Campbell, William Stalcup, John Nelson, Michael Musser, George Smith, Isaac Stalcup, Samuel Musser, Samuel Kincannon, Dorylap Fulcher, Theophilus Debosen, William Cox, Edward Faris, John Edward, Isaac Reed, John Killinger, William McCready, John Goodman, Robert Sanders, Zachariah Mitchell, John McClure, Elias Stalcup, William Buchanan, John Jones, Valentine Greever, Benjamin F. Davis, Joshua Hubble, Stephen Keesling, Samuel Graham, Cheslin Ashlen, William R. Buchanan, Jacob Wassum, Michael Killinger, Henry Criger, Mose Robertson, Zachariah Hester, Pleasant J. Davis, John Sifer, John Currin, John Dutton, Adam Fox, Thomas Crow, Daniel Nelson, Nathaniel Atkins, William Snavely, William Sinclair, John Thomas, Jr., William Dean, Allen Currin, George Goodman, William Black, Solomon Glessing, John Miller, Thomas Sexton, William Detherage, Andrew H. Cox, Richard Williams, John A. Pritchett, Madison Williams, Joseph Williams, John Snavely, Champion Wynn, George Burket, Henry E. Sprinkle, Joseph Davis, George Hayten, John Allen, Jacob Snider, William Shannon, John Hill, Charles Shumaker, Ephriam McFartridge, Nicholas Thompson, John Grubb, Runson Tilson, Jacob Fulks, Elijah Dungans, Leonard Hutton, William McFartridge, George Killinger, Jr., Lewis Jones, Sr., Oswalt Roberts, Sampson Cole, David Blessing, Peter Snider, John Blankenbeckler, John Goodman, John W. Schoolfield, William Buchanan, Peter Musser, Alexander Buchanan, Andrew F. Buchanan, John Comer, Nicholas Snavely, John Snider, Jr., William Cole, James Houston, John Roberts, John

Houston, Jeremiah Spratts, George W. Scott, Robert Houston, James Shannon, William Porter, Saml. D. Hooser, William Campbell, William Scott, John Totten, William Hopkins, Daniel Hoofnoggle, Jacob Dutting, Mustin Davis, George Killinger, Sr., John Scott, John Wassum, James M. Wilson, Wm. Johnson, Jr., Charles Talbot, Samuel C. Williams, William Love, Rolan Wolf, Erastus Tomilson, John Anderson, Thomas J. Davis, Adam Groseclose, Adam Camper, Joseph T. Comb, John Buckhanan, John Cegley, John Cullop, Conrad Faris, Richard T. Johnston, William Pretchete, Joseph W. Davis, George Dungans, Philip Pickle, John Sexton, John F. Johnson, William Graver, Thomas Snider, Jacob Anderson, James Cole, Joseph Newton, Jacob W. Killinger, Charles McCrady, James Taylor, William Goodpasture, Hiram A. Greever, Solomon McDaniel, Robert Lewis, Joshua Ross, and Andrew Debusk. Thus, 220 votes were cast for Fulton.

For William Byars: Jonathan Bishop, Elia Roland, Joseph Jones, Robert Grimes, James Wortham, Stephen Grimes, Perry G. Mance, John McCready, —— Dennison, —— Hacks, —— Whitehead, —— Harris, —— Davis, —— Jayne, Michael Burgen, William Wilson, Robertson Clements, Oliver Wheeler, John Bowlin, Thomas Williams, A. Dyer Sherwood, Armons Wells, Thomas Jones, Lawrence Naff, David Copenhaver, Turner Urp, Andrew Scyfer, Isaac Patrick, Thompson McGhee, Ezekiel Nelson, Hugh Cole, William Johnson, Sr., Thomas Measle, Ezekiel James, William Mingle, Nat Harris, James Morris, Jr., William Philips, Andrew Edmondson, Abram Blessing, Martin Wolf, George Blankenbaker, George Umberger, William Thompson, James Harris, James W. Roavark, Fairs Morriss, Peter Fox, John Wolf, John Byars, Jacob Thomas, John Burket, Simson Wolf, Philip Umberger, John Fudge, George Pierce, Mahlam Scott, Benjamin Wolf, Jacob N. Beatie, Isaac Sayers, William Forester, Christopher Vaught, John Snider, Sr., Andrew Aker, Thomas Thomas,

George W. Davis, Andrew Shannon, Isaac Collins, James Umbager, Peleef Bishop, John Pugh, John Pafford, William Scott, Jr., Daniel Wolf, Elijah Umphrey, Davis Denton, William Tilson, Martin Houston, Tucker M. Page, Nat Harris, Sr., Joseph Wolfe, John Hutton, John W. Smith, Berry St. John, Richard Minton, Joseph P. Bonham, Thomas Hull, Joseph Thomas, George T. Lansdown, Joseph Clement, James Johnson, Michael Wolf, Arthur B. Byar, John Wheeler, Chrisly Copenhaver, John M. Campbell, George Byars, Henry Copenhaver, Adam Rosenbaum, Jacob Copenhaver, James S. Grimes, and Joseph Dutting, making a total of 103 votes for Byars against 220 cast for Fulton.

Chapter VIII

CHURCHES

APPARENTLY the first people who came to make homes in what is now Smyth County were of Presbyterian, Baptist, Lutheran, and Reformed families with an occasional Methodist and Episcopalian among them. Those of Scotch-Irish extraction predominated both in numbers and in influence, and the Scotch-Irish element was all Presbyterian at first. On the South Fork some of the first settlers were Baptists. The Coles, coming from Connecticut, were either Baptists or Congregationalists before they came and were certainly Baptist soon after they arrived. Thomas Woolsey, one of the earliest South Fork settlers, was a Baptist preacher. The founder of the Smyth County Tilson family came from England to settle on the South Fork and his descendants have been Baptist for the most part. The Rouses were of German origin and therefore presumably Lutheran or Reformed at the start, but have been Baptist for generations. The same may be said of the Gollehons. The Bonhams were Episcopalians when they came from Loudon County and the first Thomas coming from Wales via Southampton was probably an Episcopalian or a Presbyterian. The Sinclair, James, Nelson, Williams, Pierce, Griffitts, Britton, and Bishop families would presumably be of Episcopal origin but may have been Baptist or Methodist when they arrived in Smyth territory. The Anderson, Bowen, Houston, McClure, Scott, Kincannon, Henderson, and many other South Fork families were Presbyterian when they came. The Wolfe, Blankenbeckler, and other German families were of Lutheran stock.

All of which is recited to show that from the first the people of Smyth have been denominationlly scrambled. In the Middle and North Fork valleys the same sort of mixture prevailed but with a much stronger predominance of Presbyterians. From the Revolution on through the first decade of the nineteenth century, German folk came in considerable numbers and were mainly Lutheran. The old Chilhowie country was settled by the founders of the Wolfe, Wassum, Snavely, Cullop, Goodman, Fox, and Copenhaver families who founded the old Lutheran Church at Mt. Zion.

The first houses of worship were the log Presbyterian houses in Washington County built at Abingdon and on the Huff place along the Middle Fork in 1772. The people from all the valleys of Smyth would ride or walk down to the meeting house at Ebbing Spring, several miles below the present Washington line, to hear Parson Cummins preach, until the first houses of worship were built in Smyth.

In 1776 John and Arthur Campbell made good on the promise given to their sister Margaret, ten years before, when she agreed to come out to the wilderness and keep house for them, by building on John's land the first meeting house in Smyth, and the third on Mississippi waters. This was the first building of the present Royal Oak Presbyterian Church.

Soon after this the Rev. Tidence Lane, pioneer Baptist preacher of Tennessee, stopped on the South Fork long enough to form a congregation out of the Baptists he found there, and the converts he made, and to build a log church in Sinclair's Bottom. One date given for this is 1777, and if that is correct this would be the first Baptist church erected on Mississippi waters. The dates for both of these buildings are traditional, but well substantiated. The deed for Sinclair's Bottom church was recorded in 1792 and that of the

Royal Oak in 1796, and both merely state that buildings were standing before the deeds were made.

The Methodist movement began to take shape with the first of Bishop Asbury's visits in 1788, and, riding the crest of the waves of revivalism that swept the country around the turn of the century, made great inroads upon the membership of all the older denominations. Methodists took root in every section of the county through their classes and camp meetings, and from 1820 on have grown so vigorously that they now outnumber all others combined. The Episcopal church had no organization until after the Civil War, and the Christian church started later still. The Holiness orders and the lone Dunkard Church, on Roland's Creek, are of recent origin.

The union church has been a characteristic feature of Smyth ecclesiastism.

The old Bethel Church, a log building that stood near Chatham Hill, was used jointly by Presbyterians, Baptists, Methodists, and Lutherans for nearly a hundred years and all the neighborhood would worship together under whatever preacher who might officiate. Legrand Sexton was a Methodist steward and T. K. Sexton, his brother, a Presbyterian elder.

The Lutherans and Presbyterians had joint possession of a church on the Middle Fork in 1818, which was either the Pleasant Hill Lutheran Church near Groseclose or a church on Nicks Creek near Atkins, probably the latter. By deed recorded in Wytheville, February, 1818, Frederick Cullop transferred to "John Snavely and George Killinger, elders of the Lutheran and Presbyterian congregations—a lot of land for use of said congregations whereon their meeting house now stands——lying and being in the County of Wythe on the Middle Fork of Holston." Similar arrangements existed near Sugar Grove in a house owned by Methodists and

Baptists and used at times by Presbyterians, and in other parts of the county.

Presbyterian

The Presbyterian was the first denomination to organize in the county. The organization was first called the Upper Holston Congregation and met in the house built on the Campbell land at Royal Oak in 1776. It is not certain when the organization was effected. The people who were pious, and many were, belonged to Rev. Charles Cummins' Ebbing Spring flock and some were officers. William Campbell and William Bates, and most likely some others, were elders in the Ebbing Spring Church. Charles Cummins would ride up to the Upper Holston meeting house and hold services there, and his successors in the Ebbing Spring pastorate, Craighead and Crawford, would do likewise.

The earliest reference I have found to Royal Oak as a distinct entity is in the records of Abingdon Presbytery and shows that Presbytery met in the Royal Oak Church in October, 1829, but gives no further information about the church.

John Campbell sold his farm to Abraham Goodpasture in 1789, and June 18, 1896, Abraham Goodpasture and Martha, his wife, conveyed two acres and thirty-five poles of land on which the meeting house was standing to Edward Crow and Samuel McReynolds, trustees for the Upper Holston Congregation. The old log building was used for some years after Marion was started, extra services being held at times in the village at the courthouse. In 1853 E. L. Watson conveyed to the trustees the lot on which the Marion Grammar School stands. A brick house was on it when the deed was made and when it was built is not known, but probably a short time before this date. In 1880 Mrs. Eleanor Sheffey deeded to the church the corner it now occupies, and, in 1885, the third building was completed on this site. It was remodeled in 1897, and in 1923 was torn down and replaced by the present house, Mrs. Virginia Haller donating the additional land for the site. The erection of the present building was proposed by Mr. W. L. Lincoln at a Sunday School Workers' Conference held in the home of Mrs. Eleanor Sheffey Buchanan, and Mr. Lincoln as vice chairman of the committee, charged with supervision of construction; his brother, Charles C. Lincoln, chairman of the committee; Mr. J. C. Campbell; and Mr. H. P. Copenhaver led the congregation to the successful completion of the enterprise. Mr. Copenhaver personally solicited nearly all the subscriptions and personally collected the greater part of the money that paid for it. These, with Mr. C. P. Blackwell, Mr. W. A. Reith, Mrs. B. F. Buchanan, and Miss Edna Brown composed the building committee. C. B. Kearfoot drew the plans, and Rogers and Leventhall did the work under contract. The corner stone was laid with Masonic ceremonies on Saturday afternoon, June 16, 1923, Rev. Tyler Frazier, patriarch of the Methodist Conference, delivering the address. It was dedicated on the first Sunday in April, 1924, by Dr. W. W. Moore, President of Union Theological Seminary, the last church dedicated by Dr. Moore. Pastors of the Royal Oak Church as a separate charge have been: Philip Woods, David Palmer, —— Clymer, Edward McMahon, W. V. Wilson, W. H. Groves, C. D. Waller, J. McD. A. Lacy, W. M. McFerren, J. M. Sedgewick, and G. A. Wilson, Jr., the last coming on Jan. 8, 1922.

Of the pastors, Palmer lived on a farm in the Royal Oak addition, and he and Woods both taught school in Marion. They were the last preachers to use the old log house with its big cord-length fireplace at one end and pulpit in the middle of one side. It would be interesting to know the nature of the congregations that assembled there when the county was formed. Thompson Atkins and the Crows above Atkins would come. Thomas Thomas and his wife, Freelove Cole, at Thomas' Bridge, perhaps, worshiped there and may have been members, since their children were, Abijah Thomas being an elder. The Shugarts, Sheffeys, Irons, Killingers, Scotts, Byars, Bowens, Crows, Pruners, and other families from Atkins to Seven Mile Ford belonged there. Some would drive a coach hung on leather straps for springs; some would drive a chaise; some came by road wagon; most came horseback, and many would walk.

McMahon, a Scotchman, enlisted in the Confederate army and was promoted to rank of colonel. W. V. Wilson came in 1865 and stayed until 1874. He preached all over the county and was widely known as "Father Wilson." He was famous for sitting on the back of his neck with his feet propped up on wall or mantelpiece. When I, his grandson and the present pastor, came to the charge fifty years after he left the county, I was received with open arms by people of all denominations and all stations in life in all parts of the county, simply because I was "Father Wilson's" grandson. Folks like to talk to me about him and say complimentary things, but the finest compliment I ever heard paid to him, or any other man, was voiced by Mrs. Dickey of Grayson, Mrs. C. C. Lincoln's mother. She said to me: "I knew your grandfather, and I thought he was a very humble Christian."

Dr. McPheeters, Dr. McFaden, Dr. Lacy, and Dr. McFerren are the only living ex-pastors and they are all honored and beloved men of note in the Southern Presbyterian ministry.

For fifty years and more the Royal Oak was the only organized Presbyterian church in the county, but in various sections groups of Presbyterians worshiped in union churches. In the forties the Pleasant Hill Church was organized in Rich Valley. Matthew and "Good John" Buchanan were the first elders. Aaron Whitehead, Wilson Buchanan, and Franklin

Grayson were soon afterwards elected elders. The first church was opposite the dwelling house on the Fulton farm. In 1858 the present building was erected by Jacob Wolfe on land deeded by Franklin Grayson. The old church, being an abandoned building, was made a public nuisance by soldiers quartered at Saltville and in the Valley during the Civil War and was burned by order of the commanding officer. Ministers who served the church as supply have been Reverends Ruff, McClure, W. V. Wilson, John R. Sullivan, and J. C. Pullin. The first pastor was Rev. J. B. Bittinger, installed in 1896. He preached his farewell sermon on March 15, 1914, and has been succeeded by Reverends R. D. Carson, C. M. Chumbly, and John Martin.

Churches at Saltville and Chatham Hill were organized by Rev. W. V. Wilson; at North Holston by J. D. Bittinger and in Locust Cove by C. M. Chumbly. They have been united with the Rich Valley pastorate.

Rev. W. V. Wilson conducted services in an outbuilding on Capt. John M. Preston's place at Seven Mile Ford. A church was built on land donated by Captain Preston and dedicated on July 4, 1880. The first elders of the Seven Mile Ford Church were Capt. John M. Preston, Capt. C. H. C. Preston, and William Alexander. The first deacons were Robert Humphrey and John A. Copenhaver. Among the ministers who served as supply for the church are: D. E. Frierson, W. H. Groves, and F. E. Eversole. Pastors have been I. O. Sullivan, F. T. McFaden, C. D. Waller, J. McD. A. Lacy, M. M. McFerren, J. M. Sedgewick, G. A. Wilson, Jr., and John H. Grey.

Capt. John M. Preston, one of the first and for years the sole elder of the Seven Mile Church, was a lovable and beautiful character whose life was a benediction to his community. Mrs. Preston's Christian service, especially in teaching the children of the community, is of far-reaching influence. Captain Preston's funeral was conducted in the little church he loved and served so well, on Sept. 29, 1928, and his body was laid to rest in the historic Preston graveyard in the ninetieth year of his age. His son, John M. Preston, III, and Gilbert McCormack, grandson of John A. Copenhaver, one of the first deacons, are now elders.

Mr. Peter Killinger, an elder of the Royal Oak Church, was greatly interested in carrying the gospel to the unprivileged people in the mountainous sections of Smyth. His grandson, Rev. Kenneth Killinger, inspired originally by his zeal, has taken that as his life work and as a minister of the Lutheran church has built up a great mountain mission work. The Royal Oak Church under Mr. Sedgewick's leadership began expanding through mission outposts, establishing the first one on Hook's Branch. During the present pastorate this work has been continued. Rev. O. V. Caudill was secured in the winter of 1922–23 as mission worker, and with his assistance additional missions have been established and chapels built on Spruce Creek, Walker's Creek, and Nicks Creek. Mr. Caudill left the work in 1926. Rev. John H. Grey succeeded him, serving two years. Mr. T. E. Ross, a layman of the congregation has been employed in the work since Mr. Grey left.

The chapel on Spruce Creek was built as a union church; in the winter of 1922 an evangelistic meeting was held in the building; a considerable number professed faith in Christ, and followed their saintly Sunday School Superintendent, Mrs. Ellen Mitchel, into the Presbyterian Church.

The other denominations then sold their interest to the trustees of the Royal Oak Church. The Walker's Creek and Nicks Creek chapels were built under the leadership of Mr. Caudill. A large part of the money for the Walker's Creek Chapel was donated through him by a Christian Endeavor Union centering around Holland, Michigan. Abingdon Presbytery authorized the sale of an abandoned Presbyterian church at Meadow View, with the consent of the surviving members, and the proceeds were invested in the Nicks Creek building. Messrs. J. R. Pafford and Frank Hutton, two leading Methodist laymen of that community, rendered invaluable aid in the building and maintenance of the Nicks Creek Church. Messrs. R. M. Richardson, T. E. King, C. P. Blackwell, and J. W. Sheffey have rendered large service in this extension work.

BAPTIST

Dr. S. W. Dickinson, born and reared in Louisa County, came to Marion to practice medicine in 1880, married Sarah Look, and has been prominently identified with the health of Marion and the life of the Baptist Church ever since. He kindly furnished the following sketch:

While there is evidence of the existence of individual Baptists at earlier dates, Baptist historians agree that the first church of their faith to be organized in Virginia was founded by Robert Nordin and two associate ministers, emigrants from England, at Burleigh, Isle of Wight County, in 1714, and soon after another was organized at Brandon, Surry County.

About 1743 there was a movement of Baptists from Maryland to Northern Virginia, where they organized several churches in rapid succession. This was the period of the great migrations of Scotch-Irish and Germans from Pennsylvania, and along with them came Baptists from Pennsylvania and Delaware. Most important of all came Shubal Stearns, who, born in Boston and converted by the preaching of Geo. Whitefield, after some years became a Baptist preacher and moved to Berkeley County, now West Virginia, and with his brother-in-law, Marshall, in answer to the call of other Baptists who had moved on ahead, settled in the Yadkin Valley section of North Carolina, where he began a wonderful work.

From some one, or maybe all of these sources most likely,

originated the few Baptists who first settled in Southwest Virginia. They had moved across and over the mountains partly to escape persecution, but chiefly looking for better living conditions and plenty and better land. They were, or had become, great movers, and whole churches and communities moved when news of some Eldorado was brought to them.

Their preachers were not so much noted for learning as for fervent zeal, and were men who preached with power, sparing neither effort nor sacrifice to carry the gospel to the remotest settler. Many a rude arbor, shaded grove, and private dwelling, unlicensed by the general court as places of worship as the law required, were bravely used as such by these Baptist preachers. Tradition, or maybe a chance associational minute or record, has preserved the names of a few of these noble men and pioneer preachers who were here before church work had taken organized shape, and we yet hear called the names of Timothy Burgess, Moses Foley, Simon Cockrell, John Frost, A. Baker, W. Brundrage, and Jonathan Mulker. About Holston Mills you may yet hear the name of Thomas W. Woolsey, whose remains lie buried in the Maiden burying ground near the home of Mrs. Wm. Britton; and a few years ago a monument was erected at his grave bearing his name and date of death, 1794, and the simple inscription: "A Pioneer Baptist Preacher." He owned land, probably that now owned by the Dutton family, and was a worthy man. The county surveyor says this land is one of the oldest surveys in that section. There appears strong reason to think he helped to start, if not to organize, St. Clair's Bottom Church.

There are several Baptist churches in Smyth County whose organization antedates the formation of the county.

Semple's *Virginia Baptist History,* written in 1810, gives St. Clair's Bottom Church as organized with 45 members in 1791, and A. Baker is named as pastor. This is an antimission church, but has maintained a regular organization and worships now in a neat brick house, built in 1851, on the site of the previous log house. (All first churches were built of logs and called "meeting houses.")

Rich Valley Church was organized with 26 members in 1802, somewhere near or about Chatham Hill, and A. Foley was pastor about 1810. The church house now at Chatham

Hill owes its existence to this one-time organization. Middle Fork Church was organized in April, 1821, and for a number of years worshiped in a log house near where Mr. Bascom Leonard now lives. In 1875 they erected a neat brick house on land donated by Mr. Robert Bonham one mile east of Chilhowie. This church has practically complete minutes of its meetings since its first organization. The Marion church is the next oldest and was organized in 1845, with 17 members, in the Courthouse, with Rev. N. C. Baldwin as pastor. This church continued to worship more or less regularly in the courthouse until they built the house on Broadway on a lot bought from Mr. Wade Strother in 1859. The present church building was erected in 1891.

Some thirty years ago Mr. N. C. Baldwin, telling me about the organization of this church, said that he then lived in Marion in a house near where Miss Grace Buchanan now lives, and probably fronting the old stage road. He said that until the Methodist Church was built all the religious services of the town were held in the courthouse, the churches each having regular Sundays. After the Methodist Church was built, he sometimes preached there, as the circuit rider did not in those days come with either regularity or frequency because of the number of his appointments.

The Baptists worshiped in the courthouse with more or less regularity until they built the house on Broadway (now used as a garage) about 1858 or 1859, on a lot bought from Mr. Wade Strother, for $125, the deed being dated Nov. 21, 1859. The Baptist congregation worshiped in this house until 1891, when they sold it to the Farmers Alliance for $375. During this time the membership was greatly increased, and the Cedar Bluff Church at Atkins organized by members from the Marion church. During this period, after Mr. Baldwin, the church had the following pastors: A. J. Davis, William Huff, Mr. Noffsinger, R. B. Boatwright, and D. A. Glenn.

While Mr. Boatwright was pastor in Marion, his son, Frederick William, fell into Staley's Creek when at flood. He fell in above Main Street and was brought ashore unconscious some distance below. His father was called, and, while workers were trying to resuscitate the boy, dropped on his knees and prayed fervently that his life be spared. The lad came to all right and is now the president of Richmond University.

On June 27, 1890, Mr. W. C. Seaver and the trustees of the Methodist Church sold to the Baptist Church, for $250, the lot which the Methodists had used since 1846 and from which they had recently moved.
On this lot the Baptist Church now stands. The first parsonage was built during the pastorate of Mr. D. A. Glenn, since which time the church has had the following pastors: Mr. Vernon I'Anson, John W. Hundley, J. Manning Dunnaway, C. W. Trainham, E. M. Harris (during whose pastorate the Sunday-school room was added), C. W. McElory, J. R. Edwards, H. K. Williams, and Hugh Carter. In 1924 the present parsonage was built.

The Lebanon Association minutes for 1931 show 15 churches reporting 2,006 members in Smyth County.

Rev. H. W. Bellamy, of Abingdon, served many country churches of Smyth County and is greatly beloved by the people of these churches.

The Lutheran Church in Smyth County

By C. W. Cassell

Was the "German neighborhood on the Holston," where the Rev. Paul Henkel, Lutheran Missionary from Shenandoah County, visited and preached in 1787, in Smyth County? Of this we cannot be certain. The wording in his diary indicates that he and his wife rode in one day from the home of Jacob Dobler on Reedy (Reed) Creek in Wythe County to this settlement. Certain it is, there were those of the Lutheran faith among the early settlers in Smyth. Their names bespeak their nationality and their faith. Not all Germans were Lutherans, but in well nigh every case where the German pioneer settled, Lutherans were found among them. Not speaking the language of the country, few of them became civil officers or committee chairmen. In the old court records seldom do their names appear as overseers to open up wilderness roads or as military captains, but in the rank and file they loom large. They were primarily home builders. They loved their church and brought with them their Bibles, hymn and other devotional books, establishing family and public worship, churches, and schools. They traveled long distances, and their pastors traveled long distances to serve them. Paul Henkel tells of one Elias Wacker coming thirty miles to service on the visit mentioned above. The first Lutheran church in Southwest Virginia, St. Peter's in Montgomery County, established as early as 1745, kept in touch with their brethren in the faith as they located further west in Virginia and Tennessee. Further research will doubtless reveal definite dates and names. The absence of documentary evidence of a Lutheran organization in Smyth until 1798 does not argue that Lutherans were not living here before that date, nor that they did not gather for preaching and the administrations of the Sacraments.

Who were the first ministers? Possibly Brugell and Daser from St. Peter's in Montgomery. Paul Henkel made occasional visits here in the eighties and nineties. About this time Leonard Willy labored in Wythe and Smyth. Geo. D. Flohr, who located near Wytheville in 1799, traveled throughout Southwest Virginia until his death in 1826. Andrew Secrist was here in the twenties. Jacob Scherer, who lived near Rural Retreat, 1830–53, and Elijah Hawkins, who lived near Groseclose, 1838–68, both served as faithful shepherds to the several flocks in Smyth. He whose life has meant more to the Lutheran churches in the county than any other one minister is the late Rev. J. J. Scherer, D.D., who as president of Marion College from 1873 to 1909 also served as pastor of one or more of the churches nearly all of that time.

Our space does not permit a full statement of the labors of the many faithful men who have served as Lutheran pastors in the county. Their names, in addition to those already given are: J. A. C. Schoenberg, J. A. Brown, J. K. Rader, John Boone, Wm. C. Sloop, F. Hickerson, L. A. Mann, J. A. Bell, W. E. Hubbert, S. R. Smith, E. H. McDonald, J. C. Repass, J. B. Greiner, W. B. Oney, J. P. Brodfurher, I. P. Hawkins, E. Studebaker, W. P. Huddle, D. S. Fox, W. R. Brown, E. W. Leslie, S. D. Steffey, P. D. Leddin, H. N. Miller, E. C. Cronk, M. Q. Boland, J. W. Strickler, W. W. J. Ritchie, J. A. Arndt, H. P. Counts, J. L. Smith, R. E. Kern, S. W. Hahn, E. H. Copenhaver, W. G. Cobb, L. W. Strickler, W. C. Buck, S. C. Ballentine, Geo. H. Rhodes, P. E. Shealy, Frank H. Miller, S. L. Nease.

Those now serving in the county are: Hugh J. Rhyne, Marion; Kenneth Killinger, Mountain Mission; A. L. Hahn, St. James; P. L. Snapp, Pleasant Hill; C. W. Cassell, at Konnarock.

Where have the Lutheran people worshiped and what about the churches? The first congregation to be organized appears to have been that near Atkins. In 1798, Leonard Willy drew up a constitution for St. John's, St. Paul's, and Kimberlin, in Wythe, and St. Mark's (Collups), in Smyth. This Collups Church (Collops, Colleps) stood about 300 yards south of the Lee Highway and about 100 yards west of the road leading up Nicks Creek (Nicks Creek is the first stream west of Atkins.) It was a log building. When it was built is not now known. The old stone house standing near the highway just west of the creek is said to have been built in 1775 by one Frederick Collup. It is likely the old church goes back near that date. In those days groups of people are known to have met regularly for worship for a period of years without having a formal organization or a church building. In 1857 a frame church was built about 100 yards east of the old building, between the road and the creek. This was known as Cedar Grove. It served as a place of worship for the congregation until 1888 when a new frame building was erected at Atkins. Since then it has been known as St. Matthew's. Owing to the removal of many members from the community, the congregation has ceased to exist as an active organization. Occasional services are held in the church. For a long period it was a large and influential congregation. Among her members in the early days were the names: Collup, Aker, Wassum, Bear, Atkins, Henderlite, Kegley.

Ebenezer, in the neighborhood of old Chilhowie, at times called the Chilhowie Church, first existed as Zion, two miles north of the present Ebenezer Church. Zion was a log building. When it was built is not known. Geo. D. Flohr preached here in 1799. Ebenezer was built in 1854. The community has been the home of the Copenhavers and the Rosenbaums. There is a large cemetery here. The Rev. Hugh J. Rhyne of Marion is the pastor.

Pleasant Hill, on south of highway near Groseclose is the next oldest Lutheran church in the county. It first finds a place on the roll of congregations of the Synod of Virginia in 1843, having been organized under the ministry of Elijah Hawkins. A church was built that year. It was frame and stood until 1907 when it was replaced by the frame building now standing. The cemetery on the opposite side of the highway is a large and well kept one. The Rev. P. L. Snapp, of Rural Retreat, is the pastor.

Pleasant Hill appears to have been a preaching place for years before the date of the organization of the congregation and the building of a church. There are those who believe the old Schneble Church, listed in the "Register of Churches in Virginia" in the minutes of the "Special Virginia Confer-

CHURCHES 135

ence," by Dr. Solomon Henkel, 1809, was in this neighborhood. John Schneble and John Schneider were officers. This was then in Wythe County.

In the western part of the county, in the neighborhood of St. Clair's Bottom, is St. James, an active congregation with a neat frame church, and a cemetery not neglected. It was organized in 1859, under the ministry of the Rev. F. Hickerson with seven charter members. The church was built that year. It was repaired in 1882, again repaired in 1892, and rebuilt in 1908. The church site was deeded by Josiah and Sally S. Cole; and the cemetery by James and Ellen Edmondson, John and Martha Edmondson, and Geo. and Mary Edmondson to trustees F. Hickerson, Davis Jones, Samuel Cole, Daniel Wolfe, and John Copenhaver. The congregation is served by the Rev. A. L. Hahn, of Damascus.

The congregation at Marion came into existence in 1874 when twenty-four members belonging to Ebenezer and Cedar Grove united in forming an organization. The Rev. J. J. Scherer was the pastor. Messrs. G. D. H. Killinger, T. M. Rosenbaum, Thomas Copenhaver, and M. M. Musser were the first officers. The congregation worshiped in the Methodist Church until 1887, in the Episcopal Church until 1896, and in the College Chapel until 1910 when the church was built. It is a brick structure with Sunday-school rooms. The pastor of the church is the Rev. Hugh J. Rhyne.

Four miles southeast of Marion on Staley's Creek is the Attoway Church. Here was a preaching point for a number of years before the organization in 1910. The Rev. J. J. Scherer was the pastor at the time. That same year the church was built. Before building the church the schoolhouse was used as a place of worship. The Rev. Kenneth Killinger is the pastor.

The youngest congregation in the county is the Church of

the Atonement, on Bear Creek, four miles North of Atkins. It was organized in 1928, by the Rev. Kenneth Killinger. The church is a frame building.

This church is one of the large number of preaching places in the Mountain Mission work under the care of Mr. Killinger. The Mountain Mission work began by his holding Sunday school and lay-services in the isolated regions of the mountains south of Marion. The missionary extended his work to other parts of the county and also into Grayson and Washington counties. His preaching places in Smyth County, besides those mentioned, are: Buck Eye Hollow, Currin Valley, Slemps Creek, and Mitchel Creek.

Lutheran ministers who have come from Smyth County Lutheran congregations are, by congregations, as follows:

Levi Groseclose	Pleasant Hill
W. C. Buch	Pleasant Hill
R. G. Rosenbaum	Ebenezer
E. H. Copenhaver	Ebenezer
J. J. Scherer, Jr., D.D.	Marion
B. A. Copenhaver	Marion
Kenneth Killinger	Attoway

Time would fail me to attempt to name the large number of laymen who have gone out from the congregation mentioned above and have become prominent in church and state. Special mention should be made of Mrs. Catherine Scherer Cronk, daughter of the late Rev. Dr. J. J. Scherer, Sr., prominent in the work of the Women's Missionary Society of The United Lutheran Church in America, and in the Missionary Movement of America, a woman Smyth County is ever glad to honor.

No doubt at other places in this memorial volume mention will be made of the educational institutions within the county.

In this sketch, should be included, however, something of the Konnarock Training School for Girls, established by the Women's Missionary Society of The United Lutheran Church in America. It is located in the southwestern part of the county, on a foothill of the White Top Mountain. The first session opened in 1924. The capacity of the building is thirty-five boarding pupils. The purpose is to provide schooling and home training for the underprivileged girls of the mountain districts. The faculty consists of a corps of well-trained teachers who are there for the work's sake. The institution has become a center of missionary activity. In addition to the religious training given by the faculty, the Lutheran pastor at Konnarock gives regular religious instruction, and holds services in the chapel each Sunday for the school and the people of the community.

Two miles from the Konnarock Training School is the Iron Mountain School for Boys, now in the process of establishment by the Brotherhood of The United Lutheran Church in America. The purpose is to provide industrial training for the underprivileged boys, under positive Christian influences. While most of the buildings lie just across the line in Washington County, a very large part of the property is in Smyth, and many of the boys will come from Smyth County homes.

METHODIST

Dr. Dickinson and Mr. Cassell kindly consented to write the sketches of the Baptist and Lutherans of Smyth and it was my hope to have a Methodist prepare this sketch, but not finding one to do it I must needs try it myself. Methodist churches are too numerous in Smyth for me to go into detail with many of them or into much detail with any of them. All I can hope to do is to trace the broad outlines of the denomination's growth with notes on a few of the outstanding figures and a few representative churches.

Bishop Francis Asbury, the father of American Methodism, made biennial trips through Southwest Virginia over a period of about twenty-five years, starting in 1788. In May of that year he held the first Methodist Conference west of the Alleghanies in the home of Stephen Caywood, in Washington County between Glade Spring and Saltville. On this trip he was most cordially entertained in the home of Gen. William Russell, who, having married Gen. William Campbell's widow, had come to live at Aspenvale and had removed to Saltville in February, 1788. General and Mrs. Russell attended the conference and it is probable that the General became actively enlisted in the cause of Methodism at this time. His wife became a Methodist two years later. As the sister of Patrick Henry, she was reared an Episcopalian and as the wife of William Campbell she had been a worshiper in the Presbyterian church. Bishop Asbury in his diary says:

On Sunday, April 18, 1790, I preached at General Russell's house, and had a "good prayer meeting" there on Wednesday the 21st. On Sunday the 25th I preached there again, and the next day set out for Kentucky.

Returning from Kentucky he made the following entry:

Friday, May 28, Saturday 29, and Sunday 30 I spent at General Russell's whose wife is converted since I left the house last. I thought then she was not far from God.

From this time on she lived an ardent Methodist and is rightly styled the mother of Methodism in Smyth. The Russells, like Philemon and other New Testament saints, had a church in their house. After her husband's death, Jan. 14, 1793, Mrs. Russell built a house at Chilhowie in which she lived until her death in 1825. She had a church in this house, and her church, her house, and herself are thus described as they were seen in 1822, by Mrs. Julia A. Tevis:

Both she and General Russell were faithful members of the Methodist Church. They were converted in the good old-fashioned way, when nobody objected to shouting, if it came from an overflowing heart filled with the love of God. The General walked worthy of his vocation until he was taken home to a better world, leaving his excellent widow a true type of Wesleyan Methodism. "Madam Russell," as she was generally called, was a "Mother in Israel"; and the Methodist preachers in those days esteemed her next to Bishop Asbury. She lived for a while in Abingdon, but as the gay society of that place, particularly among her own relatives, was uncongenial to her, she withdrew to a retired spot near the "Campground," in the vicinity of the Sulphur Springs. At this place a wooden house had been erected under her special superintendence, and according to her own ideas of consistency.

There were two rooms below, large and spacious—the one first entered being her common sitting-room. A door from this opened into one much larger, which contained a pulpit and seats for a moderate-sized congregation. When a preacher visited her she said: "Brother, how long will you tarry? There's the pulpit; shall I send out and call together a congregation?" No visitors came to see her, and remained an hour, without being asked to pray. If they declined she prayed herself, mentioning every person for whom she prayed by name.

She dressed in the style of '76—full skirts, with an overgarment, long, flowing, open in front, and confined at the waist by a girdle, and made of material called Bath coating. In this girdle were tucked two or three pocket-handkerchiefs. The sleeves of her dress came just below the elbows—the lower part of the arm being covered with long, half-handed gloves. She wore a kerchief of linen lawn, white as snow, and sometimes an apron of the same material; and on her head a very plain cap, above which was usually placed a broad-brimmed hat given her by Bishop Asbury in days long gone by, and worn by the old lady with probably the same feeling that Elisha wore Elijah's mantle. She was erect as in the meridian of life, though she must have been seventy years old when I first saw her. A magnificent-looking woman, "she walked every inch a queen," reminding me of one of the old-fashioned pictures of Vandyke. She never shook the hand of a poor Methodist preacher in parting without leaving in it a liberal donation; she knew the Gospel was free, but she also knew that "The laborer was worthy of his hire."

Madam Russell gave the land for a church and cemetery at Saltville, which was called Elizabeth Church. The cemetery is still Elizabeth Cemetery. This building which stood on a knoll across the road from the cemetery is supposed to have been the first Methodist church built in Smyth County.

Bishop Asbury would sometimes come into this county through Grayson and sometimes up Cripple Creek. He was entertained at least once in the James home at Sugar Grove, and he formed strong classes in the Blue Spring and Cedar Spring neighborhoods on both sides the county line. From these nuclei, Saltville and Chilhowie in the northwest corner and Cripple Creek in the southeast, the Methodists spread over the whole county. In both of these sections were famous camp-meeting grounds. The camp meeting is the explanation of the phenomenal growth of Methodism in Southwest Virginia among people who by inheritance belonged to other denominations. As one reads Mrs. Tevis' description of the camp meeting at Chilhowie and thinks of the beauty and mysticism of it, of the fellowship and devotional spirit, of the strength of the preaching, the fervency of the praying, the heartfelt melody of the singing, and of its peculiar adaptation to the people and condition of its period, one can readily understand that the Sulphur Springs and Asbury camp grounds have made Smyth a preponderantly Methodist county. I quote her excellent description at length both because of the importance of the camp meeting to the theme of this sketch and because of the light it throws upon the country as it was then:

In September, 1823, the annual camp-meeting was held near the Sulphur Springs, in Smyth County, Virginia. A beautiful grove of grand old trees in a lovely mountain gorge marked the spot that had, for this special purpose, been generously donated to the Methodists for the term of a hundred years by Colonel Thompson, the son-in-law of old Mother Russell. Mother Russell's unobtrusive dwelling was in the immediate vicinity, and she not only attended constantly this means of grace herself, but her house was the temporary home of many who came from a distance. The camp-meetings held on this spot were widely diffusive of good, and were really necessary in a country so sparsely settled as was this part of Western Virginia at that time. It was not uncommon to find persons attending from Tennessee and North Carolina.

We reached the camp-ground late in the afternoon of a brilliant Autumn day. Near by, but hidden under the foliage of the water willow, whose branches hung over the clear stream, was a spring widening into smooth, deep water—a miniature lake, throwing back the sunshine like a mirror, and keeping all its secret depths unlighted; then contracting into a narrow stream it ran, glittering like a silver thread, through the valley beneath. Beyond it rose a magnificent mountain, skirted with woods and, even to the very summit, dotted with farms and dwellings rendered quite distinct on a clear day. Nearer, and upon one side of the green and goodly valley where the tents were pitched, was a less elevated mountain, covered with every shade of green foliage, interspersed with flowering shrubs; among which predominated the luxuriant and richly-tinted "laurel," with its deep green leaves so refreshing to the eye. The declining sun touched everything with a soft and tender light, and the fleecy clouds, visible in the fathomless blue air, seemed like white doves of peace, floating with wings outspread in benediction over the assembled multitude of God's people, who had come up into the wilderness, apart from the dust and heat and hurry of existence, that they might hold sweet communion with each other, and bow with united hearts before their great Creator, here to worship him under the over arching skies in a "temple not made with hands."

A winding pathway up the mountain side, quite concealed from the passers-by, led to a spot high up, where, under the spreading oak and chestnut, prayer was offered up during the intervals of public preaching for earnest seekers of religion. Pious and experienced women, who were ever laboring for the good of souls, and who felt that a cup of cold water given to famished lips in the spirit of the Gospel is a pearl of great price in the sight of Him who has pronounced it "more blessed to give than to receive," were accustomed to pray there with and for the female penitents and seekers of religion. All along its steep ascent were quiet nooks and shady dells, where no prying eye or careless footstep would be likely to intrude.

I had come to the meeting by the special invitation of Aunt Betty, whose hospitality I was to share, and whose large heart and simple provision made it a pleasant resting place for many of her friends. Her tent—or, rather, cottage—was erected by her kind husband, with great attention to comfort and convenience, having an upper story containing small sleeping apartments, while the lower story was appropriated to prayer meetings and the reception of transient visitors. The bountiful table was spread under the shade of the trees, near the little temporary kitchen where old Solomon presided as chief. To his heart's delight, he found ample time not only to wait on the preachers, whom he almost worshiped but also to attend prayer-meetings among his colored brethren, and occasionally fill their preaching-stand as an exhorter; besides, he never neglected the preaching hour among the whites. It was pleasant to see his shining black face, softened by a magnificent fleece of white wool, with dilated eyes and half-open mouth, as he sat at a modest distance during the service, drinking in large draughts from the same pure fountain of mercy as his white brethren; and it was exciting to hear his deep, suppressed, "Amen, Massa! bress God!"—in tears flowing fast as he occasionally exclaimed, "Free salvation, glory to my Massa in heaven!"

My first night at the encampment was full of beauty. At each of the four corners of the camp-ground was left the stump of a large tree, four or five feet high, the tops of which were rendered fire-proof by a layer of brick mortar, and upon these blazed burning pine knots, lighting up all the surroundings with their tall flames. Among the dark, green foliage glittered the flickering lights of numerous lamps attached to trees; beautiful white vapors floated in the star-lit sky, now resting an instant, then glancing onward, hiding the face of the full moon like a snowy veil cast over the jeweled brow of a queen.

In the stand were reverend, good-looking men, whose very appearance inspired confidence. The trumpet was sounded, and long lines of people were seen wending their way to roughly constructed seats, made for the occasion. I never saw more perfect order, more attention to politeness and decorum, in any assemblage of people. The hymn was announced—all sang together; in those days singing was worship—the beginning, as it were, of prayer. The assembled multitude rose up to sing, and, after repeating the last two lines of the hymn, fell upon their knees, to continue that act of devotion in prayer; and there was a power in it felt by all. When we arose again a well-known melody poured forth from the hearts of the whole congregation, full of freedom, of simplicity, of feeling, and of energetic sentiment. It was as the wings of seraphim, upon which the assembled multitude were borne heavenward, thus elevating preachers and hearers in the introductory, so that the whole subsequent service showed its effect. Never did truer music gush from the human heart; and a more efficacious means for inspiring the minds of the hearers with the love of religion could hardly be conceived than when its sublime sentiments are clothed in sweet musical harmony that captivates the senses, and touches the soul through the medium of the ear and heart. Many of the old tunes, habitual in the worship of those days, seem instinctive to the devotional feelings of our people. If our congregations had not then the artistic appreciation in the execution of music which belongs to the present day, they had, at least, more of that heart-gushing piety which flows in sweet music from the exhaustless fountain of true religion; and their choice tunes showed a higher musical taste than now prevails among us.

Our surroundings were favorable to devotion. We were too remote from the cities and towns to be annoyed by the curious and the idle. Public services never continued later than ten o'clock P.M.—at that hour all were expected to seek repose; yet in some of the tents the voice of prayer and praise was heard at a much later hour, and, at intervals, the prolonged shouts of happy souls.

The sound of the trumpet at early dawn awakened all slumberers for morning prayer; after which a frugal meal—nothing hot but tea or coffee—was prepared, and then an interval of two or three hours spent in private devotion before the eleven o'clock preaching. We dined at precisely one o'clock, giving an opportunity for the serious and penitent to withdraw again for private prayer. Religious exercises, thus conducted, even the most censorious and fastidious must acknowledge to be productive of great good, and was the very thing most needed in a thinly settled country, where the visits of a minister were only occasional, and preaching-places were few and far between. Here rich streams of Gospel grace caused all hearts to overflow with love to God; and the hallowed music of many voices mingled with the songs of the redeemed in heaven.

The first camp meeting at the Sulphur Springs camp ground was held in August, 1819, and at this time Robertson Gannaway was converted. He was licensed to preach in 1823 and in 1827 was assigned to the New River circuit which then embraced most of Wythe, Grayson, Carroll, and Pulaski counties and half of Smyth. Later he was instrumental in forming the Marion circuit, and in the late thirties he organized the Marion Methodist Church. Members of this first class were:

Mr. and Mrs. John W. Schoolfield, Mrs. Dudley, Dr. and Mrs. Hiram Daily, Mrs. Broomfield, Mr. and Mrs. William Francis, Mr. and Mrs. James F. Pendleton, and Mr. and Mrs. F. P. Staley.

The class met for organization in the home of Mr. and Mrs. William Francis. In 1847 the first church building was erected on the lot now occupied by the Baptist Church. In 1877 the Marion Church was taken from the circuit and made into a station. In 1887 the lot where the present church stands was secured and shortly afterwards, under the pastorate of the Rev. George W. Miles, the present church building was erected. The splendid Sunday School plant was erected under the pastorates of H. B. Brown and F. B. Shelton.

Rev. George W. Miles was one of the strongest and most influential of Smyth County preachers. When he came to the Marion circuit about 1870, there was a split in the village church. He talked with the leaders of both factions and found each set in condemnation of the other. He then decided it was time to hold a revival, and that revival not only healed the breach in the Methodist Church but stirred the town from center to circumference. Nearly all the old whisky soaks came to the altar. Then, Mr. Miles said, was the time to get rid of liquor; so he rounded up the temperance forces and had all the barrooms closed. Representative St. John had an act passed by the Legislature of Virginia amending the town charter so that no liquor could be sold in Marion, or its immediate vicinity, except by unanimous vote of the council, and, as there has always been at least one born dry on the council, Marion has been saloonless since. It was the first town in the state to banish the saloon.

Mt. Carmel Church had its beginnings in services held in the home of "Aunt Sukie" Atkins, a first cousin of Parson Gannaway and sister of his wife. She was a notable and beloved woman whose memory is still affectionately revered in that end of the country. William Gannaway and his wife, living on Cripple Creek between Asbury Church and Speedwell, were pious Presbyterians. Many of their twelve children became devoted Methodists through the power of the Asbury camp meetings. Catherine married Joseph Brownlow and was mother of "Parson Brownlow," governor of Tennessee. Sally married Robertson Gannaway. Frances married William Atkins, and Susan, the beloved "Aunt Sukie" of the Mt. Carmel neighborhood, married Joseph Atkins. From one or the other of these twelve Gannaway children a great many present-day Smyth County people descended.

"Aunt Sukie" would have prayer meetings and preaching in her house. In 1854 the first Mt. Carmel Church was built nearby in a locust thicket back from the present site. The present church was built in 1871 while Rev. George W. Miles was on the circuit. On Oct. 3, 1871, Jacob Carsel, A. P. Sprinkle, and William F. Scott, building committee, entered into contract with Levi Brown and W. F. Bonham to erect the building.

In the upper end of Rich Valley, Methodists long worshiped in the old union Bethel Church. Sometime in the fifties the first distinctively Methodist church in that section was erected by the twin brothers William L. and Robert H. Richardson on the line between their farms. It was known as Richardson's Chapel and was in use until the present building, jointly owned by Methodists and Presbyterians, was erected at Chatham Hill.

There was an old log union church near Robert's Mill in Rye Valley. It was moved to Sugar Grove. It was used by Methodists and Baptists, principally, until differences arose, and then the Methodists built Wharf Hill Church at Sugar Grove, and the Baptists their own church near by. A Methodist church, which has disappeared, used to stand on the upper end of Walker's Creek. Denton's Chapel stood along the stage road in the corner of the field where Mr. Henry Copenhaver has for years provided the public with a delightful picnic ground. The old graveyard, connected with Denton's Chapel, is on a hill opposite, between the railroad and the new section of highway. Denton's Chapel was abandoned at the building of Laurel Spring Church, and after the Methodists had bought old Mt. Zion from the Lutherans. A Methodist church was built on the Newman farm up Hutton's Branch in the eighties. It was abandoned so that its membership might affiliate with the Mt. Carmel and Davis Memorial Methodist churches, and then the Northern Methodists stepped in and built Centenary Church on Hutton's Branch. A Methodist church was built between the old Madam Russell home and the Sulphur Spring at Chilhowie and was later removed to the present building in the east end of the town. Tate's Chapel was erected by the mother of James D. Tate on the Tate farm near the mountain. Davis Memorial at Atkins was built in the early nineties while Rev. George A. Maiden was on the circuit.

Emory and Henry College has exerted a powerful influence on Methodism in Smyth County. Its founder, Rev. Creed Fulton, was a Smyth County boy reared in Rich Valley.

Dr. L. L. H. Carlock, former president of Sullins College, was in charge of Marion station for four years.

In 1865 the first session of Holston Conference after the War sat in the Marion Church. It was at this conference that J. Tyler Frazier was licensed to preach. He says:

At the close of the War between the States, with my army blanket, a suit of jeans clothes, a borrowed hat, and a borrowed horse I made my way across the mountains from my home in Giles county to Marion to try to gain admittance into the Holston Conference, holding its first session after the close of the hostilities at this place. This was in September, 1865. I had preached all during the four years in the service but had few of the qualifications considered necessary for admittance into that august body. I was young, only 25, strong, with a willing mind, but I have always believed that a dearth of material at that particular time was the reason my application was successful.

On this occasion he was assigned for entertainment to the hospitable home of Mr. William C. Sexton, for a long time clerk of the Smyth County court, and shared a room with a famous hunter of wolves and bears, Wilburn Waters. He induced Wilburn to tell him of some of his more notable hunting adventures, and he can repeat those stories now as he heard them from the lips of the mighty hunter himself.

The Rev. J. Tyler Frazier, grand old man and patriarch of the Holston Conference, Southern Methodist church, celebrated his ninetieth birthday Saturday, Nov. 22, 1930, and on Sunday, at the recognized hour of morning worship, broadcast from Emory a sermon, with music rendered by his children, grandchildren, and great-grandchildren. His brother, the Rev. George A. Frazier, celebrated his eighty-fifth birthday Saturday, Nov. 22, 1930, and on Sunday at eleven o'clock broadcast a sermon from Tuscola, Ill. The Frazier brothers, born on the same day of the month in 1840 and 1845, respectively, one gone to the West, the other remaining to live his long, constructive life of labor in Southwest Virginia, were trained in the school of the primitive evangelist and sylvan camp meeting, preaching over the radio what may well be their last sermons. Those were more than sermons. They were the voices of a changing epoch sounded by the messengers of an unchanging gospel.

Born in the mountain wilds of Giles in an humble primitive home, the Rev. J. Tyler Frazier learned, as he said, the Bible from his mammy as she plied the spinning wheel and loom. He imbibed the poetry of Nature from the mountain laurels, the hemlocks, and the spruces, the clear woodland streams, and the songs of mountain birds. He learned of the Omnipotent and All-Wise from the wild grandeur of his native hills. With very limited opportunities for schooling, he educated himself, laying the foundations from his mother's Bible under his mother's tutelage. Down to old age there was in his preaching something of the haunting mystery of the deep forests, the spirit of the clear mountain brook, the melody of the hermit thrush, the rugged strength of the eternal hills. He passed away at his home in Chilhowie, Feb. 23, 1932.

Episcopal Church

Christ Episcopal Church at Marion, the first of the denomination in Smyth, was erected in 1869. To the energy and fidelity of Mr. and Mrs. James H. Gilmore is chiefly due credit for the pretty little edifice now owned by the Episcopal Church.

In 1885 Mr. Gilmore, whose family constituted nearly the entire membership of the church, was elected one of the professors of law at the University of Virginia, and moved with his family to Charlottesville. The Episcopal services in the church were discontinued for twelve years; and the Lutherans occupied it from October, 1887, to May, 1895.

The corner stone of St. Paul's Episcopal Church, at Saltville, was laid in 1896, by the Wm. King Lodge A. F. & A. M. No. 22, on land deeded by the Mathieson Alkali Works. The money for the building, which was consecrated May 14, 1900, by Rt. Rev. A. M. Randolph, Bishop of Southern Virginia, was raised by the rector, Rev. Claudius Smith. Until 1906 the church was a part of Holston Parish of which Abingdon was the center. While a member of this parish the rectors of St. Paul's were: Rev. J. S. Alfriend, E. R. Carter, and Rev. R. E. Boykin. In May, 1906, Preston Parish was formed, composed of Saltville, Marion, and Glade Spring with Saltville as its center. The rectors of Preston Parish have been: Rev. M. B. Marshall, Rev. W. T. Elmer, Rev. W. H. Pettus, Rev. T. E. Opie, Rev. W. R. Noe, Rev. John R. Matthew, Rev. E. C. Burns, Rev. H. C. Fox, and Rev. A. W. Taylor. In 1916 a parish house was built on N. P. Row on land deeded by the Mathieson Alkali Works.

Rev. Thomas Apil and Rev. J. C. Smith also served the Marion Church.

Christian Church

The first Christian church established in Smyth County grew out of a union Sunday School conducted in Perryville Chapel at Saltville. The Perryville Chapel was built in 1896 by the Saltville Land Company for the Saltville Circle of King's Daughters who conducted the Sunday School and arranged for preaching services. Mr. Vincent Hobbs, a member of the Christian Church, led the Sunday School work until his death. When the King's Daughters disbanded in 1906, the building was turned back to the land company, who turned it over to the Christian Church. In 1909 Rev. H. D. Coffey held a revival by which many members were added to the church. In 1918 the Mathieson Alkali Company donated a lot upon which a church was built.

Along about the middle nineties the Rices and other Christian families moved into the Seven Mile Ford neighborhood. Rev. A. C. Maupin began services in the Dungan schoolhouse northwest of Seven Mile Ford and led the movement that resulted in building the Sugar Grove Christian Church near the schoolhouse. The land was deeded by Joel Boothe and Mary Boothe on Aug. 31, 1897. Mr. A. C. Rice built the house. It was dedicated by Rev. W. H. Burleigh, free of debt. At the time of organization there were some twenty-five or thirty members. The church has had a steady and healthy growth.

The Chilhowie Christian Church was built and organized some time after Sugar Grove.

Among the Christian ministers who have served the county were: A. C. Maupin, P. C. Hasselvander, G. W. Headon, W. A. Wise, G. H. Easly, J. D. Coffey, William Barnett, Minor Zuderman, Samuel Sutton, L. A. Morton, Arthur Wake, and H. O. Crow.

CHAPTER IX

SCHOOLS

So FAR as can be ascertained the first school teacher to carry on in the bounds of Smyth County was an Irishman named Turner Lane who conducted a school at the Royal Oak prior to 1786. Lane was a big man of good appearance and a good teacher, maintaining good order and discipline and getting good work from his pupils without being tyrannical. He left Royal Oak and opened a school at Abingdon in 1786. After teaching there for a number of years he removed to Tennessee. He may have had his school in the church building or perhaps in another log house of which tradition tells nothing. If the latter, it was probably similar to the first schoolhouse in Abingdon, thus described by Mr. L. P. Summers: "The ground was the floor and the seats for the scholars were made of hewn slabs placed on forks driven into the ground around the walls, and their writing table was of the same material placed on forks in the middle of the room."

In 1786 or 1787 Col. Arthur Campbell had a good school in his house, as appears from a letter written by his nephew, Gov. David Campbell, in which an incident is told to illustrate Col. Arthur's "disposition to have his own way without regard to the opinions or desires of others."

Gen. William Campbell having died, the Court appointed Col. Arthur Campbell guardian of his daughter, Sarah. Sarah's mother, the famous Madam Russell, and Arthur Campbell could not get along at all, but quarreled heartily over the management of Sarah and her affairs. This letter says an open rupture took place over Sarah's education, Colonel Campbell as her guardian wishing to control and direct it, and her mother refusing to allow him to do so. "When the daughter was ten or eleven years old, that is about 1786 or 1787, Colonel Campbell was one day passing Aspenvale, the residence of Mrs. William Campbell (then Mrs. William Russell), when he met Sarah with some companions near the gate of the dwelling house. After conversing with Sarah about her education and the manner in which it was being neglected, he proposed to her that she get on the horse behind him and go to school, as he had a good school then at his house. She consented, and he thus carried her home. The girls who were with her went to the house and reported to Mrs. Russell what had happened. Next day she, accompanied by General Russell, went to Colonel Campbell's house to bring home her daughter, but the colonel would not let them see her. I do not recollect how long Sarah remained at Colonel Campbell's —some weeks though—when the matter was compromised and she taken home again."

The first music teacher of record in Smyth was a German named Aaron Palferras, who, as a redemptioner, or indentured servant, in Gen. Francis Preston's household at Saltville taught music to the Preston children, and thereby hangs a tale. This young German, when on a visit to England, went on a drinking bat one night with a party of gay young blades, and when he sobered up the next day was horrified to find himself legally married to a woman of the streets. He ran off to Liverpool and boarded the first ship to America. Not having any money he was sold in Philadelphia to the highest bidder, being bound to serve the master who bought him for a period of years to pay the cost of his passage. Francis Preston was in Philadelphia at the time and, struck by the young German's appearance, bought him. Finding his servant to be an educated gentleman and an accomplished musician, he assigned

SCHOOLS

him the task of teaching music in the family. When the music teacher's term of service had expired, he continued to live in the Preston home on the basis of a friend and equal until he learned that his wife was dead and then he returned to Germany.

A notable teacher of the early days was Master Burns, tutor in General Preston's home at Saltville, where he instructed a future university president, a university professor, a noted patron of art, a United States Senator, and wives of a famous preacher, of two generals and three governors, all children of Francis Preston and his wife, the little Sarah Buchanan Campbell about whom Col. Arthur Campbell and Mrs. Russell quarreled. He is buried in the Preston graveyard at Seven Mile Ford.

The more prosperous families in the early days would employ tutors for their children. Some of the early preachers taught community schools. Among these was the Rev. Thomas Woolsey, first resident Baptist pastor of Smyth County. He lived and owned land on the South Fork near the present residence of Mrs. William Britton, where he had a log building, long known as the Blankenbeckler schoolhouse, that he used both as a church and school. In recent years a monument has been erected to this devoted servant of the Cross whose life of faithful, humble service brought the gospel to the people of Smyth and trained their children in Christian citizenship.

The Rev. Joseph Pendleton, an ardent Methodist, came to Smyth prior to 1800 and for many years taught a school four miles east of Seven Mile Ford, near the head springs of the branch that comes down south of the Preston home. He made his own books. His son, Philip, grandfather of Mrs. W. H. Copenhaver of Chilhowie, assisted him in the school. His daughter, Lucinda, when sixteen years old, eloped with one William Morgan. Morgan went to Batavia, N. Y., where he published a book on Masonry and was murdered, a combination of circumstances which so stirred the country as to lead to the formation of the National Anti-Mason political party.

"Lucinda, then 23, with two children, was left without support and among strangers. Her father never did relent. She married afterward a Mr. Harris, went to Iowa, was divorced from him, and entered a convent where she served in Memphis, Tennessee, as a nurse during the Civil War and died there."

The Rev. William Bishop, a Methodist minister conducted an excellent classical school in the old Elizabeth Church building at Saltville, attracting students from other counties who boarded in the vicinity.

Many communities, in ante-bellum days, had schools conducted on a subscription basis. The teacher was sometimes a local resident, sometimes an unmarried man or woman who boarded about among the patrons. Some were elementary schools, some classical schools or academies, and some a combination, starting the little tots with their A B C's and carrying them through pre-collegiate preparation. The Presbyterian ministers, the Rev. David Palmer and the Rev. Philip Wood, taught classical schools in Marion, the latter at one time having a school in the oft-remodeled building now known as Hotel Marion. The Rev. Luther Ambrose Mann, a consecrated and much beloved Lutheran minister, described by some of those he taught as "one of the best men who ever lived in Smyth," resided before, during, and after the Civil War in the neighborhood of Ebenezer Church. Near his home he taught an excellent classical school. He taught music and, lacking textbooks, he wrote the notes and scales all over the walls and ceiling of his schoolroom. Besides Mr. Mann, a Mr. Gannaway and a personage known as "Drunken John" Miller taught school at some time in this building.

SCHOOLS

The most noted of those old ante-bellum classical schools was Liberty Academy which stood a half mile due north of the Methodist Church at Chilhowie. Mr. A. F. Bonham, born June 25, 1848, says he started to school there when ten years of age, and that it was an old school of high reputation long before then. It continued in operation for some years after the War.

Mr. Bonham recalls the following teachers: Chancellum, a Methodist preacher whose wife taught a primary school at their home near the Sulphur Springs; Taliaferro; Logan; Hutton; Judge D. C. Miller; Miss Angelina Bishop; Overton; Gen. James Greaver, and Col. Robert H. Dungan.

The old White Oak Branch School near Chatham Hill is remarkable for its alumni. Among those who went to school in this old building, that is now a shed in a pasture field, were: two Lieutenant Governors, B. F. Buchanan of Virginia and Barry Miller of Texas; two Supreme Court judges, John A. Buchanan of Virginia and George W. Buchanan of Missouri; George W. Richardson, county judge of Smyth; John W. Richardson, register of the land office of Virginia; Albert Sexton, Secretary of the Commonwealth for Alabama; G. Beauregard McDonald, candidate for United States Senator from Nebraska; Dr. J. D. Buchanan, beloved physician of Smyth; and John L. Buchanan, who at various times in his career was Superintendent of Public Instruction of the Virginia Agricultural and Mechanical College at Blacksburg; President of Randolph-Macon College; President of Emory and Henry; Professor of Greek in Vanderbilt University; and President of the University of Arkansas. The latter years of his life were spent in Rich Valley at the home of his brother F. Grundy Buchanan. He died there Jan. 19, 1922, and was buried in Fayetteville, Ark., beside his wife.

By a compromise arrangement between patrons in the upper and lower communities, this school for a time at least was taught for one half session in the White Oak Branch house and the other half session in a house at Chatham Hill.

Among the teachers in this school were James R. Hubble and his sister, Mary, afterwards Mrs. Jerome Whitehead; William E. Evans and his wife; Judge D. C. Miller; B. Frank Buchanan; and Robert M. Richardson. Judge George W. Richardson leaves this interesting account of his school days there:

I first attended school at White Oak Branch, taught by either or both Esquire Jas. R. Hubble or his sister Miss Mary, who afterwards became Mrs. Jerome Whitehead. The school room was about eighteen by twenty feet, into which forty to fifty children of all sizes were packed, and had to sit on benches, without backs, with a slanting board fastened to the walls, where we learned writing as our turns came. The door was at one end and a large fire place at the other, and as those near the fire place would become too warm, they would move back and allow others to take their places, and this process of firing and falling back was continuous during the school hours in cold weather. We learned our "A B C's" and the sounds of the different letters, and the method of combining these so as to make words, from McGuffey's Old Blue Back Speller, and then to read, from McGuffey's Reader, and got our first knowledge of figures and mathematics from Pike's Arithmetic. We studied out loud and sang geography, all methods now regarded as crude, and yet I cannot but believe that as rapid progress was made in those days as now, when children are taught to read by sight, without knowing a letter in the book. Our good teachers did not spare the rod, and children who went home with a tale of mistreatment by the teacher, were likely to have the dose repeated at home, so that little trouble of that character ever arose. We had to rough it in those days, but at recess and dinner hour we had great times playing marbles, "Bull-Pen" and chasing the fox over the hills and through the woodland surrounding the school house. Later in life, I taught one session at this place, but in a somewhat better building. Hubble's Sugar Camp, the largest in that section, and from which great quantities of tree sugar and molasses were produced, was adjacent to the school house, and it was regarded a valued privilege to be there at "stirring off" time. A more delicious sweet than pure maple syrup was never invented or tasted.

What seems to have been the first free school in the county was established by Henry Copenhaver, veteran of the War of 1812, grandfather of Mr. Henry P. Copenhaver and son of Frederick Copenhaver, progenitor of all that tribe now living in Smyth. He had eleven sons and two daughters and to educate them built a log schoolhouse near the present Greenwood Church, and employed a teacher. He then rode around the community and told all parents to send their children to school. Those who could afford it might help to pay the teacher, but all were free to send whether they paid or not. This old log house was moved but is still standing about a quarter of a mile from its original site.

The Mitchell home on College Street was built as an academy, and many men now prominent in Smyth were educated there. This building was erected soon after the Civil War by private subscription. The first teacher was William E. Evans, one of the ablest pedagogues Smyth County ever had. From Marion he went to Jeffersonville as head of a school, and one of his former pupils, A. T. Lincoln, taught with him there for the session, 1880–1881. Mr. Lincoln was advised not to apply for reappointment when it was learned that he had voted for Garfield in the Garfield-Hancock election, because at that time Tazewell people would not stand for a Republican teacher. Judge D. C. Miller came to Smyth as a Confederate refugee from a Yankee neighborhood in east Tennessee. He taught in the Liberty Academy near Chilhowie, in the White Oak Branch School in Rich Valley, and for many years in the Marion Academy, varying his teaching with law practice, a five-year term as County Judge and a term as County Superintendent of Schools. His son, Phipps

Miller, after graduation from West Point taught here with his father. Other teachers in this Marion Academy were: Dr. Grace, a minister; Prof. R. H. Brown; Walthall and his son, Wilburn Walthall; Frank A. Kelly; Dr. J. J. Scherer, and Dr. J. B. Greiner, Lutheran ministers; and Judge George E. Cassell, now living in Radford.

The first free school in Marion is said by some to have been taught in the old building on Broadway beside the first Baptist Church, in the upper story of which Masons once held their lodge meetings; by others this honor is ascribed to the old building now standing on the corner by the Baptist Pastorium, which was the home of Mrs. Henrietta Desmond for many years. Certainly this house was the first built in the town for a free school and school was taught there for a term of years and then transferred to the Presbyterian Church building, which stood across the street from it, where the Graded School now stands.

In the later fifties William Farmer of Wytheville taught a boy's school in that old Masonic building on Broadway, and about that time the Misses Marissa and Mary Gordon, sisters whose father was killed in the War of 1812, taught a girls' school in a large brick residence on the site now occupied by Marion College. Two sisters, the Misses Sally and Mary Van Meter, who with their parents had removed to Marion from Botetourt County, taught a private school for smaller children in the house on Main Street now occupied by Mrs. Julia Rider and her sons.

Dr. Scherer started Marion College in the brick residence that had formerly housed the Misses Gordon's school for young ladies, and continued to use this as his college building until it was replaced by the first unit of the present plant. Mrs. Sally Van Meter Helms was closely associated with Dr. Scherer in the earlier years of Marion College as assistant in charge of the younger girls. At the time of her death she was living in Wytheville. Her body was brought to Marion for burial and her funeral was conducted in the college chapel by her pastor, the Rev. Mr. Hall of the Wytheville Presbyterian Church, assisted by Dr. Scherer.

MARION JUNIOR COLLEGE

By President Eldridge H. Copenhaver

Marion College was founded in 1873 under the name, Marion Female College. It was chartered by the state of Virginia as a liberal arts college for women in 1874. Its first president was the Rev. J. J. Scherer who for thirty-six years directed its affairs wisely and economically. He retired as president emeritus in 1909. After his retirement, until the beginning of the present administration in the fall of 1927, his successors have been the Revs. J. C. Peery, J. P. Miller, H. N. Miller, and C. Brown Cox.

In the work of starting and establishing the college, President Scherer had valuable helpers in his beloved wife, Mrs. Katherine Killinger Scherer, who was not only a true helpmate and advisor, but a veritable mother to the girls in College, and in the Rev. J. B. Greiner who was associated with him as teacher for sixteen years, and "who took an active part in shaping the course of instruction and in general management of the College." No history of the College would be complete without honorable mention of Mrs. Scherer and Rev. J. B. Greiner and their constructive work in the cause of Christian education.

In 1912 Marion Female College was made a standard Junior College and its name changed to Marion Junior College. It is controlled by the Lutheran Synod of Virginia through a Board of Trustees consisting of twenty-five men— five of whom are nominated annually by the Board itself and elected by the Synod for a period of five years. Some of the first members on the board were: the Hon. J. P. Sheffey, Dr. H. C. Stevens, M. Jackson, James H. Gilmore, N. L. Look, G. D. H. Killinger, John S. Copenhaver, C. K. Coley, William McCauley, Benjamin Phleager, Joseph Groseclose, the Hon. Fayette McMullin, and Judge John A. Kelley.

The idea of the founders of Marion College "was to provide a liberal education under Christian influences and environment for girls of the territory in which the College is located." But a larger program than they at first had in mind was laid out and enlarged to include students from any or all sections of the country, and patronage comes from ten or more states, north and south.

With a modern equipment and an efficient corps of University trained teachers, the College has aimed to keep abreast with every progressive but conservative educational movement and to meet standard requirements. In addition to four years of preparatory study, two years of college work, along with special courses, are offered; the curricula are sufficiently full and varied to afford students wide range in the choice of their courses of study. To meet the requirements of the State Board of Education and to qualify for the Normal Professional Certificate, the Education course has been extended to include ninety hours of practice teaching in the grades of Marion Grammar School under a trained critic teacher.

Because of very moderate rates, many girls of limited means have obtained a college education at Marion, which otherwise would not have been possible for them. During its long history the College has made worthwhile contributions to the cultural life of the town and community.

Of the hundreds of young women who have studied at Marion College many are not only civic, social and church leaders in their communities, but scores are rendering a more pretentious service as teachers, social workers, nurses, physicians and home and foreign missionaries. It is worthy of note that the first missionary society in the Southern Lutheran Church was organized at Marion College. This organization was effected even before any very great interest in missionary endeavor was manifested anywhere.

The Scherer family, so intimately associated with Marion College, through Dr. J. J. Scherer, its founder and first President, and his daughters Mrs. Laura S. Copenhaver, at one time teacher of English and Miss May Scherer, teacher of Bible and other subjects and since 1916 Dean of the College, are descendants of Jacob Daniel Scherer, who came to America in 1764 from Alsace-Lorraine. Jacob's grandson, the Rev.

SCHOOLS

John Jacob Scherer, travelled through Southwest Virginia in 1815 and organized thirteen Lutheran Churches. His son, the Rev. John Jacob who for forty years was President of Marion College, went to Texas after his graduation from Pennsylvania College and began the study of law, supporting himself in the meantime by school-teaching. His diary relates: "The first day I went into the school room a dozen boys had pistols and bowie knives swinging about them. I had no trouble until a boy of eighteen who had been a murderer got into a fight with another boy." After a few months of school-teaching Dr. Scherer decided that ministers of the Gospel were needed even more than lawyers in the West as well as the East. After several years in Texas he came to Virginia and founded Marion College "in the face of obstacles that would have balked a less determined or less faithful man." He was proud of the fact that for forty years of teaching he never missed a day because of illness, and in his eighty-eighth year he wrote, "It seems to me that it would be murderous to lay an old servant away—segregating his ability and his desire to serve." He read his Greek Testament every morning to the last three days of his life and he could quote verbatim large passages from the King James version. In the Richmond News Leader at the time of Dr. Scherer's death in his ninetieth year, Dr. Douglas Freeman wrote of him:

"Born in the year of Nat Turner's insurrection, his observant eyes saw changes such as few Virginians have known. But those changes never bewildered nor depressed him. Sometimes he was puzzled for a moment but he always found the answer in the Gospel of Jesus Christ. That was the remedy he sought always to apply—to the ills of society, to the maladies of ignorance and to those complex pathological conditions that mystify the man who cannot see with the eye of faith."

His son, the Rev. John Jacob Scherer, D.D., is Pastor of the Monument Avenue Lutheran Church of Richmond and Judge of the Juvenile Court.

The College Gymnasium was erected and other improvements made to buildings and grounds during the administration of Dr. C. Brown Cox.

The present State school system became effective in 1870,

but the old academies and private schools continued to function until the first decade of the present century when the modern high schools began to supplant them.

The Smyth County School Board

The organization at the present time is as follows:
Superintendent: B. E. Copenhaver.
Trustees: First District—F. L. Sanders, Chairman; Second District—A. W. Ristine; Third District—J. B. Keesling; D. D. Cole, Clerk.

Marion

W. W. Scott, Clerk; W. M. Sclater, Chairman; Geo. F. Cook.

Saltville

Mrs. Henry Chapman, Clerk; H. A. Reutschi, Chairman; T. K. McKee.

There are six standardized high schools in the county:
Marion High School, 1914; Saltville High School, 1916; Sugar Grove High School, 1928; Rich Valley High School, 1927; Atkins High School, 1931; Chilhowie High School, 1922.

Four of these have Vocational Agriculture Departments, instituted at Sugar Grove and Rich Valley in 1927, at Chilhowie in 1929, and at Atkins in 1931.

The office of county superintendent of schools was begun in 1870. Hon. D. C. Miller was the first superintendent, serving until 1875 when he went on the bench as County Judge. He was succeeded by Maj. A. G. Pendleton. Judge Miller was reappointed at the close of Major Pendleton's term, but the Major contested the appointment and won it, to be succeeded at its close by Frank Kelly. Then Major Pendleton was appointed again to succeed Kelly, after which Charles E. Anderson came in for one term, winning the appointment over Kelly and Pendleton. The present incumbent, Bascom E. Copenhaver, has served continuously since 1901. Mr. Copenhaver, born and reared about two miles north of Marion, has been associated with Smyth County schools all his life as pupil and teacher. He served for a while as Principal of Marion College during the presidency of Dr. J. J. Scherer and did much to establish that institution on a sound financial basis.

Chapter X

NEWSPAPERS

The first newspaper in Smyth County was the *Marion Visitor* launched in 1858 by George J. Curtis and James W. Kennedy. Mr. R. A. Anderson found in the papers of his brother-in-law, Mr. Joseph Wolfe, a copy of the Prospectus of this enterprise and also one sheet of the *Visitor* published Feb. 15, 1861. The Prospectus is a little leaflet of about three by six inches in size and reads as follows:

PROSPECTUS OF THE
"MARION VISITOR"

We, the undersigned, propose establishing, as soon as a sufficient number of Subscribers can be obtained, in the town of Marion, in the County of Smyth,

A FAMILY NEWSPAPER

Neutral in Politics, and devoted to Literature, News, Science, Agriculture, and General Intelligence.

News of both a general and local character will be fully reported in its columns, and it will comment with freedom and fairness on whatever it may think worthy of condemnation or approval.

The *Visitor* will be of a Double Medium size, and printed in good style, and will contain information of value to its readers of all pursuits, and will, if possible, prove acceptable to all.

By strict attention to business, the Subscribers hope to obtain for the *Visitor* an extensive circulation in Smyth and the adjoining Counties.

TERMS:—$2, to be paid in advance.

George J. Curtis
James W. Kennedy.

Mr. E. S. Watson, of Marion, is our authorized Agent to receive subscriptions.

The first page of the *Visitor*, Feb. 15, 1861, announces that it is published every Friday, by James W. Kennedy, and that the subscription rate is two dollars a year. It also carries the following advertisements and professional cards:

A. G. PENDLETON, JR.
ATTORNEY AT LAW,
Marion, Smyth County, Va.,

WILL practice in the courts of Smyth, Wythe, Washington, Grayson and Tazewell counties. Office in Courthouse yard.

DRS. E. J. & S. B. GOODWIN,
Chatham Hill, Smyth County, Va.,

Offer their professional services to the citizens of Chatham Hill and the surrounding country. We can be found, at all hours, in our office, except when professionally engaged.

J. W. & J. P. SHEFFEY,
ATTORNEYS AT LAW
Marion, Smyth County, Va.,

Practice in all the Courts of Wythe, Smyth, Washington, and Tazewell; in the Federal Court of Wytheville, the District Court of Appeals at Abingdon, and Supreme Court of Appeals at Lewisburg. Business intrusted to them will receive prompt attention.

DR. I. P. HOYT,

Having located in Marion, offers his professional services to the citizens of the town and surrounding county.

Residence—South side of Main street, first house west of the bridge.

A. P. COLE,
ATTORNEY AT LAW,
Marion, Smyth County, Va.,
Strict attention given to all business intrusted to his care.

A VERY large supply of BALE COTTON, of all Nos., just received and for sale by
R. J. VENABLE & BROS.

THE QUESTION SETTLED
FUSIONISTS DEFEATED

EVERYBODY wears Boots and Shoes, and as a good article and a genteel fit are desirable, the fashionable world should call at the old stand of P. J. Gregory, on Main Street, Marion, Va. He makes
(Picture of   BOOTS AND SHOES   (Picture of
a boot)   a shoe)
of the very best quality, and at the lowest possible price. He will also repair Boots and Shoes in the most durable manner, and being the best workman in the Southwest, none will have a bad job put on them. He hopes by strict attention to business, to merit a liberal portion of public patronage.

I have on hand a lot of Shoemaker's tools, pegs, and other articles used by them, which I will dispose of upon reasonable terms.

P. J. GREGORY.

TO THE LADIES

OUR MAC being a great Ladies man, always keeps his eyes open in purchasing, we can now sell a first-rate Ladies Calf Shoe for $1.

McDONALD, BEATIE & CO.

READY-MADE CLOTHING, of excellent quality for sale by
R. J. VENABLE & BROS.
Marion Depot

More Goods Wanted.

As the time is close approaching when we must buy our FALL AND WINTER GOODS, we hope those indebted to us will call and pay us a part, if not all, of their indebtedness, as we are in want of funds.

Aston and Hull

Just after the War a newspaper was operated in Marion for a short time by Mr. John Wright.

The *Visitor* having proved a war casualty, James W. Kennedy and M. P. Venable tried another newspaper venture in 1869, and called their paper the *Herald;* and about the same time the Hon. Fayette McMullin established a newspaper that he called the *Patriot*. McMullin after a short while sold the *Patriot* to Marcellus P. Venable and the two were combined into one known as the *Patriot and Herald*. In 1874 Wm. C. Pendleton purchased a half interest in the *Patriot and Herald*. The great Readjuster conflict that was to stir the political life in the state of Virginia to its foundation began to take shape, and in the early days of that movement Pendleton bought out Venable's interest in the paper. Pendleton was a Readjuster and made his paper a Readjuster paper. The Funders of the county attempted to secure control of his paper or at least to have their side of the question set forth in its columns, but Mr. Pendleton desired to continue it as an organ on the principles which he advocated and the advocates of the other side established a paper known as the *Conservative Democrat,* with T. Marion Anderson as the Editor.

This paper was edited by different men and has passed through the hands of various owners and under the name of the *Marion Democrat* is still published every Tuesday.

Eugene Jones was one of the early editors. Prof. R. H. Brown was one of the early owners. Brown was a one-armed man and a teacher in the old Marion Academy. He married

Miss Cynthia Scherer and left her a widow with two small daughters, Anita and Edna. Mrs. Brown taught music and other subjects for many years in Marion. She was a woman of fine business ability and by thrift, industry, and wise management was enabled not only to rear and educate her daughters but to acquire along with other property a home on Main Street opposite the Marion College campus in which she spent her last days, dying there on July 22, 1924.

Following Mr. Brown, B. F. Buchanan had control of the *Democrat* for a while and sold it to the Rev. George W. Miles, who with his son, Geo. W. Jr., published it for a number of years and then sold it to W. H. Twombly. Twombly sold it to J. G. Stephenson and Company and they carried it on until about 1918 when it was bought by R. A. Anderson, owner and publisher of the *News*.

Mr. Pendleton sold the *Patriot and Herald* in 1889. It was removed to Wytheville and died there. About that time the *Southwestern News* was established in Marion and published by Wilmer Williams, and then by Jas. H. Francis.

On May 15, 1896, Messrs. R. A. Anderson and C. B. Francis bought it and changed its name to the *Marion News*. Two years later Anderson bought out Francis and from then until 1918 published the *Marion News* as owner and editor. In 1918 he turned the management over to his son, Marvin, and about that time bought the *Marion Democrat*. Since then the two papers have been owned and published by the Marion Publishing Company, one with a Republican and the other with a Democratic editor. The Andersons sold the business to A. L. Cox. In 1925 Sherwood Anderson in his roamings through the gloamings stumbled on the hills of Southwest Virginia and fell so thoroughly in love with them that he bought a mountain farm in Grayson just over the Smyth line and built himself a house there in 1926. Then he came to Marion and on Nov. 1, 1927, bought the Marion

Publishing Company with its two weekly papers from Mr. Cox, and had a big time running them for several years. His son, Robert Lane Anderson, came in to help, and in 1931 a controlling interest in the business was transferred to him. Robert L. Anderson had taken over from his father the active management and editing of the papers two or three years previous to this date.

In 1914 Col. W. C. Pendleton founded a paper known as the *American* which he published in Marion for four years in competition with the other two papers.

Chapter XI

INDUSTRIES

The oldest and most important industry of Smyth County is farming and grazing. The pioneers cleared patches of land and planted corn. At times they had no bread but substituted the white meat of turkeys and pheasants until the corn crop ripened. But the rich virgin soil soon yielded far more foodstuff than could be consumed. Wheat and other small grains were planted from the first; tobacco was raised in the early days but its cultivation was practically abandoned before the county was formed, to be revived on an extensive scale within the last three years; fruit trees were planted by the first settlers; hemp and flax were important crops until comparatively recent years, when home weaving gave way to factory-made goods.

The census of 1840, the first after the county was formed, shows that Smyth had 9,000 cattle; 11,000 sheep; 16,000 hogs; 52,000 bushels of wheat; 221,000 of corn; 7,000 of rye; 178,000 of oats; and 34,000 of potatoes. In that year Smyth produced over seven bushels of wheat and thirty bushels of corn for each man, woman and child, black and white, in the county, and there were one and a third times as many cattle, one and a half times as many sheep, and two and a third times as many hogs as there were people. Practically the only market for surplus grain was afforded by the great herds of cattle, horses, and mules, and droves of hogs that were driven through the county to eastern markets; by stage-coachmen and travelers through the county with people and animals to feed; and by drivers of covered wagons passing

INDUSTRIES

through and coming into the county. In the days of the crowded wilderness push to Kentucky and Tennessee the traffic on the Wilderness Road bought considerable quantities of grain. The covered wagons going to and from the salt works and plaster banks of Rich Valley and, after 1856, hauling goods from back counties north and south to the railroad, provided an appreciable market for surplus farm products.

From the very beginning the main money supply on Smyth farms has come from live stock, driven afoot to markets at Philadelphia, Baltimore, Lynchburg, Richmond, Petersburg, and North and South Carolina towns, until the railroad shipments began. Although shipments by rail began in 1856, this driving of stock afoot to distant markets continued until long after the Civil War.

Grass was growing in many an open glade and along the river bottoms when the white men first came. It grew spontaneously wherever the woods were cleared away, and the flocks and herds of settlers increased.

In the late eighties and early nineties of the last century, Col. George W. Palmer had on an estate of 6,000 acres in Rich Valley the largest herd of registered shorthorn cattle in the world, shipping annually large numbers of animals for breeding purposes all over the South and West, some going to California and several carloads to Central America. He did much to improve the cattle of Smyth. At that time and until cold storage was perfected fat export cattle were shipped from Smyth County pastures to Liverpool. Now most of them go to Lancaster, Pa.

The annual Smyth County Fair with its display of farm products and live stock is one of the biggest and best in the country. Mr. E. K. Coyner, Secretary of the Association, has very kindly furnished the following account:

The beginning of the Smyth County Fair in 1908 was at Broadford, Va. A number of citizens met together and agreed to hold a county fair. There were no exhibits other than saddle and draft horses, and very few cattle. In 1909 it was moved to Chilhowie and held in the Sanders bottom in front of Marvin Sanders' house. A number of nice saddle horses were in attendance and more draft horses with a few cattle.

In the fall of 1909 the citizens had a meeting in the courthouse and it was greed to issue shares at $10 per share and begin with what was known as the Smyth County Fair Association. A committee composed of J. E. Thomas, J. W. Stephenson, W. W. Hurt, and Bob Williams were to locate a site and begin a real county fair.

Land was purchased from Henry Sprinkle and Jonas Groseclose on top of the hill and a number of small buildings were erected, together with a fence around the grounds, and a track was graded. A fair was held in the fall of 1910. J. E. Thomas was made secretary and W. W. Hurt, president. Quite a lot of interest was displayed in this project as people visited from all sections of the county and adjoining counties, coming in buggies, hacks, farm wagons, coming in the early morning and spending the entire day.

The third year John W. Stephenson was elected secretary and ran the fair for two years. There being a very small amount of money appropriated with considerable obligations, no premiums were paid and the fair association went into the hands of a receiver and was sold. It was purchased by practically the same stockholders as before and was called the Smyth County Fair, Live Stock and Agriculture Association. E. K. Coyner was elected secretary. It has been operating since that date under that name, growing to be a very large fair. The track was made into a regulation one, free attractions put on, fireworks displayed, and a very large cattle show developed. All exhibits were brought up to a strictly district fair scale with entries from other counties and other states. It has never missed a single year from the beginning, holding a fair each and every year.

INDUSTRIES

Presidents have been: R. C. Gwyn, H. P. Copenhaver, and R. C. Gwyn, Jr.

Mr. H. P. Copenhaver has been in charge of the agricultural exhibits since the fair started.

County agricultural agents of Smyth have been: Nelson Rue, 1915; A. W. Hendrick; Lee Cole, 1919–1926; and P. E. Bird since 1926.

The county raises every sort of grain and vegetable, all fruits of temperate latitudes, and melons. In the old camp meeting days negroes, children, and white owners of small patches made a good thing out of selling melons and fruits to the campers.

The first manufacturing enterprise in Smyth County was Arthur Campbell's grist mill on Staley's Creek, built in 1770, the first mill on waters west of the New River streams. The Fincastle County Court "ordered that a Road be cutt from Arthur Campbell's Mill to Blue Spring at the head of Cripple Creek by the way of Rye Bottom," and the same day, Dec. 6, 1774, "ordered that a Road be cutt from Arthur Campbell's mill to Archibald Buchanan's on the north Fork of Holston." William Campbell, Gentleman, was ordered to appoint titheables to work on both of these roads.

The first mill in Rye Valley was on Comer's Creek and was run by a man named Jones. The stream was then called Jones' Mill Creek. When this mill was built is not known but it was there on May 6, 1783, when Hugh Fulton ran the line between Washington and Montgomery counties from a "Walnut and buckeye above the Royal Oak south crossing the middle fork of Holston, Campbell's mill creek, three mountains, the south fork of Holston above Jones' mill, his mill creek, four mountains, Fox creek to six white pines on the top of Iron mountain by a laurel thicket."

The first mill in Rich Valley was Thomas Tate's on the

site where McCarty's Mill now stands. This mill was designated by the Virginia Board of Public Works survey as the head of batteaux navigation, and improvements in the river were made at state expense to this point. Every year flatboats laden with beeswax, homespun, maple sugar and other nonperishable farm products, and with pig iron, plaster, and salt, were floated down the river to market on the spring floods, or "tides" as they are still locally called. They would go regularly to Kingsport and Knoxville and occasionally to New Orleans. They were launched as far up the stream as Chatham Hill, where a boatyard was operated for the making of flatboats in the middle of the past century. Indeed, boat building was a very considerable industry in Rich Valley until the railroad supplanted the rapid, rocky North Fork as a freight carrier. These flatboats were made of the poplar trees growing straight and tall and large in profuse abundance. The tree was peeled, split with an axe and wedge, and the heavy timbers dressed and snugly fitted. The boats were often ninety feet long, rarely less than sixty. A ninety-foot boat would be sixteen feet wide. These long, narrow craft required skillful handling in the rapids of the turbulent, swollen stream.

Record is found of the following mills in operation when the county was formed: Keesling's Mill, at Cedar Springs; Groseclose's Mill, near the present village of that name; Preston's Mill, at Seven Mile Ford, and Humphrey's Mill, on the river above Seven Mile Ford; Cole's Mill, in Sinclair's Bottom; Hume's Mill, on Staley's Creek in Marion; an old mill on the Middle Fork, between the Royal Oak Cemetery and Ellis's quarry. The mill now occupied by the H. B. Staley Company was built soon after the county was formed by Zachariah Shugart. On July 19, 1832, the court acted on his application to erect a dam across the Middle Fork

INDUSTRIES

of Holston River for the purpose of running a saw and grist mill. Shugart owned one side of the river and John Irons, Jr., infant heir of John Irons, deceased, owned the other. Court appointed twelve men to lay off an acre for the purpose with due regard to the interests of all parties concerned and to appraise the same; also to examine above and below as to probable damage to other property from overflow to mansion houses, gardens, and orchards; and to inquire into what degree the passage of fish and ordinary navigation would be affected; and to form an opinion as to whether the health of the neighbors would be injured by the stagnation of the waters. In August the Commissioners—Adam Groseclose, John Sprinkle, John Steffey, William Goodpasture, Joseph Dutton, Jacob Snider, Richard T. Johnston, William Thompson, John D. Fudge, Mitchell Scott, Roland Wolfe, and Jacob Neikirk—reported. They had laid off the acre for abutments and so forth and for the same had allowed John Irons, Jr., $7.66. For damage to John Irons, Jr., and William Humes from overflow by a nine-foot dam they allowed them forty-six cents each. They asserted that in their opinion no damage would be done to mansion house, garden, orchard, or office, and no inconvenience to fish, or obstruction of navigation, or menace to health would result from said dam.

In 1856 Shugart had a partner, W. H. Ancil, and in that year either built a new mill or remodeled the old one. In 1871 it was sold to Joseph Atkins, who sold it the next year to J. A. and J. W. S. Taylor. In 1875 Capt. D. D. Hull bought a half interest from the Taylors. In 1880 W. S. Staley bought the Taylor interest and until 1905 it was run under the style of Hull and Staley. In 1895 they installed the first roller process to operate in Smyth County, and began the making of Snow Flake flour, a brand that won the gold medal in the Jamestown Exposition.

In 1905 Henry B. Staley bought the Hull interest and after his father's death bought out the other Staley heirs, and has owned and operated it since.

The Mt. Carmel Mill, owned and operated by J. Emmet Thomas, is on the site of a mill run by John Sprinkle when the county was formed. The Copenhaver Mill is also probably on the site of a mill which operated when the county was formed, for a Mr. Dungan had one there either then or shortly afterwards. Dungan's Mill was washed out by a flood. Another was built on the site and operated by Mr. Glenn. This Glenn Mill was the first one built by Oscar Stone, a noted millwright. It was taken over by Mr. Goodell and Mr. Copenhaver to grind baryta. The Goodmans had a mill on the creek above the present Stephen Meek residence and Aunt Polly Goodman, who spoke English with a German accent, was a miller there. An old mill on the site of the Roberts mill in Rye Valley probably dates back a hundred years or more, but the historian has no definite data on it. Catherine's mill, probably near Cedar Springs, existed in the Fincastle County days. Besides the Tate mill, where Jack McCarty now grinds, there were ante-bellum mills in Rich Valley above Ellendale, at Chatham Hill, and other points.

Next to grinding grain the pioneer manufacturers turned their attention to forging iron. The first iron forge in the county was located immediately below Sugar Grove on the Williams land. Its old timbers were washed out by a flood within the memory of men now living. Tradition says that cannon for use in the Revolutionary War were made in this old forge, the truth probably being that long, heavy barrels of the muskets with which pioneers did such deadly work were made there. When the county was formed a man named Nichols had a forge in the gorge above the mouth of Comer's Creek. At one time there were three forges in operation at this place, which, with a store, covered wagons from North Carolina and Grayson, and other activities, made it the leading business point on the South Fork.

Abijah Thomas went into the foundry business on a large scale and at the beginning of the Civil War was successfully operating forges in Rye Valley. He had large iron works on Staley's Creek above Marion, which were destroyed by Major Harrison of Stoneman's Raiders, Dec. 16, 1864. He kept a large force working in the iron mines he owned or leased to supply metal for his foundries. Samuel Graham operated a foundry on the Ward place at Chatham Hill, and before Graham's day Col. Thomas Tate had iron mines and a furnace somewhere in that vicinity.

G. G. Goodell came from Fulton, N. Y., in 1859 and bought the old Grist Mill on Staley's Creek in Marion that had been operated by William Humes, and started a foundry close by.

Goodell and Quiaf, both Northern men, operated this foundry during the Civil War, and made in it gun barrels with which Confederate soldiers shot Yankees.

Upon the Smyth reaches of Cripple Creek where the head streams come sparkling out of the mountains are the remains of a noted furnace. It is the White Rock Furnace, for many years operated and still owned by the Lobdell Carwheel Company. Before the Lobdell Carwheel Company bought it, it was known as the Panic Furnace. In the great depression of 1873 there was a man named Gallegher in Southwest Virginia who had vision and courage and faith. In that panic year he started this furnace on the head of Cripple Creek and from it went the iron that made the wheels on which prosperity rolled into all parts of the country.

The Lobdell Carwheel Company bought Gallegher's Panic Furnace and after years of prosperity closed it down because it was cheaper to buy their iron than to mine and make it and haul it to distant shipping points, not because of diminishing ore, which is still there in finest quality and great quantity.

For over a hundred years iron was made in Southwest Virginia by the primitive, wasteful, small charcoal-burning furnace. Even after the introduction of coke and well into the present century charcoal was largely used. The White Rock Furnace of the Lobdell Carwheel Company, for instance, used large quantities of charcoal.

One day I took a long tramp through the Glade Mountains over the lands of that company. "Uncle Billy" Myers was with me. He told me a lot about the charcoal burners who used to live back in those hollows when he came to this country to work as a lumberman in the woods some twenty-five or thirty years ago. He would point out a pile of stones overgrown with bush and brambles, and say: "There is where an old cabin stood. That is the chimney. There is the line of the foundation. A charcoal burner lived there."

We came to an overgrown clearing in the mountain wilderness, miles from any present habitation. There is a great old cherry tree, several old apple trees, the remains of a huge chimney, rotting hewn logs lying about. "That," he said, "was a big two-story log house. All around here was cleared, with garden and pasture, and fields. The foreman of the works in all the charcoal pits lived there." Every once in a while we would pass by a space of open ground, with black soil and little vegetation, a portion perhaps twenty feet square and smoothed off level, frequently in the bottom of a sink hole, sometimes on the general level. "That," he would say, "was an old coal pit. They would pile cord wood up there in big heaps and burn it. Had to know just how to burn it. They kept a man watching it all the time, day and night. I used to see the charcoal burners coming out of the mountains, their faces so black you couldn't tell whether they were niggers or white men. Sold it to the furnace by the bushel. How would you like to walk from here to Marion and come back with a hundred pounds of sugar on your back? That was common for the men who used to live in here. Women and children would walk out of here to town and back, too. Nearly all the timber on these mountains right through here was cut out to make charcoal. Gave work to people living in the mountains, cutting timber for the charcoal burners."

As I walked and talked with "Uncle Billy" I realized more vividly why the mountaineers are leaving the mountains, and I wondered what will be the means of livelihood for those who stay on and continue to breed prolifically.

In 1880 Pierce's Forge, below Sugar Grove about three and a half miles, was making excellent bar iron from ores mined in that vicinity. These two were the only forges or furnaces then operating in the county, Thomas' enterprises and the Chatham Hill foundry not having been revived after the War, and Goodell having turned his attention to the more profitable business of baryta digging and grinding.

Iron mining started in Smyth before the Revolution, the first ore being dug in the neighborhood of Sugar Grove. At a very early date iron was mined on the North Fork of Holston somewhere in the neighborhood of Chatham Hill, and iron mining has been a more or less important industry in Smyth ever since.

Lead was also taken out in Smyth in small quantities by the early settlers, and there has been a deal of prospecting for lead in Rye Valley and some serious attempts to mine it on a large scale but with no great success. That there are large deposits of lead in the South Fork Valley is generally recognized as a fact.

Manganese has been mined in large quantities. Baryta mining was a very profitable industry until the deposits were exhausted. There are vast deposits of gypsum and of salt in Rich Valley which have been worked in various ways and for various purposes for a century and a half, and still appear to be inexhaustible.

The enormous deposits of limestone are the basis of great industries in the county. There is marble, and marble companies have been formed for the purpose of getting it out, but it has never paid.

In 1901 Dr. John S. Apperson and Thomas W. Lumsden purchased the old Goodell plant and reëstablished the foundry business under the name of the Marion Foundry and Milling Company. In 1906 Dr. Apperson formed a corporation styled the Marion Foundry and Machine Works which took over this property and erected new buildings on the north side of Foundry Street. The Company made wagons and did the repair work of the Marion and Rye Valley Railroad as well as run the foundry. Dr. Apperson's sons continued the business after his death until 1925.

These three men, Thomas, Goodell, and Apperson, figured largely in the industrial development of Smyth, in their successive generations.

Abijah Thomas, a man of rare vision and enterprise, was the foremost industrialist of Smyth County before the Civil War. His developments of the iron industry in mines, furnaces, and foundries along the South Fork and on Staley's Creek, made him a wealthy man for his day, and if the Civil War had not destroyed these properties and involved him heavily he would in all probability have amassed one of the great fortunes of the state, and have set his county fifty years ahead in industrial development. His father, Thomas Thomas, born in Wales in 1776, came to Smyth from Southampton County, Virginia, and on April 5, 1791, married Freelove Cole, born Dec. 24, 1773, and died March 22, 1848, daughter of Joseph Cole, pioneer settler on Sinclair's Bottom. Abijah, their youngest son, was born on the South Fork May 21,

1814, in the same house in which Mrs. Freelove Cole Thomas gave Marion its name. He married Priscilla Scott on June 2, 1836. He built a large octagonal house that still stands on a beautiful location near Thomas' Bridge and died there on Dec. 1, 1876.

G. G. Goodell came to Marion from New York state in 1859 and went into the foundry business. He was a Democrat of Northern sympathies. When the war broke out he took his wife and daughter, Ella, who later became Mrs. Henry P. Copenhaver, to his old home in New York, where the children would taunt her by calling her a "Copperhead." He continued his business in Marion during the War and because of his Northern connections was in position to render valuable services during the reconstruction period. He was appointed postmaster at Marion and in that capacity controlled extensive political patronage. He discovered the extensive deposits of baryta in the county and developed them. He died in December, 1886.

Dr. John S. Apperson first came to Smyth as a boy and worked at getting out cordwood for a Mr. Shuler until the War started. He learned medicine and surgery in the army and came to Marion to practice. His first wife was a Miss Hull and his second wife was Miss Mary Black, daughter of Dr. Hugh S. Black. He was a business man of vision and careful, sound judgment, and among other things created the Marion Foundry and Machine Works Company, and with George W. Miles and others promoted the building of the Marion and Rye Valley Railroad.

Spinning and weaving of cloth, from flax raised on the farms and wool, clipped from sheep in the pastures and carded by hand, was an important home industry in Smyth from the earliest settlements until comparatively recent years. There are a few old residents who still understand the art of weaving and some are even now making money out of handwoven carpets and coverlets that bring fancy prices from meticulous customers.

When Smyth County was formed in 1832, and for some years thereafter, William Humes had a cotton mill on Staley's Creek. He seems to have operated on a small scale in the old mill on the foundry site and to have ground grain there at the same time. October 25, 1833, the court acted favorably on a petition of John and William Humes to build a ten-foot dam across the river between the present dams of the Look and Lincoln, and Marion Ice and Coal Company plants. This dam and a grist mill were built. The mill, or another built there, was later operated by Snavely, then by Killinger, was purchased by Look and Lincoln, and became the nucleus of the great Lincoln industries of Smyth. The "other machinery" mentioned in the Humes petition was no doubt the cotton mill machinery and was probably operated in the new plant. Thompson Atkins, grandfather of Z. T., W. J., and George Atkins, bought the old plant and ran it as a grist mill.

Two successful woolen mills have been operated in the county, one at Olympia and the other at Holston Mills. Capt. John Buchanan Whitehead established the Olympia Woolen Mills about 1870 and they continued in successful operation until late in the nineties.

The Holston Woolen Mills on the South Fork was a flourishing enterprise with a busy and growing community about it when it was sold and removed to Salem. The mills were started before the Civil War by that very enterprising captain of industry, Abijah Thomas. He disposed of the property to a stock company which continued their operation until some time in the eighties. William Alexander was superintendent of these mills at the time of their removal to Salem and for some years before. He was a native of Scotland and

INDUSTRIES

had learned the business in his father's mills in the old country. A breakdown in a train led to his taking this position. He was traveling through with no intention of stopping when the engine of the train on which he was riding broke down near Seven Mile Ford. There seemed to be no prospect of moving on for some hours, so he walked over to Capt. Charles Preston's home and asked for something to eat. Capt. Charles Preston, with his wonted hospitality, not only gave him something to eat but insisted on his staying over. Finding that the young Scotchman was skilled in manufacturing woolens, Captains Charles and John M. Preston took him out to the plant and he went to work for the company, becoming superintendent.

Hand-made furniture has been manufactured in Smyth from the days that pioneers fashioned rude benches, chairs, tables, and beds for their cabins until now. Some of the cupboards, desks, tables, etc., made in the home shops of the earlier settlers, were beautifully done, and before the days of mass production skilled cabinetmakers in many communities made the bulk of Smyth County furniture.

The Crewey family of Rich Valley have been noted for several generations for their skill in the art. One of them now makes cedar chests and cherry and walnut furniture by hand in his cabinet shop on the North Fork in a building resting on foundation timbers that were originally placed there to support Thomas Tate's first mill.

In 1843 William C. Seaver came to Marion from Wytheville where he was born March 17, 1823, and where he had learned the trade of cabinetmaker. He opened a shop in a log building on the corner of what is now the Seaver Block and prospered from the start. Soon after the War he enlarged his shop by the erection of another building and in 1884 enlarged again to house his cabinet shop and the warerooms of his undertaking and furniture business. In 1875 he built a saw and planing mill on Staley's Creek and in 1905 added a furniture factory to the planing mill. He died June 5, 1909. At the time of his death his sons were in the business with him and one of them, M. M. Seaver, still carries on the undertaking and furniture phases under the style of W. C. Seaver and Sons.

In 1907 a company of local men organized The Virginia Table Works, built a plant in Marion, and manufactured tables. In 1912 this property was acquired by the Virginia Table Company in which Charles Clark Lincoln held a controlling interest. He was president, and E. A. Rhodes was superintendent of the works. These two had exclusive management of the business and from the start it prospered tremendously.

For some years it confined its output solely to tables, then to dining-room furniture, and in twelve years grew into the largest factory in the world making dining-room furniture exclusively. From 1922 to 1929 the plant was greatly enlarged, and a bedroom furniture factory was built at Bristol, operated from the Marion offices. After Mr. Rhodes' death, L. E. Gordon became superintendent and still holds that position. At the time of his death in 1929, C. C. Lincoln and his sons owned the company and it passed to his widow and boys, Charles and John Dickey. Under a reorganization with Charles C. Lincoln, Jr., president; John D. Lincoln, vice-president, and J. W. Horne, secretary, the business is being successfully carried on under the firm name of The Virginia-Lincoln Company.

The old firm of Look and Lincoln, under the management of Mr. A. T. Lincoln and W. L. Lincoln, began the manufacture of furniture in 1922 and continued until its dissolution, when the business was bought by the Lincoln Furniture

INDUSTRIES

Company, which continued to make furniture in the plant until the fall of 1931.

Col. William C. Pendleton, in a special illustrated edition of his paper, *The American,* of Jan. 8, 1914, writes as follows of the firm of Look and Lincoln:

Charles F. Lincoln died Oct. 13, 1891, and was sixty-one years old at the time of his death. Nathan L. Look died May 2, 1907, and had reached the venerable age of eighty-eight years at the time of his death. These two men are recognized as among the most progressive citizens Marion has ever had, and are admitted to have accomplished more in the way of making the town a place of industrial activity than any men who have ever lived here. They came to Smyth county in 1856, and settled first in Rich Valley on the celebrated Taylor farm, where they engaged in agricultural pursuits for four years.

In 1860 they conceived the idea of establishing a manufacturing enterprise at Marion. Acting upon that idea, they came here in 1860 and purchased the old grist mill that stood where the plow handle factory of Look and Lincoln is now located. The mill was built by William Snavely, but in the late fifties of the last century had become the property of Peter Killinger, from whom it was purchased by Look and Lincoln. Here they established a plow factory, which they operated in a small way until the close of the Civil War.

Immediately after the termination of the War they established a plow handle factory in connection with their plow factory, and soon were manufacturing and finding a ready market for the heavy output of handles that became noted for their superior quality.

In 1880 the industry was greatly enlarged by adding a wagon factory at a point on the north side of the river, just west of the iron bridge that spans the river west of the plow handle factory. This wagon factory was successfully operated until the present large one was erected in 1901.

Shortly after the death of the junior partner, C. F. Lincoln, in 1901, a disastrous fire destroyed the plow handle factory and sawmill. These were the same buildings that were purchased by the firm in 1860, and that had been built and used by William Snavely about the middle of the last century.

Shortly after Mr. Lincoln's death the business was incorporated under the old firm name of Look and Lincoln, N. L. Look retaining one half the stock in the incorporated concern and the Lincoln heirs retaining the other half.

As before stated, N. L. Look died at a venerable age May 7, 1907. Since his death the Lincoln heirs have acquired all the stock in the corporation and now are the owners of one of the most valuable industrial enterprises in Virginia, but continue to run it under the old and popular firm name of Look and Lincoln. The following members are its officers: C. C. Lincoln, president; W. L. Lincoln, vice-president; A. T. Lincoln, secretary and treasurer. These three are men of rare business ability and under their intelligent management the enterprise has continually advanced in importance and largely increased in value. A. T. Lincoln is one of the most popular citizens of the town and county. He represented Smyth County in the late constitutional convention, was elected twice to the State Senate from this, the First Senatorial District of Virginia, and last November was elected without opposition to represent Smyth County in the present House of Delegates.

The Look and Lincoln plants, as they now exist at Marion, have an annual capacity of 400 wagons and 600,000 plow handles, and fifty men are employed in these plants.

The firm has been engaged extensively in the lumber business in Rye Valley for more than ten years. They are operating there regularly from six to eight large mills and are conducting a large store at Sugar Grove. They have 125 men on their sawmill pay rolls, which evidences the character of these operations.

It can be stated without fear of successful contradiction that the old firm of Look and Lincoln was the first to give impulse to manufacturing enterprise in Marion, and the Lincoln boys, who now have charge of the business founded by Nathan Look and their father, Charles F. Lincoln, are fully alive with the spirit that imbued their predecessors.

INDUSTRIES

Alanson Taylor Lincoln died in the Abingdon Hospital and was buried from the Royal Oak Presbyterian Church on Jan. 30, 1925, in the sixty-seventh year of his age. Charles Clark Lincoln died of pneumonia at his home just east of Marion Dec. 23, 1928, in his sixty-third year. The passing of these two men cast a shadow of gloom over the town of Marion that was extended to the county. A. T. Lincoln was a genial, kindly man of many interests—business, social, civic, and political. A large number of newcomers to his home town have said that he was the first man to greet them so as to make them feel at home. He owned the first bicycle and the first automobile in Smyth County. He was identified with every popular movement and was the instigator of many a public enterprise for the advancement of community life and prosperity in town and county. In his later years especially he was very active in his church, teaching a large Bible Class for women in his Sunday School. He was an invaluable patron of the Woman's Club and the father of the Kiwanis Club of Marion.

Charles Clark Lincoln was a brilliant business executive and probably accomplished more to advance the business interests of Marion than any other one man. He went to school to Judge Miller in Marion and for one term at King College. At the age of fifteen he went to work in the Look and Lincoln factory and from then on bought his own clothes. He was postmaster in Marion for four years, 1898–1902. When he built his first home there was no electricity available but he wired his house, the first wired in the town, and soon afterwards was one of the promoters of the local power company that lighted the town. He promoted the first telephone company and personally installed the first telephone system in Smyth and Grayson counties. Besides building up his great furniture factories he was chairman of the building committee of the present Presbyterian Church, built

Hotel Lincoln, the Lincoln Theatre, his beautiful home in the Royal Oak Addition, and other buildings in the town. He had a phenomenal memory, having the details of his large business affairs always at his instant command and being able to recall figures and dates over periods of years with uncanny accuracy. He would, for instance, send a clerk to the courthouse to look up a deed recorded twenty years before and tell him in what book and on which page to find it. His widow, who was Miss Laura Dickey of Grayson before her marriage, now lives in the beautiful gray stone mansion he built in the Royal Oak Addition near Marion. Her son, John D., and his family make their home with her.

Under the management of Charles C. Lincoln, Jr., and John D. Lincoln the business has been maintained on a paying basis throughout the present period of depression and has every prospect of continued success.

In the early nineties Atkins Brothers, George and John, started a hub factory in a small way at Attoway. They found a ready market for the hubs and prospered. They expanded and made broom handles, then built a real factory, and began the making of tool handles of all sorts and spokes as well as wheels. Much of their output was sold in foreign countries. They shipped to Hamburg, Germany, great quantities of Walnut squares, that is small walnut logs cut into square sizes of varying lengths. During the World War the Government commandeered the plant and Atkins Brothers made locust nails, or wooden pins for the Shipping Board's wooden fleet, under a good war time contract. The Atkins Brothers' handle factory burned in 1923 or 1924 and was not rebuilt. John Atkins had died some years before. George A. Atkins still lives at Attoway. They were sons of Squire Joseph Atkins of Marion and Elizabeth Shugart, and grandsons of Henry Shugart and Thompson Atkins. A brother, W. J.

Atkins, is now living in Marion, the father of six most attractive daughters. Another brother, Zachariah T. Atkins, lived in Marion all his life, dying Friday, Oct. 9, 1931, in the eighty-fifth year of his age, and was buried from the Royal Oak Presbyterian Church, Sunday morning at eleven o'clock, the hour at which he had been in his pew for worship, unless providentially prevented, every Sunday morning for more than half a century. For many years he had been an honored elder in his church, a loyal Mason, and one of the most beloved citizens of his community. He was a farmer. The first binder to cut Smyth County wheat was driven by him in a field now occupied by the Southwestern State Hospital and a great crowd assembled to behold the wonder. For several years after his eightieth birthday he would celebrate his birthdays by driving the binder in his harvest fields.

A nephew of the Atkins brothers, J. P. Killinger, son of Mrs. Margaret Atkins Killinger, was in charge of their handle factory for a number of years before it burned. In 1926 he with Mr. Lee Cole and six other stockholders organized the Marion Handle Mills, Inc., and revived the business in the old Apperson foundry plant in Marion. Mr. Cole later withdrew from the firm and the enterprise is now managed by Mr. J. P. Killinger and his son, Ralph Killinger. They have prospered. About half of their output has been sold on the foreign market, large shipments going to South Africa and South America.

The Rich Valley Handle Company, owned and operated by D. B. Handshew, ran a small factory in the Nebo neighborhood from 1925 to 1928. The plant closed not from lack of orders, but because of its inaccessible location.

Lumbering has been a major Smyth County industry. In 1900 the Glade Mountain Lumber Company built a band mill on Nicks Creek and for three or four years cut timber out of Glade Mountain under the management of Hyler and Randolph. In 1914 the Atkins Lumber Company under the management of Hunter, Clark, and Gwynn began operations at Atkins and cut the timber off 15,000 acres bought by H. G. Gwynn and transferred to the company, and other holdings extending from Bear Creek to Reed Creek. The Lincolns for many years had extensive lumbering operations in Rye Valley.

The Spruce Lumber Company, J. C. Campbell, president; C. W. Amsler, vice president, and L. A. Amsler, secretary and treasurer, operated a band mill on Staley's Creek above Marion and another at Fairwood in Grayson County. Their logging over a wide area was done largely by contract. Mr. Campbell, when asked about this work, said: "We heard about this timber from some Cumberland, Md., people who had an interest in it. We came down here and looked over the timber in 1902. At that time there was dispute in the title and we did not care to invest, but afterwards the title was cleared up and we came here. We purchased about thirty thousand acres from the Douglas Robinson estate and erected a mill here at Marion. We started the mill in the year 1905 and we purchased the Marion and Rye Valley Railroad. The next year we purchased the Fairwood property from Williamsport partners and later on we organized another company. Later we consolidated both companies into the United States Lumber Company. We manufactured from three hundred and fifty to four hundred and fifty million feet of lumber. For the Marion Mill we cut timber on South Fork of Holston, Comer's Creek, and Roland Creek. My mill burned in 1910. I built it up again. Sold out about 1918. Sold railroad to John Buchanan, Horace Buchanan, and C. B. Buchanan."

The Hassinger brothers came from Pennsylvania and started

operations at Konnarock about 1907. They cut the timber off the mountain drained by the Laurel Fork, completing their work and closing down in 1929 or 1930.

Mr. H. L. Bonham of Chilhowie carried on an extensive lumber business for many years.

Through the influence of Mr. Campbell's brother, Mr. W. H. Teas, of Ridgeway, Pa., was induced to come to Smyth and look into the possibilities of the extract business. The result of his investigation was the incorporation of the Marion Extract Company in 1910 and the beginning in July of the erection of the plant and building of the village of Teas in Rye Valley. Shipments commenced in February, 1911. Col. Pendleton's *American* of Jan. 8, 1914, says:

It is the second largest extract works in the world, with a capacity for handling 200 cords of bark and wood each day of 24 hours. The plant is equipped with twelve 200 horsepower boilers. The largest engine is of 600 horsepower. There are 48 large leaches or tanks where the ground wood and bark is leached, and the liquor is then conveyed to a quadruple-effect vacuum pan, where the extract is concentrated. This pan has a capacity of 300,000 gallons per day of 24 hours. Chestnut wood, hemlock bark, and oak bark are the materials used for manufacturing the extract.

Between eighty and ninety men are employed by the company, there being both day and night shifts.

Nearby and around the main works forty-one neat cottages have been erected for the use of the employees at a moderate rent, each one supplied with an abundance of as pure and fine water as ever flowed from the earth, and with ample ground for vegetable gardens. Five prizes of $10 each were given last year to the five employees who kept the neatest yards and had the best gardens. The sanitation is excellent, the cottages being fitted up with screen doors and windows, and cleanliness of the premises being a requirement of all who live or work there.

The officers of the company were as follows: W. H. Teas, president; E. M. Campbell, vice president; J. C. Campbell, secretary and treasurer; G. H. Tilson, superintendent.

Mr. and Mrs. Teas and their three boys lived in Marion for a number of years and endeared themselves to many friends in town. Mr. Teas became deeply attached to the place. He developed other and larger plants in North Carolina and Tennessee, and when the supply of extract wood became exhausted he was compelled to curtail more and more the operations at Teas, finally dismantling the plant. But he kept the company offices in Marion until his death, May 1, 1930. About 1918 he purchased a beautiful home on the Chesapeake in Maryland where he made his home until he died. Mrs. Teas and her sons, John and William H., Jr., are now living in Nashville, Tenn.

Saltville is explained by the great salt deposits located in the valley in which the town is situated. Prior to the coming of the white man this valley constituted a "salt lick" where deer, buffalo and other animals licked the salt from the crusts formed on the surface at the upper end of the valley, and Indians made salt by boiling water from salt springs which at different points broke out around the margin of a lake which filled the lower end of the valley. These springs were in existence as late as 1853.

The patent to the lower end of the valley, containing 330 acres, was granted by Lord Dinwiddie, Governor, in the name of George II, to Charles Campbell on Oct. 23, 1753, and describes the tract as being in the county of Augusta on the north fork of Indian River. This covered the lower end of the valley and extended up to what is now known as "the old store." One-third of this patent was lake, and another third swamp, which took in the section up to where the salt plant was a few years ago. The lake was a gathering place for wild fowl of all sorts, and as late as 1848 thousands of

INDUSTRIES

wild duck and geese would rest on it in their migrations. That it was a favorite resort of the Indians is shown by the many relics found. In 1846, when the field in the rear of the present hotel was plowed, the locations of former buildings were distinctly traced by lines of ashes, periwinkle sheels, and pottery.

The property was inherited from Charles Campbell by Gen. William Campbell. General Campbell left two children, Sarah and Charles Henry, the latter dying when five years of age. Col. Arthur Campbell and Col. William Christian were appointed guardians of the children and under them the salt properties were considerably improved. The Virginia Assembly gave the young son of General Campbell 5,000 acres of land in consideration of the splendid services which his father had rendered to both the state and nation. Col. Arthur Campbell, the boy's guardian, selected the land voted by the assembly adjoining the Salt Lick tract and when Charles Henry died this land passed to his sister, Sarah, who later married Gen. Francis Preston. Some years afterwards, General Campbell's widow became the wife of Gen. William Russell and they, with their family, moved to the Salt Lick in 1788. Russell sunk a well on the margin of the flat in front of his home. Salt water was obtained and he built a furnace and salt houses. The furnace was an open shed and the kettles were the camp kettles of that period with a capacity of from eight to ten gallons. A dispute over the properties soon arose. Gen. Arthur Campbell, as the guardian of Sarah Campbell, and General Russell engaged in a controversy. The court appointed Col. Thomas Madison as guardian of Sarah Campbell in lieu of her other guardians. Colonel Madison in 1790 settled at Salt Lick. He built a log cabin, dug a well, and commenced the manufacture of salt. He continued in the salt business until three years later, when his ward married General Preston. General Preston built an addition to the log cabin in 1795, and two years afterwards retired from Congress and settled at Salt Lick with his family. He immediately began to increase the output of the properties, digging another well and enlarging the furnaces and kettles.

Competition began to develop when the 150 acres at the upper end of the valley were patented to one Evan Lee. He sold to James Crabtree, Crabtree sold to John Musgrove, and in 1795 Musgrove sold the original tract to William King for 500 pounds sterling. King dug a well just above his line, which was about fifty yards beyond "the old store," and in 1799 struck water at 200 feet. In 1801 King rented the Preston Salt Works for a period of ten years. King died in 1808, a rich man, with mercantile establishments over a number of Southern States. His executors continued the operation of the salt works until 1819, when in court proceedings, brought to straighten out the estate, the salt works was leased to John Sanders for five years at $30,000 a year. The next year James White bought this lease and operated the works until 1833. At this time the King and Preston estates were leased to Alex. McCall and William King. In 1845 they defaulted in the rent for the Preston estate and Col. Thomas L. Preston was put in charge. In 1846 Thomas L. Preston rented the King salines for five years. At the end of his tenancy they were rented to Wyndam Robertson for five years. At the expiration of this lease Thomas L. Preston again rented the property for five years.

The salt furnaces during this time consisted of long sheds with large kettles of various sizes under which ran flues to short chimneys. These furnaces were fired by wood and this fuel was used until some years after the Civil War. The first furnace built after the plan of those used at Syracuse, N. Y., was erected in 1846 by Thomas L. Preston, opposite "the old store."

INDUSTRIES

The lake remained in the lower end of the valley until 1847, when Colonel Preston dug a ditch from the foot of "Sugar Loaf Hill" to the gap leading to the river and thus drained the whole valley. The dirt thrown out of this ditch formed the road which now runs across the valley from the present home of Mr. Charles Wiley to the company's store.

In 1858 Preston leased the two saline estates of Spencer Ackerman and Company, and George W. Palmer of Syracuse, N. Y., took charge of the operations, making his home in the old Preston house at the southeast corner of the valley. In 1863 George W. Palmer and Wm. A. Stuart, father of ex-Governor Henry C. Stuart, purchased the Preston estate from Robert Gibbony, trustee of Thomas L. Preston, and in 1864 a corporation under the name of Holston Salt and Plaster Company acquired titles to both the King and Preston estates. This company was owned and operated by Palmer and Stuart until 1893, when the property was acquired by the Mathieson Alkali Works.

During the Civil War Saltville was the source of the sole salt supply of the Confederacy. So important a point was it that forts were dug on the top of every hill surrounding the valley and breastworks for riflemen were thrown up on both the outer and inner slopes of these hills below the forts on top. Most of these old earthworks are still in evidence on the hills around the valley.

At this time there were a great many furnaces (consisting of sheds with rows of kettles) in operation in the valley. Each southern state had a furnace from which it got its supply of salt. There was an old furnace located on the site of the present alkali plant at the river, where salt was manufactured and loaded on flatboats which in high water were floated down to the Tennessee and so on into the South. Many tales are told of conditions during the War. The currency was the Confederate bill. There would be hundreds of wagons lining the roads for miles waiting their turn for salt. Each wagon would bring a load of wood to be applied as part payment for the salt and the rest would be paid in Confederate currency. So plentiful was this that the bookkeeper, Mr. Ernest Middleton, would sometimes find his cash thousands of dollars over and no way to account for the surplus. On inquiry, Mr. Stuart would tell him that he had put some thousands of dollars in the safe and forgot to tell him about it. Frequently, on the other hand, he would be thousands of dollars short. Inquiry would develop the fact that Mr. Stuart had in that case taken out a lot of money to make some purchases and had neglected to notify the bookkeeper. Such was business in the old days.

In addition to developing the salt and plaster properties, Palmer and Stuart operated a tremendous farm through which they built up a large cattle business. During the eighties they owned what was then said to be the most valuable herd of registered shorthorn cattle in the world and many of their animals were bought and sold for fabulous prices. They also developed a herd of Clydesdale horses, many of them magnificent animals, and so numerous were they that frequently colts would be three or four years old before they ever had a bridle on them. They shipped many registered cattle all over the world and exported thousands to England. The cattle business, however, did not prove a financial success with them and was partly the cause of the failure of the firm. After the death of Mr. Stuart about 1890 the company was found to have become seriously involved financially and this led to its sale in 1893. The Mathieson Alkali Works was the purchaser this time of the entire works and the 12,000 acres of land.

While the Mathieson Alkali Works did not obtain its charter until 1892, the plan for the organization of the company had been conceived several years prior to that time and defi-

nite steps taken to put it into effect. Mr. E. E. Arnold, who was then active head of an old established wholesale drug and chemical house known as the Mason-Chapin Company, Providence, R. I., was the originator of the idea and later interested sufficient New York capital in the project to make it a reality. The site for the plant was selected in 1891 and arrangements made for its construction and management about the same year, which is generally regarded as the beginning of the company's history.

The Mason-Chapin Company had for a good many years imported large quantities of the products of an English firm known as the Neil Mathieson Company, whose soda ash and bleaching powder had always maintained a high standard of excellence with the trade of this country. In 1890, after negotiations which had been under way for some time, the Mathiesons sold out their plant at Wildnes, England, to the United Alkali Company and retired from business. Mr. Neil Mathieson, senior member of the firm, however, consented to come over to this country and undertake the construction and operation of the proposed ammonia alkali plant. His duties as defined in the plan would be to build the works and equip it, install the methods and processes used in England, and supervise the first manufacture of the "Eagle Thistle" products. This trade-mark, which was already so well established in the chemical world, had been bought by the new company and would thereafter designate their output.

With a view to selecting a site for the plant, Mr. Robert L. P. Mason had been employed in Western Pennsylvania watching for rock salt in the gas wells being drilled by the New York and Pennsylvania Company. In August, 1891, Mr. Mason was succeeded by Mr. Charles M. Perry, a chemist of Providence, R. I., who later found that there was no promise of salt in that section, and in September left for Warfield, Ky., to consider possibilities there. This field also proved unpromising, so the next move was to Saltville in October, 1891, to investigate the property owned by the Holston Salt and Plaster Company, of which Mr. George W. Palmer was president. This location offering advantages superior to any others visited, it was definitely decided upon and active steps taken to start its development.

Application for a charter was made on Aug. 4, 1892, as required by the laws of the State of Virginia, before Hon. John A. Kelly, judge of the Circuit Court for Smyth County, the petitioners being Edward E. Arnold, George W. Palmer, W. F. Sayles, William Grosvenor, John Waterman, James T. Kennedy, Alfred Harrison, James Gee, John R. Gladding, Louis W. Arnold, and Samuel L. Peck. On Aug. 13, 1892, the charter was entered as a matter of record in the office of the Secretary of the Commonwealth at Richmond.

A change was later made in the arrangement to have Mr. Neil Mathieson supervise the building of the plant, when his son, Mr. Thomas T. Mathieson, was designated to take his place. This being agreeable to the interests concerned, a small staff of assistants who were formerly employed at the Wildnes plant accompanied Mr. Mathieson to this country, arriving Jan. 12, 1893. The newly formed Mathieson Alkali Works having taken over the property of the Holston Salt and Plaster Company, building operations were begun very soon after they reached Saltville and the Valley was the scene of busy construction activities from this time on for several years.

The site chosen for the plant was the southeastern bank of the North Fork of the Holston about a mile and a half from the location of the Norfolk and Western depot at that time. Active construction work was begun in the late fall of 1892 and was carried on during 1893 and 1894 under the direction of Mr. Mathieson and Mr. Perry, who represented the interests of the new company. In the summer of 1895, the first product was manufactured on July 4 and since that date the plant as an operating entity has been in continuous motion.

During 1895 negotiations were entered into with Mr. H. Y. Castner for the control in this country of his electrolic cell for the manufacture of caustic soda and as a source of chlorine for making bleaching powder. An option was secured and the construction of a one-unit plant of 250 horsepower was undertaken at Saltville to demonstrate the efficiency of Mr. Castner's cells before closing the deal. This plant was completed and put into operation during the winter of 1896. During the period the plant was demonstrating and proving the efficiency of the new process, Mr. Castner's interests were represented by Mr. Harry Baker, who had been his principal assistant in the development work at Oldbury, England, and the Mathieson Company employed Mr. W. D. Mount as their representative. Both of these men had had training that fitted them admirably for their work.

After the completion of the demonstration work Mr. Baker returned to England and the plant was closed down for a general overhauling, afterwards being placed in operation under Mr. Mount's supervision as a school for training operatives. It had been previously determined that no enlargement of the plant would be undertaken at Saltville, as the location did not seem desirable either from the standpoint of cheap power or proximity to the chief points of consumption of the products. For this reason Niagara Falls was later decided upon as the proper site and the plant there represents an expansion from the original Saltville unit. Important improvements worked out in the experimental plant and later embodied in the development at Niagara Falls include the method of continuous brine saturation. As a matter of interest it may also be noted that the first bleaching powder in this country manufactured on a commercial scale from electrolytic chlorine was produced at Saltville. The Niagara Falls plant of the Mathieson Alkali Works is today one of the largest of its kind in this country.

Mr. Mathieson's contract with the company as general manager in entire charge of operation did not require that he should live continuously in this country, but that after the completion of the construction work and starting the plant operating, he was required to give it only such supervision as in his judgment should be necessary to insure the best results. He left for England in July, 1895, spent the winters of 1895 and 1896 there, and in June, 1896, virtually severed his active connection with the plant. He was succeeded temporarily by Mr. J. V. Johnson as general manager, with Mr. Charles M. Perry his assistant. On July 1, 1897, Mr. J. Findley Wallace was made general manager, but resigned Jan. 1, 1898, Mr. Johnson then serving again temporarily until August, 1898, when Mr. Mount was promoted to this office. In 1900, Mr. James Edwards of New York City succeeded Mr. Arnold as president of the company.

Shortly after the plant had been in operation, it was realized that the original equipment as installed by Mr. Mathieson (being of English design and construction, and based on the then English method of producing soda ash) was inadequate, and the entire plant was practically remodeled and rebuilt. These early changes were all made while Mr. Mount was general superintendent, and Mr. E. M. Davis, superintendent of operations. Mr. Davis, familiarly known as "Teddy," made the statement that the plant made alkali on the same spot as before, but that the remodeled layout bore no resemblance to the old. For this splendid achievement, managed without the loss of a single day's time in the operation of the plant, too much praise cannot be given. Mr. Davis continued in his work until 1909, when he was killed in an automobile accident. Mr. Mount continued in active charge of the operation of the plant as general superintendent and general manager until Nov. 9, 1918, when he severed his connections with the Mathieson organization to become a mechanical and consulting engineer.

In November, 1918, Mr. Mount was succeeded by Mr. J. H. MacMahon. Prior to coming to Saltville Mr. MacMahon was acting general manager of the Niagara operations, and before coming to this country and entering the Mathieson fold he had been actively associated with the large ammonia soda plant in England. With this early experience and ammonia soda training, he was in excellent position to take on the management of the operations at Saltville. Mr. MacMahon, together with the chemical organization, developed a new process for the manufacture of certain barium products, and successfully carried out experiments for establishing a suitable plant to manufacture these products on a commercial scale. Early in 1920 it was discovered that the process could be greatly facilitated by the application of certain improvements. Mr. MacMahon was actively engaged and interested in investigating these possibilities which promised to be of a very material benefit to Saltville. The necessary investigations and research work were accordingly carried on in this connection and in April, 1921, the officials of the company decided to have Mr. MacMahon devote his entire time and energies to this, and on that date he left Saltville to take up his duties at Niagara Falls.

In April, 1921, Mr. Eugene A. Hults was placed in charge of all operations at Saltville. Mr. Hults was born at Perth Amboy, N. J., and completed the high school course there before entering Pratt Institute, where he graduated in electrical engineering. At the age of twelve he entered the employ of S. B. Greacen, engineers and machinists, working after school, on Saturday and during his vacations until his graduation from Pratt Institute. Here he served his time as machinist and acquired the first trade of many which can now be listed along with college degrees after his name. In order to take a special course in chemical engineering, Mr. Hults entered Columbia University and on completion of his work there became connected with the construction department of the General Electric Company. Afterwards he went to the Testing Department of Schenectady, N. Y., where he was later made head of the Induction Motor Testing Department. In 1907, upon the advice of officials of the General Electric Company, he accepted a position with the Universal Portland Cement Company at Buffington, Ind., as assistant electrical engineer and in direct charge of the construction of their new "Number Four" cement plant. Later he was made chief electrical engineer in charge of all electrical operations of both of their large plants. Early in 1910, after resigning his position with the Universal Portland Cement Company, Mr. Hults entered the selling organization of the General Electric Company at Chicago and was given charge of the engineering sales of all electrical equipment to cement plants and chemical industries. He also introduced for the General Electric Company their centrifugal exhausters for blowing engines and installed the first large centrifugal blowing machines at the blast furnace plant of the Pickens-Brown Company at Chicago. In 1914 he resigned his position with the General Electric Company to take charge of the North Iowa Brick and Tile Company at Mason City, Iowa, the largest clay products plant in the state. At this time the company was bankrupt, but in the face of this unfortunate condition Mr. Hults reorganized the plant and put it on a handsome paying basis. This position was sacrificed in December, 1917, when Mr. Hults enlisted in the Air Service Division of our army. The call of his country during the first months of our participation in the World War found him engaged in one of the "essential industries," but it found him also a real

INDUSTRIES

man, ready to serve regardless of a justified exemption. After the signing of the Armistice he was engaged in consulting engineering and organization work in Chicago, and prior to coming to Saltville, was president of the Ceramic Equipment Company, a subsidiary organization of Proctor and Swartz of Philadelphia. In September, 1920, he came to Saltville as assistant to the president to aid the management in its operations, and in December, 1921, he became manager.

Charles E. Wiley, assistant general manager, was born at Emory, Va., in 1872, but came to Saltville when only eighteen months old and liked the town so well that he has been there practically ever since. His early education was received in the local public schools and he continued his studies later at Emory and Henry College. This old institution of learning, which has seen four generations of the Wiley family within its halls, was the reason for the grandfather's coming to this section, he having accepted the presidency of the college in 1848, coming from Baltimore by stagecoach to take over the office he filled for twenty-five years.

William Wiley, father of Charles E. Wiley, was born in Emory, Va., and came to Saltville during the time of the Holston Salt and Plaster Company with whom he served as sales agent. At his death in 1894 the son left college and in October, 1895, started to work for the newly organized Mathieson Alkali Works as a chemist. He was promoted successively to laboratory chemist, operating chemist, assistant process foreman, process foreman, assistant chemical superintendent, and in November, 1909, after the death of Mr. E. M. Davis, chemical superintendent. In 1918 he became assistant manager to Mr. MacMahon and still retains that office with Mr. Hults.

Space demands that with one exception the remaining interesting personnel of the Mathieson Alkali Works be passed by. That one exception is Rufus Kincannon Sanders, born

June 25, 1863, died in 1924. He was the youngest child of a family of sixteen children equally divided into brothers and sisters. His father's house was between the firing lines in the Battle of Saltville and the women and children were within it barricaded behind feather beds and other things. Rufus K. grew up amid the bare hard times following the War, a hard-working, happy country kid, with a farm to keep him busy, fishing and swimming and hunting to play with, and the salt works with their covered wagons and flatboats to keep him interested.

At the age of sixteen he went to work in the mines at Plasterco. His first job for the Mathieson Alkali Works was hauling sand, his first load being the first load for the foundation of the tower house. For over thirty years he was with the company in many capacities, but his distinctive job was that of superintendent of quarries. The getting out of an ample and sure supply of rock is vital to the operation of the plant and it is not always easily done. "R. K." was known to the company as the one and only "old reliable" who never failed on the job. Mr. Sanders was a man of fine business ability, executive force and practical sense. He was also a man of genial, jolly disposition, who could tell a good story and had many a one to tell, who made folks laugh, and whom people liked and respected for the geniality of his disposition and the bigness of his heart. At the time of his death he was a member of the State Highway Commission. He was postmaster for six years, appointed in Cleveland's second term. And he was always identified with public and welfare projects advancing the interest of his town and county.

The Mathieson Company owns and operates a quarry at Rich Valley. An aerial tramway with buckets passing along its wires transports the stone from quarry to plant over some five or six miles. The Culbert quarry at Marion was formerly operated by the Mathieson Company, but the Rich Valley quarry has been developed to supply the full demand and eliminate this long railway haul.

James R. Sparks, former foreman of the Marion quarry, had been connected with the company since he was a water boy when only fourteen years old. During the War he entered the service at Camp Lee and because of his experience in quarry work was sent almost immediately to France. Here he was put in charge of the first crusher used in that country and had under him 500 German prisoners who were used to get out stone for the railroads and highways. After two years of this important work he returned to his old place with Mr. Sanders at the quarry.

The enormous gypsum deposits underlying a great part of Rich Valley were discovered early and were worked on a small scale for fertilizer about the time the county was formed. Before the Civil War various land owners had opened plaster banks from which farmers of this and many other counties would annually haul covered wagon loads. Mr. Alexander Stuart of Wytheville became interested in this plaster business in the fifties, which eventually brought him to Saltville as part owner of the salt works. In 1880 there were four plaster companies operating in the Valley on properties that had been producing more or less commercial plaster for decades. They were the Holston Salt and Plaster Company and the Buena Vista Plaster Company at Saltville and Plasterco, Pearson Plaster Bank at North Holston, and the Buchanan Plaster Bank in the Cove. The last had been opened long before in an attempt to develop a salt operation in the Cove. A shaft eight by ten feet was sunk 592 feet through fine plaster and then struck a saline solution. The salt making idea was abandoned. The first diggings of plaster banks were made on the highest ground where it could be found to avoid water and facilitate the digging. The Pearson bank was opened in the fifties. Great quantities were shipped on flatboats. A great deal was loaded at the banks on covered wagons, either ground or in lumps. The commercial banks would be equipped for grinding the plaster ready for sowing, but some farmers thought to save money by buying in lump and pulverizing it themselves.

In 1907 the Pearson property was purchased by the Southern Gypsum Company, who immediately began the erection of their great plant there and the building of the village of North Holston. The officers of the company were: Dr. F. A. Wilder, president and manager; A. W. Ristine, vice president; C. H. Ewing, secretary and treasurer; E. T. Archer, superintendent of works. The Southern Gypsum Company was succeeded by the Beaver Products Company, incorporated Feb. 4, 1927, with J. Hume Taylor, R. T. Bilisoly, and N. B. Ferebee, all of Norfolk, as officers and directors.

Quarrying of limestone rock has been an important industry in Smyth from the beginning. The rock was first used for building the great stone chimneys and foundation walls of log houses and some of the masonry work was beautifully done. Then some stone houses were built. The old Cullop house on the Lee Highway at Nicks Creek was the first built, and was erected about the close of the Revolution. Tradition says it was built in 1776, a date that is too early to be probable. This old house was a stopping place on the Wilderness Road in tavern and stagecoach days. Mrs. Julia Tevis gives this description of a night spent there at Christmas time, 1822, when she left Abingdon for Wytheville in a stagecoach before daylight on a cold morning with the prospect of "a two day's journey over the rough roads; but we were made of sterner stuff than to dread cold or personal inconvenience. We traveled all day, through a violent snowstorm, over frozen ground and ice-bound torrents, stopping only twice to change horses, ere we reached the old stone tavern where we were to tarry for the night. It was near ten o'clock, the family were all in bed; one little tallow candle burned in the window, casting a feeble light upon the pathway that led to the door standing wide open for the expected stage passengers.

"The cheerlessness of the room we entered was made visible by the flickering rays of a few expiring embers. In the middle of the apartment was a square table, upon which were heaped in pewter dishes, cold beef, fat pork, cabbage, potatoes, with a large dish of cucumber pickles. A brown jug of milk and a show of teacups and saucers intimated arrangements for tea or coffee. My head ached so violently that I turned from the supper table with disgust, and stepped into an adjoining room in search of fire and some place upon which to rest my weary limbs. I threw myself upon what I supposed to be an empty bed, and in doing so awakened squalling children. Rising hastily, and turning toward another, I saw the vision of a red flannel nightcap popping from under the bedclothes, which so frightened me that I flew to the other side of the room, and sunk despairingly into an old armchair, where I remained until my companions had supped, after which we were shown upstairs into a cold room. The feather bed, which I immediately appropriated, was made up like a grave, and surmounted by two little pillows, either of which I might have put into my pocket, and both of which I lost somewhere in the recesses of the bed during the night."

From the earliest days rock was burned for lime and until recent years the crude limekiln was a common feature of Smyth County farms. Mortar made by the old stone masons was sometimes of a hardness and whiteness that defies time. In some old cellars mortar laid over a hundred years ago is as hard as the rocks it binds and so white it appears to have been newly painted.

In 1896, W. F. Culbert, the "Rock Man," came to Smyth and went into the quarrying of limestone on a commercial scale. He soon began supplying chemical limestone to the Mathieson Alkali Works and until the quarries in Rich Valley with adequate bucket lines were developed to eliminate the haul from Marion, he shipped thousands of tons from his Marion quarries to the great chemical plant at Saltville. His firm, W. F. Culbert and Sons, Denny C. and Guy Thurston being the sons, has marketed many a truck and train load of lime, powdered limestone for fertilizer, and crushed stone for railroad ballast, macadam roads, and concrete work.

The Ellis quarries, east of Marion, under the management of E. P. Ellis have produced great quantities of crushed and powdered limestone. Mr. Ellis came to Marion from Tennessee in 1905 to work for the Spruce Lumber Company. In 1915 he opened this quarry and has been engaged in that and the lumber business ever since. During the World War his plant was taken over and run for the government by the Mathieson Alkali Company.

Mr. William Francis Culbert, born in Carter County, Tennessee, has had a varied and interesting career. While a boy on the home farm he furnished iron ore and charcoal to nearby furnaces. When twenty-one he left home to seek his fortune and spent a number of years in railroad construction work at various places in Tennessee, Kentucky, and Southwest Virginia. Then he started for California, but stopped at Tombstone, Ariz., and walked nine miles to get a job in a copper mine. Here he found employment at good wages, but the wild life of the camp did not appeal to him, so after a short time he went on to California, where there was considerable work in railroad construction. He was given charge over about fifty Chinese laborers. They were so treacherous that he found it necessary to carry a revolver for protection. Murder was very common, and conditions exceedingly unpleasant. After a year of this he decided to leave California for the gold and silver mining sections in the Northwest Territory. He went by boat from San Francisco to Portland, Ore., thence by rail to Butte City, Mont. Near here he found work in a gold mine, but shortly afterwards was crushed under a fall of stone and was confined in a hospital about six months. Having spent three years in the West, he returned home and found employment on a railroad construction job in Clinch Valley, Va. It was here that he met Miss Evelyn Jessee of Russell County and was married to her May 28, 1891. Railroad construction work did not, he considered, fit in with married life, so he went from there to Big Stone Gap, Va., where he furnished iron ore and limestone to the iron furnace at that place. This work lasted about four years. From there he moved to Foster Falls, Va., where he engaged in furnishing iron ore to another furnace. But this did not last long. He then returned to Big Stone Gap, where he thought it would be possible to keep the iron furnace in operation, but after a short period it closed. Then he made his last move. From 1896 to the present time he has lived in Smyth County. He at last found a place he felt was unexcelled as a home place for his family.

His business in Smyth County has continued almost uninterrupted from 1896 to the present time. He has in the meantime conducted business in Georgia and Florida, but his home has always been in Smyth County. He would never consider any business opportunities that would in any way interfere with his maintaining his home in Smyth County.

The fine brick clays of Smyth have been used for making brick since the era of brick houses started in the last decade of the eighteenth century. In the first half of the last century a large number of handsome brick houses were erected in the county and the bricks were usually made locally, the owner or contractor either making them or having them made for each project. In the 1890's the Virginia Vitrified Brick and Sewer Company established a large plant and did a good business for several years at Chilhowie. In the 1920's a company with Mr. Maurice Hale as manager began making brick on Staley's Creek. They sold out to the present owners, E. L. Knight and his associates, who are making a good thing of it.

Chapter XII
BANKS

The charter for the Bank of Marion was approved Feb. 11, 1874. The first meeting of the board of directors was held in the counting room of H. B. and D. D. Hull, in Marion, March 17, 1874.

The first officers were:

M. Jackson .... President
G. G. Goodell .... Vice President
J. W. Fell .... Cashier

The first board of directors:

Frank Alexander	John P. Sheffey
D. D. Hull	Jas. H. Gilmer
G. G. Goodell	N. L. Look
Fayette M. McMullin	A. G. Pendleton
Geo. W. Palmer	A. P. Cole

John S. Copenhaver, Clerk

The following have served as officers:

Presidents

M. Jackson	D. D. Hull	E. H. Copenhaver
	W. M. Hull	

Vice Presidents

G. G. Goodell	E. H. Copenhaver
D. D. Hull	R. C. Gwyn
	H. P. Copenhaver

Cashiers

J. W. Fell
H. B. Haller
E. H. Copenhaver

W. B. Jackson
J. W. Sheffey
W. Lynn Copenhaver

(Walter S. Staley was elected cashier but did not serve. John S. Copenhaver became acting cashier.)

Assistant Cashiers

W. B. Jackson
J. W. Sheffey
Geo. H. Miles

A. T. Buchanan
J. R. Collins
Dan M. Buchanan

Bookkeepers

W. M. Hull
J. W. Sheffey
J. T. Brosius

A. C. Hankla
A. T. Buchanan
J. R. Collins

Thomas Ewald

Stenographers

Beatrice Steffey
Mary Sue Robinson (Funk)

Louise Tilley
Bessie Wolfe

The following stockholders have served as directors:

Frank Alexander
D. D. Hull
G. G. Goodell
Fayette McMullin
Geo. W. Palmer
John P. Sheffey
Jas. H. Gilmer
N. L. Look
A. G. Pendleton
A. P. Cole

J. B. Rhea
Geo. E. Penn
R. J. Haller
J. W. Fell
B. F. Buchanan
V. S. Morgan
S. D. Jones
C. L. Clark
W. M. Hull
R. C. Gwyn
Geo. H. Miles

Samuel Wilkerson
Thomas H. Thurman
John S. Copenhaver
M. Jackson
John S. Apperson
H. P. Copenhaver
E. H. Copenhaver
H. L. Morgan
W. B. Jackson
J. W. Sheffey

BANKS

Present board of directors:

W. M. Hull	W. B. Jackson
E. H. Copenhaver	Q. A. Calhoun
Walter E. Johnston	W. Lynn Copenhaver
George F. Cook	E. K. Coyner
H. P. Copenhaver	J. Herman Buchanan

Present officers and employees:

W. M. Hull	President
H. P. Copenhaver	Vice President
W. Lynn Copenhaver	Cashier
J. R. Collins	Assistant Cashier
Dan M. Buchanan	Assistant Cashier
Thomas S. Ewald	Bookkeeper
Bessie Wolfe	Stenographer
Present Capital	$61,650
Present Surplus	63,350
Undivided Profits including Reserves	53,000

The Marion National Bank was organized in 1903 with a capital stock of $25,000.

The first officers were:

George W. Richardson	President
W. F. Culbert	Vice President
Otis L. Williams	Cashier
W. P. Francis	Assistant Cashier

The first board of directors:

W. F. Culbert	B. H. Baylor	John M. Gwyn
Geo. W. Richardson	H. B. Staley	Geo. M. Atkins
L. P. Collins	W. L. Lincoln	Jno. A. Groseclose

On Feb. 15, 1907, George W. Richardson, President, and W. F. Culbert, Vice President, resigned and W. L. Lincoln was elected President and B. H. Baylor, Vice President. The following shareholders have served as directors:

    W. P. Francis*   R. Brittain Peery*
    Jno. A. Groseclose*   B. F. Buchanan*
    J. G. Fry   W. E. Dungan
    W. H. Teas*   F. M. Young*
            R. M. Richardson

Since the bank's organization the following have served as cashiers:

J. G. Fry, now Assistant Reserve Agent of Federal Reserve Bank Richmond, Va.
T. R. Keys, now President of Erwin National Bank, Erwin, Tenn.

Assistant Cashiers:
John A. Groseclose*
A. D. Brockman, now Vice President and Cashier of First National Bank, Kingsport, Tenn.
S. M. Danewood, present address and occupation unknown.

Others who have served as tellers and bookkeepers:
H. P. Gillespie, now Assistant Vice President of First and Merchants National Bank, Richmond, Va.
G. A. Wheeler,* J. V. Copenhaver, Miss Charmie Williams, and Mrs. Roxie Wolfe.

The present board of directors:

    R. A. Anderson   J. Arthur Peery
    J. D. Buchanan   T. E. King
    J. C. Campbell   W. L. Lincoln
    E. M. Copenhaver   H. B. Staley
    Frank Copenhaver   James D. Tate
            R. T. Greer

* Deceased.

BANKS

The present officers and employees are:

James D. Tate .... Chairman of the Board
W. L. Lincoln .... President
H. B. Staley .... Vice President
T. E. King .... Vice President and Cashier
W. A. Wolfe .... Assistant Cashier
H. Frank Peery .... Assistant Cashier
George F. Britton .... Teller
L. P. Haywood .... Bookkeeper
Lloyd Currin .... Bookkeeper
Miss Ruth Maiden .... Stenographer

Present Capital ....$ 135,000
Present Surplus 135,000
Undivided Profits and Reserve 45,000
Total Resources 1,550,000

The First National Bank of Saltville, Virginia

($25,000 Capital Stock)

The Saltville Bank was organized in 1903 with $25,000 capital stock.

Presidents	Vice Presidents
W. W. George....1903–1913	J. D. Buchanan....1903–1919
J. S. Geotchius....1913–1921	R. K. Sanders.....1919–1921
R. K. Sanders....1921–1924	J. L. Early.......1921–1924
J. L. Early.......1924–1926	Jno. R. George....1924–1926
Jno. R. George....1926–1931	Clyde Crafts 1926–
Chas. E. Wiley....1931–	

Cashiers	Assistant Cashiers
H. C. Cecil.......1903–1906	C. M. Shannon....1908–1927
T. J. Harris......1906–1920	James McCarty ...1926–
Clyde Crafts......1920–	

The following men were directors when bank was organized in 1903: W. W. George, R. K. Sanders, J. S. Geotchius, H. L. Morgan, T. W. Buchanan, J. A. Gollehon, J. M. Gass, W. D. Mount, J. H. Dunkley, T. T. Taylor and T. J. Hughes.

1904:
  V. M. Scott
1905:
  Jno. R. George
1908:
  A. H. Finks
  Frank A. Wilder
1909:
  H. C. Chapman
1910:
  W. S. Jennings
  W. M. McCready
  W. B. Porterfield
1912:
  J. L. Early
1915:
  J. L. Easter

1918:
  E. E. Routh
1922:
  E. J. Conrad
  J. H. MacMahon
  C. E. Wiley
1923:
  B. F. Buchanan
1926:
  E. A. Hults
1928:
  Clyde Crafts
  G. J. Wallinger
1931:
  J. D. Tate
  H. A. Reutschi

Reorganized as the First National Bank in 1918 with $50,-000 capital stock.

THE SALTVILLE SAVINGS BANK

(Founded 1920)

T. K. McKee .... President
J. S. Roberts .... Vice President
R. M. Shannon, to 1932 .... Cashier
Jackson Buchanan, 1924 .... Assistant Cashier

BANKS

Directors

T. K. McKee
J. S. Roberts, deceased
J. F. Watson
F. B. Henry, resigned
M. S. Durham, resigned
J. M. Goss, resigned
E. A. Holmes,
   Vice President
R. W. Holmes

Geo. W. DeBusk,
   Vice President
W. W. Buchanan
T. E. King, resigned
A. W. Ristine
R. M. Shannon, Active
   Vice President, 1932
R. E. Hughes

J. Archie Buchanan, Cashier, 1932

Capital ....$ 40,000
Surplus 12,000
Total Resources 276,000

The National Bank of Chilhowie
(Organized June 12, 1907)

Officers

Dr. R. F. Young .... President
L. M. Cole .... Vice President
W. E. Umbarger .... Cashier

Directors

H. L. Bonham
A. C. Beatie
L. M. Cole
E. H. Copenhaver
J. W. Heninger
Martin Houston
A. J. Huff

W. W. Hurt
Walter Kelly
C. R. Mercer
Dr. T. K. McKee
F. L. Sanders
R. W. Scott
Jos. N. Umbarger

Dr. R. F. Young

On Jan. 11, 1910, Dr. R. F. Young, resigned as president and E. H. Copenhaver was elected.

On March 2, 1914, E. H. Copenhaver resigned as president, and L. M. Cole was elected to serve remainder of this term, and W. H. Copenhaver was elected vice president. On January 12, 1915, I. M. Cole resigned as president, and W. H. Copenhaver was elected to succeed Mr. Cole, and L. M. Cole was elected vice president.

On March 6, 1920, W. E. Umbarger resigned as cashier, and G. P. Cox was elected to succeed Mr. Umbarger, and S. A. Cole was elected assistant cashier.

On Jan. 12, 1932, L. M. Cole resigned as vice president, and J. T. Frazier, Jr., was elected to succeed Mr. Cole.

The present officers are as follows:

W. H. Copenhaver .... President
J. T. Frazier, Jr. .... Vice President
G. P. Cox .... Cashier
S. A. Cole .... Assistant Cashier

Directors

A. C. Beatie	W. H. Copenhaver
H. L. Bonham	W. T. Smith
Lee M. Cole, Jr.	J. E. McSpadden
S. A. Cole	W. J. Daly
G. P. Cox	J. T. Frazier, Jr.

Capital .... $ 25,000
Surplus 25,000
Undivided Profits and Reserve 7,500
Total Resources 430,000

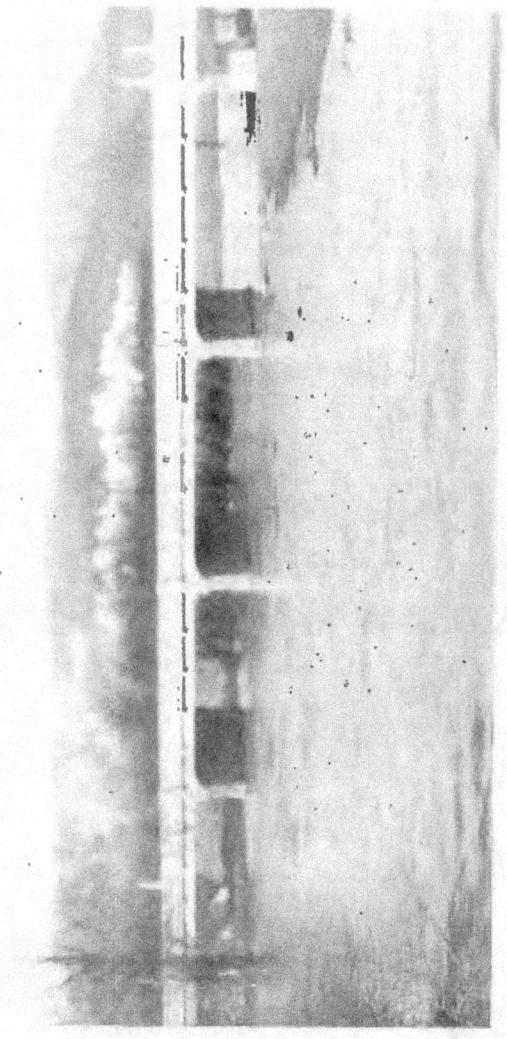

Memorial Bridge at Seven Mile Ford

CHAPTER XIII

TRANSPORTATION

The first roads in Smyth County were made by the buffalo, and that the buffalo were natural engineers is attested by the fact that many of the main roads today follow the old buffalo trails with minor variations. Indians used these paths that the great beasts had marked out, and traders to the Indians followed then, horseback and afoot. The first surveyors and explorers rode them, riding with an extra horse or so laden with what goods and implements they cared to bring along. The early settlers brought in their goods secured on the backs of horses by means of pack saddles made of tree branches that forked at an angle and in a shape to fit a horse's back. These pack saddle forks were keenly sought for in the woods and those of proper shape and strength were highly prized. Sleds such as those still occasionally used on some mountain farms were also employed. Rude wagons and ox carts were also built by the first settlers but were rare.

The first wagon road was built while the country was uninhabited between the running out of the first comers by the Indians and the beginning of permanent settlement with the coming of the Campbells, when Col. William Byrd in command of an expedition to relieve Fort Loudon in the distant Cherokee country of Tennessee exasperated the frontier militiamen by making them cut out a wagon road from Fort Chiswell to the Long Island of Holston. Little more would have been done than cutting out the trees and brush along the buffalo trail, and it was probably pretty well grown up in brush again when John and Arthur Campbell came to Royal Oak in 1766.

Some of the early road orders are: Botetourt Court, Feb. 14, 1770, Arthur Campbell made surveyor from Stalnaker's near Chilhowie to the Royal Oak and James Davis from the Royal Oak to Davis' Valley; then on Jan. 5, 1773, Fincastle County Court appointed Arthur Bowen overseer of the road from the lower end of the Royal Oak to Alexander Wiley's and Alexander Wiley from his house to William Davis'; on May 4, 1774, Fincastle County Court ordered that John Hays, James Hays, Archibald Buchanan, and Robert Davis view the nighest and best way for a road from Rich Valley over the mountain by Robert Davis' unto the leading road from Holston; and on the sixth day of December, 1774, Fincastle County Court directed a road to be cut from Arthur Campbell's to the Blue Spring by way of the Rye Bottom and from Arthur Campbell's mill to Archibald Buchanan's on the North Fork. Other orders in the Fincastle courts are: "that William Edmiston, George Adams, John Beaty, Joseph Drake, David Snodgrass and James Kincannon, or any three of them, being first sworn, do view the nighest and best way from the Town House (now in Smyth County, Va.) to the Eighteen Mile creek (now Abingdon), and report."

It seems that there was some contention among the settlers on Holston as to the location of this road; for, on the 2nd day of March, 1773, the above order was set aside by the court, and on that day it was ordered that John Hays, Benjamin Logan, William Campbell, Arthur Bowen and Thomas Ramsey, or any three of them, being first sworn, do view the several ways proposed for said road and make a report of the conveniences and inconveniences attending the same. The viewers thus appointed made their report to the County Court on July 6, 1773, recommending that the lower road be established, which report was confirmed and the road established,

TRANSPORTATION 221

and William Campbell, William Edmiston and James Bryan were appointed overseers of the said road.

On May 2, 1773, that Robert Davis, Alexander Wylie, Robert Buchanan, and Hugh Gallion, any three of whom being duly sworn, do view the nighest way from James Davis' (at the head spring of the Middle Fork of the Holston) to James Catherine's (near the head spring of the South Fork of the Holston), but the records of Fincastle fail to show that this road was established.

On March 3, 1773, James McCarthy, Matthew Mounts, John Smith, Thomas Byrd, Nathan Richerson and Peter Lee, or any three of them, being first sworn, were ordered to view the nighest and best way from the Town House on Holston to Castle's Woods on Clinch river, and make report.

The commissioners made their report on July 6, 1773, and the road was partially established, beginning at John Dunkin's in Elk Garden thence over the mountains to Poor Valley, about five miles to the westward of the old path, and from thence by the Big Lick, through Lyon's Gap to the Town House.

On March 2, 1773, the court directed John Maxwell, Robert Allison and Robert Campbell, or any three of them to view the nighest and best way from Catherine's Mill to Charles Allison's, and so on to Sinclair's Bottom, and report.

On July 6, 1773, the commissioners reported, and the court directed a road to be established from Catherine's Mill to Charles Allison's house on the condition that the people on the South Fork or any others on same road who think it useful, to cut the same themselves.

On the same day the court ordered that William Edmiston, Robert Edmiston, Alexander McNutt, Robert Buchanan, and John Edmiston, any three of whom may act, do view a road from Charles Allison's house down the South Fork to Robert Edmiston's house and report.

At the first court of Smyth County in 1832, the following road overseers were appointed, which indicates the roads in the county and also people living along them:

It is ordered that William Love be appointed over-seer of the public road leading from the Branch at John Thompson's to the seven mile ford; and that he with the list of tytheables to be furnished him by Abram B. Trigg gentlemen keep the same in legal repair.

Others named were: Henry Neaff from Seven Mile Ford to Arthur M. Bowen's; Jacob Blessing, from Arthur M. Bowen's to the creek at the widow Byars'; James Johnston, from the branch of the widow Byars' to the branch west of Mitchell Scott's; Henry Copenhafer from the branch west of Mitchell Scott's to the branch at Isaac Collins'; Isaac Collins, from the branch at Isaac Collins' to the crossing of the river near Henry F. Shugart's; George Killinger, from the ford of the river near Henry F. Shugart's to the Royal Oak ford; Daniel Hoofnogle, from the Royal Oak ford to the house of Joseph Atkins to Acre's branch; Thompason Atkins, from Acre's branch to the Branch of Thomas Crow's; George W. Davis from the Branch at Thomas Crow's to Pleasant Hill; Henry Snavely from Pleasant Hill to the county line; which carried the Lee Highway through the county. A journey over this road in the eighteen twenties is thus described:

We left Wytheville in the early dawn of a most beautiful Summer morning. It was a journey of only sixty miles to Abingdon, but it would take two days to accomplish it. We wended our way slowly over a broken mountain road which had never been graded—a macademized turnpike was unknown. We traveled in an old-fashioned nine seated stage coach, drawn by four horses changed at long intervals. We lunched and rested at mid-day beneath the spreading trees, whose interwoven branches made network of the dark blue light of day. Water from a gushing stream, the depth of whose source defied the heat of Summer, quenched our thirst, while we inhaled the fragrance of rock-hung flowers, the sweet brier and the health-inspiring pine.

For the road to the valley through Lyons Gap, Peter Talbert, from the forks of the main road at Mrs. Saunders' to the branch at Hughes; John Hughes, from the branch at Hughes to the top of Walker's Mountain; John S. White, from the top of Walker's Mountain to the fork of the valley.

In Rich Valley: Andrew Shannon, from the county line to Wilson Buchanan's; John Buchanan, from Wilson Buchanan's to Beaver Creek; Jeremiah Spratt, from Beaver Creek to Mrs. McCarty's Branch; James Smith, from the county line at the Salt Works to the Cedar Branch; Jacob Lyon, from Cedar Branch to the deep ford near the widow Poston's; Jeremiah Ayeres, from the widow Poston's to the Laurel forks; Andrew Smith, Laurel fork to the mouth of Cove Creek; Calvin McCarty, the mouth of Cove Creek to the first ford of the Creek above Lamie's meadow; Robert Buchanan, the first ford of the Creek above Lamie's meadow to Robert Buchanan; Greenbury Patrick, from Robert Buchanan's to Zadoc Sexton's house; Zadoc Sexton, from Zadoc Sexton's house to the foot of the Yellow Hill; Benjamin F. Davis from Yellow Hill to the county line; John M. Tate overseer of the road from the ford of the river at the mouth of Cove Creek to the valley road near John Shannon's.

Moses Rector was overseer of the road from Jeremiah C. Gardner's by the way of the Sulphur Springs to the salt works and John Pierce, from the forks of the road near the house of John Pierce to Preston's mill.

In Rye Valley: Henry Cryder, from the county line in the Rye Valley to the Blue Spring; John Scott senior, from the Blue Spring to the western foot of the Wharf Hill; Ezekial James, Wharf Hill to the first ford of the river west of Nichol's Iron Works; Samuel Kincannon, west of Nichol's Iron Works to Mrs. Matthews'; Ryland Roland, from Mrs. Matthews' to the ford of the river near Thomas Thomas'; George Reed from the ford of the river near Thomas Thomas' to the forks of the road east of John Anderson's; Thomas Allan, from the forks of the road east of John Anderson's to the seven mile ford; Joseph Brown overseer of the road from the forks of the road east of John Anderson's to the main stage road at Blessings; Andrew Bucahnan overseer of the road from the forks of the river on the south side of the south fork near Thomas Thomas' to Major Joseph Thomas; Sampson Cole, from Major Joseph Thomas' to St. Clair's Bottom meeting house; John Edmonston from St. Clair's Bottom meeting house to the county lines near Coles' mill; William Scott, from the county line at Keesley's mill to the Blue Spring road; Andrew Lasley, the road from the forks of the lead mine and Grayson road east of the Blue Spring to the Grayson line.

Mr. L. P. Summers in his *History* says:

On the twenty-eighth of January, 1846, the General Assembly of Virginia incorporated the Southwestern Turnpike road, which road was to be a macadamized road from Salem, Virginia, by the way of Christiansburg, Newbern, Wytheville, Marion, Abingdon to the Tennessee line, and appropriated seventy-five thousand dollars to carry into effect the object of the act.

The said road was to be graded to a width not less than twenty-four feet, and to be macadamized to a width not less than twenty-two feet.

This act provided for the condemnation of the lands over which the road was to pass, said road to be, at no point, on a grade exceeding three degrees.

The construction of this road was begun during the same year and the work upon the road was carried on with commendable speed until the year 1848.

In January of this year, the road had been completed as far as Wytheville, and there was an urgent demand for its immediate completion to the Tennessee line, by the citizens living in the counties of Smyth, Wythe, Washington, and Scott, and the General Assembly on the seventeenth of January, 1848, appropriated the sum of three hundred thousand dollars to complete said road, not exceeding seventy-five thousand dollars of said sum to be expended in any one year.

Fifty thousand dollars of the public money appropriated

for the construction of this road was paid to William L. Lewis, the contractor, but for some reason, which cannot now be explained, the work of constructing said road was delayed, and but little progress was made until the year 1851, when it was completed to Seven Mile Ford.

The failure to complete this road has been attributed to different causes, among the number being:

First. The anticipated construction of the Virginia and Tennessee Railroad.

Second. The principles actuating Governor Johnson and his advisors, which principles were opposed to internal improvements by the Commonwealth and favored a strict construction of the Constitution of the Commonwealth.

Third. The indisposition of the representatives from Eastern Virginia to interest themselves in the welfare of Western Virginia.

In 1851 a resolution introduced by a delegate from eastern Virginia requiring the Board of Public Works to suspend further construction of the Southwestern Turnpike was passed by the legislature, and no work was done on it west of Seven Mile Ford.

"Resolved, by the General Assembly, That the Board of Public Works be and they are hereby authorized and required to suspend the further construction of the Southwestern Turnpike road, except so much as may be necessary to finish any intermediate sections between the eastern part of said road which has been finished, and the extreme western part of said road upon which the contractors may have commenced work."

This substitute was eloquently and energetically opposed by Colonels Hopkins and Imboden, but was adopted by a vote of fifty-two to forty-four, and the friends of the road were unable to obtain a reconsideration of the vote.

A number of unsuccessful efforts were made by the friends of this road to have work on the same resumed, but without success.

The newspapers of Abingdon charged that Governor Johnson and the Board of Public Works were responsible for the suspension of work upon this road, and Governor Floyd was severely censured for his course in the matter. The road was never completed west of Seven Mile Ford, and while Southwest Virginia and Washington County have had to bear their portion of the great public debt created for public improvements previous to 1860, they have received no benefit therefrom.

This is one of the historic roads of the state from the days of the buffalo and Indian. After the traders with packs of wares for Indian traffic on their pack horses, and after Patton, Buchanan, Walker, and other explorers, came Byrd's military expedition. Then came the sleds, creaking wagons, and oxcarts. There followed the thousands pushing westward over the Wilderness Road afoot, in wagons, oxcarts, and pack horse trains to people Kentucky and Tennessee. Then the colorful stage coach and the picturesque Conestoga wagon came, hauling passengers and goods from Nashville to Philadelphia. The covered wagon of varied pattern continued as an important freight hauler in Smyth until the gasoline truck was introduced.

Since 1920 road building has received a tremendous impetus in state and nation, and Smyth County has felt the impetus. There has been great improvement in roads over the whole county. The state has completed the Lee Highway and is constantly improving this great road. Also the state has put into its primary highway system the road from Troutdale, down Comer's Creek and the South Fork to the Washington line, from the Grayson line near Troutdale through Marion, towards Chatham to near the top of Walker's Mountain; and from the Washington line, through Saltville and Broadford, up Poor Valley to the Tazewell line. The county roads have been greatly improved by the Board of Supervisors under the chairmanship of Mr. June Eller. Supervisors C. B. Rouse, in Rye Valley, and Samuel and W. W.

Buchanan in Rich Valley have done much for better roads in their respective districts.

Flat boats on the North Fork carried a great deal of freight and along about 1820 the State Board of Public Works gave serious consideration to developing a water freight route from New River up Walker's Creek, with a wagon portage and then down the North Fork of Holston.

The Virginia and Tennessee Railroad was chartered in 1849, and soon thereafter numerous railroad meetings were held to arouse interest and secure subscriptions for its building. In October, 1851, a great railroad meeting was held in Abingdon. The following delegates from Smyth County attended this boosters' meeting: "James F. Pendleton, Thomas L. Poston, James Saunders, Dr. Thomas M. Tate, H. D. Poston, Esq., Meade E. Smythe, Richard Haller, John C. Poston, William T. Campbell, E. S. Watons, Esq., Dr. William T. Thurman, William Porter, Esq., Robert Houston, Esq., A. H. Campbell, James C. Smythe, Dr. Robert Thurman, John C. Rogers, James Campbell, John Campbell, Thomas H. Thurman, Colonel Hiram A. Greever, John H. Barton, John Pride, and Robert Goolsby."

On the twentieth of September, 1850, a railroad meeting was held at Elizabeth Chapel at Saltville, having for its object the election of delegates to a railroad convention to be held at Jeffersonville, on the seventeenth of October. The object of this convention was to have the Virginia and Tennessee railroad located from New River along Walker's Creek and Holston Valley, passing Saltville. The proceedings of said meeting were as follows:

On motion, Major A. B. Trigg was called to the chair and William P. Bishop and William King were appointed secretaries.

The object of the meeting was explained by Dr. Robert Thurman, and the following-named persons appointed to report resolutions for the action of the meeting: Dr. Alex. McCall, Major Thomas Tate, Dr. Robert Thurman, H. D. Poston, Theo. G. Pearson, D. M. Hunter and John Roberts.

The Committee retired and afterwards reported the following resolutions which were unanimously adopted:

Resolved, That it is expedient for the carrying out of the objects of this meeting that the committee hereby appointed shall solicit the concurrent support of the people of Russell, Tazewell, Washington, Smyth, Wythe, Mercer, Giles, Boone, Monroe, Logan, Wyonming, Kanawha, Fayette, and Greenbrier counties, in behalf of obtaining a survey for the Virginia and Tennessee railroad from New river along Walker's creek and Holston Valley, passing the Gypsum bank and Salt Works to the Tennessee line for intersection with the Tennessee railroad at the most convenient point.

Resolved, That a general meeting of the citizens of the aforesaid counties and others interested be held on the 17th day of October next, at Tazewell Courthouse, in aid of the aforesaid objects.

Resolved, That the following-named persons be appointed delegates to said convention: Tobias Smyth, James Kelly, W. W. Harvey, James McNew, J. M. Ropp, Wyndham Robertson, Alex. McCall, D. M. Hunter, Thos. L. Preston, James T. Morehead, Robert Thurman, James Saunders, T. G. Pearson, H. D. Poston, Whitley Fullen, O. H. Ward, John Roberts, Charles C. Taylor, Charles C. Campbell, Jerome Campbell, Jezrell Harman, P. C. Buchanan, Jr., Joseph Sexton, A. H. Cox, James Cox, Ransom Tilson, Martin Davis, William P. Milner, C. F. McDonald, G. W. Buchanan, John B. Tate, C. J. Shannon, P. C. Buchanan, Sr., and J. F. Baugh.

The railroad with branch line to Saltville was built through the county in 1856. Sundry unsuccessful attempts were subsequently made to have the line from Glade Spring extended up the valley to Tazewell.

On June 17, 1870, the Virginia and Tennessee was merged with other companies holding sections from Lynchburg to Norfolk to form the Atlantic, Mississippi, and Ohio Railroad, which in turn became the Norfolk and Western on April 4, 1881.

When the Cripple Creek line was built there were lively prospects of having it run on through Rye Valley and down the South Fork to reunite with the main line, but they came to naught.

The Marion and Rye Valley Railway Company promoted mainly through initiative of Dr. J. S. Apperson and George W. Miles, men of vision, was chartered in the year 1891, and in 1893 built for about six miles to haul manganese ore out of Currin Valley. By the energy and indomitable will of George W. Miles, it was extended in 1896 to Sugar Grove to form a junction with the Virginia-Southern which was built about the same time by J. W. Moltz and associates to develop resources in western Grayson. The two companies were placed under one management. P. S. Swain of New York was the first president. He was succeeded by B. F. Buchanan who served for several years and was succeeded by George W. Miles who held the office until 1905 when the United States Lumber Company purchased the properties, and operated them with J. C. Campbell as president until they wound up their lumber business and sold the railroads.

After that the road from Marion to Troutdale was operated as a passenger and freight carrier until the fall of 1931 when the corporation commission allowed suspension of operations.

Mr. George W. Miles was one of the great business men of Smyth. Mr. C. C. Lincoln and others who were close to him have expressed the opinion that his untimely death set Southwest Virginia's business development back at least twenty years.

Mr. George W. Miles, Jr., son of Rev. George W. Miles, was born at Rheatown, Tenn., Jan. 19, 1861, on Gen. R. E. Lee's birthday and in the first year of the War between the

States. His career was brilliant and his death in the prime of life, February, 1905, was calamitous to Smyth County and Southwest Virginia.

Much of his boyhood and young manhood was spent in Marion. He graduated from Emory and Henry College and the University of Virgina, being an intimate friend at the University of his Marion schoolmates B. Frank Buchanan and John Stuart, with them belonging to the Phi Delta Theta Greek letter fraternity. From 1882 to 1892 he was professor of Greek, English, and other subjects at Emory and Henry.

On Dec. 23, 1884, he was married to Miss Martha E. Morgan, daughter of Vincent Morgan of Marion. Frank Buchanan and John Stuart were the only groomsmen at the wedding. Mr. and Mrs. Miles spent their summers at the old Morgan home in Marion and their three children were born there. Vincent M. is now a distinguished lawyer of Fort Smith, Arkansas, and the leading candidate for the Democratic nomination for United States Senator from Arkansas. George Holland has made his home in Marion, engaging in farming, stock raising, and in the insurance business. Mary married Stuart B. Campbell of Wytheville and lives at "Loretta" the beautiful old Stuart and Campbell home of that town. Mr. Miles' ambitious spirit led him to resign the professorship at Emory and Henry to launch out on an educational venture of his own, and the remaining thirteen years of his life were crowded with achievement. He founded the St. Albans School for boys, erecting the buildings on a beautiful site above New River just opposite Radford and operated this school with brilliant success for ten years. Radford was then a booming young city with possibilities unlimited in the visions of its promoters, and George Miles found himself in his element. He at once became a leader in the building of Radford. Acquiring control of the water, street railway and electric power works, he developed them

TRANSPORTATION 231

into splendid properties with his dam on Little River. He built a short railroad line from Radford up Little River. In 1893 he and Dr. J. S. Apperson pushed through the building of the railroad from Marion six miles up to Currin Valley. Then he carried this line on over to Rye Valley. In 1904 he was offered a partnership in the firm of Chapman and Company of New York City, which would have enabled him to command all the capital needed for the far-reaching projects evolved in his busy creative brain for the development of resources in Smyth and other Southwest Virginia counties. While making his arrangements to remove to New York he fell a victim to cancer of the liver and died in a Richmond hospital.

He was a valued member of the Board of Visitors of the University of Virginia, and proposed and carried through that body the plan to place a president at the head of the University. As a member of the committee to select a president his choice was Professor Woodrow Wilson of Princeton and he had a very extended correspondence with Dr. Wilson before that gentleman finally decided that he would not accept the office. Then came developments, entirely unthought of by him, which led to the great disappointment of his life. He and Mrs. Miles attended a celebration in honor of Col. William E. Peters when that veteran retired from the active duties of the Latin chair in the University. At this celebration Mr. Miles made a speech that tremendously impressed his hearers. The afternoon of the same day he attended a meeting of the Board of Visitors where a committee was awaiting him with a startling proposal that he accept the presidency of the University. The idea having never before occurred to him, he could give no answer but asked for time to consider it, the members of the board then present urging it upon him. One of them, Col. Joseph Bryan, later went for a long walk with him and expressed the hope that he would find his way clear to accept the position, saying that in his opinion the only possible objection would be that Mr. Miles might have a greater future in the work he was then doing than the presidency of the University could offer. Colonel Bryan remained his staunch supporter, but the Colonel's son, John Stewart Bryan, an alumnus of the University and editor of the Richmond *Times-Dispatch* came out against him, threw the weight of his paper into the scale, and stimulated opposition to him among the alumni. Opposition developed in the faculty and in the Board of Visitors. Mr. Miles, hesitant before, was aroused by the challenge of opposition and threw his whole soul into the tense fight to win the presidency. Dr. Edwin A. Alderman was elected by a majority vote of the Board.

Mr. Miles was a man of persuasive power who managed boys and men. He persuaded the Virginia Iron, Coal and Coke Company to move their offices from Bristol to Radford. He persuaded the government of Virginia to put a normal school at Radford. He persuaded Mr. J. C. Campbell to build his band mill at Marion instead of Troutdale.

When building his railroad across the mountain to Rye Valley he ran out of money and persuaded the workmen to stay on the job without pay until he found the money to pay them. Mr. Robert Ward of Sugar Grove says that once a banker from Lynchburg whom Mr. Miles had persuaded to invest heavily in this road came out to look it over. Ward took him across the mountain to Sugar Grove by muleback. It was a cold sleety day and the farther they went the madder he got and the sicker of the whole business. He told Mr. Ward that his money was gone and he would never sink another dollar in the made-up enterprise. Ward on their return to Marion reported to Miles who said he just had to have some more money out of that man. He got on the train and went to Lynchburg and came back with thirty thousand dollars of the banker's money. Some years later Mr. Ward saw that banker and said to him: "Why is it that you told me you would not put another dollar in this road and then turned right around and let George Miles have thirty thousand dollars?"

"Because," he answered, "George Miles is smarter than I am. He got on the train with me that night and persuaded me. George Miles can persuade almost anybody into almost anything he wants. Well, I am mighty glad he persuaded me, because he was right. This is the best paying investment I ever made."

That was the way with George W. Miles.

The following court orders are cited as of interest in the history of county transportation:

Whereas by an act of the General Assembly of Virginia passed the 26th March 1860, it was provided that the County Courts of Smyth and Tazewell be authorized a majority of all the Justices of said respective Counties being present, to subscribe to so much capital stock of the Jeffersonville Marion & Rye Valley Turnpike Company on behalf of their Counties respectively such sum as to them shall see proper &s and whereas all the justices of the County of Smyth having been summoned for the purpose and a large majority of them being present they by a vote determined to subscribe on behalf of the County of Smyth to the capital stock of the Jeffersonville, Marion and Rye Valley Turnpike Company the sum of $2000 or one hundred shares. And it is further ordered that James W. Sheffey be appointed proxy to represent the interest of said County of Smyth in all general meetings of the stock holders of said Company and with full power and authority to confer said appointment on anyone he may select by letter of attorney to act for said proxy in his absence.

Ordered that Robert A. Richardson be and he is hereby appointed to have horse racks put up on the west side of the public square so that the enclosure will not be damaged by horses &c tied to the fence; and if the person or persons owning the property on the west side of the alley, west of the Court house lot refuse to put up the horse rack as above specified, according to an agreement formerly made by which a portion of the public square was thrown into said alley, then the said Richardson shall have the fence on the west side of the Courthouse Square let out on the line corresponding with the Alley on the South side of the Street.

It appearing to the Court that The Rail Road, which "The Southwestern Virginia Mining Smelting and transportation Company are authorized by 'Act of assembly of the 19th Dec. 1866,' to construct from same point at or near Kings Saltworks, so as to connect with the Virginia and Tennessee Railroad running to that point, and thence in an eastwardly direction through the Valley between little Bushy and Walker's big mountains to Sharon, and from thence in the same direction down Walker's Creek valley to the confluence of Walker's big and little Creeks, and from thence the best practical route to the Virginia and Tennessee Railroad at or near Dublin Depot, passing through the Counties of Smyth, Bland & Giles and perhaps a portion of Pulaski," is likely to be beneficial to the county of Smyth. The Court doth order that a Poll be opened Saturday the 12d day of October next, at the several election permits in said County of Smyth for the purpose of "taking the sense of the persons qualified to vote for members of the General Assembly," on the question whether the Court of said County, on behalf of said County, shall subscribe a sum not exceeding $25,000—to the stock of said Company.

It being represented to this Court that the Engineers on the Va. & Tenn. R. Road when approaching Marion Depot from the West are in the habit of giving the signal whistle, as they come out of the Cut west of Wm. A. Jones' house and that this habit is dangerous to the public travel on the McAdam Road, at that point than any others, and that serious accidents have happened in consequence of that habit, Therefore the Court requests that the Superintendent direct its Engineers not to give Signal until they pass the house of Wm. A. Jones.

Chapter XIV

THE WAR BETWEEN THE STATES

EARLY rumblings of impending war are reflected in court records of 1860. In December of that year, six squads of patrols were used to keep order in the county. They were to serve a term of three months. The captains of these patrols were A. T. Starritt, Henry C. Patrick, C. W. Beattie, E. A. Scott, Geo. W. Davis, C. J. Gregory, Robert H. Hubble, and James T. Porter. The privates were John Byars, E. L. Roberts, Augustus O. Sanders, Alec Gollehon, John L. Shannon, Jr., John A. Sayers, Alec Whittaker, John W. Roberts, A. J. Talbot, James Harmon, Wm. Gillespie, Charles Sexton, Francis J. White, Clayton Hubble, Geo. W. Buchanan, Samuel A. Buchanan, Geo. Harmon, Jr., Reece Davis, James Greever, John L. Sanders, James M. Rector, Andrew J. Sanders, Stephen Walker, Levi C. Bishop, Jasper Grinstead, A. J. Copenhaver, John Rouse, William Copenhaver, Marvin Tilson, Anderson Wolfe, Geo. J. Wheeler, Joseph Umberger, Clayborn M. Byars, William Thurman, Isaac C. Anderson, Martin Roan, Robert C. Green, J. M. Fuller, D. D. Hull, A. G. Copenhaver, John L. Copenhaver, Charles W. Venable, E. F. Bates, Henry Groseclose, Geo. W. Musser, Robert Buchanan, George W. Aker, Jacob Castle, William A. Mays, Samuel Wilkinson, James A. Scott, John T. Nelson, John M. Williams, Levi M. Scott, William C. Jones, Rufus James, and Larvis Sheets.

At the June term of Court the following order was entered:

Ordered that the patrols heretofore appointed by this court and those appointed at this term of said Court be and the same is hereby established as the regular police of Smyth County under the provision of an ordinance of the Virginia Convention passed the 1st of May 1861. For the prevention and punishment of offences against the Commonwealth of Virginia, where upon the following persons appeared in Court and severally took the oaths prescribed by said ordinance.

Captains—G. W. Henderlite, Geo. Hubbard, William F. Hurst, James H. Gilmore, P. J. Gregory, William D. Wilmore, R. G. Owry, and John S. Copenhaver, John Irons, James M. Pruner, E. L. Watson, Nelson Fudge.

Privates—D. D. Hull, V. L. Morgan, John W. Sprinkle, H. Clay Jones, Thomas H. Thurmon, William E. Moore, John P. Wright, Jesse G. Rice, John Gullion, James G. Monroe, James D. Wolfe, William Henritze, W. W. Pruner, John Austin, William P. Sheffey, H. J. Garrett, William C. Sexton, George W. Johnston, William H. Trucks, Fountain Prater, John H. Townsend, William Francis, George S. Venable, H. S. Oaks, W. R. Johnston, Henry Henderlite, James H. Francis, P. H. McGruder, A. Phipps, G. W. Wolfe, W. H. McDonald, R. S. Campbell, and F. Newman.

One reason for appointing these police patrols was the danger of trouble from negroes aroused by men of the John Brown stamp. But there is no indication that there was ever any trouble of this sort in Smyth County.

Mr. James W. Sheffey was elected to represent this county at the State Convention which passed on the question of secession. He was opposed to secession, but was compelled by developments finally to vote for it. At the February term of court, 1861, the county court deemed it expedient to appropriate the sum of one thousand dollars for the purpose of uniforming a volunteer company in the town of Marion under the title of the "Smyth Blues." A. G. Pendleton was the captain of this company and at the March term court allowed the "Smyth Blues" to use the upstairs of the courthouse for a drill room, holding Captain Pendleton personally responsible for any damage inflicted upon the building. At the

May term of court, 1861, it was ordered that the Company then enrolled and called the "Smyth Home Guards" commanded by Capt. E. L. Watson, should be appointed a police patrol for a term of three months. At the May term of court a committee composed of Joseph Sexton, James M. Rector, James A. Buchanan, James B. Lowder, William P. Dungan, and John H. Barton was appointed to investigate the families of volunteers who might need assistance and to report them and the probable amount needed for their relief to the court.

At the same term of court, Robert Goolsby and James Rector were named commissioners to purchase horses for troopers. The horses were to be owned by the county, paid for by county bonds, and if any survived the war they were to be returned to the county.

The following list of Smyth County Companies has been compiled by Mrs. John Sexton after many years of investigating:

1—First company organized at Marion, Smyth County known as "Smyth Blues" Co. D, 4th Va. Reg. Infantry. Stonewall Brigade, organized April 21, 1861, A. J. Pendleton, Captain, James W. Kennedy, 1st Lieut., A. E. Gibson, 2nd Lieut.—(Dr. T. L. Sexton is the only member of this company now living)

2—Second Company F, 50th Va. Infantry, known as "Smyth Greys" organized in Rich Valley, May 1861, C. F. McDonald, captain, Wm. King, 1st lieutenant. Gannaway 2nd lieutenant. Whitehead, 3rd lieutenant.

3—Co. B, 48th Va. Reg., organized at Seven Mile Ford; known as "Jackson's Old Division," James Greever, captain; Robert Dungan, 1st lieutenant; John M. Preston 2nd lieutenant; Gollehon, 3rd lieutenant.

4—Co. A, 8th Va. Cavalry, known as "Smyth Dragoons" Jankin's Brigade, organized at Marion, John H. Thompson, captain; J. P. Sheffey, 1st lieutenant; Hezekiah Harman, 2nd lieutenant; Fulton St. John, 3rd lieutenant. They were under Wm. C. Jones, then Bradly T. Johnson, then they wound up with Fitz Hugh Lee. This company was mustered into service at Wytheville on May 27, 1861, under A. F. Cook, colonel of 8th Va. Cav.

5—Then there were made up three at one time, July 1861, Co. A, 23rd Battalion, organized at Holston Woolen Mills. Wm. Blessing, captain; John T. Killinger 1st lieutenant; Elchanah Bishop 2nd lieutenant; John Gollehon, 3rd lieutenant; Henry Hubble, Orderly Sargt.

6—Next was Co. F made up at Marion, W. H. McDonald, captain; Hiram Greever, 1st lieutenant; Wm. Greever 2nd lieutenant; Madison Scott, 3rd lieutenant.

7—Next was Co. A at Chatham Hill, Paddy Buchanan, captain; Rush Campbell, 1st lieutenant; J. M. Pratt, 2nd lieutenant; L. L. S. Campbell, 3rd lieutenant. All three companies belonged to Col. Clarence Derrick's Battalion under John B. Floyd first year, then Echols Brigade, Breckenridge Division.

8—Two Companies of volunteers 45th Va. Reg. were made up about Rural Retreat in May and June 1861, of Wythe and Smyth county men. All the officers were Smyth County men except one; John R. Buchanan, captain; his brother James Buchanan, 1st lieutenant; Chas. Bumgardner, of Wythe Co., 2nd lieutenant; James M. Snavely, 3rd lieutenant.

9—Next Co. (perhaps B), 29th Va. Reg., Wm. Horn captain, George W. Mercer, 1st lieutenant, Henry Groseclose, 2nd lieutenant; John Phillipi, 3rd lieutenant. (Mr. Geo. W. Davis belonged to Co. B, 29th Va. Reg.)

10—In January and February of '62 the conscript law was passed taking men between eighteen and thirty-six years. Co. K, 63rd Va. Reg. organized at Marion: John C. Killinger captain; John C. Owry, 1st lieutenant; D. D. Hull 2nd lieutenant; Sam Cole 3rd lieutenant.

11—In Rich Valley Co. E, 21st Va. Cavalry, was made up: Wm. Cox, captain; Frank McDonald, 1st lieutenant; John S. E. McGee, 2nd lieutenant. Belonged to Col. Wm. E. Peter's Reg. 22nd Virginia Cavalry. Same Brigade as the 8th.

12—In April '64 there were two companies made up of boys between the ages sixteen and eighteen and men between forty and fifty known as the Smyth Co. Reserves, called the North Side Co. and the South Side Co. The North Side was commanded by Capt. Evan Richardson, Col. Smith's Battalion. This company was in the severest of the fight in the Burbridge raid; South Side Capt. J. W. Sheffey.

13—The South Side Company was Co. A, 23rd Va. Battalion, Richard Brown, captain; Joseph L. Gollehon, 1st lieutenant. These companies belonged to a battalion of boys and old men of Southwest Virginia, Col. Bob Smith in command, who with the help of a Kentucky regiment, whipped Burbridge at Saltville.

14—In the spring of 1864 eighty-four men of Smyth county who had been detailed to make saltpetre under the superintendence of Dr. John L. Buchanan, were organized into a company. F. G. Buchanan was captain; Wesley Fell, 1st lieutenant; G. W. Campbell, 2nd lieutenant. This company was ordered out several times and was in the battle at Saltville when Burbridge attempted to destroy the works.

Mrs. Sexton also informs us that Edward McCready, killed at the first battle of Manassas, was the first Smyth soldier killed in the War and that the Gibson-McCready Camp United Confederate Veterans organized at Marion April 20, 1869, was named for him and Capt. Andrew Gibson, who was killed early in the War; that Sidney Painter, who lived and died in Marion, was the first wounded soldier brought to Southwest Virginia; and that Mr. and Mrs. Martin Davis of Rich Valley furnished ten sons to the Confederacy. This district was represented in the Confederate Congress by the Hon. Fayette McMullin, a citizen of Smyth County, and by Walter Preston, a half brother of Capt. John Preston, who defeated McMullin. A sister of Gen. Jubal Early, Mrs. John Clarkson, lived in Smyth County and the widow of J. E. B. Stuart made her home at Saltville after his death. John Clarkson had owned and operated salt works on the Kanawha River, and, being driven out by the Yankees, refugeed in Smyth with about one hundred of his negroes. He hired the negroes out in the county. Miss Kate Korff, a worker in the Confederate Hospital, became Mrs. Legrand Sexton and lived at Chatham Hill. The surgeon, who gave the anæsthetic when Dr. Hunter McGuire amputated Stonewall Jackson's arm was Dr. Harvey Black, who spent the latter part of his life in Smyth.

At the April and May courts of 1862, $3,780 was appropriated along with a gift of $500 from Mr. James W. Sheffey for equipping volunteers. From 1863 until the close of the War, requisitions of slaves were made for work on fortifications in various parts of the State and the court records show that Smyth furnished its quota and gives the names of the owners of the slaves requisitioned. When the slaves were sent off to a distance, their masters would see to it that a proper person went along to see that the slaves were properly cared for.

On March 2, 1863, a meeting was called at the courthouse to take steps for supplying the people of the county with cotton yarn and cotton cloth and the following resolutions were adopted:

Resolved that Governor Vance of North Carolina be respectfully requested to allow our county agent to purchase cotton yarns and cotton cloth from the respective factories in his state, and that he allow the same to be brought out of the state of North Carolina to this county, we hereby pledge ourselves to see that no speculation is made in the articles purchased by our agent, whom we hereby endorse as an honorable and reliable man.

2nd. That Montgomery F. Baker is hereby appointed agent of this county to purchase the articles above referred to.

3rd. That the people of the respective Magisterial Districts are here requested to assemble on or before the 9th Inst. and appoint a District agent who shall report on the 13th. at the Courthouse to the County agent, the amount needed by his district, reporting a list of the several families and the amount needed by each. And the Clerk is hereby directed to make out a copy of the foregoing and affix the seal of his office thereto, and deliver the same to the County agent.

THE WAR BETWEEN THE STATES 241

And it is further ordered that the Commissioners appointed in the several Magisterial Districts to make out and return a list of citizens to be instructed to give notice to the citizens of their district to meet at a time not later than the 9th. Inst. to appoint District agents, to report to the County agent at the courthouse not later than the 13th. Inst. the wants and necessities of the citizens of their respective Districts, in pursuance with the third resolution above.

At the June term of court, 1863, Patrick C. Buchanan, Jr., was appointed to receive and distribute the proportion of salt allotted to the people of Smyth County and he was authorized to borrow the money to pay for the salt, giving bonds of the county as security. From a record of the March term of court, 1864, it appears that one thousand two hundred people, families of volunteers, were dependent upon the county for support and that three thousand six hundred bushels of grain would be required to maintain them until the first of the next August. The Confederate Government was collecting grain in payment of taxes and court made application to purchase the amount needed from this tax in kind. Mr. Oury, Jailor of Smyth County, was made an allowance for the keep of prisoners confined here because the train on which they were being conveyed had broken down.

In August of 1863, a unique and daring raid aiming at destruction of the railroad was defeated in Smyth County. Captain Wilson, described by Mr. Grundy Buchanan, who talked with him, as a very brave and unusually intelligent man, started out from Cincinnati with twenty-five or thirty men for the purpose of destroying bridges, depots, and tracks of what is now the Norfolk and Western Railroad. Mr. Wilson told Mr. Buchanan that he and his men had been promised a promotion if they could succeed in this attempt. They came up the Tug Fork of Sandy, one of the favorite routes of the old Indian marauders from Ohio, and crossed into Tazewell County at Horse Penn Cove. They would hide by day and travel by night. Mr. Charles Taylor looking for cattle in the Horse Penn Cove ran into them and was made prisoner. They released him when he took oath not to reveal their presence. They were later discovered by an old woman named Patsy Hall. Patsy also took that oath, but, as soon as she got away from them, she hurried to tell all of the neighbors that these Yankees were in that Cove. But as Patsy told it there were hundreds of Yankees there and considerable excitement prevailed in Tazewell County. Confederate troops were called up and struck the trail of the raiding party. They saw that the raiders were traveling on foot, straight through the woods and fields toward the railroad in Smyth County, near Marion. Word was sent across the mountain to Rich Valley and Marion. Mr. James W. Sheffey, of Marion, assembled the "Home Guards" and picketed Hungry's Mother Creek far back into the mountain. The Tazewell troopers came around to Marion and joined Sheffey's men on Hungry's Mother. The raiders, in the meantime, traveling by compass, had walked straight across the mountains.

Mr. Grundy Buchanan, who was then engaged in getting saltpetre from the Valley says: "The first we knew of their presence in our county, they were said to be on Spratts Creek about one mile east of Chatham Hill. The time being about an hour by sun P.M. By order of Capt. Joseph M. Thomas of the "Home Guards" the Rich Valley road was picketed and they crossed this road about one o'clock A.M. Captain Thomas having been thrown from a horse on the previous day was unable to take command of about thirty home-guards, assembled at Legrand Sexton's store and Lieut. James V. McDonald was placed in command to follow the trail made by the Yanks across the mountain. The Yanks had found water about one-third the way down south of the mountain, built a fire and were roasting green corn for their breakfast. Jonathan Olinger some sixty odd years of age, leading our squad, when in sight of them, without orders, fired on the Yanks and they scattered like partridges and we could find but fourteen of twenty-eight, two having given out on the way. Of course we should have surrounded them before firing on them. John Atwell, one of my saltpetre men, was wounded in the thigh which exempted him from further service. Lieutenant Wilson commanding the raiders told us that if we had sent down a white flag they would have surrendered as they had given up hope of accomplishing their purpose. When we took the prisoners to the foot of the mountain, we found Marion Home Guards and Tazewell rangers picketing Hungry's Mother so that they could not possibly have reached the railroad."

Mr. Stephen Groseclose, Confederate soldier, at that time was at his father's on Snider's Branch on furlough. He says that walking out in the fields he was very much surprised to come upon two soldiers in Federal uniform and still more surprised when they threw up their hands and surrendered to him. As he took them prisoners, they told him that they were of the raiding party and described the attack upon them by "Home Guards," in these words, according to Mr. Groseclose: "We tried to surrender to the "Home Guards," but the damn fools kept on firing so we broke and ran and we are mighty glad to find a Confederate soldier to whom we can surrender."

Mr. Groseclose took them into his father's house, gave them supper, and in the evening, he and his father put them on horses and rode into Marion. They turned them over to the jailor. The other fourteen prisoners were in the jail and seemed very happy. It is not known how many the "Home Guards" fired upon, but none of the raiders were hurt. These raiders traveling by night, afoot, directed their course by compass. They seemed to have had two compasses. One was picked up by Mr. Washington Pratt, who sold it for $300, Confederate money; the other was found near the spring where the raiders were captured by Mr. Stephen Groseclose and it is in his possession now.

Bushwhacking and guerilla warfare accompanied by intense neighborhood bitterness and marked with murders, whippings, burnings, and stealing, particularly of horses and other stock prevailed in the Civil struggle of eastern Tennessee and slashed over into bordering southwestern Virginia counties. There is evidence of this sort of thing having appeared in Smyth in vague traditions of bushwhackers and horse thieves, and some documents of the period. The only definite account of this sort of warfare that I have found was furnished by Mr. Robert M. Richardson, who was born on the old Richardson place where "Buckeye Billy" the original Richardson settler lived in Rich Valley. He was born July 18, 1863, and on that night Yankees raided Rich Valley. They came across the mountain from the direction of Marion, reached William Richardson's farm about sundown, and immediately began tearing down rail fences for camp fires. A group of officers came to the house and demanded food. Miss Elizabeth Richardson, an aunt of the baby that was born that night, and a lady of dignified mien and impressive presence met them at the door, told them there was a very ill woman in the house and requested them to leave without causing disturbance. They courteously apologized for their intrusion and left, after being fed. Mr. Richardson had sent his negroes with all the horses on the place into the woods to hide them. During the night he looked out of the window and by the light of his burning fence rails saw one of the negro men in the yard directing the Yankees to the horses. This negro went off with the raiders the next day but all of the others remained faithful. Through his treachery the horses were found and

THE WAR BETWEEN THE STATES 245

carried away down to one old blind mare. All the other stock on the place was either butchered or driven off. Mr. Richardson asked that they leave him one horse to ride to mill. They refused, saying: "Your people stripped us bare and we will give you the same treatment." This indicates that these raiders were a bushwhacking outfit from East Tennessee, but it is not now certain who they were.

Late in September, 1864, Gen. Stephen G. Burbridge with a Federal Army of 500 men left Pikeville, Ky., came up the Big Sandy River through Buchanan and Tazewell counties attempting to capture the Salt Works. He was met on the morning of October 2, at Cedar Creek on the Western limits of Saltville, and defeated by a force of Confederates under the command of Gen. John S. Williams. Detailed accounts of this battle are given in Summer's *History of Washington County* and Pendleton's *History of Tazewell County* and will not be repeated here. There are several instances of the battle, however, which we will note. The Sander's home lay between the lines and was repeatedly struck during the firing. Mrs. F. G. Buchanan, daughter of "Governor" Sanders, was a child at the time and she says that she, her mother, and other children remained in the house throughout the batte, huddled behind feather beds. There was a double log house standing within the line of fire with a huge chimney. An old negro woman climbed into this chimney and stayed there until the battle was over. Saybird Walker, a little boy, living near Chilhowie, ran off from home to see what was going on at Saltville and he watched the entire fighting from a hilltop back of the Confederate lines. The last regular company to go from Smyth was made up of eighty-four saltpetre and iron men who had been detailed to work in the saltpetre caves in Rich Valley and in Thomas' Iron Works in Rye Valley and near Marion. F. Grundy Buchanan was captain of this Company. In the spring of '65, they started to join

Lee's army but at Ellison they learned of the surrender, turned back and disbanded at Christiansburg. Captain Buchanan and Esq. Sam McClure are the only members of that company now living. The company was engaged in the Battle of Saltville where Mr. McClure had a remarkable vision of his brother's death while lying out on the battlefield that night. He saw his brother shot and killed and lying dead in the field. He came to his captain and told him what he had seen and asked permission to go to his brother. Captain Buchanan answered: "Sam, you have been dreaming. Your brother is probably all right." He answered: "No, I have been wide awake all night." Captain Buchanan said: "I have orders to send out a detail to bury the dead. You may go with them and look for your brother." He did so and found him several miles away on the spot and in the exact position in which he had seen him during the night.

Stoneman's Raid

The greatest turmoil, destruction, and distress of the War in Smyth County was caused by Stoneman's raid in December of 1864 made for the purpose of destroying the Lead mines, the Salt Works, and the railroad. Four thousand troops under Gen. Stephen Burbridge in eastern Kentucky and fifteen hundred under Gen. Alvan C. Gillem at Knoxville united at Bean Station, Tenn., under command of Gen. George Stoneman and on the twelfth of December, 1864, started out of Southwest Virginia. Gillem moved from Knoxville on December 10, and Gen. John C. Breckenridge, commander of Confederate forces in Southwest Virginia, and Eastern Tennessee, was at his headquarters in Wytheville. He had something over two thousand men under his command but they were scattered in small groups from Monroe County, West Virginia, to Greeneville, Tenn. General Vaughn with the largest contingent, of approximately one thousand men, was at Greeneville, Tenn., opposing Gillem. Gen. B. W. Duke with the remnant of Morgan's troopers was near Rogersville. Gen. George B. Cosby had just arrived at Wytheville with a small force from the Valley of Virginia. Col. Henry L. Giltner was in Russell County. Col. Robert Smith was at Saltville with a battalion of reserves. Gen. John Echols was at Dublin, and Colonel Witcher, with his cavalry, was at Centerville in Monroe County. On the thirteenth Stoneman defeated Duke at Kingsport and drove him to Bristol. Vaughn had moved up to Paperville. Breckenridge, thinking the Federal objective would be Saltville, attempted a concentration of all his scattered forces at that place and directed Generals Duke and Vaughn to fight and retard the enemy at every possible point, falling back on Saltville. General Echols was directed to assemble reserves and detail men; Colonel Witcher, marching ninety miles in twenty-five hours from Narrows through Tazewell, reached Gillespie's Gap at noon of the fifteenth, rested men and horses there, and arrived at Saltville the next morning. General Breckenridge himself with a battalion of reserves under Colonel Robert Preston arrived at Saltville at daybreak on Thursday, the fifteenth. General Cosby marched through Marion on Wednesday, the fourteenth and was at Seven Mile Ford at 3:30 that afternoon, writing that he intended to push on to Saltville that night. Duke had made a stand at Bristol, but was driven out and arrived at Saltville on the fourteenth. Giltner had also arrived so that Gen. Breckenridge succeeded in concentrating all his scattered forces at Saltville by Thursday, the fifteenth except the Reserves that Echols was assembling near Dublin at General Vaughn's command. Vaughn had taken position at Paperville where Burbridge tried to strike and destroy him, but Vaughn under cover of a dense fog eluded Burbridge and retreated up the south side of Holston. Stoneman hurried Burbridge ahead to cut him off at Abingdon, but Vaughn keeping up the South Fork road passed by Abingdon and reached Marion before the Federals struck his rear. The Yankees, coming down the Lee Highway, however, prevented his junction with Breckenridge at Saltville. From Abingdon, Stoneman sent Gillem, Thursday, the fifteenth, on up the Lee Highway with instructions to catch Vaughn. He also sent three hundred men under Major Harrison to push ahead and destroy the railroad. That day Major Harrison cut the railroad at Glade Spring, pushed on up ahead of General Vaughn destroying bridges and sections of track. A portion of Vaughn's command spent the night of the fifteenth in and near Marion, his wagon trains continuing through Rye Valley towards the Lead Mines. The next day he moved his wagon trains and his main force down Cripple Creek to the Lead Mines while Colonels Bean and Gillespie, commanding part of his force, skirmished with Gillem in Marion and up the pike to Wytheville. Gillem in his official report says:

We arrived at Marion, about one hour before daylight on the 16th, when we were fired upon by a large party of the enemy posted in the village of Marion and either by soldiers or citizens from many of the houses. The enemy was immediately charged and driven from the town, and took a position on the heights beyond.

As it was perfectly dark and the country unknown to me, and as I found it impossible to procure a guide, I re-formed my command and awaited until dawn, when I again attacked and drove the enemy from their position, pursuing them closely for twelve miles, driving them from every position they attempted to make a stand. Thirteen miles west of Wytheville they began to use their artillery, which was immediately charged and captured, the enemy losing eight pieces between that point and Wytheville. When within one mile of Wytheville, and after pursuing the enemy thirty-one miles, I halted for a short time to allow my command to close up, it having been reported to me from several sources that a force

THE WAR BETWEEN THE STATES 249

of some seven hundred or eight hundred infantry had arrived at Wytheville from Lynchburg.

This was not, as Gillem seems to think, Vaughn's main force, but a detachment under Colonels Bean and Gillespie keeping Gillem amused while Vaughn escaped with his wagon trains. Colonel Bean was killed on the main street of Marion nearly in front of the Sheffey home, and a Yankee officer was killed in front of the courthouse; also a Confederate and a Yankee officer were killed between the courthouse and the Marion National Bank.

Stoneman with Burbridge's troop came on from Abingdon spending the night of Thursday, the fifteenth in Smyth. Their men camped from the county line at Greever's to Captain Preston's at Seven Mile Ford, chopping beeves on the mahogany tables of the Preston dining room. On Friday the sixteenth he pushed through Marion to the vicinity of Mt. Airy where he was joined on Saturday, the seventeenth, by Gillem. He sent a force of six hundred men under Colonel Buckly with orders to destroy the lead mine works and return down Rye Valley to Seven Mile Ford. Buckly carried out his orders, put the lead mines out of commission, and marched down Rye Valley through Adwolfe to camp at Seven Mile Ford on Sunday, the eighteenth, while the Battle of Marion was being fought.

When General Breckenridge learned that Stoneman had passed Saltville by and kept on up the valley by the main stage road, he decided to follow him and moved out of Saltville with all his troops except about four hundred, mainly reserves, under command of Col. Robert Preston. His advance under Colonel Witcher came up with the Federals between Atkins and Mt. Airy, formed line of battle and engaged in skirmishing there. Breckenridge took a strong position on the high ground north of the river from the bridge east of Marion down towards Mt. Carmel, and Witcher fell back to this line. Stoneman with his united forces moved up to the attack occupying positions on the south side of the river. The battle began on Saturday evening, December 17, and continued into Sunday night. General Stoneman on Sunday morning sent Gillem with a strong force around the Confederate right to attack Saltville while he kept Breckenridge engaged at Marion. Gillem, marching up Snider's Branch by the Groseclose place through Mitchel's Valley struck the Chatham Hill road and got within eight miles of Saltville when a courier overtook him with orders to hurry back with all speed to Stoneman's assistance. He came back and went into position late in the evening on the Confederate left flank and rear. There were less than one thousand Confederates engaged in the battle of Marion but they occupied an exceedingly strong position from which Stoneman's four thousand or more could not budge them by repeated attacks Saturday evening and all day Sunday. Sunday night the exhausted armies lay in the trenches. Breckenridge found his ammunition nearly exhausted. Gillem's men were on his left and rear cutting him off from Saltville in that direction. Buckly's six hundred were behind him at Seven Mile Ford, blocking that route to Saltville. Stoneman's four thousand were in front of him. Under cover of darkness he quietly slipped out of the trenches and retreated up Staley's Creek getting safely across the mountain by daybreak of Monday, the nineteenth. That night he reached the pike at Mt. Airy. The next day, his men rested and a new supply of ammunition secured, he turned back down the Lee Highway in pursuit of Stoneman, passing through Marion again, and his advance, composed of the freshest men under General Duke, reached the picket lines at Saltville at daybreak on Wednesday, the twenty-first, the main body following a few miles behind.

On Wednesday evening, December 19, Stoneman, having discovered that the Confederates were gone, put his forces in motion for Saltville. Burbridge's division halted in the middle of the day at Seven Mile Ford to feed and rest. Gillem's bivouacked that night west of Chilhowie, his camp fires extending through the Greever farm and on towards the Huff place. Generals Stoneman and Gillem spent the night in Colonel Greever's house. On Tuesday, the twentieth, they captured Saltville, Gillem's division approaching from Glade Spring and Burbridge's through Lyon's Gap. The forts at Saltville were defended by about four hundred men under Col. Robert Preston, three fourths of them old men and boys. Some of the defenders of Saltville were killed and some were captured but most escaped to the mountains and eventually rejoined Breckenridge's army. The Yankees burned the works at Saltville on Tuesday night, December 20, and spent Wednesday breaking salt kettles and stopping up the wells. Thursday morning, the twenty-second they evacuated Saltville, Gillem returning to Tennessee and Burbridge to Kentucky by way of Pound Gap. Breckenridge reëntered Saltville. According to official reports of the Federal generals the destruction at Saltville was complete, all the kettles were smashed to bits and the wells so effectually choked that it would be easier to dig new ones than to re-open them. According to General Breckenridge's report, corroborated by Mr. Alex Stuart, owner of the works, about one-third of the kettles were destroyed and the damage to wells could be repaired in a few weeks.

During the Battle of Marion General Breckenridge maintained his headquarters in the James W. Sheffey home. Capt. D. D. Hull, at home on furlough, reported to General Breckenridge and was assigned to duty as a courier. He carried the message ordering retreat across the mountain. Thomas' Iron

Works on Staley's Creek were burned by Harrison before the battle.

The hardest fighting in the Battle of Marion occurred about the bridges near the Allen home. This house with the family in it was between the armies and the line of hottest firing. Mr. Ferd Allen was a baby about a year old. The Michael Killinger house was back of the Yankee lines, and Miss Betty Killinger, later Mrs. Stephen Groseclose, accompanied by women of the Allen family, carried the baby boy under fire from the Allen house to the comparative safety of her father's home. To lessen the chances of being shot, she kept pinching the baby to make it cry, hoping to make sure the soldiers would note that they were women and children. In the Killinger home they barricaded themselves with feather beds, etc. Old Michael Killinger refused to get behind anything but calmly sat before the fire smoking and chewing tobacco and grumbling because he was too old to get in the fight. He was not hit, though bullets coming through the windows grazed his chair and penetrated a heavy wooden chest close by.

The covered bridge across the river above Marion figured prominently in this battle. The first fighting occurred there on Saturday evening, and Federals attempting to cross from the east were driven back by fire from the Confederates on the hills across the stream. Some of the planks were torn up in the bridge and after dark two of the Federal generals went down and examined the bridge and had the planks relaid. They then ordered Colonel Mannagan's Kentucky regiment to advance across the bridge. This regiment had cleared the bridge and had advanced up the road some distance when the Confederates surprised them with a torrent of shot and shell, and the Federals, thrown into confusion, rushed back jambing into the bridge. The Confederates had perfect range and their shells knocked down large timbers and the balls of

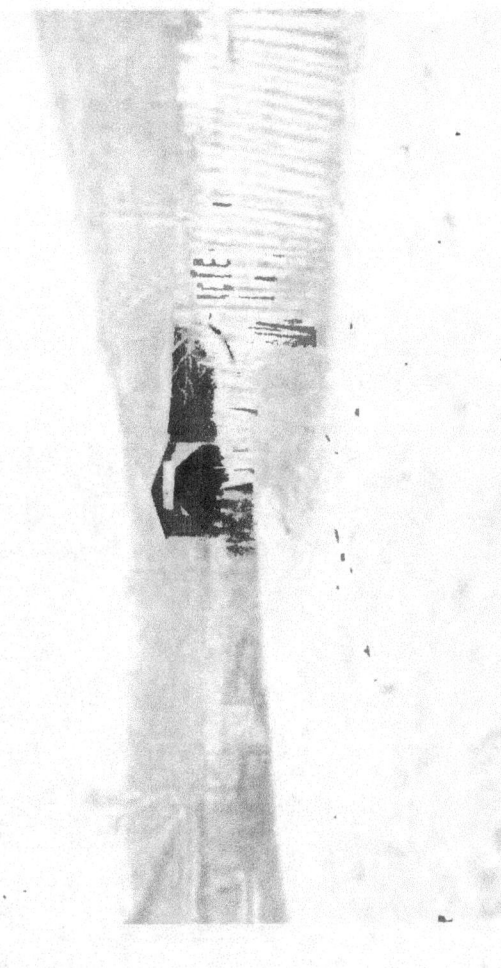
Covered Bridge on Marion Battlefield

THE WAR BETWEEN THE STATES 253

their sharpshooters riddled it like a sieve. It became a shambles until Colonel Mannagan finally got what was left of his men out of it and safe on the other side. Before daybreak on Sunday morning the Confederates opened the battle, and by nine o'clock the roar of an artillery duel was reverberating through the hills. All of the Federal troops were called into action, and Stoneman was so hard pressed that by the middle of the day he was forced to send a courier post haste to call Gillem to his assistance.

There was a regiment of negro cavalry under the command of Colonel Cole. These negroes charged the Confederate works and were driven back. Some of the bitterest fighting of the battle was this hand to hand struggle with negro troops. A Confederate calvary troop charged one time in the rear of the Yankees and came very near capturing their pack train.

After the battle and the departure of Stoneman's troops for Saltville, a detail was ordered to burn the covered bridge which crossed the Middle Fork of Holston where the iron bridge now crosses. Just east of it there was a toll house kept by the Allens. Susan Allen, sister of baby Ferd, was a little girl in her early teens. When the soldiers fired the bridge and left, she ran out with a bucket, waded into the stream, and douched the flames. The soldiers saw her and came back. They scolded her and set it afire again. Again she put it out. They threatened to do all manner of things to her and at last with their fire making headway and having to hurry back to their command, they told her if she put it out again, they would come back and run their bayonets through her. They had scarcely passed out of sight around a nearby bend in the road before she had the fire out and the remnant of that shot-riddled old covered bridge was saved. Susan Allen is now Mrs. Snavely Groseclose and lives with her daughter in Kentucky. This incident is placed after the battle as a more probable time, though it may have occurred on Thursday or Friday before when the Yankees were on their way to Wytheville.

Elizabeth Catherine Killinger was a heroine of this time as appears from the following account written by her daughter, Mrs. Laura Scherer Copenhaver, in 1912:

Major Harrison, with three hundred picked men, was sent ahead to destroy the iron works near Marion, having received orders to burn bridges and tear up railroad tracks along the way.

By this time confusion reigned in the town of Marion. Reports of the ravages of the Federal troops in the villages along the line ran from mouth to mouth. The knobs and mountains surrounding the town received fugitives of all classes. Women waited, white-faced and trembling, in their homes.

William Sexton, clerk of the county, was hauling corn on his farm near Marion when a frightened courier told him of the rapid approach of the enemy. Thinking first, not of his own safety, but of the records of the county intrusted to his care, he mounted his horse and galloped into the panic stricken town. Here he secured a wagon and a negro driver. Going into the courthouse he gathered up the files, thrusting them into a large box, which he put into the wagon. Mr. Thurman, a merchant, whose store was just across the street, threw in a number of bales of dry goods. Just as Major Harrison's men came into town the wagon started, Mr. Sexton accompanying it on horseback.

He turned up the Staley's Creek Road hoping that the Federals would take the main road to Wytheville. But they were bent upon the destruction of the iron works; and, therefore, took the same road, turning in at the iron works, while Mr. Sexton continued along the Rye Valley Road.

The wagon had just reached the foot of the hill below the old Killinger place when a messenger from the iron works came across the country with the news that Harrison's men had destroyed the iron works and were on the road to Rye Valley. At that moment the clatter of the approaching cavalry was heard, and Mr. Sexton realized the uselessness of any

THE WAR BETWEEN THE STATES 255

further efforts at saving the records. Just as the Federal troops came into sight he put spurs to his horse and rode into the hills. He was pursued for a little distance by the enemy. Several shots were fired at him, but he made good his escape into the mountains.

The Federal commander, after examining the contents of the wagon, set fire to it. He then dispatched two of his men to the house on the hill with orders to search it, and, if rebels or firearms were concealed in it, to burn it to the ground.

The messengers were met at the door by Katherine, the youngest of the house. They asked for a drink of water, and then most courteously inquired if there were any rebel soldiers or firearms concealed about the house. They were told that the men of the family were away with the Confederate army. As to firearms, behind the door were stacked two new guns captured from the Yankees and left there by one of the sons who was at that moment home on furlough and hidden in the knobs around the house. The quick-witted eldest daughter heard the question, and, knowing Catherine's habit of fearless candor, grasped a rusty and battered old rifle and came forward with a disarming smile.

"Here's Dad's old gun," she said.

The courteous Northerners laughed at the dilapidated old weapon and made no further effort to search the house. Instead one of them politely remarked:

"I hear that calico is scarce in the South now. There are several bales of it burning in that wagon at the foot of the hill. Go down and help yourselves."

The girls watched the soldiers march down the hill to their regiment, encamped for a brief rest near the spring which now supplies the town of Marion with water. Calico was indeed scarce in the South in December, 1864. But neither of the girls was minded to accept a dress on such terms. They went back into the room where their mother was.

From the window could be seen the smoke of the burning wagon and the camp fires of the Federal soldiers. Catherine watched it, thinking of the contents of the wagon. She knew of the burden it carried, since Mr. Sexton had stopped in the road to warn the family of the coming of Harrison's men. She understood that the loss of the records would involve the

county in an endless succession of lawsuits, and she declared her intention of going down and trying to save the books.
Her mother and sister begged her not to make the attempt. They told her that the dangers of venturing so near the dreaded troops from the North were too real and terrible to be faced by an unprotected girl. But Catherine persisted. She was confident that she could save the books; and under cover of the approaching twilight, she went down to the wagon, accompanied by a girl, a servant of the house.

The books were burning slowly; and she was able to carry them one at a time over a footbridge to a clump of bushes, into which she threw them. The servant became alarmed at the firing of several shots in succession and ran back up the hill toward the house with a bale of half-burned calico in her arms. Catherine stayed until the last book was saved. The charred edges of the flames she put out with her hands may still be seen in the records of the clerk's office.

The terror aroused by the presence of the Federal troops in Southwest Virginia was increased by the atrocities committed by Captain Cole's regiment of negro soldiers. One of these negroes shot down Mr. LaFayette Snavely, an unarmed citizen, who was standing in the front door of his home a few miles from Marion. The Federal General Brisbin, speaks of the barbarous behavior of this colored regiment to its white prisoners, adding as an excuse that the Confederate raiders under Witcher, had excited the wrath of the negroes by killing without mercy all of them who were prisoners, as an example to others who might think of fighting against the South.

A Court record of Jan. 17, 1865, takes note of this instance as follows:

> The Court having been informed that the records of the County of great value to the people having lands in the County or other interests in the records, were saved by the heroic efforts of Miss Elizabeth C. Killinger from destruction by fire, set to them by the Public Enemy in their late raid into South Western Virginia, and desiring to testify their appreciation of her conduct & services doth order that the cordial thanks of the Court are due and are hereby tendered

to the said Elizabeth C. Killinger for the saving of the Records of the County from destruction after they were fired by the enemy and that there be appropriated five hundred dollars as a reward for her valuable services and that a copy of this order be delivered to her by the Sheriff; and that he pay her the five hundred dollars above appropriated.

General Vaughn, having saved his wagon trains, was trying to get from Wytheville to Marion on December 22 with about seven hundred men but was obliged to halt at Reed Creek because of the suffering of his men from the intense cold. General Echols, writing from Mr. Sheffey's house in Marion at 5:30 P.M., December 22, says four hundred and twenty reserves under Col. J. F. Kent would reach that place the next day unless stopped by the extreme severity of the weather.

In Stoneman's raid a great deal of damage was done to private property. It is said that Sheridan boasted that he had left the Valley of Virginia so bare that a crow flying over it would have to bring his rations with him. General Gillem, in his official report to Andrew Johnson, makes practically the same boast in different words of his exploits in Southwest Virgina during this raid.

Aunt Mary Poole was a little colored girl, a slave of the Greevers, at the time of Stoneman's raid. She says: "Old Marse Hiram Greever and my pappy, Cæsar, was refugeeing out in the mountains with the horses and silver. Marse Jeems was off to the war and ole Miss Greever was away from home visiting some whar. The Yankees first come by and camped. Gen'ral Stoneman and Gen'ral Gillem stayed in the brick house, then they all went away up towards Marion. After they had been gone two or three days, Marse Hiram and my daddy come home with the horses and silver. They hadn't much more 'n got home until I looked up the road and I seen the Yankees was comin' back. I run into the house and told old Marse Hiram the Yankees was comin' back. Marse

Hiram and my daddy, Cæsar, grabbed up a bag full of silver and took out of the back door and up through the garden and the branch back of the house and got out of sight just as the Yankees come in the front gate. The generals stayed in the big house that night and I waited on them. Thar was a barrel of apply brandy in the cellar and they had some soldiers knock the head out of it and poured it all out because they said that if the men got hold of it, they would all get drunk and burn down the house. And that night the soldiers camped all up and down the road as far as you could see both ways. They come in about dark and before you knowed it, they had all the fence rails tore down and was making fires out of them. And they had caught up all the chickens, hogs, and what cows was on the place and killed them and was cooking them for their supper."

Aunt Mary Poole is now upwards of ninety years old and lives on a little place back of Mr. Levi Cole's house. She also says that at the beginning of the war the Confederates had a company of soldiers drilling on the lands in front of Capt. Charlie Preston's, the present home of Mrs. H. L. Morgan. She says that "Marse Jeems" was captain of that company and that Capt. John M. Preston was lieutenant and that every day she used to carry a big hamper of "vittles" to them on horse back. She remembers vividly an occasion when a flag was presented to the company by Mrs. Arthur Campbell Cummings, sister of Captain Preston, and that there was big speech making. This flag was made from Mrs. Cumming's wedding dress and is now in the possession of Mrs. E. L. Greever. Aunt Mary also recalls vividly the departure of the company when the mothers, wives, and sweethearts, weeping, told the soldiers good-by.

For several years after the war, a detachment of Federal soldiers was quartered at Marion in barracks located south of Lee Highway between the Colored Methodist Church and Mr. Henry A. Pruner's residence.

Judge George W. Richardson published the following in the *Marion Democrat:*

During the war rye coffee tasted fine, sweetened with tree sugar. Wearing apparel was made from raw materials by the good women, and looms, cards and spinning wheels were in almost every home. The women wore lindsey dresses, and the men and boys flax linen shirts and tow breeches, and coats of homemade jeans, and knit yarn "Galluses." These tow breeches were the most lasting things a boy ever wore, and the "Galluses" would stretch and knots would be tied in them and this would be repeated until they became as full of knots as a dog of fleas.

Straw hats were made from wheat straw, plaited and then sewed into proper shapes and sizes. Boys' hats were mostly wide brimmed, and sometimes after being out in a hard rain, or dipping them into water they would push the tops up with their hands until they would much resemble the Mexican sombrero. Socks and stockings were knitted of yarn, mostly white, but often of a conglomerate, nondescript color, occasioned by the experiments made in the use of walnut hulls, barks, and leaves, as dye stuffs. Nobody knew just what color would be forthcoming, but, however hideous it might be, it had to be worn, for times were squally in those days and there was nothing to waste. Women wore long, wide dresses in those days, with hoop skirts of amazing sizes. It has been a long time ago, but according to my best recollection, some of them were about six feet in diameter, and about eighteen feet in circumference. Just how they managed to ride horseback in those days, with these tremendous hoop skirts, I do not recall but they did.

In those days mothers went visiting and spent the day. They went on horseback, riding a side saddle, with a satchel hanging to the horn, a baby in her lap, and two or three children on behind and enjoyed it.

I can remember soldiers drilling on the hill back of Richardson's Chapel.

According to his own statement Mr. William E. Copenhaver of Smyth County was the last man at whom a shot was fired at Appomattox. Mr. Copenhaver said that he rode out to the top of a ridge and sat his horse there silhouetted against the sky line, watching a bloody engagement between a North Carolina Brigade and the Federal troops, the last action by the army of Northern Virginia. Fighting had ceased; the Yankee battery was unlimbered and the guns moved to another position. Not thinking that he was in danger or, in fact, seen by the Yankees, he was watching the proceedings with interest and with some curiosity as to why one of those cannons should be pointed in his direction. Then he saw a charge rammed home and the gun fired and a cannon ball whistled over his head. They had evidently taken a crack at the lone horseman against the sky line and with a cannon. He turned his horse and got away from there. When he reached his own lines, a short distance away, the report of Lee's surrender had just been sent in. No more shots were fired. Thus it seems that a Smyth County man, Philip Greever, fired the first shot at King's Mountain and another Smyth County man, W. E. Copenhaver, was the target for the last shot at Appomattox.

CHAPTER XV

NEGROES OF SMYTH

ALONG with the first settlers of Smyth came the negroes, slaves brought to the wilderness by their owners, and many of the negroes in the county today are descendants of these slaves of the original settlers. Others were brought in later and still others have moved into the county voluntarily from time to time. Madam Russell and various other slaveholders freed their slaves from religious conviction. Others set individual slaves free for one reason or another. At the first census, after Smyth County was formed, 1840, there were in the county 838 slaves and 145 free colored.

Among the most notable of the earlier colored men was John Broady, body servant of Gen. William Campbell, a man of intelligence and fine character, who accompanied his master in his military campaigns. In compliance with Gen. Campbell's request that John be set free after his death, Gen. Francis Preston, Campbell's son-in-law, had him manumitted by order of the Washington county court and deeded to him a fertile tract of land west of the present Saltville corporate limits that is still known as Broady's Bottom.

Among the free negroes of the Civil War period were Aunt Jane Smith and her children, one of whom, John Trucks, is still living; Obadiah Hayden; Fanny Cooley; James Cooley, a brick mason; John Ross; John Fowler, Marion's first barber, and others.

James Cooley and John Ross were enlisted soldiers in the Confederate Army. James and Fanny Cooley were the parents or grandparents of John Cooley and his descendants now living in Marion. They are still brick layers. The firm of Cooley and Smith contractors and brick layers have had large contracts not only in Smyth but other parts of the State. Morgan Stuart, who was killed by a fall from a truck, was also a contractor who did a lot of work. John Fowler had in his shop a clock which is now in Will Sharp's Barber Shop and is one of the oldest clocks in the county.

In all three of the Valleys there were numerous slave-holding families. The principal negro settlements since emancipation have been around Saltville, Marion, and Sugar Grove, with quite a few living about on farms over the county.

During the Civil War the negroes of Smyth as of the South as a whole were generally loyal to their masters. There were exceptions to this rule.

The colored people have churches and schools about over the county where the colored population is thick enough to support them. Henry Smith, born in Marion in 1862, gave me the following account of the church and school development in Marion.

Just after, during and before the War, the colored people worshiped in the white churches, where galleries were provided for them and whatever their white folk's creed was that is what they were. The colored Baptist Church was the first organized, Samuel Cyrus, a local preacher in War times, Henderson Goode, Pleasant Blount, Creed Borroughs, and Archie Johnson being among the charter members. This was about 1867.

Major George Smith, a Northerner, donated the lot in the west end of town, now occupied by the Methodist parsonage, for school and church purposes, and deeded it to the colored race. It is still held on that deed, and any colored person who gets in there you can't get him out. James Cooley and his boys, Steve Richardson, and the public generally of the colored people made a kiln of brick on the lot intending to build a brick house, but they sold the brick and built a frame house which was used as a school and jointly as a church by Methodists and Baptists, one using it one Sunday and the other using it the next. After a while the Baptists moved out into their new house and the Methodists bought the adjoining lot from Mr. Nelson Fudge, and had it deeded to the colored race. They built a frame house of worship on it. There were so many colored people in the town then and coming to prayer meeting and preaching for five or six miles around that the two churches would not hold them all. Now there are not nearly so many and those who are here are harder to get to church.

The presiding elder came along and called for the church deed and finding it deeded to the colored race told them that was all wrong and it should be changed to the Methodist Conference. Reece Boyd, one of their members, had been a slave of the Pendleton's and Major Pendleton running for the Legislature then told Reece if he would get his people to vote for him he would have that deed changed by the Legislature. Reece delivered the vote and the Major got his act through changing the deed to the Methodists. That building got dilapidated and the congregation decided to build a new church. They began with $154 all told in the bank to the church's credit. They held rallies, one rally netting $1020.40. They got some help from the white folks and finally had enough to go ahead on. When they started to tear down the old church the Baptist trustees objected on the ground that it was deeded to the colored race.

Henry Smith says:

The Baptists employed a counsel, Judge G. H. Fudge, and they took out injunction against us and ordered us not to move that church, that it didn't belong to us; so the trustees came on up to town and informed Judge George W. Richardson. Judge Fudge had wrote this first deed that the church stood on deeding it to the colored race so they come up to the courthouse and gets this old deed and was holding them at bay with it, not knowing that we had another deed that was made by the Legislature of Virginia. When that come to light, Judge Fudge informed the Baptist trustees who were pursuing the matter "Boys they've got you," and we went ahead and built the church in 1914, all paid for.

The first colored school after the War was taught by a colored man named Lemons in an old stable set on the corner of the right side of the creek after crossing Seaver's bridge. The teacher stayed around a week at a time with families of children that went to school.

After the government took it up a free school was organized. The first one, in a log hut where Mr. Wythe Hull's residence now stands, was taught by a white woman from Massachusetts, Miss Libby Bayton; she boarded with Major Smith, where the College is now. She taught Sunday School in the same building, assisted by George Smith, Jr.

The next session was taught by a colored woman named Lottie Ussher. She taught two terms in the same log hut.

The school building was then changed to where the Methodist parsonage is now. The next teacher was Lottie York from Washington City. Then James Ricks, who later practiced law in Washington and had a good practice, was examined by Judge Kelly and admitted to the bar in Marion.

Major Pendleton was then superintendent of schools. He went to the colored people and told them that the white and colored children were coming into contact going to the west end and if the colored people would grant it the white people would buy a lot and build a house on Needmore Street. Sally Smith owned a lot for which she had paid $75 off the old McDonald land and sold it to them for $62. On it was built a clapboard house with two rooms and a partition. They used that until the white school was torn down when they took the timbers and built the school standing there now, which about collapsed in 1930. Now a modern building equal to any in the state for its purpose houses the colored school. Prof. Floyd Broady has taught many years in the Marion school.

The colored people of Smyth are as a class industrious, thrifty, and well-behaved citizens. Of late years many have been leaving the county for higher wages and wider opportunities in northern cities.

CHAPTER XVI

THE WORLD WAR

SINCE the World War was a world war with its centers of destruction overseas, one Virginia county with no concentration camp or similar scene of activity would be of so little significance to the whole as to afford small scope for history writing. Smyth, like all other Virginia counties, made its full contribution.

Some of the boys volunteered. Others went through the draft. Some remained on this side in various forms of service. Some went overseas. Some did not come back. Many went through hard fighting. General Otho Rosenbaum, Major Ralph Dickenson, and Major Glenn Anderson, Smyth boys, were West Point men and officers in the regular army throughout the War period.

The following Smyth boys were killed or died in the service: George W. Arden, W. H. Grubb (first Smyth boy killed "over there"), Carl Repass, Emory Chaffon Shrader, John G. Spangler, Charles A. Whiteley, Camel Poe, Joe S. Olinger, Joe Crewey, Jas. M. Gass (colored), Robt. Rector, O. J. Burkett, Marvin Testerman, Charles Atkins, C. A. Vogt, and Ben Parson.

The Draft Board was composed of Rush C. Gwyn, Chairman; R. T. Greer, Secretary; Dr. S. W. Dickenson and Dr. J. D. Buchanan, examining physicians. Mr. H. P. Copenhaver successfully put across the Y. M. C. A. drive for funds. Mrs. George W. Miles was chairman of the Liberty Loan drives. Under her leadership, supported by the splendid field work of T. E. King, George A. Collins and others, the county oversubscribed its quotas. The first Red Cross unit in the county was formed at Chilhowie with Mrs. James D. Tate as the moving spirit. There being no chapter in Smyth the Chilhowie unit at first affiliated with the Bristol chapter. Saltville also organized a Red Cross unit. About this same time, a little later than the others, the chapter at Marion got under way with Mrs. George W. Richardson at the head of it and Mrs. George W. Miles her second in command. The Chilhowie branch transferred its allegiance to the Smyth County Chapter. Saltville has maintained its own distinct chapter organization.

The Ordnance Department of the Army decided to build a plant for the manufacture of atmospheric nitrogen. A plant for this purpose, dismantled after the war, had been built in Saltville in 1914 by the Nitrogen Products Company whose officers were officers of the Mathieson Alkali Works. Saltville was selected for the location of the government plant as the nitrogen coming from the Mathieson Alkali towers would be available and because of the fact that the Nitrogen Products plant was conveniently located for the training of the enlisted men who would operate the new plant.

Work was started early in 1918, and at the same time a number of drafted men were sent to Saltville to learn the process of the Nitrogen Products plant and others to learn the operation of gas production at the Mathieson Alkali Plant. The demand for labor in building the plant, which was done under the Quartermaster's Department of the Army, brought to Saltville more men than the town could accommodate and the first work done in connection with the new plant was the erection of barracks to take care of this surplus. Later these were used to quarter the enlisted men. The plant was turned over to the Chemical Warfare Service Department for operation at about the time the armistice was signed so that its output was never available for war purposes. A few units however operated for a short time after the end of the war to determine the practicability of the plant, and while many minor changes were found to be necessary, it was demonstrated that if the war had been continued Saltville would have been shipping from Chemical Plant No. 4 a chemical that would have been a great factor in its outcome. The cost to the government for the erection and operation of the plant was over two million dollars. The number of enlisted men necessary to operate and guard the plant was four hundred. The plant has been scrapped and there is practically nothing to show for it.

The government also made extensive use of the Mathieson Alkali Plant and other Smyth County industries for producing war materials.

MUSTER ROLL SMYTH COUNTY IN THE WAR WITH GERMANY

William Adams, Printus Clayton Aker, John W. Alexander, David S. Allen, Jake A. Allison, William Allison, Worden Allison, James Anders, Byron F. L. Anderson, Marvin J. Anderson, James F. Anderson, Alex Apperson, George W. Arden, James M. Archie, Kelly Armstrong, Louis G. Arnold, Louis E. Ashlin, Charles E. Atkins, James P. Atkins, Soloman E. Atkins, Price W. Atkins, Thomas Jefferson Atkins, and Oscar Gleason Ayers.

Charles F. Biase, Frank Fay Bales, James H. Bales, George W. Baldwin, Lee Baldwin, James H. Bates, Douglas Barberry, Wiley O. Barton, Willard S. Barr, W. M. Baumgardner, Henry W. Beasley, Charles Wm. Bennett, Early M. Bennett, Wm. V. Birchfield, Wm. McKinley Bise, George R. Bise, George C. Bishop, Newton C. Bishop, Andrew L. Blankenbeckler, Rush Blankenbeckler, Walter R. Blankenbeckler, Henry Blankenbeckler, Wm. A. Blankenbeckler, Ray C. Blankenship, Burton Blevins, Conley Wm. Blevins, Gather

THE WORLD WAR 269

Blevins, Granville Blevins, Dudley Blevins, Leonard Blevins, Lincoln Bolden, Tony Bolt, James B. Bonham, James F. Bonham, S. L. Bonham, Edward T. Bowling, Hobson L. Bowser, Anderson G. Boothe, James J. Boothe, Robert Muncie Boothe, — Bowers, Roy Branson, Andrew W. Brickey, Dooley D. Bridgeman, Alexander M. Britton, Fred S. Britton, Wm. Duke Britton, Frank C. Broady, J. Bascom Brockman, John Brooks, John T. Brosius, Fred Wm. Broski, Emmett Brown, John Q. Brown, M. M. Brown, John Brown, Willie B. Brown, David B. Buchanan, John L. Buchanan, Jr., Frank Buchanan, Luther L. Buchanan, Albert T. Buchanan, James W. Buchanan, George E. Buchanan, Thomas Buchanan, Walter E. Buchanan, Thomas Sam. Burgess, Robert Thurman Burgess, Henry Raymond Burgess, James Greek Burkett, O. J. Burkett, Frazier Burkett, Harry E. Burkett, Ollie Burns, and John A. Burnop.

Allen E. Cahill, Joseph R. Campbell, Leslie Calhoun, Ellis M. Calhoun, James Hamplion Calhoun, Alex F. Cole, Edward Call, Harvey Call, Charlie Call, Thomas F. Call, Worley F. Carico, Henry Hurley Carter, Garnet F. Carter, Rush E. Carter, Hirst Carson, David H. Cassell, H. Bailey Cassell, Arthur M. Catron, Martin L. Catron, Robert L. Catron, J. E. Cassidy, Andrew Chadwell, Bruce Chapman, Wm. M. Chapman, C. C. Caudill, James Frazier Clear, John A. Clear, Dean B. Clear, Homer Floyd Clear, James E. Coe, Clay S. Cole, Dean B. Cole, Fred Newton Cole, Alex F. Cole, Harold M. Collins, Roy L. Comer, Wm. A. Conner, Claude W. Conner, Edward F. Conner, Frank Copenhaver, Dave Concoran, Ellis Cornett, Robert P. Coulthard, Clarence Cox, Julian Crankfield, John Craven, Wm. T. Craven, Toby C. Cress, Arthur G. Cress, John Creggar, Brady Crewey, Jos. A. Crewey, Ianson Crouse, Albert Charles Crouse, W. Carl Crow, Bert McKinley Crumley, Guy Thurston Culbert,

Homer A. Cullop, John B. Cullop, Wm. J. Cullop, Grover C. Cullop, Earnest C. Cummings, Silas C. Cummings, Charles L. Currin, and William H. Currin.

Ralph R. Daniel, Leonard Davidson, James Davidson, George Davidson, Hyter Davidson, James E. Davis, Harold F. Davis, Hezero Davis, George Ed. Davis, James Debord, Roy C. Debusk, Charles O. Debusk, Claude T. Debusk, S. C. M. Delp, Edward H. Dempsey, Ben Densmore, William C. Dennison, Emory N. Dinsmore, Nathan L. Dickinson, James M. Dillman, Bruce W. Donnelly, Reid H. Duncan, and James Richard Dutton.

Bert H. Eastridge, Floyd Leslie Echols, George Roy Edmiston, Perry Frank Edmiston, Wm. Henry Edwards, David R. Elan, Russell McKinley Elledge, Carl Early Elliott.

William Wesley Fadis, Elijah M. Faris, Ralph White Farris, Graham J. Ferguson, Walter J. Ferguson, James M. Ferguson, Guy Earl Fisher, Frank W. Ford, Marvin C. Ford, Leonard S. Fry, L. Sanders Fry, Riley Robinson Fry, Wm. Toby Fry, Clifford W. Fuller, and Charles P. Fulton.

Wm. R. Galliher, Ben Gammond, Esquire Gambill, Samuel Starritt Gass, James S. Gass, Wm. F. Gates, George W. Gates, John M. Gilbert, Lawrence M. Gills, Reed Goins, John W. Gollehon, James H. Gowdy, John Vint Goodman, Robert Goodman, Milton W. Goodpasture, Wm. E. Goodpasture, William Goolsby, Peyton H. Gregory, Robert Green, Hobert Green, Ernest Vint Greever, Willard A. Grinnon, Willie Meek Grinstead, Leander Groseclose, W. H. Grubb, Heber B. Grubb, Jackson Gullion, and Robert Gullion.

Everett M. Hale, Floyd Jackson Hale, Robert Lucian Hall, Charles M. Hall, Andrew G. Hall, John B. Hankla, Jesse T. Hankla, Edward Hankla, Robert R. Harman, David Harman, Jr., Benjamin H. Hart, Virgil Madison Hart, Brady Harris, Wm. Dick Harris, Arthur Harris, Seldon Harris, Olin Harris, James Harrison, McCoy Hash, John A. Hash, Floyd Y. Haw-

THE WORLD WAR 271

thorne, Charles Hawthorne, John A. Hawthorne, Wm. Haynes, Claude M. Heath, Robert Heath, Onie C. Henderlite, Thomas Henegar, Charles Henegar, Reese Tolbert Heninger, Dewey G. Hester, Carl P. Hester, John B. Hester, Frank S. Hester, Wyndham Hicks, McCoy Holman, James D. Holdman, J. Roy Horne, Robert R. Hogsdon, Turley Howington, Robert R. Hubble, Garland Leroy Hubble, Harmaon Brown Hubble, Manuel Huffman, Scott A. Hughes, Phillis Washington Hughes, Jesse M. Hughes, Leeland Humphrey, Lewis O. Hundley, Samuel R. Hurt, Walter G. Hutton, James H. Hutton, Walker Hutton, Wm. K. Hutton, Hester Hutton, and Carl E. Hutton.

John P. Inscore and William M. Ivey.

Benjamin F. Jennings, Walter C. Jennings, Charles B. Johnson, James A. Johnson, Charles D. Jones, Charles K. Jones, John B. Jones, and Jethro Jones.

Adam W. Kegley, G. A. Keese, John H. F. Keesling, James M. Kell, Harry Douglas Keller, Jacob Wesley Keller, Walter W. Kelly, Frank A. Kelly, Floyd Kendrick, Walter S. Kent, John H. Kerley, Hugh White Killinger, Frank Kindrick, John H. King, Ward King, John C. King, George Washington Kirk, Roby Gordon Kirk, Robert C. Kirk, Wiley M. Kirk, William G. Kirk, Conley G. Kirk, Archie Kirk, Otto Deland Kitts, Melvin C. Kitts, Walter Kitts, and Frank W. Kregor.

George S. Lawrence, Roy E. Leach, Dent Leftridge, Peter Leonard, Albert Theodore Leonard, Seymour J. Leonard, George Lomans, Gillespie Lomans, Thomas Walker Louthan, Merl M. Lovelace, and Ed. Luster.

Floyd McKinley Madison, Virgil E. Maiden, Benton Maiden, Leroy Martin, John H. Markum, George Washington Mash, Lotus D. Marshall, William A. Mason, John David Mason, James C. Medley, Edward Mercer, Walter J. Mercer, William James Mercer, Herbert C. Mercer, Willie B. Merideth, James Mitchell Miller, Charlie Miller, James Whitten

Mills, William D. Mitchell, Ralph Montgomery, Glenn R. Montgomery, Everett S. Moody, William Snavely Moore, John Geo. Moore, Grover C. Moore, Haynes L. Morgan, Carl B. Morris, George R. Morris, George Vance Moxley, Roy Mumpower, Henry H. Musselwhite, John W. Musser, Wm. S. Musser, and Claude D. Myers.

S. E. McClannahan, Charles Willis McCloud, Samuel C. McCormick, Robert B. McCready, Charles C. McCready, Frank McCready, John McElrath, John P. McGhee, John Wise McGhee, Randall McGhee, Wm. L. McGinnis, Wm. M. McIntyre, Hurley C. McKinnon, Gyp McNew, John McNorman, and James H. McVey.

Ezra E. Neff, William C. Neff, Hubble Neikirk, Garnet L. Nelson, L. Marvin Newman, James A. Newton, and James G. Nutter.

John Robert Oday, James S. Olinger, and Robert McKinley Osbourne.

Luther T. Pafford, Muncie B. Pafford, Ben. R. Parsons, Avery Willard Parsons, Robert W. Pendleton, Rufus Pennington, Wm. H. Pennington, Ephriam H. Phillippi, M. Leslie Pierce, Harry Pierce, Earnest C. Pickett, Luther G. Pickle, Charles Pickle, John Piper, Camet Poe, Charles Rhudy Poe, Grover Pollard, Joseph Hiram Prater, George D. Prater, William Bowen Prater, Roy S. Prater, Frank Pruitt, William H. Pruner, Roscoe F. Pruner, and Carl W. Pruner.

Nathan C. Quillin and Vernon E. Quillin.

Fred Harvey Rector, Emery P. Rector, Robert C. Reedy, Strother C. Redmond, Carl Repass, Andy M. Rhudy, Early S. Rhudy, Eugene Richardson, William M. Richardson, George Allen Richardson, Walter W. Rigsby, Howard Rigsby, Edgar L. Ritchie, Robert Roark, James E. Roe, James Robbins, James K. Roberts, Benj. H. Roberts, Edward S. Roberts, James K. Roberts, E. Hiter Robinson, Conley T. Robinson, George T. Roland, France Rose, Kin Ross, Glea Ross,

THE WORLD WAR 273

Lillard Roten, Newell Orland Routh, Conley L. Rowland, Bedford Russell, John Wiley Russell, and John Calvin Russell.

Joseph B. Sanders, Graham W. Sanders, Onyx E. Sayers, Charles B. Scott, John W. Scott, Louis Scott, A. Dickey Scott, Harry W. Scott, Will Scott, Wm. Edwin Seaver, Marvin Seaver, John L. Sheets, Norman Judson Sheets, Lester Ray Shelton, James Pugh Shelton, George W. Short, Charles L. Shorts, Emory Chaffon Shrader, Andrew Simons, Burrell Frank Sisco, Walter Chesterfield Smith, Joseph Defon Smith, Kelly Smith, Aught Smith, James V. Snavely, Henry T. Snider, Raymond Snider, Arnold R. Snider, Charles S. F. Snider, Bruce Snider, John T. Snider, John L. Snider, George M. Snow, Charles L. Sparks, James R. Sparks, John G. Spangler, Sidney Sprinkle, Willie P. Sprinkle, Harry L. St. Clair, Gordon C. St. Clair, William B. St. John, Charles K. Steele, Marvin Stone, Joseph Sult, Albert Surber, E. K. Surber, Robert Surber, Frank L. Swain, and Frank Sweeney.

Albert Taylor, Luther H. Terry, James Ezra Tester, Marvin Testerman, Robert Thomas, Robert T. Thomas, Charles Herbert Thomas, William B. Thompson, Bertram B. Thornton, Stanley L. Tibbs, Everett B. Tibbs, William R. Tilson, James T. Tilson, John J. J. Tilson, Wm. Brazzle Todd, William Tolbert, George Tolbert, Walter C. Totten, Arthur G. Totten, John S. Trexel, Clyde Tribble, John R. Tual, Edgar F. Tuell, Charles Tucker, and James A. Turner.

Edgar Lee Umbarger and William Robert Urps.

Charles A. Vogt and James Emory Vogt.

George S. Waddell, Arnold Walt, Gustave J. Wallinger, A. Scott Ward, James Louis Ward, Charles F. Wassum, Hugh Clayton Watson, John Webb, Luther K. Webb, Henry B. Welch, Reson H. Welch, Arthur Van West, L. Ray West, Conley J. Wheeler, Gayle A. Wheeler, Glenn H. Wheeler, Wm. J. Whisman, Lee Taylor White, James F. White, Edward

Whiteley, Charles A. Whiteley, James Whiteley, James Marvin Wilson, John Wm. Wilson, Robert Wilson, Edward F. Williams, Jesse Williams, Albert Lee Williams, Thomas Frank Williams, Edward Winston, Joseph B. Wolfe, Roy A. Wolfe, Joseph T. Wolfe, John H. Wolfe, Walter C. Wolfe, Edward Wood, Dan Woodward, Wythe B. Woody, George Wyatt, and Mike Wymer.

Walter T. York.

Chapter XVII

SOUTHWESTERN STATE HOSPITAL

With Williamsburg and Staunton hospitals full to overflowing, and scores of helpless mentally sick in jails and almshouses over the State, the thoughtful people of Virginia realized in the winter of 1883–1884 that immediate steps must be taken to build and equip another public institution for the care and treatment of these unfortunates. It was to meet the end demanded that the Hon. W. G. Mustard, of Tazewell County, introduced in the lower branch of the General Assembly, March 5, 1884, a bill creating a commission to select a site somewhere in the mountains of Southwest Virginia, for establishing the "Southwestern Lunatic Asylum," even at that late day the laity of Virginia, as in many other states, failing to distinguish between either the ethics or the object of a name or characterization now fallen into disuse. The "Southwestern Lunatic Asylum," conceived during those early days of 1884, is today officially known and publicly esteemed as the Southwestern State Hospital.

This commission was composed of some of Virginia's most distinguished sons. They were empowered to visit towns and cities in the southwest portion of Virginia situated west of New River. One of the conditions named in the original bill was that the site should be commanding and where the air is pure and the water plentiful. Every town in the mountains of Southwest Virginia could meet that requirement. Another instruction the commission had from the legislative body was that material assistance should be given the State by whatever town was favored with the "lunatic asylum." Every competing point from the west bank of New River to the Tennessee line rose splendidly to the occasion. It was a difficult undertaking the commission assumed when it met June 4, 1884, at Central Depot, now the beautiful little city of Radford, for the purpose of visiting sites and inspecting and choosing from the many offered the final location of Virginia's newest, and what was later to become, one of her most famous hospitals.

From the records of the commission, it appeared that the little town of Marion appealed strongest to the nominating board. The citizens of Marion and the people of the county tendered the Atkins farm, with added lots, just on the corporation line, comprising in all 199 acres of splendid farming and grazing land, in addition to which deeds were tendered to four springs having a daily water supply of more than a million and half gallons. Judge D. C. Miller and Capt. J. P. Sheffey conducted the negotiations for the citizens of Marion and Smyth County and at Roanoke, July 16, 1884, the Commission formally located the institution at Marion.

On August 26, Governor Cameron and the Board of Public Works approved the findings of the commission, and the General Assembly, in November following, passed two important bills relating to the proposed institution, one appropriating a sum not exceeding $100,000 for construction purposes, and the other bill authorized the people of Smyth County to vote $30,000 in bonds for payment of lands and water rights deeded to the Commonwealth.

The building was completed and received by the commission Feb. 12, 1887, and upon formal tender to Governor Fitzhugh Lee, he appointed as the first board of directors of the new institution: Dr. Samuel W. Sayers, of Wytheville, President; Daniel Trigg, Abingdon; A. M. Bowman, Saltville; Judge S. C. Graham, Tazewell; H. C. T. Richmond, Lee County; S. P. McConnell, Scott County; Henry C.

SOUTHWESTERN STATE HOSPITAL

Stuart, of Russell County, who in November, 1913, was the choice of the Democratic primary for Governor of Virginia; Dr. S. W. Dickinson, Marion, and Capt. D. D. Hull, of the same place. March 1, 1887, the board elected the following chief officers: Dr. Harvey Black, physician and superintendent; Dr. Robert J. Preston, first assistant physician, and Dr. John S. Apperson, second assistant physician. C. W. White was elected steward; A. H. Gibboney, clerk; J. L. Groseclose, treasurer. The last office was abolished after the first year.

The labors of Dr. Black in organizing, and the constant strain upon him as the responsible head of an institution which he had largely directed from the date of its birth in that legislature of 1884, proved too much for his health, and on Oct. 19, 1888, a year and seven months after taking up his new and more exacting duties, he breathed his last. Dr. Preston succeeded Dr. Black. Dr. Preston died Aug. 29, 1906, and Dr. Daniel Trigg acted as superintendent, pending the appointment of Dr. A. S. Priddy, of Bristol, Virginia, as superintendent, Nov. 1, 1906. Capt. Gibboney served as clerk for six years, being promoted to the office of steward Oct. 13, 1891, afterward serving the State most acceptably as clerk and supervisor of farm and garden.

Dr. J. C. King, superintendent and chief medical director of the Hospital, first became connected with the institution April 15, 1901, as second assistant physician, was elected first assistant physician in 1907, and advanced to superintendent Dec. 8, 1908. Under the administration of Dr. King, the Legislature has appropriated a sum sufficient to erect a tubercular building, and the general arrangement is to meet every possible demand for sunshine and air. Begun in 1911 and completed in 1912, the building now gives comfort to fifty patients who are fed from their own diet kitchen. Carrying out the segregation idea, a commodious cottage has been pressed into service for the old and chronic dements.

In 1910 the General Assembly decided to locate at Marion, in connection with the Hospital, a building for the care and treatment of the criminal insane. Dr. King visited a number of the eastern institutions of this character and finally plans were drawn following the general idea of Mattewan. This building is 44 x 174 feet, two stories, with basement, and was designed with the idea of giving patients and those confined there awaiting trial, or under observation, every opportunity for exercise and freedom of movement.

The first assistant physician at each of the State hospitals is a male, while a woman physician in charge of female patients is second assistant. Dr. E. H. Henderson is first assistant physician at the Southwestern State Hospital, and Dr. Carolyn A. Clerk occupies the office of second physician.

Dr. Black opened the Hospital for the reception of the first two patients, May 17, 1887.

Dr. J. C. King resigned in 1915 and has since established and operated a private sanitarium near Radford, in the old St. Albans School plant. This school was founded and run by one of Smyth county's ablest sons, Mr. George W. Miles, Jr. He was succeeded as Superintendent by Dr. E. Henderson on Nov. 10, 1915. Dr. Henderson was a native of Giles and before coming to the institution as first assistant physician in 1909 had practiced medicine in Pulaski County. He continued in office until his death in February, 1927. During the twelve years of his very successful administration, many improvements were made on the property and additional land was purchased. The most notable event of this period was the establishment of the Davis Clinic.

Dr. George A. Wright, first assistant physician under Dr. Henderson, was then and is now a reader of the Congressional Record from which he learned of the Federal Government's intention to establish such an institution for the treatment of war service men suffering from mental and nervous disorders. He proposed to his chief that they go after it and Dr. Henderson immediately took it up, and with Mr. A. J. Huff, Chairman of the Board of Directors, authorized Dr. Wright to institute negotiations. Blue prints and plans for a building were submitted to Washington and a committee came from there to look over the site. The government agreed to utilize the proposed building under contract, provided it was completed according to specifications and ready for occupancy in the year 1921. Work was begun. The appropriation was insufficient for completion. Governor Westmoreland Davis arranged for a loan from the State Treasury which made possible the completion of the building and securing of the Clinic, so that it was named in his honor. The Clinic was opened for patients in the fall of 1921 and has been in successful operation ever since.

Dr. George A. Wright is a native of Giles County and descendant of Peter Wright, a famous pioneer hunter and one of the earliest to live and hunt in that New River country, and the first to come to Smyth County to practice medicine at Chilhowie.

Then, as now, he was recognized as a physician of rare skill, a veritable genius for sympathetic contact with his patients, and as a sportsman, passionately fond of hunting, fishing, and all forms of outdoor sports and recreation. In 1906 he was married to Miss Lula Buchanan of Rich Valley. In 1918 he came to the institution as First Assistant Physician and resigned in 1922 to become surgeon in the George Ben Johnson Memorial Hospital at Abingdon. After Dr. Henderson's death he was recalled as Superintendent, taking the office June 1, 1927. Under his administration a very extensive building program has been carried forward, landscape improvements have been made, and two farms have been added to the real estate holdings.

The resident officers of the Southwestern State Hospital have been:

Officers	Service Began	Service Ended	Remarks
Superintendents			
Harvey Black, M.D.	Mar. 1, 1887	Oct. 19, 1888	Died in office
Robt. J. Preston, M.D.	Nov. 30, 1888	Aug. 20, 1906	Died in office
Daniel Trigg, Jr., M.D., Acting Supt.	Aug. 21, 1906	Nov. 1, 1906	Resigned
A. S. Priddy, M.D.	Nov. 1, 1906	Nov. 10, 1908	Resigned
J. C. King, M.D.	Dec. 8, 1908	Nov. 10, 1915	Resigned
E. H. Henderson, M.D.	Nov. 10, 1915	....	Died in office
Geo. A. Wright, M.D.	June 1, 1927	....	....
First Ass't. Physicians			
Robt. J. Preston, M.D.	Mar. 1, 1887	Nov. 30, 1888	Elected Supt.
E. J. Brady, M.D.	Nov. 30, 1888	April 15, 1889	Elected Second Ass't. Phys.
T. D. Kernan, M.D.	April 15, 1889	June 18, 1896	Died in office
Z. V. Sherrill, M.D.	July 24, 1896	April 15, 1891	Resigned
A. S. Priddy, M.D.	April 15, 1901	June 22, 1903	Resigned
S. R. Sayers, M.D.	July 14, 1903	Dec. 10, 1904	Resigned
Daniel Trigg, Jr., M.D.	Dec. 8, 1904	Feb. 5, 1907	Resigned
J. C. King, M.D.	Feb. 5, 1907	Dec. 8, 1909	Elected Supt.
J. W. Stephenson, M.D.	Dec. 10, 1908	Dec. 21, 1909	Resigned
E. H. Henderson, M.D.	Dec. 21, 1909	Nov. 10, 1915	Elected Supt.
R. E. Chumbley, M.D.	Dec. 1, 1915	Dec. 15, 1917	Resigned
W. T. Chitwood, M.D.	Dec. 15, 1917	May 11, 1918	Resigned
Geo. A. Wright, M.D.	May 11, 1918	May 15, 1922	Resigned
James King Gray, M.D.	April 14, 1922	....	Still in office
Second Ass't. Physicians			
T. D. Kernan, M.D.	Nov. 30, 1883	April 15, 1889	Elected First Ass't. Phys.
Jno. S. Apperson, M.D.	Mar. 1, 1887	Nov. 30, 1888	Resigned
E. T. Brady, M.D.	Apr. 15, 1887	June 1, 1892	....
C. K. Kernan, M.D.	July 24, 1899	Apr. 15, 1901	....
J. C. King, M.D.	Apr. 15, 1901	May 25, 1903	Resigned
Eliz. F. Collins, M.D.	Aug. 1, 1903	June 1, 1905	Resigned
Margaret V. Painter, M.D.	June 15, 1905	July 15, 1911	Resigned
Alice N. Pickett, M.D.	July 15, 1911	Sept. 26, 1912	Resigned
Carolyn A. Clark, M.D.	Sept. 26, 1912	April 1, 1922	Resigned
Malcolm H. Harris, M.D.	Sept. 9, 1922	April 18, 1923	Resigned
Preston E. Wolfe, M.D.	May 7, 1923	....	Still in office

SOUTHWESTERN STATE HOSPITAL 281

Officers	Service Began	Service Ended	Remarks
Ass't. Physicians Davis Clinic			
James King Gray, M.D.	Oct. 1, 1921	Apr. 14, 1922	Elected First Ass't. Phys.
Malcomb H. Harris, M.D.	June 15, 1922	Sept. 9, 1922	Elected Second Ass't. Phys.
Leroy L. Sawyers, M.D.	Feb. 4, 1923	Nov. 14, 1924	Resigned
Wm. H. McCarty, M.D.	Nov. 17, 1924	....	Still in office
A. D. Hutton, M.D.	July 6, 1928	....	Still in office
D. C. Boatwright, M.D.	Nov. 1, 1928	....	....
Stewards			
C. W. White	Mar. 1, 1887	Apr. 15, 1899	....
A. H. Gibboney	Oct. 18, 1901	June 1, 1917	Died in office
Walter E. Johnson	June 7, 1917	....	Still in office
Clerks			
A. H. Gibboney	Mar. 1, 1887	Apr. 15, 1893	....
H. B. Staley	Apr. 15, 1893	Apr. 15, 1897	....
J. B. Richmond	Apr. 15, 1897	Sept. 24, 1901	Dead
Walter E. Johnson	Oct. 18, 1901	June 17, 1917	Elected Steward
Will Spickard	June 7, 1917	Mar. 1, 1931	Resigned
W. S. Robinson, Jr.	Mar. 1, 1931	....	....
Matrons			
Mrs. L. B. Crockett	Mar. 1, 1887	Apr. 15, 1889	....
Mrs. A. H. Gibboney	Apr. 15, 1889	Apr. 15, 1893	....
Miss Bettie Scott	Apr. 15, 1893	Apr. 15, 1897	....
Miss Nannie Akers	Apr. 15, 1897	Apr. 15, 1901	....
Miss Channing Goode	Apr. 15, 1901	Oct. 19, 1903	Resigned
Miss Margaret Shannon	Oct. 19, 1903	May 4, 1905	....
Miss Fannie Withers	May 4, 1905	Feb. 1, 1911	Resigned
Mrs. Lena J. Sprague	Feb. 1, 1911	May 12, 1913	Resigned
Miss Cora L. Ogle	July —, 1913	Jan. 1, 1914	Resigned
Miss Queen Shelton	Feb. —, 1914	July 25, 1917	....
Miss Victoria Scott	Aug. 1, 1917	Sept. 22, 1919	....
Miss Nora D. Carter	Dec. 15, 1919	....	....
Supervisor of Farm and Garden			
A. H. Gibboney	April 15, 1899	Oct. 18, 1891	Elected Steward (died)

Chapter XVIII

TOWNS

Population of Smyth County and Its Towns 1840 to 1930

Virginia	1930	1920	1910	1900	1890	1880	1870	1860	1850	1840
Smyth County...	25,125	22,125	20,326	17,121	13,360	12,160	8,898	8,952	8,162	8,162
Chilhowie.......	712	572								
Marion.........	4,156	3,253	2,727	2,045	1,651	919	368	445		
Saltville in Smyth County......	2,407	1,800	1,314	878						
Saltville in Washington County	557	448	314	173						
Saltville total..	2,964	2,248	1,628	1,051						

Chilhowie

Chilhowie was a substantial and notable community long before there was any Chilhowie town. It was the Town House community so named because on a hill in the center of the town is the oldest English built house on soil drained by Mississippi streams. Col. James Patton and his exploring party built it in 1748 to mark the site which Patton chose for a future city and they called it the Town House. A man named Stalnaker, perhaps the same whose wife and son were killed when his cabin on the present J. R. Shanklin farm was burned by the Indians in 1754, lived at the Town House about 1770. Whether this Stalnaker lived in the Town House itself or built another is not certain. He probably occupied it for a while at least. Capt. James Thompson, who built and lived in the stone fort and residence called Kilmackronan, now the home of Mrs. A. Huff, owned the house and a great deal of land nearby. It was transferred by his heirs to James Sanders, and sold to Robert Beattie in 1837.

Robert Beattie had moved to the place in 1833 from Seven Mile Ford, having gone to Seven Mile Ford from the Glade Spring community. He enlarged the house and made it a combination house and stage coach tavern which acquired a reputation in its day. Robert Beattie reared a large family in the old house, as did his son, Claiborne Watkins Beattie. His grandson, Alonzo Beattie, present Mayor of Chilhowie, lived there with his father after his marriage until his own house was built at the foot of the hill. The Town House was a favorite place for militia musters.

There is a good story, probably true, to the effect that at one of the earlier musters a gallant young gentleman from Kentucky was present named John Floyd. He had a very handsome, and very swift and spirited Kentucky horse. Horse and rider matching well, elicited the hearty admiration of those bold spirited, horse loving gentlemen of the Washington militia. Floyd was a likable fellow, clean and keen. Moreover his father, the elder John Floyd, killed in Indian battle in Kentucky, was a romantic hero of the Revolution, associated with glamorous adventures in the dark and bloody wilderness, leading surveying then settling parties, fighting Indian battles; on the high seas, privateering; in an English prison, escaping by making love to the jailor's daughter, coming home to romantically wed the daughter of Col. John Buchanan. Moreover, on this very muster ground he had had a strenuous time enlisting and disciplining a company to follow him to Point Pleasant back in Dunmore's War, 1774, when he was slated to lead the company that Joseph Drake wanted to lead. For his father's sake and for his own young John Floyd would be the lion of the hour.

When the time arrived for the special event arranged to do him honor he could not be found. It developed that Miss Letitia Preston, daughter of the late Col. William Preston, who, visiting with her brother Francis, had ridden over to enjoy the social festivities of the muster, was also missing. Finally some one acknowledged having seen Miss Letitia mounting the beautiful and spirited horse behind Mr. Floyd. They arrived at the old Kentucky home as Mr. and Mrs. John Floyd, but whether they stopped on the way to provide another horse the story does not say. This John Floyd and his wife later lived in the present Pulaski County. He was the Governor of Virginia who signed the act authorizing the formation of Smyth County, and as candidate for President of the United States he received the electoral vote of North Carolina. As for the truth of this story, it has been told in varied forms and it likely has foundation in fact. Col. Thomas L. Preston told it to Mr. B. F. Buchanan as true and the Colonel was careful about the truth. He, however, according to Mr. Buchanan's recollection, made the hero the elder John Floyd, and the heroine Miss Jane Buchanan. But there is substantial evidence that the marriage of the elder Floyd took place elsewhere and under very different circumstances. Soon after the signing of the Declaration of Independence Col. William Preston, Dr. Thomas Walker, Mr. Edmund Pendleton and two other gentlemen purchased a schooner, fitted her out for a privateer and put Floyd in command. Off the West Indies he captured a rich prize, a British merchant ship laden with a cargo that would have made the fortunes of all involved in the privateering venture. When Colonel Floyd had left for this voyage he was engaged to Miss Jane Buchanan, daughter of Col. John Buchanan, who had died. Among the treasures of the captured vessel was a very elaborate and costly trousseau intended for a prospective bride in some wealthy colonial family. Colonel

Floyd's exuberant spirit exulted in the prospect of presenting this to his Jane. But just off the Virginia capes a British man-of-war overhauled him, captured his schooner, and took all his prize cargo, including the trousseau, away from him. Moreover, they clapped the Colonel into a prison in England where he languished for many a month, finally making his escape, getting across the Channel to France, and thence by the help of Dr. Benjamin Franklin, returning to Virgina.

No intelligence of the privateer or its crew had reached the United States. The inference was that all was at the bottom of the sea. A year after Col. Robert Sawyer, a distant kinsman of Miss Buchanan, an officer in the army, and a rich man, addressed the young lady. Sawyer had requested her to walk with him in the garden; she consented, and whilst there she agreed to marry him. In an hour thereafter Colonel Floyd arrived at "Smithfield," much to the joy and surprise of his friends. Miss Buchanan's last engagement was immediately cancelled, and in the month of November, 1778, she married Colonel Floyd. Soon afterwards they went to John's Creek and settled there. Colonel Floyd's father and family had left Amherst and were living on John's Creek. He remained a year there and then determined to remove to Kentucky. By this time their eldest son, William Preston Floyd, was born.

This account of the elder Floyd's marriage, written by Mrs. Letitia Preston Floyd, herself, does not seem to fit in very well with the tradition that the hot-blooded Colonel finding opposition from Col. John Buchanan to his marriage with Jane, swept her on the horse behind him and rode away from the Town House muster to Kentucky with her, especially since Col. John Buchanan had died some years before. It is possible, however, that it was the elder John Floyd who ran off with his bride, Jane Buchanan, and not his son with Miss Letitia Preston, and that opposition to the match came not from Jane's father but from her brother-in-law. Joseph Drake had married a daughter of Col. John Buchanan, and they lived on Carlock's Creek not far from the muster grounds. There was an old quarrel between Drake and Floyd. Jane was visiting at the home of her cousin William Preston when John Floyd came back to life and claimed her from Sawyer. In the month of November, 1778, she might well have been visiting her sister, Mrs. Drake on Carlock's Creek. Colonel Floyd might well have attended a muster at the Town House that month, perhaps to take command of a company. And he might have learned that his old personal rival, Drake, was trying to break off his engagement with Jane Buchanan and in his heady way taken her on his horse behind him and ridden forthwith to the parson. We can keep the story anyway and until we dig up definite proof as to the marriages we may assign it to John, Jr., or John Sr., as our fancy pleases.

There is another interesting tradition in the Chilhowie vicinity whose truth has been questioned, the story that Philip Greever fired the first shot at King's Mountain and that the old musket from which he fired it is still in possession of his descendant, Mrs. Virginia Greever. Personally, I believe the story to be absolutely true, and on the following grounds: (1) It has come down by direct tradition in the Greever family; (2) The old musket of the period of King's Mountain with the initials "P. G." cut into its iron barrel, has been handed down as Philip Greever's gun; (3) Philip Greever himself in an affidavit sworn to before a notary public makes the assertion that he fired the first shot in that battle, and he made this affidavit while many veterans of King's Mountain were still living around him, who would have certainly refuted it if not true.

In the stagecoach days, certainly one, possibly two, presidents of the United States were entertained in the old Town House Tavern. In a cockpit nearby the sporting gentry would match their game roosters, sometimes for high wagers. The stage road ran up the hill and in front of the old house. Madam Russell spent her last years in a large log house she had built just west of the Town House. To the north was a sulphur spring, in a beautiful wooded location that was developed into a notable summer resort known as the Chilhowie Springs, and had attached to it a famous race track and a still more famous camp meeting ground.

In 1804 Robertson Gannaway purchased a farm near the sulphur spring. Just before marching to Norfolk with a volunteer company in the War of 1812 he leased the sulphur spring, and after the War was over began building near it. He ran a small store, a blacksmith shop, and a house of entertainment. In 1815 he opened the Chilhowie Springs and in his own words "promoted Appolyon's cause" in the running of the resort until August, 1819, when he was converted in the nearby camp meeting. He continued to run the Springs until 1821 when he went into the Methodist ministry. He was succeeded by others who carried on the hotel features of the resort, the last being George E. Palmer. Cabins were built under the trees around the Springs and all through the last century families from nearby counties would camp out there on summer vacations, and visitors from the South would come to summer in this health giving resort. Senator Wm. C. Preston of South Carolina spent many a summer there with his family.

Mr. James Tompson deeded a tract of land near the Springs as a camp meeting ground. The first camp meeting was held on the Sulphur Springs camp ground in August, 1819. It became famous not only for its preaching but also as a political hustings. The most notable political rally was held during the Polk-Clay presidential campaign of 1844. The large shed, called a tent, was furnished with rough benches to seat several thousand people and the pulpit provided an excellent rostrum. Cabins flanking the tent on both sides for use of worshiping families during camp meetings were fitted up for accommodating visitors. The hotel and cabin accommodations at the Sulphur Springs were crowded to capacity. Dozens of sheep, hogs, and beeves were barbecued, hundreds of hams were boiled, and thousands of pounds of bread, cake, pie, chicken, and turkey were heaped on rude tables which if placed end to end would have reached for more than a mile. Delegations from a distance brought wagon loads of provisions, and they came from all over Southwest Virginia and Western North Carolina, East Tennessee, and Eastern Kentucky. Processions of vehicles and horsemen extended for miles in either direction as they approached the meeting place. Most of the men were on horseback and many carried polk berry stalks and were shouting for "Polk, Dallas, and Texas." Felix Grundy, L. C. Haynes, John B. Floyd, and other distinguished orators kept the speaking going for two or three days, not only in the tent but from various other platforms set up on the ground. There was no brass band but old time fiddlers were numerous and had foot-tickling power.

When the railroad came through in 1856 and when the first wood-burning train passed by a lad in the excited crowd who gathered to see it cried out: "It makes more smoke than mammy's pipe." A post office was established where the railroad crossed the river about a mile east of Chilhowie. This office, midway between Seven Mile Ford and Chilhowie, was the Seven Mile Ford office intended to serve both communities. Mr. W. S. Staley, of Marion, once operated a store, owned by his father, at the place and was postmaster. The original post office at Chilhowie was called Town House. After the building of the railroad a siding was put in near the Town House and the place was called Greever's Switch. Mr. George Palmer, proprietor of the Sulphur Springs, suggested that the village growing up around Greever's Switch be called Chilhowie and he worked until he had the name adopted. The name is an Indian phrase which means "valley of many deer," and was applied by the Indians to the northern part of the Middle Fork Valley between Seven Mile Ford and Marion.

The first store built in Chilhowie was put up by Minter Jackson in 1870 and the second was built by Hiram Henegar. There was an old store house on the Sanders property near Beattie's stable where store was kept by one John Summerfield before the village started, patronized by the guests at the Springs and people around. This old house was torn down and made into a residence by Mr. Hiram Henegar—the first dwelling in the town of Chilhowie.

Mr. Minter Jackson fathered the first Chilhowie industry—a pottery plant—and in 1890 and 1891 Adams Brothers and Payne, of Lynchburg, acquired extensive holdings of brick clay lands, and built and operated a plant at Chilhowie under the style of the Virginia Vitrified Brick and Sewer Pipe Company. This firm carried on an extensive and profitable enterprise at Chilhowie for a number of years.

One of the oldest families of Chilhowie is the Sanders, the old homestead now occupied by Mr. Marvin Sanders being one of the landmarks of the community. The Sanders family came to Smyth from Wythe when John Sanders leased the King Salt Works at Saltville in 1819 at an annual rental of $30,000. Col. James White of Abingdon purchased this lease from John Sanders and entered into contract with James Sanders by which he agreed to take all the salt the latter could make at one dollar per bushel, estimating that he could handle the capacity output of the wells for a handsome profit at that figure, but Sanders built additional furnaces and opened more wells and threatened to glut the market and bankrupt Colonel White. To avoid the threatened bankruptcy,

Colonel White offered Sanders large sums to cancel the contract. At last it was agreed that if Colonel White would purchase the beautiful estate on the Middle Fork of Holston, lying west of the Aspenvale tract, and extending to Colonel Greever's, below the present Chilhowie, and deed it to Sanders, the contract would be cancelled. Tradition says this purchase cost Colonel White $75,000.

The old Sanders home, east of Chilhowie, was built by James Sanders when he acquired this great farm, and his widow was living there when Smyth County was formed. His descendant, Marvin Sanders, lives in the old place now. Frank Sanders, a brother of Marvin's, acquired a part of the old Capt. Charles Preston estate still farther east, and has developed it into one of the finest farms in the county. Dr. Dan Sanders, another brother, has practiced medicine in Chilhowie for many years, and Dr. Ben Sanders, living there, has specialized on the eye. Dr. Ben Sanders once ran a drug store in the town. The first drug store was kept by one Hickman, who was succeeded by Mr. Joseph Sechler and Dr. T. K. McKee. Dr. Ben got it from them and passed it on to Mr. Greever who has it now.

> "Meet me at Chilhowie—howie
> I am bound to go———"
> Don't you hear the horses prancing
> Meet me at the show;

This was the song at a horse show held at Chilhowie on July 4, 1910. It was a gala occasion. Horses from many Southwest Virginia counties were shown, riders dressed in gay uniforms put on a drill of fancy figures, a tournament was ridden, a game of baseball was played, and in the evening a ball was given in the School House. Dr. J. Glenroy Harris, "The Knight of Spottsylvania," won the first prize in the tournament and John M. Preston, "The Knight of the Holston," the second.

Among the prize winners in the horse show were C. S. Wassum, J. R. George, Miss Maggie Pratt, Miss Nellie Preston, Miss Gladys Vance, Miss Bessie Hutton, Charles McKenny, J. W. Stephenson, R. C. Gwyn, G. C. Huff, J. E. Thomas, and Lee Umbarger.

In the boys' and girls' riding contest Mattie Preston Wassum won the first prize and Ike Huff, the second.

The Vance Company are dealers in general hardware, building and farm supplies, and manufacture and sell fertilizers. It has a capital stock of $250,000, owned by one hundred and forty stockholders composed largely of farmers in Washington and Smyth counties. It has four branch stores located at Abingdon, Glade Spring, and Marion, and does an annual business of approximately $600,000.

This business has a successful history of over thirty years. It originated in the nineties of the last century in the firm of Vance & Umbarger, which was organized at Chilhowie by Mr. James L. Vance. To succeed the old company, Mr. Vance—in 1902—organized the firm of James L. Vance & Company. His partner in this enterprise was Mr. Q. A. Eller, whose connection with the business has continued to the present time. This firm did a large business in farm machinery and supplies throughout Southwest Virginia, and organized a number of branches at different points in the succeeding years. Some of these branches afterwards became independent stores, and some remain as part of the present organization.

The policy of Mr. Vance and his associates was to foster the development of agriculture in this section by the introduction of improved machinery and the promotion of improved methods of farming. To meet the needs of the section, the company began the manufacture of fertilizer—having in mind the production of brands especially suited to Southwest Virginia. The company was also active in finding outlets for, and marketing the products of, their customers.

The business of the company grew as agriculture developed, and the company became not only a source of supply, but a source of information in regard to the best methods of farming. It has always worked hand in hand with the Experimental Station at Blacksburg, and has kept in touch with the latest developments in agricultural methods with a view to making them available to the farmers in its territory.

About the same year that James L. Vance and Company was organized, Mr. Vance also organized a hardware store at Chilhowie under the name of W. H. Copenhaver & Co. In partnership with him were R. W. Scott and W. H. Copenhaver. This business also developed and expanded in the hardware field, and in the course of time, it also acquired branch stores.

In 1926 the hardware business, which had broadened its scope of activities, merged with the farm supply business under the name of The Vance Company in honor of the founder of both companies. It has continued under this name up to the present time. Mr. Copenhaver and Mr. Eller are in active charge of the business at Chilhowie.

Its President is J. T. Frazier, Jr., and the Vice-Presidents are Jas. D. Tate and H. L. Bonham.

Its Board of Directors consists of: F. L. Sanders, T. B. Rector, Geo. F. Pierce, W. P. Buchanan, W. T. Smith, Jas. E. McSpadden, Jas. D. Tate, J. T. Frazier, Jr., W. B. Porterfield, Noell Craig, and H. L. Bonham.

Its policy is to maintain an efficient organization of local men at each store who know the needs of the public, and take an interest not only in rendering good service in the store, but in promoting whatever is of value in the community.

The original founder, Mr. James L. Vance, was a man of many interests; of broad vision; and of unusual foresight. His labors for the development of this section have extended beyond his lifetime through the organization which he founded.

Mr. Vance, descendant of a pioneer who figures in the first militia musters at the Town House and in Indian and Revolutionary warfare, lived and died at Chilhowie. Mr. Q. A. Eller came up from North Carolina to go into the farm supply business with Mr. Vance in 1902 and has lived since then in the town. His brother, June A. Eller, for the past dozen years, has rendered splendid service to their adopted county as Chairman of its Board of Supervisors. Mr. William H. Copenhaver was born and reared on a Smyth County farm. Mr. J. Tyler Frazier, Jr., son of a beloved old Methodist minister of sainted memory, President of the Vance Company, is Smyth County's present representative in the House of Delegates. Mr. W. N. Neff, another member of the firm formerly lived at Chilhowie but now resides in Abingdon and represents Washington County in the state House of Delegates. He is a scion of the pioneer Neff family who settled on the Middle Fork above Seven Mile Ford on the farm owned until recent years by Henry Tilson. James D. Tate, another associate of the firm, was reared on the old Tate farm north of Chilhowie, son of a shrewd and convivial old Virginia planter and a pious Methodist mother who built a church on the farm known as Tate's Chapel. Colonel Tate acquired his title by appointment on Governor Lee Trinkle's staff. He is an able business executive with many large and varied interests and is active in the promotion of many public improvements.

The Bonham Orchards and Farms are a great industry

in and around Chilhowie. Mr. H. L. Bonham, after profitably working in the lumber business, began planting apple and peach trees in 1911 and 1912. In 1916 he built a warehouse in his orchards south of town. After a season he put a cold storage plant in the town warehouse, and has been adding to it ever since, until it now has a capacity of a hundred thousand boxes, a bushel to the box. He barrels some apples but packs the bulk of his crop in boxes and disposes of it on the domestic market, mainly in the South and West. In addition to his orchards, comprising all told some fourteen thousand trees in Smyth and Wythe counties, he has large farming interests. On his pastures near Chilhowie he has a fine herd of thoroughbred Herefords. He devotes a great deal of effort to the improvement of blue-grass pastures, and every year for the past several years he has entertained the countryside in a great farmers' picnic, with speakers on scientific farming. His work in improving agriculture has received wide recognition. Mr. Bonham represented Smyth County for a term in the legislature. He ascribes a large share of the credit for the success of his business to his sons who are associated with him.

The Bonham family has lived from pioneer days in Smyth County, the first Bonham having built his cabin on South Fork. His name was Hezekiah Bonham and he came from Loudon County to settle in Sinclair's Bottom. Either his father or his grandfather was an Episcopal minister, who had twelve sons and gave all of them Bible names ending in "iah." Mr. Robert S. Bonham was sheriff of Smyth County for nine years, and his son, A. F. Bonham, was County Surveyor for a number of years. The latter has in his possession a clock made by Johnson and Ides and purchased by his father from an agent who was going about the country peddling clocks in the eighteen-twenties. This was the last clock the agent had and he offered it to Mr.

Robt. Bonham for thirty-six dollars. Mr. Bonham was a young fellow just married and had very little money. He said to the agent: "I have eighteen dollars. If you would rather have the eighteen dollars than the clock, take it and leave the clock. If not, take the clock and leave the eighteen dollars." Since the clock is still running in the Bonham home it is inferred that he took the eighteen dollars.

The town of Chilhowie was incorporated by order of Smyth County Court in 1915. Mayors have been: James D. Tate, John W. Hennegar, and A. C. Beattie.

Chilhowie has fine spring water derived from a spring at the head of Grosses' Creek about which this letter tells:

CHILHOWIE, VIRGINIA
STAR ROUTE BOX 30
January 25, 1932

Mr. G. A. Wilson, Jr.

DEAR SIR: I saw in the Smyth County News that you wanted help to get information concerning your History of Smyth County. I live on Grosses Creek close to the Washington county line. The line runs through our farm. You wanted to know why the Creek was called Grosses. I suppose it was because so many Grosses lived here when it was named.

I was a Gross. I was born and raised on the head waters of Grosses Creek. My father owned the Spring that now gives water to the town of Chilhowie.

The folks that lived here when I can first remember are about all gone. Garrett Marshall, Paulser Surber, Rachel Barlow, uncles John and Rufus Gross, Grandmother and her four unmarried children, Josiah Shupe, Mary Gentry, James and Sallie Houston, Katie Meek and Mr. Davenport are about all the families. Cousin Abraham Gross was our closest neighbor. Just a few descendants of these families are here now, two of Rachel Barlow's children, James and Amanda, two of Josiah Shupe's children, Hannah and Sallie, one grandchild, Washington Shupe, one of uncle Rufus Gross's, Eliza Anna Blevins, and myself.

SARAH ELEANOR PENNINGTON.

Marion

The founding of Marion may well be dated from May 25, 1832, as on that day during its second term the newly established Smyth County Court ordered that "George W. Davis, Edward Fulton, Henry B. Thompson, Charles E. Harrison, and James F. Pendleton be appointed commissioners to lay off the Town at the place designated by the Commissioners appointed by an act of the General Assembly of Virginia to fix upon the seat of Justice of this County; and it is further ordered that the said Commissioners lay off a cross street east of the Public square fifty feet wide and two other cross streets forty feet wide and the said commissioners are directed to map off the said town and after giving sufficient notice make sale of the lots upon Twelve months credit requiring bond and approved security and make a report of the whole proceedings to the court."

This order was promptly executed and the town laid off in the wheat and rye fields of William Humes. Lots were duly laid off and sold. The town, as first laid, began at Broadway and extended to the western limits of the present Marion College campus. The Main Street was seventy feet wide; the cross street, which is now Church Street, was fifty feet wide; another cross street which passes between the residence of Mr. J. C. Campbell and the Presbyterian Church was fifty feet wide; an alley on the west end of the court block was sixteen feet wide; and alleys by the Episcopal Church and east of the present Rider property were sixteen and one-half feet wide. The stage road ran north of the town through a ford in Staley's Creek below the present residence of Dr. Thompson, ascending the hill north of the Grammar School and passing in front of the houses now occupied by Miss Grace Buchanan and Mr. B. E. Copen-

Marion

haver, through the college campus and the Look lot back to its present location.

At the west end of town the road ran so as to cut lot corners, making three triangular lots of four poles frontage in one block that is now part of the college campus. All other lots were four poles frontage and ten poles in depth, running four to a block. On the north side of Main Street was the Court Square, with two four-lot blocks on either side and the stage road some distance north of them. On the south side of Main Street were five blocks of four lots each, and in the west on either side of the street was a three-lot block.

The first purchasers of lots were: On the north side of the street beginning at Broadway, Samuel Scott, Jos. W. Davis, Joseph Atkins, Foster and Davis. Then the Courthouse came. Robert Beattie purchased two lots in the middle of the block where the old Haller house now stands. T. Brumfield and John Thomas one lot each in the block where Mr. Campbell's house stands. On the south side: John Thomas first bought the Piggly Wiggly lot, and M. Hutton had another lot in this block. Crockett Ingles had two lots in the next block, one being the corner now occupied by Hotel Marion. Opposite the courthouse, I. Wauhof had the second lot from the east corner and the Sprinkles the corner now occupied by the Post Office. The next block was either reserved or purchased entirely by Humes. John Thomas and J. W. Larvis had lots in the block where Mr. George Collins now lives and Mr. Lloyd one lot opposite the college grounds.

The area comprised within the original town was without houses. The old Thurman home was standing just across the stage road from the northern town limits, and had stood since before 1800. It is still standing and is the home of

Mr. and Mrs. B. E. Copenhaver, the oldest house now in Marion. Humes had his cotton and grist mill at the ford, on the site later occupied by a foundry. John Irons' family lived across the river in the neighborhood of the present Staley Addition. Henry Shugart lived in a log house that stood on or near the railroad right of way back of the East End Filling Station or back of the Francis home. The old Arthur Campbell house was standing on the hill southwest of the D. D. Staley property. The church and probably the preacher's home and John Thomas' house were in the Royal Oak addition. One Isaac Collins lived west of town where Mrs. Hull's home is now, and a man named Hoosier had some kind of wayfarers' tavern near the spring in the corner of the Look lot.

The first store was on the corner now occupied by the Bank of Marion and was opened for business in 1832 by Spiller and Company, a firm composed of William Hickman Spiller, of Wytheville, and Francis Preston Staley. The present generation of Sheffeys and Staleys are grandchildren of this Spiller and Staley respectively. Staley owned land south of the town and up Staley's Creek, which he had no doubt inherited from Abram Staley with whom Arthur Campbell had land arguments in Botetourt and Fincastle courts. Soon thereafter another store was opened on the corner now occupied by the Marion National Bank. This was owned by E. S. Watson, who married one of the Thurman girls. Samuel Vernon and W. H. Spiller were granted license to run stores by the same order of court, May 24, 1832.

The courthouse was completed in 1834, and about this time Zachariah Shugart built a saw and grist mill where the H. B. Staley Mill is, and the Humeses built a mill that was later operated by one Snavely, then by J. Peter Killinger, and converted by Look and Lincoln into that firm's plow, wagon, furniture and other kinds of a factory. Mr. Zachariah

Shugart also built, about this time, a large frame house that served as a tavern, and was bequeathed by him to his niece, Mrs. Joseph Atkins. It is known now as the old Atkins house. Zachariah Shugart was a bachelor, a large man of striking appearance. He, the colonel of militia, E. A. Scott being major, drilled troops at the semi-annual musters. He entered the Confederate army when past the age limit and died shortly afterwards while in the service.

The first hotel in town was built where Hotel Marion now stands. Mr. E. K. Coyner, who came to Marion from the vicinity of Waynesboro, Virginia, in 1909, has supplied this information concerning the site:

At the first sale of lots, Crockett Engles bid off lot 16 for $220.00 but it was never deeded to him, but was deeded to Robert Beattie, on the 25th day of May, 1832. This was the lot on which Hotel Marion now stands. On Oct. 8, 1835, it was sold to James P. Strother and James P. Strother called it the Continental Hotel. Then James Strother sold it to Abijah Thomas in 1856 on May 9, and a man by the name of Ellis Perkins kept a barroom in the building. Then Abijah Thomas sold it Dec. 1, 1885, to John V. Thomas, who used it as a residence. It was sold from John Thomas by Commissioners V. S. Morgan, B. F. Buchanan, C. D. Carter, W. W. George and S. D. Jones. Sept. 10, 1888, E. D. Groseclose, of San Jose, California, and B. P. Groseclose, of Barton, Kansas, bought it from the Commissioners and started the Valley House. In 1909 E. K. Coyner bought the Valley House from the two Grosecloses and ran it as the Valley House until 1915, then changed its name to Hotel Marion, still owning it.

Lot No. 15, which is now a part of the hotel property, was bought by John Schoolfield on Feb. 18, 1835, and sold to Shepherd Brown.

The various denominations—the Methodists, Baptists, and Presbyterians—held services in the courthouse until their churches were erected.

The Methodist Church was built in 1846 south of the then town limits on the lot now occupied by the Baptist Church. The Presbyterians were continuing to use their old log house east of town, but in 1853 Edward S. Watson deeded to the Royal Oak Presbyterian Church the lot where the Graded School building now stands. The church building was on it at the time of the conveyance; when it was built is not known but probably about 1850. The Baptist Church was organized in 1845 and the house was built east of Broadway in 1859.

Howe's History of Virginia, published about 1840, speaks of Marion as a recently established village on the great turnpike from Baltimore to Nashville and describes it as a small neat town containing three stores and about thirty dwellings. One of these stores was Spiller's or Staley's; the others were probably Vernon's, and either Watson's or McDonald's.

In 1843, Mr. William C. Seaver came to Marion and started business in a log building which stood on the corner of the Seaver block. He was a skilled mechanic, industrious, and economical, and from the very first prospered and continued to prosper until he died June 5, 1909. His son, M. M. Seaver, is still carrying on under the firm name W. C. Seaver and Sons.

Marion of the early fifties is thus described by an old resident:

The town had possibly five hundred population. No manufacturing plants, two churches, Presbyterian and Methodist, a half dozen general merchandise stores, wheelwright shops, cabinet shops, blacksmith shops, shoe shops, saddle and harness shops, two tailor shops, two taverns, two schools, one for boys and one for girls, two grist mills, and one barber shop. The people were industrious, religious, social and happy.

Soon after the founding of Marion, Madison Crockett built a brick residence west of the old Thurman house. This house was later occupied by the Misses Gordon who conducted a school in it. Then, just after the Civil War, it was sold to Col. George Smith, a Northerner, and his son George, Jr., lived with him there. Dr. J. J. Scherer bought this property from the Smiths and opened Marion College in the old brick residence.

Isaac Collins lived in a brick house west of Marion when the town was formed. Judge George W. Jones later owned and lived in this house. Then his brother, William Jones, a farmer and civil engineer, bought it and lived in it. Capt. D. D. Hull bought it from William Jones, demolished the old brick house and built on the site the residence now occupied by his widow and daughter, Miss Banie Hull.

Francis Preston Staley built and reared his family in the house now occupied by W. M. Sclater.

The railroad was built through Marion in 1856 and F. P. Staley was the first depot agent. His son W. S. Staley also worked in the depot and may have been in charge at one time. Nicholas Perkins was depot agent after the Staleys, then came F. H. Cowden, who served for many a year, and after him came Messrs. Dungan, J. B. Neal, I. B. Wells, and C. P. Blackwell. Mr. Blackwell was born and reared in Wytheville. He worked in the Marion station as a young man in the early nineties, left, and then came back to take charge Jan. 10, 1910. He is still on the job, and long may he continue. The first depot was where the freight station now stands and freight and passenger business was handled at the same stand. The frame building across the tracks was operated as a hotel and trains would stop at meal hours long enough for the passengers to be fed. A negro with a big dinner bell would meet the trains.

About the war period, just before and after, the following were among the Marion concerns:

Mr. Walter Pruner, who lived where Mr. Newell Atkins now lives south of Hungrys Mother, was a cabinetmaker and had a shop in his house. Mr. Alexander Campbell was a silversmith who operated what would now be called a jewelry store where the Peery Crocery Company now does business. West of the town on the Look property Mr. Nelson Fudge operated a tannery. Mr. Madison Pruner was a wagon maker who lived and worked near the Episcopal Church. Messrs. Milburn and Clayburn Galliher had a blacksmith shop on Staley's Creek and hammered iron with a tilt hammer worked by water power. Milburn lived in a house where Mr. George Seaver later lived. Frank Newman operated a blacksmith shop where the Episcopal Church now stands. Mr. William Francis was a tailor and had his tailor shop where Weiler's Store is. He lived where the Royal Oak Apartments have been built. The Collins Department Store stand was occupied by Mr. William Moore, a saddle maker. On the corner where the Marion National Bank is now, Mr. E. S. Watson kept a store. Mr. Adam Groseclose operated a grist mill where the old Humes Mill had been and where Messrs. Goodell and Quaif were to build a foundry and machine shop at which they made gun barrels used by the Confederates during the War. Messrs. Look and Lincoln made the stocks for the guns at their plow, chair, and broom factory. Mr. Goodell came to Marion from New York in 1859 and started this foundry. About the same time Messrs. Look and Lincoln moved from Rich Valley, starting their manufacturing business where Mr. Peter Killinger had formerly operated a grist mill.

Through the reconstruction period Federal troops, commanded for a part of the time by a Colonel Hambright, were quartered in barracks lying south of the road between the present Colored Methodist Church and the residence of Mr. Henry A. Pruner.

Rev. W. V. Wilson, D.D., came to Marion as pastor of the Presbyterian Church in 1865, and continued to live in

Marion until 1874. At one time some other officer than Colonel Hambright was in charge of the troops policing Marion, a little man with much more sense of his own importance than sense of propriety. He gave Dr. Wilson a peremptory order to pray for the Federal soldiers in his public worship. The minister ignored the order and the officer had him arrested and brought to trial before a court-martial. A very able lawyer, Mr. J. H. Gilmore, volunteered to defend him before that court, but he had difficulty in handling his client, for the indignant old preacher would not keep quiet and burst out on the officer with this: "Man, are you such a jackass that you don't know better than to try to dictate to a minister what he shall pray for? If you have any sense at all you ought to know that a prayer is nothing unless it comes from the heart, and the only prayer I could make from the heart for you or your soldiers is that the Lord would take the last rascally one of you back north where you belong." The officer was stubborn and his pride was wounded and it might have gone hard with the preacher had not Mr. C. F. Lincoln and Mr. G. G. Goodell, well known northern men, immediately gotten in touch with this fellow's superior officer, who required him to release Dr. Wilson with apologies, and to refrain from any future interference with any minister of the gospel in the discharge of his duties.

Dr. Wilson in his nine years residence in Marion established a reputation for wisdom and piety, and for ability as a fisherman as well as a preacher and pastor which still endures.

Marion in 1880 had a population of 919 distributed in part as follows:

At the western limits a tannery was just north of the road and Mrs. Fudge lived across the road from the tannery. Mr. N. L. Look lived on the hill above the tannery and Judge Fudge lived just across the road from him, where Graham

Hull now lives. The road was called West Street. Main Street extended straight ahead, and William Dodd, A. P. Cole, the Baptist Parsonage, the Presbyterian Manse, G. W. Henderlite, H. C. Pruner, W. O. Austin occupied the north side from the Look place to the College. There were no buildings on the south side. The only building on College Street was the Marion High School, now the Mitchel home. Then came the College and Rev. J. J. Scherer's residence; then Judge Jones' home and Dowdy's right back of it, where Miss Grace Buchanan lives. Judge J. P. Sheffey's house and land occupied the ground between Judge Jones' home and Sheffey Street. In the corner of his yard was his office and a drug store. Back to the river were gardens, barns, orchards and fields. West of Church Street there were no houses between the alley back of the courthouse and Presbyterian Church and the river. The Presbyterian Church was where it is now, with Mrs. Ellen Sheffey living next to it, and the Jackson building was then called the Exchange Hotel. In the west corner of the courtyard was Robert A. Richardson's law office and Mr. James H. Gilmore's was in the east corner, both some distance back from the streets. F. Alexander had a store on the northeast corner of Church and Main Streets, then Willmoore's house and saddle shop, W. P. Francis' house with the Post Office attached, then the Episcopal Church, A. Pruner, R. M. Goodell, and A. G. Pendleton on the Broadway corner. One building where Groseclose's Variety Store is, Seaver's ware rooms, the Seaver home and Galliher's place carry us to Staley's Creek. Across the creek was Mrs. F. Pruner and then Depot Street. On the west side of Depot Street was R. C. Vaughn in the little old house still there, W. R. Johnson, J. H. Francis, D. F. Carrier, and J. B. Rhea whose holdings ran to the river and had no buildings other than his home, where the Philip Francis' house is now. In his back yard was the town spring. On the other side of

OVERFLOW FROM MARION TOWN SPRING

Depot Street were the Methodist Parsonage and homes of A. Campbell and F. Cowden. Joseph Atkins lived in the old Atkins house and his farm ran back through the hospital grounds. Dr. James Sheffey lived where his widow now lives and Mr. J. B. Rhea had a store across the road from him. John W. Stallard lived in the house where Mrs. Oscar Stephenson now lives. J. H. Gilmore lived on the Piggly Wiggly and Marion Drug Company site and the south side of Main Street was occupied with residences, stores and Mrs. Sprinkle's hotel out to the Odd Fellows' Hall.

There was yard space between most of the buildings. The colored school and colored Methodist Church were standing where the church and parsonage are now. Houses and factories with open spaces between extended from Main Street to the river east of Church Street. The Baptist Church was on Broadway and the Methodist Church where the Baptist is now. Lots with some houses on them extended south of Main Street between Church and Cemetery Streets. D. C. Miller and John S. Copenhaver lived in there on opposite sides of Cherry Street and back of John S. Copenhaver's was a block marked "Town Reservoir." It is now occupied by the high school building and grounds.

In the old days the water supply came from private cisterns, from the "Town Spring" in Mr. Rhea's yard, the Shugart Spring near the N. & W. Station and the town pump, which with its horse trough was on Main Street in front of Moore's Saddle Shop where the Hotel Lincoln is now. Water was hauled in wagons at times from Shugart's Spring. On April 1, 1888, the Preston Spring on Staley's Creek, now known as the "Old Town Spring," was bought and a six-inch pipe laid. Some years later the Short Spring on the Killinger place was purchased and an eight-inch pipe laid to it from the end of the old line.

Mr. W. L. Lincoln and Mr. John Sexton were in charge

of this work. Mr. G. G. F. Killinger, after declining to sell the spring, finally agreed to sell it for a $3,000 insurance policy on his life, the town to pay the premiums. The town paid only one premium as Mr. Killinger died six months later. In 1910, while J. P. Sheffey was mayor, the great springs above Attoway were leased from Mr. George Atkins for ninety-nine years and have furnished Marion with an almost unlimited supply of the finest water, delivered by gravity from spring to faucet. Mr. W. L. Lincoln was chairman of the committees that put through these various water deals and laid the lines, his associates being at different times Messrs. O. C. Sprinkle, John Sexton, and J. C. Campbell.

W. L. Lincoln, O. C. Sprinkle, and John Sexton were also a committee appointed to have the Norfolk and Western build a new passenger station. George W. Cook, Superintendent, came down from Roanoke and they entertained him with the biggest banquet Marion had known up to that time, given in an old hotel that was opposite the Presbyterian Church property on Main Street. They got the depot, and N. & W. officials for years teased Mr. Cook with the charge that Marion bought a depot from him with a dinner. Mr. W. L. Lincoln was also superintendent of construction and treasurer of the committee in charge of building the new courthouse and for his work was presented a gold watch by the committee.

The Smyth County Telephone Company with A. T. Lincoln, President, C. C. Lincoln, Manager, and W. L. Lincoln, B. F. Buchanan, and F. M. Young, stockholders, put in the first telephones.

The Marion Light and Power Company with B. F. Buchanan, President, C. C. Lincoln, Manager, and H. P. Copenhaver, O. C. Sprinkle, A. T. Lincoln, and W. L. Lincoln, stockholders, lit up the town in 1900 and supplied electric current until they sold out to the Appalachian Power Company. At first they got power from Copenhaver's Mill dam, then built a dam farther down the river.

The Bank of Marion was established in 1874, and was then the only bank between Wytheville and Abingdon and the only one in Smyth, Tazewell, and Grayson counties. Its first stand was in the Jackson building. In the nineties H. E. McCoy, President of the Old Dominion National Bank of Bristol, established the Farmers and Merchants Bank in Marion, which failed.

In 1903 the Marion National Bank was established. An auxiliary of the Marion National Bank known as the Smyth County Trust Company was tried out with Mr. W. H. Teas as President, but after a few years was discontinued. The Peoples Bank operated for a time and then consolidated with the Marion National Bank. O. C. Williams started the movement to organize the National Bank and was the first cashier. He was followed by J. G. Frye, who went to the Federal Reserve Bank in Richmond. Mr. Thomas E. King, the present cashier, came to Marion in 1908 and has been one of the town's most active, useful, influential, and beloved citizens ever since.

Riley Thomas Greer came to Marion from Watauga County, North Carolina, on April 18, 1905, and started a unique business that has developed into the largest of its kind in the world: The R. T. Greer Crude Drug Company, dealers in roots and herbs. He selected Marion because it is a good shipping point and lies in the center of an area producing more natural medicinal herbs than any other area of its size on earth.

Mr. Greer was born in Watauga County, North Carolina, March 14, 1875, son of Finley and Mary Greer. He married Miss Eunice Josephine Todd Feb. 17, 1896. When they came to Marion they lived in a little four-room house rented from H. B. Staley, where the Virginia Lincoln Company is now. Then moved to another little house just across the street from the present offices of that company, then to the house on Cherry Street where Mrs. Crockett now lives, then built their present home. After Mr. Greer had done business in Marion for a few months he needed two hundred dollars for sixty days to carry on, and could not borrow it in the town. Now anyone in town with the money to lend would be glad to take his note for many times that amount.

He had a general merchandising business at Riverside, North Carolina, where he dealt in roots and herbs. He with his partners in that business, Messrs. G. H. Tatum and F. P. McGuire, and his cousin, George W. Greer, decided to go into the root and herb business. They put up a working capital of $2,000 and opened in Marion April 20, 1905, with a branch at Pikeville, Ky., under George W. Greer, starting at the same time. The business capital is now around $200,-000. The Greer cousins bought out McGuire and Tatum, and later took in C. C. Stafford, of Paintsville, Ky. R. T. Greer, George W. Greer, and C. C. Stafford are now owners of the business.

Marion for years was the trading and shipping point for Grayson, and the bordering North Carolina counties—great numbers of covered wagons constantly coming in, the wagons camping around the town. Copper mines operating in North Carolina shipped most of their output by wagon to Marion and thence by rail. Merchants and farmers from all that country would come in for supplies.

The town has long been a busy trading and industrial center and in the eighties and nineties was quite a resort for summer boarders. The fare at the Sprinkle House was famous and the Exchange Hotel enjoyed lucrative patronage. Livery stables did a lively business in riding horses and buggies for pleasure seekers, and in renting hacks to drummers who drove all over the mountains calling on country stores.

Marked growth of the town came with the turn of the century after the Marion and Rye Valley R.R. was built, and Mr. Campbell and associates came with their lumber mill. The development of the great Lincoln factories has carried on this impetus. In the past ten years about half of the old town has been rebuilt and much new town has grown up. The new bank buildings for both banks, the Hotel Lincoln, Wassum Apartments, Lincoln Theatre, Piggly Wiggly Stores, New Hotel Marion, and the Presbyterian Church are some of the more notable buildings put up in that time. The filling station has come in flocks like unto the old covered wagons for number.

Charles S. Wassum has developed a new business in his Royal Oak Boxwood Farms which has been remarkably successful. He maintains offices in New York City and sells boxwood and other shrubbery to a large and wealthy clientele.

The two very excellent department stores of Marion, Collins Brothers and Weiler Department Stores, started from small beginnings.

The firm of Collins Bros., Marion, Virginia, was established in 1898. The founders of this business were L. P. Collins and George A. Collins, who were originally from Augusta County, Virginia. At the time this business was established, L. P. Collins had business connections in the city of Baltimore, and Geo. A. Collins was with the Bertha Mineral Company of Wythe County. The business first started in what was known as the Richardson building opposite the present location, which was purchased from the late W. P. Francis in 1911, and continued until the death of L. P. Collins in 1917, at which time the present owner took over the entire business, which he now conducts as Collins Brothers Department Store. Mr. Alex Hutchins, associated with this firm, started as messenger boy and has grown up with it.

Mr. Max Weiler came to Marion on October court day,

1884. There was big excitement in town. The Blaine-Cleveland presidential campaign was at its height and distinguished orators from Louisiana and Michigan were addressing the voters of Smyth at Marion when he arrived. There was drinking and there was fighting. When he came there were only two brick residences, the D. D. Hull home west of town and the Stallard house in the east end. The college buildings were brick. There was only one brick store —Fell and Jackson's. He started the first men's clothing store in Marion in 1884 in a little frame building located where he now does business. He was married in 1890. The Weiler-Wolfe Store, under Mr. Weiler and J. Fleet Wolfe, was opened in 1921 across the street, below Rouse and Greenwood's Store which then stood on the corner now occupied by the Marion National Bank. A combination of the two makes the Weiler Department Stores. The Weiler family and that of their son-in-law, Mr. Stern, are the only Jews who have lived for any length of time in Marion. They are popular and highly valued citizens. Mr. Weiler made his first sale to W. C. Seaver, Jr.—a fifty-cent pair of white overalls.

The Marion Clothing Company is, next to Weiler's, the oldest clothing house in town. Hawkins-Taylor did a good business for many years under Mr. W. W. Hawkins. After they closed, McDonald's, Inc., opened in the new Wassum building.

J. L. Thornton came to Marion in 1881 and opened a photograph gallery, which he operated until 1894. Seibert and Jewell also had a gallery for a time. Frank Farris had a photograph gallery for a number of years and was succeeded by A. P. Snider, Marion's present photographer.

Mr. Thornton purchased the mercantile business of Irons and Neighbors in 1883 and established the store which his widow has conducted since his death. Mr. Thornton also founded the Marion Bottling Works, in 1905, a successful enterprise that has passed through various hands and is now owned and operated by Shanklin and Hull.

The Marion Hardware Company was organized Oct. 1, 1900, with B. F. Buchanan, President, C. E. Thomas, Vice President and Manager, and J. E. Thomas, Secretary and Treasurer. On Oct. 20, 1900, they opened in the Seaver Block, with a capital of $4,000, the first hardware store in Marion. In 1908 they built and occupied the present building. Under the Thomas management it became the leading hardware store in Southwestern Virginia. It is now a part of the Vance Company chain. D. D. Staley operated the Staley Hardware Store for many years at the stand now occupied by the Stidham Hardware.

Drug stores have been operating in Marion since the Civil War. Dr. James Sheffey ran a drug store in the corner of Judge J. P. Sheffey's yard. Dr. James F. Pendleton had a drug store on the corner occupied now by the Marion Motor Company, and *The Democrat* was published in the rooms above his store. A gentleman by the name of Edmunds from Eastern Virginia came to Marion and opened a drug store in an old frame building that stood where the Bank of Marion is. Dr. S. W. Dickenson bought Edmunds out and ran the store for nine months, then sold to Onyx C. Sprinkle who had returned to his home town after a sojourn in Baltimore.

Dr. Sprinkle put up the building now housing the City Drug Store in 1893, and did business there until he sold to Sanford Carson and associates of the Carson Drug Company. This company after some years of successful operation failed and the business was taken over by the Marion National Bank, who employed Dr. J. A. Thompson to run it. Dr. Thompson and W. O. Walton bought it from the bank and still have it.

Dr. O. C. Sprinkle, Dr. J. D. Buchanan and C. Lee Richardson organized the Marion Drug Company and started business in their new building erected in 1913. In 1922 they sold the business to W. M. Sclater. Dr. Sclater also ran the D. M. Smith Drug Company organized in 1907, and doing business for some eight or ten years. He opened the branch in Hotel Lincoln in 1927.

Scott Brothers is the oldest grocery store in Marion, having been started by J. Walter Scott at the present stand on Feb. 1, 1911. Frank Copenhaver, Charles Glenn, and Bruce Copenhaver started the cash and carry grocery stores with the Piggly Wiggly in 1922, the Jamieson, now Kroger, and Clarence Saunders Stores following shortly afterwards.

One of the town's leading enterprises is the Peery Grocery Company, which is conducting a strictly wholesale business and since its organization has enjoyed an excellent trade. In January, 1910, Messrs. J. S. and A. N. Peery and S. W. Keys, of Glade Spring, W. W., R. B. and Arthur G. Peery, of Tazewell, launched this enterprise at Glade Spring, where they continued increasing the volume of business yearly. January 1, 1913, they moved from Glade Spring to Marion, and into their own large wareroom building. The brothers R. Britton and Arthur G. Peery managed the business until the former's death. Arthur G. Peery has managed it since.

W. C. Seaver and Sons, Marion's oldest firm, had a monopoly on the undertaking and retail furniture business until Dec. 1, 1912, when the firm of Seaver and Morris, composed of W. C. Seaver and M. C. Morris, began business. Mr. Seaver was trained in the old firm under his father. Mr. Morris had previously been engaged in the business at Chilhowie and at Teas. Mr. Seaver later withdrew from the firm and Mr. Morris carried on the undertaking business until his death in 1930. Several years before his death he sold out the furniture business to the Boggs-Rice firm, of Bristol, who opened their branch at Marion. Mr. Morris' son, Raymond, is now carrying on as undertaker. W. C. Seaver and Sons are still carrying on their large business at the old stand. The Medical Society of Southwest Virginia was organized in Marion. Dr. S. W. Dickinson, of Marion, is perhaps the only living doctor who was present at its first organization. I say its first organization for it lapsed into desuetude and was revived and reorganized several times before it got going good. It was along about 1884. Dr. Black, of Blacksburg, Dr. Gleaves, of Wytheville, Dr. Gildersleeve and Dr. Estil, of Tazewell, and Dr. Preston and Dr. Barr, of Abingdon, signed a call to the doctors of Southwest Virginia to meet in Marion, and from this meeting attended by about twenty-five doctors the Medical Society of Southwestern Virginia grew into what it is now. Dr. Dickinson was also present at the organization of the Medical Society of Virginia in 1870, though he was not a member, but a student of medicine very much interested in the proceedings. He has served several times as President of the state society.

Among the doctors who have practiced in the town are: I. P. Hoyt, M. P. Watson, H. C. Garrett, Charles Henry Stevens, before Dr. S. W. Dickenson came in 1881. When this dean of Marion medicine came from Louisa, Dr. Garrett and Dr. James F. Pendleton were practicing in Marion. Dr. Garrett soon became incapacitated and Dr. Pendleton removed to Staunton as assistant physician in the Western State Hospital, leaving the field to Dr. Dickenson until Dr. P. W. Atkins opened his office. A short time afterwards, Dr. Z. V. Sherrill removed to Marion, and these three with Dr. J. S. Apperson, who moved up from Chilhowie, served the town and much of the county until Dr. Atkins' death. Other doctors came, stayed for a short time and left, but these remained. Dr. U. G. Jones practiced in Marion for a while, and Dr. Charles B. Baughman came and formed a partnership with him. After Dr. Jones removed to Johnson

City, Dr. Baughman continued in general practice for several years, then specialized in eye, ear, nose and throat, having his office in Marion for about a year, then in Elizabethton, Tenn. Dr. W. J. Weindell came in 1919. Dr. A. B. Graybeal moved in from Grassy Creek, North Carolina, and Dr. E. A. Holmes from Rich Valley about the time Dr. Baughman gave up general practice. Dr. Willis Sprinkle opened his office in 1930 and Dr. D. C. Boatwright left his job at the Southwestern State Hospital to practice in town in 1932. Dr. Clark quit her job at the Southwestern State Hospital to marry Dr. Sherrill and has practiced jointly with him since her marriage.

The first dentist of record to practice in Marion was Dr. William Farmer, of Wytheville. Dr. Farmer had taught a classical school in Marion before going into dentistry. Dr. Rex Phipps says:

Dr. William Farmer, "the grand old man of dentistry," was almost the first to practice dentistry in Southwest Virginia. For several years after graduation he was stationed as clinical instructor in the Baltimore College of Dental Surgeons, the first dental college established in the United States. Later he returned to this section and practiced his profession for many years. He passed away at Pulaski, Virginia, about 1915, still in active practice at the age of about 90 years.

Dr. J. P. Hill had an office at Mt. Carmel from 1875 to 1910. Dr. Robert Blackwell, in Marion, 1880 to 1893. Dr. E. M. Copenhaver opened his office in 1892. Dr. R. H. Phipps, in 1907; Dr. F. P. Repass, from 1912–1931, retiring because of ill health; Dr. W. P. McGinnis from 1915 until his death; Dr. Jesse Baughman, 1926 ——; Dr. Morris Wechsler, 1931 ——.

The first jeweler of Marion of whom I can find record was Alexander Campbell, the silversmith. A Mr. Messelwhite had a jewelry shop at one time, and also a Mr. Redfoot. In 1899 Mr. G. M. Fisher opened a little shop in a part of the site now occupied by the Marion National Bank which has been developed by his brother into the J. K. Fisher Jewelry Store. Robert Aker started his jewelry business by mending watches and clocks when he was fourteen years old. He opened his store in Marion, Jan. 13, 1919.

The first barber of record was a colored man, old Uncle John Fowler. Ben Goble opened the next shop, and passed it on to his son, Charles Goble, who with Will Sharp, has done business for many years under the Hotel Marion. Mr. Harve White, Mr. Moser, and the Hocketts have had shops in Marion for years. The Curtis Beauty and Barber Parlor was opened in 1927. Beauty parlors came into vogue with the opening of the up-to-date Hotel Lincoln in 1927.

Harness making and shoemaking shops date back to earliest days. Of the last generation Will Moore and Thomas Pruner are recalled by older residents as the harness makers and P. J. Gregory and Thomas Rider as shoemakers. Henry A. Pruner, son of Thomas the harness maker, carries on a combined harness and shoe shop and store with modern machinery and equipment.

Theodore Lorenzen started the five and ten cent store business with his variety store in 1907, and has been succeeded by the Groseclose Variety Store, Graham's Five and Ten Cent Store, and Huffaker-Faucette's more recent establishment.

The Marion Ice and Coal Company, managed by Beattie Gwyn, has been making ice for Marion and Smyth County since Mr. Gwyn bought the factory from Mr. Bruer.

Mr. G. C. Umbarger, proprietor and manager of the Laurel Springs Dairy, is the pioneer in modern sanitary dairying, and the Shanklin Dairy has been in successful operation for some half dozen years. Before these enterprises were developed the family cow was a popular and essential institution in town economy.

Judge George W. Richardson was the first real-estate agent and when Mr. Robt. G. Goolsby went into partnership with him about 1909, the firm of Richardson and Goolsby became Marion's first real-estate firm. Mr. Goolsby is still in the field, with Buchanan and Copenhaver as his competitors.

Reference has already been made to Marion lawyers of other days. The Marion bar of today is composed of comparatively young men. In order of seniority in practice they are: John Preston Buchanan, George Frederick Cook, Robert G. Goolsby, B. L. Dickinson, Charles H. Funk, L. Preston Collins, W. V. Birchfield, R. C. Gwyn, Ralph Repass, Ralph Lincoln, and Richard Rouse. All of them except Mr. Funk, who hails from Tennessee, are native sons of Smyth.

Among the writers who have lived in Marion and Smyth County Sherwood Anderson is the most famous. Mr. Anderson built his country house across the county line in Grayson County in 1926, and the following year he purchased the Marion newspapers. Since then Marion has been his place of residence. While living at Marion he has published two books, *Hello Towns* and *Perhaps Women*, besides numerous articles and short stories.

Mrs. Laura Scherer Copenhaver, for many years teacher of English in Marion College, is a brilliant writer. She is a frequent contributor to national magazines, and has produced numerous pageants and plays of a historical or religious nature and several volumes dealing with themes pertaining to church life and activities. Her sister, Mrs. Katherine Scherer Cronk, was a beloved and effective lecturer, worker, and writer of the United Lutheran Church of America and published many stories, pamphlets, and books in the field of her life work.

Dr. F. V. N. Painter, lifelong professor of literature at Roanoke College, spent his last years in Marion. Dr. Painter was widely known as a prolific and authoritative writer in the field of classical literature. Many of his books have been for years standard texts in the schools and colleges of the country. Dr. Painter died at his home in Marion, Jan. 19, 1931, and was buried in Salem.

Col. Wm. C. Pendleton was reared in Marion and spent many years of his manhood in the town as editor of the *Patriot Herald* and of *The American*. In his later years he has written two large and valuable books, *History of Tazewell County* and *Political History of Appalachian Virginia*. Colonel Pendleton, well past eighty, but active mentally and physically, now lives in Tazewell with his daughter, Mrs. Sinclair.

Miss Miriam Sheffey, who has lived all her life in Marion, has published one small volume of poems, *Spirit Mother and Other Poems*, and contributes stories, articles, and poems to current periodicals.

Mr. Denny C. Culbert, of the firm of W. F. Culbert and Sons, amused himself one winter by writing a novel, *Musty Corn*, that had a profitable sale.

Mr. John Preston Buchanan occasionally writes a short story for a standard magazine, and his wife, Mrs. Annabelle Morris Buchanan, is a frequent contributor to magazines. Mrs. Buchanan's principal efforts, however, are in the field of musical composition in which she has won wide and favorable recognition.

Col. Thomas L. Preston published a very interesting book called *Reminiscences of An Octogenarian* and Rev. J. W. Cassell, who now lives at Konnarock, is the author of a valuable history of the Lutheran Church in Virginia.

The town of Marion was established by Act of Legislature in 1835, which Act reads:

Chap. 182—An Act to Establish the Town of Marion at the Seat of Justice for the County of Smyth

(Passed March 4, 1835.)

1. *Be it enacted by the General Assembly,* That not exceeding twenty-five acres of land including that now held in trust by Robert Beattie, commissioner appointed by the court of the County of Smyth, in relation to the public land, streets, alleys and other lots lying at the seat of justice for the County of Smyth, as the same has already been laid off and may be hereafter further laid off and extended into lots, with convenient streets and alleys corresponding thereto, shall be, and the same is hereby established a town by the name of Marion.

2. *Be it further enacted,* That James P. Strother, John T. Smith, Basil C. Harley, John W. Schoolfield, William W. Hanson, Jeremiah Rogers, and Robert Thurman, gentlemen, be, and they are hereby appointed trustees thereof, who shall, before they enter upon the duties of their appointment, take an oath before some justice of the peace for the County of Smyth, to execute the same faithfully and impartially, according to the best of their skill and judgment.

3. *Be it further enacted,* That the trustees of said town, or a majority of them, shall, so soon as convenient, under their own superintendence, cause the said land (or so much thereof as may not have been heretofore laid off), to be laid off into lots, with convenient streets and alleys, and shall mark with convenient and lasting signs, the divisions, metes and bounds the relative situation and distances of the lots, streets and alleys thereof, and for that purpose may employ a surveyor.

4. *Be it further enacted,* That the trustees of said town or a majority of them, shall be, and they are hereby empowered to make such by-laws, rules and regulations for the well ordering of the police thereof, removing or abating nuisance, and for the regular building of houses therein, as to them shall seem best, and the same to amend or repeal: *Provided,* That such by-laws, rules and regulations shall not be repugnant to, or inconsistent with the Constitution and laws of the United States or of this Commonwealth.

5. *Be it further enacted*, That in order to afford the citizens of said town at all times an opportunity of knowing the proceedings of the said trustees, there shall be provided a wellbound book or books as they may become necessary from time to time, in which shall be recorded in a plain handwriting, the several certificates of the qualifications of said trustees, and their successors, and all their by-laws, rules and regulations, and other proceedings, which book or books shall be always kept in said town accessible at all times to the inspection of the citizens thereof.

6. *Be it further enacted*, That so much of the act, entitled "An Act to reduce into one act all acts and parts of acts concerning the office of trustees or directors of the several towns within this Commonwealth, and for supplying vacancies in the same," passed the second day of March, eighteen hundred and nineteen, as is of a public and general nature, shall be regarded as the law in relation to the said town of Marion, hereby established.

7. This Act shall be in force from and after its passage.

An Act of incorporation was passed March 15, 1849, which act was amended and reënacted July 9, 1870, and has been amended sundry times since then.

Since 1870 the mayors of Marion have been: R. D. Johnson, Roger Sullivan, Thomas Rector, Wade Strother, R. D. Johnson, Frank Alexander, R. J. Haller, D. F. Carrier, J. R. Sexton, Rush Nickols, A. H. Atkins, Jno. N. Hull, J. P. Sheffey, R. L. Williams, R. T. Greer, G. H. Fudge, T. J. Maxwell, R. G. Goolsby, J. White Sheffey, J. D. Buchanan, B. L. Dickinson, M. M. Brown, and R. T. Greer, present mayor.

Mr. W. P. Francis was postmaster in Marion during the Civil War, and sometime in that period the Marion office issued a postage stamp of its own. In reconstruction days G. G. Goodell was appointed postmaster, by virtue of which office he exerted wide influence in Federal patronage in this territory. Largely through his influence Mr. W. P. Francis was reappointed as his successor, and served until Cleveland's first term, when George W. Wright went in. Under Harrison's administration the postmaster was George W. Smith, and under Cleveland again George W. Wright. Then C. C. Lincoln went into office with McKinley, to be followed by R. A. Anderson until Wilson's administration gave the place to J. Blaine Richardson. Richardson was succeeded by G. H. Wheeler, and Wheeler by R. A. Anderson.

While this book is not a family register, interesting data on a few families have come into my hands, most of which have been worked into the narrative in one place or another. The Thomas family was closely associated with the founding of Marion, and the Francis, Sheffey, Look, Hull and Copenhaver families have been closely identified with town, so that having been furnished with information concerning these particular families I insert it here.

PARTIAL RECORD OF THE THOMAS FAMILY OF SMYTH COUNTY, VIRGINIA

John Thomas, father of Thomas Thomas, was born Oct. 16, 1733, married Mary Robinett March 26, 1761. Mary Thomas, wife of John Thomas, died Feb. 3, 1816. John Thomas died July 9, 1821, in his eighty-eighth year, in Pembrokeshire, South Wales, Europe.

Birth dates of children of John Thomas and Mary Thomas: Sarah Thomas, Jan. 5, 1762; Martha Thomas, March 28, 1764; Thomas Thomas, Dec. 5, 1769; Anna Thomas, June 5, 1772; Abijah Thomas, April 15, 1776.

Thomas Thomas and Freelove Cole, who was a daughter of Joseph Cole, who fought in the Battle of King's Mountain, were married on April 5, 1791.

Birth dates of children of Thomas Thomas and Freelove Thomas: Remember Thomas, March 24, 1792; Martha

Thomas, May 5, 1794; Joseph Thomas, July 9, 1796; John Thomas, Sept. 7, 1798; Mary Thomas, Jan. 23, 1801; James Thomas, July 25, 1803; Anna Thomas, Nov. 23, 1805; David Thomas, April 19, 1809; Sarah Thomas, Oct. 7, 1811; Abijah Thomas, May 21, 1814.

Marriages: Remember Thomas and Nathan Hull were married on Thursday, April 5, 1810, and had a son named Thomas Thomas Hull, who was the father of Capt. D. D. Hull. Martha Thomas and Abram Blessing were married Feb. 28, 1811, and had a daughter who married Vincent Morgan. John Thomas and Margarette Irons were married on April 30, 1818, and had a daughter who became the mother of Judge John A. Buchanan of the Supreme Court of Virginia. Mary Thomas and William Porter were married in 1819; the former, known as "Aunt Polly," lived to be 97 years of age. Joseph Thomas and Mary Morgan were married in February, 1823. Anna Thomas and George T. Lansdown were married June 23, 1829. Abijah Thomas and Priscilla Scott were married June 2, 1836.

Deaths: James Thomas, Sept. 9, 1804; Remember Thomas Hull, July, 1813; David Thomas, July 9, 1813; John Thomas, June, 1840; Anna Lansdown, September 1840; Thomas Thomas, May 22, 1838; Freelove Thomas, wife of Thomas Thomas, March 22, 1848, age 72 years, 2 months, and 29 days; she as Freelove Cole was born Dec. 24, 1773.

(Thomas Thomas came to Smyth County from Southampton County, Virginia. He is supposed to have been born in Wales.)

Birth dates of children of Abijah Thomas and Priscilla Cavinette Scott Thomas: Charles Benton Thomas, Nov. 4, 1837; Virginia Ann Thomas, May 25, 1839 (died Dec. 20, 1917, at 3 A.M., was ill only fifteen minutes); Eliza Hamilton Thomas, Jan. 27, 1841 (died Feb. 2, 1865); Thomas Jefferson Thomas, April 20, 1843 (died July 10, 1906); Missouri Freelove Thomas, Feb. 28, 1846; Asenath Wilder Thomas, Feb. 14, 1848; Mitchell Wood Thomas, Jan. 5, 1850; Martha Elizabeth Thomas, Jan. 25, 1852; Mary Ellen Thomas, Oct. 9, 1854 (died April 20, 1891); Abijah Preston Thomas, July 28, 1857; Montgomery Thomas, Aug. 10, 1860 (died April 12, 1862); Priscilla Cavinette Thomas, Sept. 17, 1864.

Deaths: Abijah Thomas, born May 21, 1814; died December 1, 1876. Priscilla Cavinette Thomas (nee Scott), wife of Abijah Thomas, born June 7, 1820; died in December, 1885.

Old deeds: Deed from Joseph Sin Clair, John Sin Clair, Robert Sin Clair and Alexander Sin Clair to Joseph Cole, dated Nov. 18, 1785, recorded in the Clerk's Office of Washington County, Virginia, in Deed Book No. 1, page 27, conveys 196 acres, granted to Charles Sin Clair, deceased, by patent bearing date of 8th day of August, 1753; the said Charles Sin Clair by his last will made July 5, 1776, left the said land to the said grantors. This tract of land is situated in the County of Washington and known by the name of "Sin Clair's Bottom" on the South Fork of the Holston River.

Deed from Joseph Cole to Thomas Thomas, dated Jan. 16, 1792, and recorded in the Clerk's Office of Washington County in Deed Book No. 1, page 239, consideration 150 pounds current money, conveys a tract of land described as follows: "One certain tract or parcel of land containing 400 acres, be the same more or less, being the same that the said Joseph Cole purchased of Henry Bowen, being and lying in Washington County on the waters of the South Fork of Holston River."

Frederick Copenhaver came from Wythe in 1804 to settle on land in the Old Chilhowie country and found the Copenhaver family of Smyth. Mr. Henry Copenhaver gives the following data on him:

COPENHAVER-COPENHAGEN-KJOBENHAVEN

During the reign of Frederick IV of Denmark, that country suffered much in the wars with Sweden under Charles XII. In 1710 a frightful pestilence cut off 25,000 in Copenhagen alone (among them the ancestors of this family), and to increase his revenue, the King let out his armies to other princes who needed and could afford to pay for foreign auxiliaries, and 12,000 Danes were lent to England to fight in the Spanish War.

This brief history is given to show the conditions of that country when in 1722 Jacob Copenhagen, a younger son of a baron, himself a captain in the army lent to England, dissatisfied with the life of strife, migrated to the New World.

Jacob Copenhagen (Kjobenhaven, meaning ship harbor) landed near Philadelphia, where he lived a number of years and married. He moved to York County, Pennsylvania, where he raised a large family, among whom were five sons, Thomas, Simon, Jacob, Robert, and Daniel. One of these sons, Thomas, prospered financially and became quite a prominent man in his day. He held commissions in Pennsylvania state troops during the Revolutionary War, from captain to colonel, gave considerable financial aid to the cause, and was well and favorably known to General Washington, having served on his staff for a time. In fact, all of these sons took an active part in the Revolutionary War, rendering service in the state troops of Pennsylvania.

Great grandfather, Frederick Copenhaver, died Jan. 20, 1836, 66 years and 19 days old. Great grandmother, Edna Phillipi Copenhaver, born July 1, 1770; died July 7, 1857; buried at Mt. Zion. Twelve children—six boys and six girls —were born to them: Henry, Christley, John, David, Samuel,

Thomas, Sallie, Elizabeth, Mollie, Christina, Katherine, Barbara.

Henry married Barbara Phillippi, Christley married Mary Cullop and Elizabeth Groseclose, John married Elizabeth Cullop, David married Virginia Anderson, Samuel married Sallie Tilson, Thomas married Rachel Tilson, Sallie married George Dutton, Elizabeth married Daniel Wolfe, Mollie married James Johnson (no children), Barbara and Christina married Adam Rosenbaum, and Catherine married John Mercer and moved West.

Grandfather, Henry Copenhaver, born Aug. 21, 1791; died July 20, 1886. He was the father of fourteen children: Mary (died in infancy), John, Felty, Frederick, Katherine, Frank, Peter, Joseph, Eliza, Thomas J., Daniel, Charles S., James H., and William Edward.

Mary, oldest, died in infancy, buried at Mt. Zion; John married Mary Brown, buried at Ebenezer; Felty married Rebecca St. John, buried at Ebenezer and Rebecca in Washington County, Virginia; Frederick married Betty Hubble, buried at Ebenezer; Katherine married Ananias Sprinkle, buried at Fort Worth, Texas; Frank married Margaret Porter, buried at Greenwood; Peter married Sue Flannagan, buried at Ebenezer; Joseph married Katherine Meyers, buried at Greenwood; Eliza married Robert Harkrader, buried at Wytheville; Thomas married Sue Carter, buried at Ebenezer; Daniel married Mary Groseclose, buried at Greenwood; Charles married Rebecca Mitchel, buried at Greenwood; James married Sue Snodgrass, buried at Greenwood; Edward married Rena Hash, buried at Greenwood.

My father and mother, John and Mary Brown Copenhaver, were married in Smyth County, Virginia, by Rev. Elijah Hawkins, Nov. 3, 1842. Raised ten children, three boys and seven girls, Joseph Brown Copenhaver, T. Pearse,

Ella D., Fannie B., Henry Polk, Sue V., Kate and Sally (twins), Marissa Garden, and Mary.

Twenty-four Copenhavers of Smyth County were in the Confederate Army, twenty-two of them brothers and first cousins.

Nathaniel Hull (born 1726) and his wife, Abigail Platt, of Fairfield and Redding, Conn., and later of Ulster County, New York, moved to Smyth County, Virginia, in 1787. They were followed two years later by their son, Samuel Hull, and his wife, Bethena Norton, whose son, Norton, was a captain in the Black Hawk War. He was the great grandfather of Graham T. and Wythe M. Hull, Sr., and also of Henry B. and D. D. Staley, now living in Marion.

Capt. Norton Hull married Remember Thomas, daughter of Thomas Thomas. She died, leaving an infant son. Capt. Norton Hull's sister, Mrs. David Denton, reared Thomas Thomas Hull, who was left motherless in infancy, and a strange coincidence was that she was later to rear the orphan children of Thomas Thomas Hull, one of whom, the late Capt. David Denton Hull, was named for her husband. Thomas Thomas Hull and his wife, Sarah Byars, are buried at Denton's Chapel, three miles west of Marion.

The Coles, of which there are two families, are among the oldest residents of Smyth County. Tradition says that they came from New England by way of New York, as did the Hull family. The oldest known Coles were Joseph (will probated 1785) and Israel (will probated 1792). They settled near the church in St. Clair's Bottom. Joseph Cole II gave the land on which the church stands. His grave is under a large pine in the rear of the church. Joseph, Samson, and Zacheus Cole, sons of Joseph Cole, Sr., married three of the daughters of Israel Cole. Joseph Cole, Jr., participated in the battle of King's Mountain. It was his daughter, Mrs. Freelove Cole Thomas, who suggested that the new court town of Smyth County be called "Marion" for General Francis Marion.

The Francis family, long and intimately associated with many phases of Marion's life and business, was founded by John Francis, an Irishman.

He was in the United States Army (i.e., the Continental Army) and received his pay for his services in Richmond, Virginia. He, after peace was signed, emigrated to Union, Monroe County, then Virginia, where he married Isabell Irskin. He settled on the "Knobs" in sight of Union, a mile or so from the town, and the place is still owned by some of the kin, namely, Mrs. Bessie Boyd, and is to this day known as the Francis Place. There John Francis raised the following children: Henry Francis, William Francis, and John Ellis Francis, who went to Marion, Virginia. John Ellis Francis had two sons, James Henry and William Preston, whose descendants now live in Marion.

(Abridged from an article written by the late Judge John Preston Sheffey.)

In the latter part of the eighteenth century, two brothers of Dutch descent removed from Maryland into Virginia. They were men of intellectual ability, culture, and refinement. The eldest was Daniel Sheffey, who came as far west as Wythe County. He was a stranger, friendless and destitute. For a while he cobbled shoes to gain the means of livelihood. He possessed an ardent desire for knowledge, read all books he could find, and was particularly fond of astronomical and mathematical studies.

He turned his attention to law, and was received into the

office of Alexander Smyth, for whom Smyth County was named. He was admitted to the bar of Wythe County, and was employed in important suits. After some years, he settled at Staunton and became a lawyer of distinction. He traveled in the practice of his profession throughout the Valley of Virginia, the New River and Holston Valleys to the Virginia border. Being able to converse with the Dutch and German people of these valleys in the native languages marked him as one of them and added greatly to his popularity. Though a master of pure English, he spoke with a decided brogue. He was also popular with the Scotch-Irish who had settled in these valleys, for there is nothing more admired by the people of that strain than mental ability, wit, and industry. So for a number of years he was sent to the House of Representatives from the Augusta district. While in Congress he became still more distinguished, especially for his power in debate, and for the flashes of genius which enlivened his speeches. He died in Augusta County in 1830.

The other brother was Henry L. Sheffey, who came out to Southwest Virginia and located in Washington County, at Abingdon. He married Margaret White, a sister of Col. James White, who was a man of extraordinary ability and of great wealth for his day. Henry Sheffey and his wife moved to Wythe County and settled on a farm on Cripple Creek. Here he, in farming and superintending his servants, and she, in household cares and the management of her children, spent the years of their married life. Five sons were born to them. Daniel, Jr., the eldest, was less than eleven years old when his mother died, and Robert Sayers Sheffey, the youngest, was about two years old. The other sons were James White, Hugh, and Lawrence. Henry Sheffey died two years after the death of his wife. The boys, Daniel and Hugh, were taken by their Uncle Daniel to Staunton and by his help and with means from their father's estate were reared and educated. When about twenty-one years of age, Daniel became totally blind, the result of laborious study. He lived to be about sixty years old, traveling frequently on horseback from Staunton to Washington county with his violin as his companion, and Randall, a negro attendant, to care for him. He was welcomed everywhere, not only because of his musical abilities, but also because he was what is called "good company." Wherever he went he had his relatives and friends read him historical and classic works, and the news of the day, so that few men were more companionable or better informed. He spent the last years of his life on a farm belonging to his brother, James, near Emory and Henry College. Notwithstanding the handicap of blindness, he managed this large estate satisfactorily. He died at Emory and his grave is near there in the College Cemetery.

James White Sheffey, the second son of Henry and Margaret Sheffey, was born on March 15, 1813, and was eight years old when his mother died. He and his brother, Lawrence, were taken to Abingdon by their maternal uncle, Col. James White, and made their home with him. James White Sheffey was educated in the excellent school at Abingdon under the tutelage of Mr. David Speaker. He read law under distinguished lawyers at Abingdon and at twenty-one years of age was admitted to the bar. His uncle, James White, soon entrusted him with important business connected with the salt works and lead mines in which Colonel White had large interests. He went early in important cases to the Court of Appeals at Lewisburg, and his efforts were crowned with remarkable success. On Sept. 9, 1835, he was married to Ellen Fairman Preston, a daughter of Col. John Preston and Margaret Preston of Walnut Grove, Washington County. The young couple made their home in Marion, moving to that place shortly after their marriage. Eleven children were born to them, four of them dying in infancy.

James W. Sheffey was eminently successful as a lawyer and farmer, investing his earnings principally in real estate. He associated his son, John Preston, as his partner in the practice of law in September, 1859, and this partnership, although interrupted by the absence of the son in the Confederate service during the War, lasted until the death of the senior partner in June, 1876. James W. Sheffey was never very desirous of political preferment, but was sometimes nominated and compelled to run. In 1861 he was elected to the Secession Convention, though it was well known that he doubted the wisdom of secession, and hoped that Virginia could work out some other plan in those troublous times. The convention was composed of able statesmen, and many of them shared Mr. Sheffey's views on the policy of secession. On the third day of the convention, President Lincoln demanded from Virginia her quota of troops to fight against her sister Southern States which had seceded. This crystallized the sentiment in favor of secession, and on April 17, 1861, James W. Sheffey became one of the signers of the ordinance by which Virginia seceded from the Union. When the War was over, Wm. Y. Brownlow, whose son Mr. Sheffey had successfully defended in a law suit, became active in securing his early pardon, which was extended to him by President Johnson. In this matter he was more fortunate than Robert E. Lee, whose application for pardon was never granted, and who died a disfranchised man. During the War, Mr. Sheffey was commissioned captain of home guards which saw some service in guarding the bridges and tracks of the Virginia and Tennessee Railroad. Upon one occasion he and his company aided in the capture of a body of raiders who were traveling through the mountains. During the War

Mr. Sheffey did everything in his power to advance the Southern Cause. His doors were open with unstinted hospitality to the Southern soldiers, and he and his family made every possible sacrifice to aid the Southern Cause. When the War was ended, his lands lay in desolation—the fences were burned or decayed, the horses and cattle gone, there was not even seed for the sowing of a new crop. He had to begin anew. He brought to this task the indomitable spirit of the South and in a few years fortune smiled upon him—there were again fields of grain ripening for the harvest, and grazing lands dotted with flocks and herds. His profession, too, became profitable and his reputation as a great lawyer was established. He chafed under the restraints of the reconstruction period and submitted with ill grace to the police regulations of the Federal soldiers who occupied his property and governed his town. In 1876 he was elected a member of the House of Delegates. At the session of 1876 he became ill at Richmond and his death occurred in June of that year at the early age of sixty-three. Among the books in his office were a dozen or more great volumes crudely bound in calfskin or cardboard. On the flyleaf of each was written, "Copied from a book lent to me by Judge Estill." These books, painstakingly inscribed in longhand on heavy foolscap paper, were the nucleus of his law library. What patience and industry and ambition the young lawyer brought to the copying of all this mass of words, these thousands of pages! It is well that he achieved success, and better still, that he deserved it.

Robert Sayers, the fifth son of Henry and Margaret Sheffey, became a Methodist preacher distinguished for his unfaltering faith and power in prayer. He was not a man of books, but one book he loved, the Book of Books which was a lamp unto his feet and a light unto his path. He was a prophet that was not without honor in his own country, and his memory still lives in the hearts and homes of the people of the mountains among whom he spent his life. He preached a plain gospel for plain people, giving his life in loving ministry to the poor and lonely. Of the five Sheffey brothers, surely none better served his generation than the mountain preacher, known as Brother Bob Sheffey.

Judge John Preston Sheffey, the only son of James White Sheffey to reach maturity, was born at Marion, Dec. 12, 1837, being in his sixty-eighth year at the time of his death. After attending the schools at Marion, he entered Emory and Henry College and graduated with the first honor of his class, in 1857. He took a course in law at the University of Virginia and in 1859 began the practice of law with his father, at Marion. When the Civil War came on, he enlisted in the Confederate Army, serving successfully as second and first lieutenant and then as captain of Company A, of the Eighth Regiment of Virginia Cavalry. He was taken prisoner at Moorefield on Aug. 7, 1864, and was confined in Camp Chase, Ohio, until February, 1865, at which time he was exchanged and afterwards joined his company at Appomattox. After the close of the War, he resumed the practice of his profession, enjoying a leading practice, until Jan. 1, 1895, at which time he succeeded the late John A. Kelly as judge of the circuit court.

Judge Sheffey was prominent in religious as well as civic life. He was a devout member of the Presbyterian Church, having been an elder in said church for thirty years.

Judge Sheffey was married on June 19, 1863, to Miss Josephine Spiller, who died on Nov. 19, 1904. He was survived by the following children: Mrs. B. F. Buchanan, Mrs. E. M. Copenhaver, Mr. James White Sheffey, Mr. John Preston Sheffey, Miss Josephine Sheffey, and Miss Miriam Sheffey, of Marion, and Mrs. P. C. March, of Bristol, later removed to Texas.

Miss Josephine Sheffey taught for many years in the Marion High School, one of the most effective and most beloved instructors that institution has known. Her influence on the young people òf Marion was both great and good. She died while in harness on Nov. 16, 1927.

Nathan Loomis Look, founder with his brother-in-law, Charles F. Lincoln, of the firm of Look and Lincoln, and active in its affairs for fifty years, was a pioneer in manufacturing in Southwest Virginia. He came of a family notable for its pioneering spirit. He was born near Utica, N. Y., March 19, 1819, where his father had moved from Massachusetts when the Mohawk Valley was newly settled, frontier country. His first American ancestor, Thomas Look, came from Scotland to Lynn, Mass., about 1643, where he engaged in manufacture of iron in the first iron works established in Massachusetts, an enterprise organized by a son of Governor Winthrop in 1643. It is interesting to note that the first ancestor of Mr. Look's partner, C. L. Lincoln, in America, Thomas Lincoln, who came to Massachusetts in 1635, was also manufacturing iron in Taunton, Mass., in 1652, where he was part owner and active with his sons and grandsons in operating the first really successful iron works in New England.

N. L. Look moved to Virginia from New York about 1847, living first in Prince William County, later in Botetourt County, and still later in Rich Valley, Smyth County, where he and Mr. Lincoln rented the farm of the late Thomas Taylor. About 1859 they moved to Marion and operated a flour and saw mill near the site of Look and Lincoln factory. They began the manufacture of plow handles, this

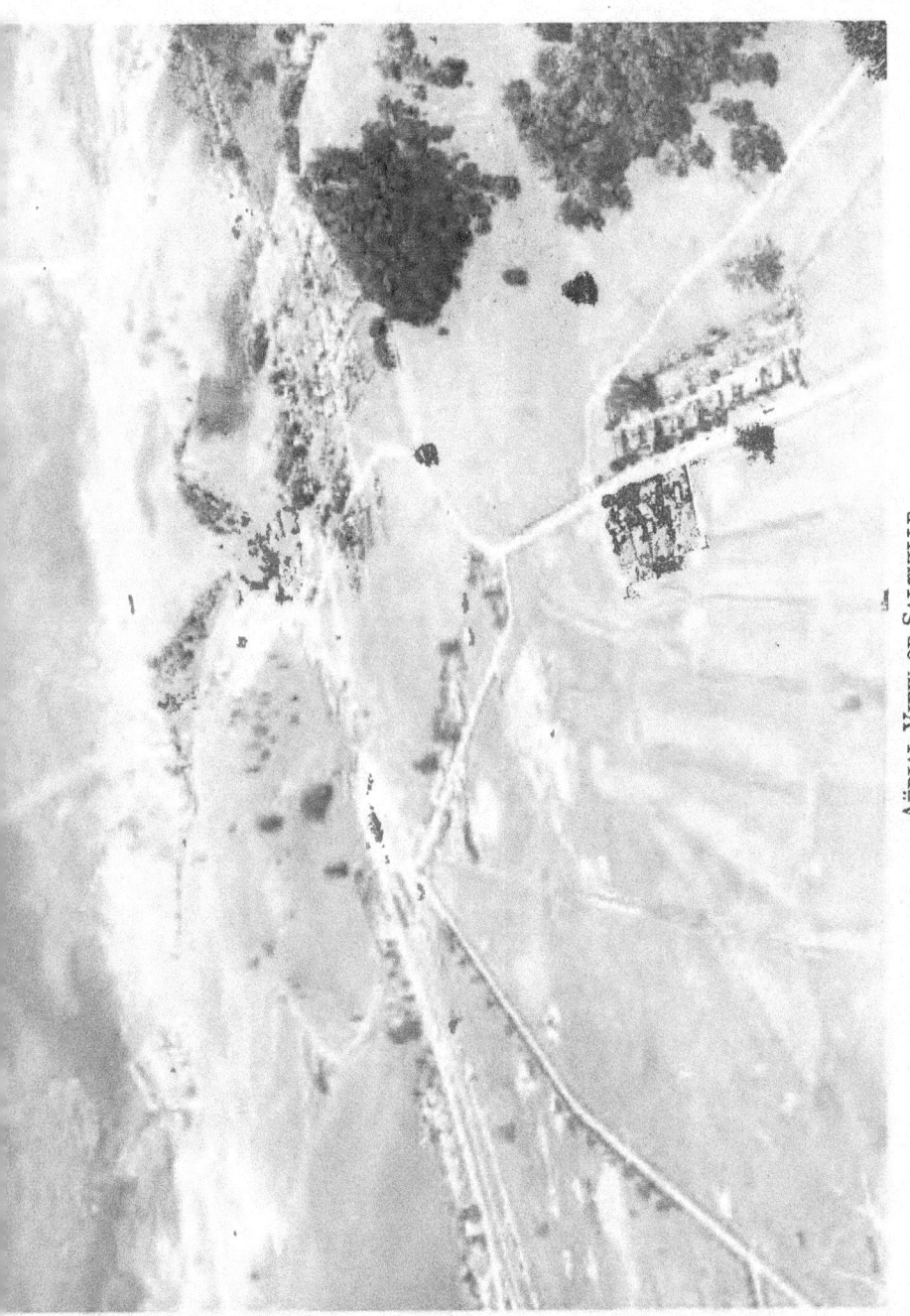

Aërial View of Saltville

being one of the first factories in the country engaged in this business. About 1880 they began the manufacture of wagons and buggies, building up a successful business, then one of the largest manufacturing plants in Southwest Virginia, selling their output over a large territory.

Mr. Look was twice married. His first wife, Sarah Ann Burt Lincoln, whom he married in 1848, was educated at Mount Holyoke College and came to Virginia to teach. To this marriage were born five children, only one of whom, Mrs. S. W. Dickinson, survived to maturity. His second wife was Columbia Thomas, a native of Smyth County and widely connected here. Mr. and Mrs. Look's home was for years a center of hospitality and a gathering place for a large circle of friends and relatives.

Mr. Look died in Marion on May 2, 1907. His long life, eighty-six years, had covered an interesting period and he could talk most interestingly about it. His recollections of his boyhood days in the Mohawk Valley from which the Indians had not entirely departed, of trips back to Massachusetts by "democrat wagon" over new roads or no roads, of seeing the first train on the New York Central line, with a wood-burning engine, of traveling horseback from Virginia to his mother's home in Western New York through the lines in Ohio in the last days of the Civil War, are still remembered. He was always interested in and informed upon public questions, and was a man who had the confidence and respect of the community.

Saltville

Saltville's salt was not found out until a good many years after the general settlement of the county. Gen. William Campbell owned the land but died before he realized what he had. He hauled salt by wagon from Williamsburg to Abingdon. Soon after his death, however, the possibilities of salt making there were realized and from then until now it has been one of the most valuable properties, making fortunes for its many owners. The place used to be called Preston's Salines. Gen. Francis Preston lived there for a while and made salt. The property belonged to his wife, General Campbell's daughter and Patrick Henry's niece. Their son, born in Philadelphia while Francis Preston was a member of the Congress in 1794, was Senator William Campbell Preston, of South Carolina, one of the most distinguished men of his day. Senator Preston spent his early boyhood at Saltville and as a young man hunted all over the hills and mountains for many miles around. Charlie Talbot, an illiterate mountaineer and the best rifle shot in all the countryside, was Preston's constant companion on his hunting excursions. In 1845 Senator Preston, then fifty-one years old, was visiting his brother at the salt works. Looking out towards the white rocks on top of the Clinch Mountain he said: "I would like to go up there once more before I die and have Charlie Talbot with me." The trip was arranged and the senator and the mountaineer hunter and cattle herdsman went side by side, as familiar and congenial and happy together as when they were boys. Passing through a cleft in the rocks the old huntsman suddenly exclaimed: "Lord, William, what a scuffle thar's been!" Then he proceeded to describe from the signs on the ground, a "scuffle" that occurred when a panther sprang from the ledge above upon a deer. Then he said, "That thar painter hain't fur from here right now, he must a run when he heerd us coming. The deer hain't fur from here nuther." Then trailing like a dog he went to a pile of leaves and pulled out the fresh carcass of a deer, torn with tooth and claw.

Senator Preston always said that Saltville, as he knew it, was the most beautiful spot on the face of the earth, and he traveled far and wide in America and in Europe. When the level basin on which Saltville is partly built was a lake alive with water fowl and the hills around were covered with virgin forests it must have been a marvelously beautiful place. Even now, the view coming over the ridge on the fine new road from Glade Spring is one to delight the eye and stir the soul.

During the Civil War Saltville was the South's main source of salt supply and from there and the vicinity came also materials for making gunpowder. It was therefore from first to near the last a strategic objective of the Federal Armies. Much maneuvering and some bloody fighting marked the long struggle for its possession. During the Civil War ten thousand bushels of salt a day were made for six months without showing any decrease in the quantity or quality of brine.

The original Salt Lick tract was patented to Charles Campbell. He had occasion to go to Orange Courthouse, then the county seat for all this Mountain Empire, and while there was arrested for nonpayment of taxes and put in jail. He wrote his wife to sell the Salt Lick tract and release him. She replied: "Remain where you are and I will pay the taxes." Then she gathered flax, spun it into hanks of thread, mounted her horse and rode to market, sold the thread and brought her husband home.

Saltville's history is so intimately associated with the great industries which have made it that there is not a great deal to be added here to what has already been told in the chapter on industries.

In February, 1788, Gen. William Russell moved from his wife's old home near Seven Mile Ford to live in a log house near the Salt Lick, making the move because of his intention to go into salt making as his major business. This house was the beginning of the modern Saltville, but before then many people had settled in the general vicinity, among them the Crabtrees, Hennegars, Scotts, Lees, Hatfields, McHenrys, and others.

In 1789 or 1790 Col. Thomas Madison, guardian of Sarah Buchanan Campbell, moved to the opposite side of the lake, across the marsh from General Russell, and built a log cabin. Colonel Madison's wife was a sister of Mrs. Russell, so that Patrick Henry had two sisters living at the Salt Lick, and it is said that they would carry on a conversation from their doorsteps, nearly a mile apart. Those Henrys had wonderful voices, and in the pure mountain air, when trees, giant hardwoods, poplars, and evergreens, and masses of laurel, covered the surrounding knobs and crags, and the stillness of the wilds was broken only by the voices of wild fowl and these ladies, they could talk to each other from doorstep to doorstep very satisfactorily. After retiring from Congress, Francis Preston moved to the Madison cabin and on the site built the Preston house, which is still standing. The stone chimney was built by Jesse Dungan, who, when it was finished, stood on his head on the top stone. Col. Francis Preston and his remarkable family lived in this house until 1810, when he removed to Abingdon to occupy a mansion he had built, which was later Martha Washington College.

The white rocks on Clinch Mountain back of Saltville probably marked the western limits of George Washington's travels in Southwest Virginia, as tradition asserts he came that far on a hunting trip with his friend Col. William Preston.

The Sanders family, prominent in affairs of Saltville, came in the 1820's from Wythe.

Col. Thomas L. Preston, son of Gen. Francis and Sarah Campbell Preston, lived at Saltville until he sold the property to Stuart and Palmer. After that he lived near Charlottesville, but would spend most of his summers with relatives

TOWNS

in Smyth. Col. Thomas L. Preston has been described by those who knew him well as being the model of an ideal gentleman, and older residents of the county yet speak of him with an inflection of respectful affection in their tone.

Mr. Alexander Stuart was a vigorous and enterprising citizen who came to Saltville from Wytheville when his son, Henry C. Stuart, the future Governor of Virginia, was five years old. His sons, Henry, Dale, and John, were reared in Saltville, and his daughter, Susie, the late Mrs. A. A. Campbell, of Wytheville, was born there. His sister-in-law, the widow of Gen. J. E. B. Stuart, and her children lived at Saltville a short while after her husband's death.

Mr. George W. Palmer came from New York. While Stoneman's men were raiding Saltville he hid out in the mountains up the Valley. Mr. Palmer built a hotel and a church, ran the company farm with the fine blooded herd of shorthorns, and was interested in many other things besides the business of making salt. He helped many a deserving boy through school. He was an honest man. When the firm of Stuart and Palmer failed he turned in his last dollar to satisfy his creditors. He kept out a gold watch which was presented to him on some occasion as a token of appreciation, and explained to his lawyer that he would turn that in too, except that he had given it to one of his children before he had any knowledge of the impending failure and felt that it really did not belong to him. His lawyer told me that a thorough check-up showed that Mr. Palmer had literally turned in everything he possessed except that watch. After the Mathieson Alkali people acquired the property he continued to live at Saltville, doing a sort of personal banking business as a representative of a Lynchburg bank.

Among the doctors who practiced at Saltville in days gone by were Dr. Thomas Dunn, Dr. M. P. Watson of North

Holston, Dr. George Wiley, Dr. Haynes Gammon, Dr. Ben Sanders, Dr. J. L. Early, and Dr. J. H. Dunkley. Dr. Thomas K. McKee is now the senior member of the medical profession in Saltville. He was born in St. Clair's Bottom and began practice in that community in 1897. In 1904 he removed to Chilhowie, and thence to Saltville in 1912. Saltville's first community nurse was Mrs. F. B. Croxton, who came in 1917 and over a period of eighteen months rendered splendid service. The Mathieson Alkali Company's Hospital renders valuable service to the people of the county generally, as well as to the company's employees. The following account of the building of the Madam Russell Church is taken from the company's publication, *Alkalite:*

The work of the Methodist Church at Saltville began in the "Union Church" back in the days of Col. G. W. Palmer, when he engaged Dr. E. E. Wiley, president of Emory and Henry College, to come to Saltville and preach a month. This was continued for several years. About 1893 Rev. D. Emory Hawk took charge of a circuit which covered this section of Rich Valley and included Saltville. During his pastorate and about the year 1893, a plan was launched to build a Methodist Church, the membership being then about thirty. The building of the church was a rather slow process and covered the years from 1893 to June 3, 1900. During that time the struggle was hard and several ministers had heart and hand in the work. Mr. J. C. Kent gave the first five dollars that was put into it. The church was dedicated on Sunday, June 3, by Dr. David Sullins.

An act to incorporate the town of Saltville was approved by the State Legislature, March 8, 1894, but this act was repealed and another to incorporate the town was approved Feb. 7, 1896. Mayors of the town have been: Paul Landman, Thomas Benton Hobbs, J. S. Goetchius, M. S. Dunham, William B. Porterfield, and Henry Chapman.

The above list was furnished me by Mr. Charles Shannon,

son of Charles Shannon, Sr., members of one of the older families of the county. Mr. Shannon represented Smyth County one term in the legislature, being one of the few Democrats to carry the county since readjustment days. He came to Saltville in 1904 as cashier of the Bank of Saltville, now the First National Bank, and held that position for over twenty years, retiring because of ill health.

CHAPTER XIX

BENJAMIN FRANKLIN BUCHANAN

COL. JOHN BUCHANAN, first surveyor to lay a chain on Smyth County soil, pushed up through the great trees, the laurel, the cane, the open grass grown glades along a large and a very beautiful and very clear creek that tumbled and splashed over boulders and foaming rapids and rested in clear still pools. He came to a tributary creek that flowed out of a long mountain cove luxuriant in its growth of walnut, oak, hickory, maple, poplar, buckeye, and locust. He made a rude survey of this fertile cove and at Staunton had it duly recorded and then gave it to his youngest sister, Martha. She married another John Buchanan, a cousin, and the young couple came to this fertile mountain cove out in the wilds of Holston to make their home. High up in Locust Cove they built a cabin, and later made them a large log house where many children were born to them. John, then a captain, was severely wounded at the Battle of Guilford Courthouse, in March 1781 and came home to die of his wounds. Martha carried on. Her children grew into strong men and women, married and made homes for themselves in the Cove and other parts of the Valley. Generations passed. The old log house became one of many happy farm homes in a prosperous farming and grazing section. Col. John Buchanan's son, Patrick Campbell, lived in it and passed it on to his own son, Patrick Campbell, Jr.

Patrick Campbell Buchanan, Jr., having inherited the house, brought his bride, America Virginia Copenhaver, to live in it, and in it on Oct. 4, 1859, was born a son whom they named

BENJAMIN FRANKLIN BUCHANAN

Benjamin Franklin. Two other sons were born to them there —William Hiter, and J. David. There were no daughters. When the boys were little fellows their mother died. Their father after a while married Miss Nancy Buchanan, his cousin, a splendid woman, greatly beloved by her stepsons whom she reared.

There was an old custom transmitted to the Buchanan clan from Scotland, by which one son in each family was selected to receive a classical education and to devote his life to scholarly pursuits while the other children were to be given the schooling essential to good citizens following the more gainful occupations of farmer, tradesman, or what you will.

Patrick Campbell Buchanan was selected as the scholar in his generation and proved a worthy choice. He was a cultured gentleman, an instructor at Emory and Henry College, a justice of the county court, a man of sense and character, influential and highly esteemed.

From his own three sons he chose Frank for the scholar's career and spent upon his education all he could possibly afford from the resources of a small estate impoverished by Civil War. He died while Frank was yet a schoolboy and willed his lands to the other two sons, saying that he had given Frank his share in the money spent for his education.

Frank went to school near his home, then to Rev. L. A. Mann's classical school near Ebenezer Church, boarding in that vicinity. He also went to school to Messrs. Evans and Miller in the White Oak Branch school house, and graduated at their male academy in Marion.

He taught in the White Oak Branch school and then went to the University of Virginia, where he graduated with degrees of Bachelor of Arts and Bachelor of Law in 1884. By teaching school, working through the summers, saving money, and borrowing a little from his stepmother, he put himself through the University. While he was preparing to go to the University his stepmother made him a nice suit of homespun clothes. She was good at that, both the making of the cloth and the making of the clothes, but that suit troubled her. Seeing him off at the Marion depot she said: "Frank, that suit looked well at home, but I don't like the idea of your going to the University of Virginia in homemade clothes."

He laughed and replied: "Well, I am not going to the University to get into society, but to work."

Though he did not go to the University to get into society the best society took him in. His innate courtesy, gentlemanly bearing, and genius for friendship won him high social standing, and his application and fine mentality won him high scholastic standing. He was a member of the Phi Delta Theta Social Fraternity, and was awarded the Phi Beta Kappa Key. In 1922 Hampden-Sidney College conferred on him the L. L. D. degree.

Governor Montague appointed him a member of the Board of Visitors of the University of Virginia, in which capacity he served until he was elected Lieutenant Governor of Virginia. Governor Trinkle re-appointed him four years later and he continued a member of the Board of Visitors until his death. When the first President of the University was being chosen in the tense fight between supporters of George W. Miles and Edwin A. Alderman Mr. Buchanan led the fight for his intimate friend, Mr. Miles. He was very close to Dr. Alderman, however, throughout the latter's administration. He was chairman of a committee to nominate Dr. Alderman's successor.

He began the practice of law in Marion as junior partner of the firm of John A. Buchanan and B. F. Buchanan, and was associated with the firm of John A. Buchanan and James L. White, of Abingdon. His association with Judge John A. Buchanan, whose high professional ideals, personal worth,

BENJAMIN FRANKLIN BUCHANAN 343

and integrity elicited admiration, profoundly affected his whole career. When his son, John Preston, came into the office with him they practiced under the style of Buchanan and Buchanan. He probably gave more valuable professional service free of charge than any other lawyer in the county. Under pressure all the time with large affairs he would at any time take a case for a poor man without charge and give it thorough painstaking attention. He frequently gave professional advice to friends and refused to accept a fee. A few months before he died an old colored woman came to me. She was in danger of being thrown out of her home. I took her to Mr. Buchanan. He was very busy, but stopped to listen closely to what she had to say. A fortnight later I learned that he had gone thoroughly into her case and had it properly settled, a matter involving considerable correspondence and several interviews that he had to arrange. He was always doing that sort of thing.

My last talk with him was in regard to writing this book, a project in which he was keenly interested. In fact, he, his brother, Dr. Dave Buchanan, Mr. R. T. Greer, and Mr. H. L. Kent were the four men whose interest decided my undertaking this work. Mr. Buchanan wrote the contract with citizens underwriting the cost, and headed the list of subscribers.

On March 2, 1887, he was married to Miss Eleanor Fairman Sheffey, daughter of Judge J. P. Sheffey, of Marion. They made their home in Marion where their seven children were born: John Preston, now a Marion attorney; Patrick Campbell, died in infancy; Frank, died in infancy; Josephine, now a teacher; Virginia B., wife of Guy B. Dennit, surgeon in the U. S. Army; Eleanor Fairman, wife of Watson Starcher, of Huntington, W. Va.; and David Hiter, a lieutenant in the U. S. Army.

The struggling young lawyer helped to educate his younger

brothers and establish them in their life work: William as a farmer on the old home place, and J. David as a doctor, who practiced all over Rich Valley from mountain to mountain for more than twenty years and then retired to live in Marion.

Mr. Buchanan's public career is thus summarized:

He was a Virginia delegate to the Democratic national convention at Kansas City, Missouri, 1900, and at Baltimore, Maryland, in 1912, and San Francisco, California, 1920. He was a member of the Virginia State Senate, 1892–1896, 1914–1916, 1924–1932; general counsel, United States comptroller of currency, 1915–1922; lieutenant governor of Virginia, 1918–1922; member of the Virginia commission to present a statue of George Washington to the United Kingdom of Great Britain and Ireland, 1921; counsel Norfolk and Western Railway Company, Mathieson Alkali Works and other large business interests, as well as conducting a large general practice; director Marion National Bank, The Bank of Marion, and the First National Bank, of Saltville; member of Virginia State Bar Association, American Bar Association, Blue Lodge chapter, commandery A. F. and A. M., past grand commander Grand Commandery of Virginia, 1900; R. A. C.; Board of Visitors, University of Virginia. He was a member of the Westmoreland Club, Richmond; Army and Navy Club, Washington; and Alfalfa Club, Washington.

He died in his room at the Westmoreland Club in Richmond about one-thirty, Sunday afternoon, Feb. 21, 1932, while attending the sessions of the Virginia Senate. He had been suffering from an attack of influenza but was much improved that day and about one o'clock a friend had left his room with the understanding that he would soon dress and go out. Shortly after one-thirty he was found dead on his bed.

Funeral services were conducted from the Royal Oak Presbyterian Church, Tuesday afternoon, at two-thirty, Feb. 23, by the pastor of the church assisted by Rev. Eldridge Copenhaver, and with Knights Templar services led by Grand

BENJAMIN FRANKLIN BUCHANAN

Commander James H. Price and Chapter Chaplain, Rev. Hugh Carter.

The following are selected from the many expressions that appeared in the papers at the time of his death:

For a quarter of a century Senator Buchanan has been an important factor on the affairs of his State. His modest demeanor, gentlemanly bearing, his comprehensive grasp of public questions and his superb ability won the respect and esteem of our people.

His very name gave weight to every measure he advocated. His associates in the halls of the legislature were willing to follow him because they knew his positions were taken only after mature thought and study and were prompted by a sincere desire to do what he thought best for the Commonwealth that he loved so well and served so faithfully.

The administration will miss his loyal support.

—Governor Pollard.

I served with him as a member of the Senate when I was governor. He was the best-loved man in public life in Virginia and enjoyed the confidence of all who knew him. In general legislative matters and especially the reform of the tax system and the adoption of the pay as you go plan for the road construction, his services entitled him to the appreciation of everyone and constitutes a lasting monument to his memory.

I was proud to be his friend and grieve deeply at his loss.

—Ex-Governor Byrd.

Always considerate of the rights of others, ever ready to lend a helping hand, giving freely of his time and talent, to me he was always the ideal citizen. Learned in the law, fluent in speech, honest and straight, to me he was always the ideal lawyer. Versed in statecraft, wise in counsel, with a heart attuned to the needs of his people, to me he was always the ideal legislator. Striking in looks, pleasing in manner, ever kind and gentle, to me he was always the ideal Virginian.

—Congressman J. W. Flannagan.

Eulogies have and will be written about Mr. Buchanan by those who were perhaps better acquainted with his public life than are most citizens of this county. Since he went down as a boy to the University of Virginia his friends at home have watched with pride his continued success and the honors that have come to him in such unusual measure. His public service to Virginia has been conspicuous beyond that of most men, but it may be, after all that his greatest contribution to the progress of humanity has been in his daily life as husband, father, neighbor and friend.

With too many men in public life, we have grown used to the rift between public and private honor. With Mr. Buchanan there has never been such a rift. His single-hearted devotion to his wife and family together with the fine intelligence and rare charm of his wife, who was Eleanor Sheffey, have combined to make his home a pleace of beauty and of stimulation to noble living.

There was about him a genius for friendship recognized by even his political opponents. It was one of these opponents who once introduced him to a mass meeting of both political parties as "the best loved citizen of the county." When he ran for the Senate of Virginia, term after term, he had as a rule no opposition.

In spite of honors that were given to him as to no other citizen of our county his integrity was not marred by any clamor for personal recognition or even by the self-assertiveness that becomes so repellent in many men in public life. It was always from others, never from himself, that his friends learned of his achievements.

When he came back from the University having won his degree *cumlaude* with grades entitling him to Phi Beta Kappa key which was later conferred on him, when he began his law practice inheriting the great tradition of his distinguished kinsman, Judge John A. Buchanan, when he was elected to the Senate of Virginia, when he would have been Governor of Virginia if he had consented to be a candidate, when he was serving on one important committee after another (at the time of his death, he was chairman of the committee to select the President of the University of Virginia), these things were known to his friends and neighbors, but never through his telling them. He seemed to think of all these happenings not as honors but as responsibilities.

"You seem to forget that I have been elected by the people to represent them in the Senate," he said when he was urged to stay home for a few days longer and rest after an attack of influenza.

There are others who will, in time, take his place in public life, but no one can ever take his place in his family or among the friends and neighbors who loved him.

—Mrs. Laura Scherer Copenhaver.

To have had the friendship of B. Frank Buchanan is one of the great privileges of my life. I saw him for the first time on Sunday morning Oct. 16, 1921, in the Presbyterian Church when, after my first sermon in Marion, he shook my hand, told me his name, and expressed his genuine pleasure at making my acquaintance. That first impression of the sincerity, simplicity, and genuine friendliness of the man has been verified and deepened by the contacts of ten years as his pastor. From the first I admired him; more and more as the years passed I loved him. Appreciation of his truly great character grew with closer and more intimate association; affection for him increased with knowledge of his mind and heart.

Gifted with an intellect of rare clearness and strength, he used it well. He was a thinker of depth and range, a student with rich stores of knowledge from many fields. His unusually strong and retentive memory kept his knowledge constantly at his command. He was a genial companion with a fine sense of humor and ever ready supply of delightful anecdote.

Mr. Buchanan was one of the purest men I ever knew. His conversation, and, so far as one can tell, his thoughts, were always clean. Men who have traveled with him in Pullman smokers and shared hotel rooms with him on political campaigns have remarked that they never heard him tell a story that was off color. He was above that sort of thing.

He was modest and unassuming, simple and approachable, yet possessed of an innate dignity that commanded respect.

He despised anything that smacked of ostentation, or pretense in any form. He had that which made men trust him and confide in him.

He was always ready to serve and I never approached him when he would not gladly and freely give of his time, his strength, and his talents for the help of an individual however humble, or for any cause that he recognized as good.

He was a high-toned gentleman, and he was an humble Christian. He was faithful in the worship of God and more than once he expressed to me his simple child-like faith in Jesus Christ as his personal Saviour. A Christian gentleman—"take him for all in all, he was a man"; one who trusted God and loved his fellowman.

—G. A. WILSON, JR.

Roanoke Times editorial:

Although death came to Frank Buchanan far from the hills of his beloved native county of Smyth, it found him at the capital of the State that he had long served with marked fidelity and conspicuous ability. And that was particularly fitting, for Frank Buchanan loved Virginia and served her with lifelong devotion, for which he was repaid with the genuine affection and sincere respect of all the people of the Commonwealth. His unexpected passing, which occurred in Richmond Sunday afternoon, has thrown the State into sadness. It is universally realized that Virginia has lost an able and distinguished son and the General Assembly is deprived of the advice and counsel of one of its most experienced and trusted leaders.

Frank Buchanan was the close friend and valued associate of successive Governors, who relied on his coöperation and support to enable them to serve the State to best advantage. He possessed a knowledge of the State Government which was equalled by few and excelled by none and when he arose in his place in the Senate to explain or defend a measure or policy, his colleagues listened with close attention, for he was recognized as a student of public affairs whose knowledge of legislative questions far transcended that of most, if not all, of his hearers.

Not that Senator Buchanan himself claimed any superiority; he would have been the very last to do so. Courteous and kindly, modest and even retiring, he was essentially a true gentleman in every sense of the word.

He could have been Governor of Virginia, unquestionably. But he never sought the office, although there was a time when he seriously considered doing so in response to requests from every section of the state that he become a candidate for the highest post in the state. Not once, but twice and even thrice, he was besought to make the race. Had he done so, it is not likely that he would have been opposed, so generally esteemed was he and so large was his following in every part of the state.

He served as Lieutenant Governor of Virginia during the administration of Westmoreland Davis and presided over the Senate with rare ability. Under Governor Trinkle he served on the commission on efficiency and economy in government and he was also a member of the Reed commission on simplification and reorganization of the government under Governor Byrd. He was the recognized administration spokesman and leader in the Senate during the Byrd administration and rendered invaluable assistance in putting through the Byrd legislative program which has had so far-reaching and beneficial effect.

In the present Senate he was chairman of the important committee on courts of justice, besides serving on the rules, insurance and banking, and finance committees. He had been in poor health ever since the beginning of the session, but despite that fact he had followed with close attention the progress of legislation and he had expected to be present this week and take part in the debate over former Governor Byrd's plan for state assumption of control of county roads.

The memory of B. Frank Buchanan will remain as an inspiration through the years, to furnish an incentive to those who came after him, for he was in all respects what a man in public life should be. A statesman and gentleman, he lived a life that was blameless and beyond reproach. Virginia is richer and better for the life and service of this stalwart son of Smyth.

Chapter XX

VILLAGES AND COMMUNITIES

Atkins

ATKINS is a town, or community, extending for quite a distance along the Lee Highway, and Norfolk and Western Railroad from an old stone house on the west to the old Thompson Atkins place on the east. That old stone house was built in the eighteenth century by Frederick Cullop and is probably the oldest house now standing in the county, unless it be that ancient log houses incorporated in enlarged and weather boarded dwellings are older. Tradition says that Frederick Cullop committed suicide and his spirit haunted the old stone house for years. This house was the center of one of the earliest settlements and was for a long time a stagecoach tavern. The Atkinses, Thompson and Joseph, the latter living in the Mt. Carmel neighborhood, were large land owners and very influential citizens when Smyth County was formed. Washington Aker was a notable and peculiar character who once lived in Atkins, his home on the site now occupied by the Church of God. The railroad station afforded a nucleus for a town and a water tank being built near the station, it was called Atkins Tank, and in the nineties it was the chief coaling station of the Norfolk and Western west of Lynchburg. The place was first called Atkins' Switch, then Atkins' Tank, now simply Atkins.

The Glade Mountain Lumber Company about 1900 built their mill on Nicks Creek and the Atkins Lumber Company built theirs on the Middle Fork in 1914, enterprises that stimulated the business life and growth of the village. Musser, Bear, Aker, Calhoun, Cassell, Shrock, Wassum, Henderlite, Hutton, Bonham, Stone, Blackard, Pafford, Crow, and others are among the names of old families who have lived long in the Atkins vicinity.

Attoway

Attoway was formally called Falling Waters. When the Atkins brothers built a handle factory there and a post office was established it is said that some official in the Post Office Department in Washington suggested the name "Attoway," why it is not known. The name Atkins was already adopted by one post office and its first syllable might have led to this peculiar name for another. Near Attoway the Zeta Tau Alpha Sorority a few years ago established a philanthropic enterprise sponsored and supported by the ladies of this national Greek letter sorority. Their health center is an attractive rustic home where a trained nurse, Miss M. L. Crosby, lives and ministers to the health of underprivileged mountain folk for miles around.

Adwolfe

Adwolfe received its name from Mr. Addison Wolfe who owned a farm where the hamlet grew.

Broadford

Broadford, where the Laurel Fork comes out of a picturesque mountain gorge to flow through splendid bottom lands into the North Fork, is one of the most attractive places from the standpoint of natural beauty of scenery in the county. It has been the home of clerks and legislators, all the active clerks of Smyth County Court having lived there at one time or another. Dr. Thomas Tate and Mr. E. L. Roberts, legislators, lived at or near Broadford. Mr. Nathan L. Look and

Mr. Charles F. Lincoln lived in that neighborhood when they first came to Smyth. Dr. Tate asked Mr. Look what were his politics and church, and receiving the reply that he was a Whig and a Baptist said: "You will never get anywhere in this county unless you are a Democrat and a Methodist."

General William Tate, an officer of the Continental line in the Revolutionary War and General of Virginia Militia after the War, moved from the vicinity of Greenville in Augusta County to a farm near Broadford on which he lived and died. General Tate planted on this farm the first weeping willow in Southwest Virginia and one of the first in America. The weeping willow was introduced into England from Egypt by means of some figs in a container made of the willow twigs, which were presented to Alexander Pope, the famous poet. Pope planted a twig in his garden by the Thames, and it grew into a splendid tree. In 1776 a British officer, coming to America to assist in putting down the rebellious colonies, cut a switch from Pope's tree which he meant to plant on the confiscated estate of some wealthy rebel which would be bestowed upon him for his services. When it had become apparent that no such estate would be bestowed upon him, he gave the switch to his friend, John Park Custis, son of Martha Washington, who planted it in the gardens of his plantation, "Abingdon," on the Potomac. General Tate's original tree, which is said to have been a fine large specimen in the year 1806, was a planting from this Custis tree, the first weeping willow in America.

Cedar Springs

Cedar Springs, a village of many waters, lies on the upper reaches of Cripple Creek. When the White Rock Furnace was in blast the Lobdell Car Wheel Company's store at Cedar Springs did a large commissary business, and now, under the

VILLAGES AND COMMUNITIES 353

management of Mr. Lantz, the company's representative in charge of its Smyth properties, does a large general mercantile business. When the county was formed in 1832 Keesling's Mill was at Cedar Springs, and when Fincastle County was in being Catherine's Mill may have been there—it was somewhere in that general section and this seems the most likely place.

Up above Cedar Springs is the Keesling place, a Southwest Virginia country home of rare setting and artistic beauty. In front of house and shady lawn there is a spring house with a water wheel on its side that is turned by force of clear spring water and generates power for the place. The stream that runs the power wheel comes from a great spring just above, and bluff and road, spring, water wheel, spring house, shade trees, residence and lawn, blend into an exquisite picture.

Camp

Camp is a prettily located hamlet in the southeast corner of the county, named from the fact that the location was a favorite camping ground for the covered wagons enroute from Grayson and North Carolina to Marion and Saltville.

Chatham Hill

Among the earliest settlers in the Chatham Hill neighborhood were Hayses, Spratts, Davises, and Richardsons. At least three Hays families were settled in that part of the valley prior to the Revolution. Robert Davis, a Revolutionary Captain, was there when Botetourt County was formed in 1869. William Richardson, known as "Buckeye Billy," came to the place still owned by his direct male descendants about that time.

Mr. William B. Spratt of Richlands has sent in this sketch of his branch of the Spratt family.

In the year of 1768, John Spratt came to Rich Valley, as one of the oldest pioneers, then in the county of Fincastle, now Smyth County from near Harrisonburg, Virginia, located on the farm now owned by the estate of Thomas W. Buchanan. He raised three sons and one daughter, namely, William, Jeremiah, Isaac, and Ellen, who married the Rev. Patton and resided at Dublin, in Pulaski County. William and Jeremiah went to Missouri, Isaac remained on the old homestead, and was in the war of 1812.

Isaac Spratt married Mary Hall, of Burks Garden, in Tazewell County; they had four sons, namely, William, James, Jeremiah, and Thomas H. Isaac Spratt was appointed by the Governor of Virginia, as one of the first justices of the peace of Smyth County in the year 1832. He died in 1883, age 97.

All of his sons went to Missouri, except Thomas H. who resided in Smyth County until his death in 1887. He married Martha Winefred Gannaway, of Wythe County, in 1856. They had five children, namely, William B., of Richlands, Virginia, Mary Shannon, of S. C., Sue C. Richardson, of Idaho, John G. and I. H. went to California, both died unmarried. Thomas H. Spratt was elected as sheriff of Smyth County, served from 1861 to 1864, he was elected to the Legislature from Smyth County, in the year 1874, only served one term.

His oldest son, Wm. B., resides in Richlands, Tazewell county. He went there in 1890. He was married in 1885 to Miss Mary E. Richardson, daughter of Wm. L. Richardson.

A brother of John Spratt, who probably came at the same time with him, settled in the Chatham Hill vicinity on the creek that took his name. The McDonalds, Grahams, Coxes, Debords, Gillespies, and other old families came later.

The Campbells of that vicinity are descendants of Colonel Arthur Campbell of Royal Oak through his oldest son, William, who inherited land and reared a large family there. He was an officer of merit in the Indian wars following the Revolution.

VILLAGES AND COMMUNITIES 355

The following was supplied by Mr. V. L. Sexton of Bluefield:

Thomas Campbell Sexton, from whom all the Sextons of Smyth County descended, was married at Hopewell, New Jersey, May 10, 1787, to Charity Current. He was born June 8, 1764, at Hopewell. He settled in Frederick County, Virginia, where he lived until 1816, when he, at the age of 52 years, moved to Chatham Hill, then in Wythe County, his brother, Joseph, having selected and purchased for him the old homestead where his granddaughter, Mrs. R. M. Gaddy, now resides. He also had a large family, ten sons and one daughter. All except his five eldest sons and one who had died in infancy, came to Southwest Virginia with him; two of the five had married and moved to Ohio, two to Alabama, and one, Aaron, remained at Kernstown, Virginia, until his wife died, June 19, 1831, when he with his three children also came to Smyth County, probably about 1836. Thomas C. Sexton's wife, Charity Current, died and was buried at Chatham Hill, March 8, 1824. Thomas C. died there March 15, 1849, at the age of 85 years.

Thomas C. Sexton and four of his sons, Aaron, Joseph, John, Gatewood, and Zadok, all lived at Chatham Hill at one and the same time, owning farms around the village and in it.

About 200 feet east of the Baptist Church, (really a union church) being of frame, and constructed long before the Civil War, now badly in decay, ready to collapse from neglect and non-use, and which stands at the southern entrance to the village, there once stood a log church, known as "Old Bethel." More than sixty years ago this old log church, which had been supplanted by the one first mentioned, was converted into a school building. The building had been weather boarded on the outside and ceiled on the inside, and to the north end had been constructed an additional room of about the same size, but built of frame, with double sliding doors dividing the two rooms. This building was used for many years for school purposes, and some noted educators taught school therein. There were a few graves, old and almost obscured from time, of the early inhabitants, but the cemetery had been located further north about 200 feet, and east of the first mentioned church, presumably because of the underlying limestone ledges that prevailed around and about "Old Bethel," but on the front, or east side of "Old Bethel" and some thirty feet distant from the building which is now gone, are two graves, side by side, and then enclosed with a plank fence to keep the school children and town cows from running over them. Marble slabs at these graves disclosed them to be the graves of Samuel Graham and his wife, who during life, had their residence not more than a half mile northeast of their graves. The old homestead was surrounded by a large orchard, and many of the trees and a part of the house which was built of well hewn logs, matched and laid perfectly, with the joists and floors of hewn poplar was still there forty years ago. This old farm sixty years ago, was owned by Thomas K. Sexton, my father, but after his death, in 1891, his estate was partitioned among his children, and later Dr. E. A. Holmes, of Marion, became the owner of the Graham farm and he now owns it.

To the west side of "Old Bethel" and about the same distance from the building were two other graves, side by side, enclosed with a wall of rough limestone. To these graves marble slabs also stand, showing them to be the graves of Thomas Campbell Sexton and Charity Current, his wife. The latter was the first buried there, which the stone shows to have been in 1824.

This Samuel Graham, tradition has it, was born on board ship when his father and mother were on their way from the North of Ireland to America. Where they landed and first resided, and when they came to S. W. Virginia, I do not know, though their descendants most probably do. It is said that his mother was a Craig before her marriage to his father, also of the North of Ireland, where many of the name still now live I am told. Samuel Graham married a Miss Montgomery, it is said, her mother being a Crockett, and they were evidently of the same family from which the Crocketts of Wythe County are descended.

Samuel Graham was the father of a large family of boys and girls, I believe nine in all that I have information of, five girls, and four boys. They all grew to manhood and womanhood, and all married and had families. One of the girls married Sam Cox and lived to a great old age. Four married Buchanans of Rich Valley, one married Patrick Buchanan, the father of Hickman S. Buchanan, F. Grundy Buchanan, Dr. John L. Buchanan, Mrs. Joseph Sanders, perhaps other children I do not know. Another married "White headed" Paddy Buchanan, one married "Black headed" Paddy Buchanan, and one Wilson Buchanan. Mr. James C. Buchanan, and Thos. W. Buchanan, both now deceased, were grandsons of Samuel Graham. I have heard many times, that when the fourth Buchanan appeared before Mr. Graham begging the hand of his daughter in marriage, that he "turned upon him" with the exclamation, "Am I to provide all of you damn Buchanans with wives?"

The four sons, William, better known as Col. Bill, Samuel L., Robert G. and James Graham, it seems all settled in Tazewell County, and there are many of their descendants living there now.

Samuel L. Graham was a lawyer, and at one time was judge of the county courts of Buchanan and Dickinson. Judge Samuel C. Graham, late, a leading lawyer of the Tazewell Bar, and at one time President of the Virginia State Bar Association, was a son of Robert G. Graham, and grandson of the subject of these notes.

The old Gaddy home referred to above was the first house in Smyth County whose walls were papered. Some of the original paper is still on and in good condition.

Dr. T. C. Sexton writes as follows:

FREMONT, NEB.
Feb. 3, 1932.

Rev. G. A. Wilson
  Marion, Virginia.

Noticing a call from you in the *Marion Democrat* to citizens of Smyth County to give any information concerning the early families of the county, I, not a citizen, but the oldest representative of two of the early settlers in Rich Valley, wish to mention especially that of my ancestors, who settled near Chatham Hill early in the nineteenth century. The McDonalds came from Maryland. The Sextons, from New Jersey. Columbus McDonald was the pioneer and ancestor of this Smyth County family. Thomas Sexton was the ancestor of the Sexton family. Both families were large and several of their children intermarried and settled in the vicinity, having in turn as was the custom in those times, large families. Hence a very common name and extended relationship in that region up to and during the Civil War period. The family demonstrated their patriotism in that conflict by the number of enlistments under the names of these families. Notably the Smyth Blues roster contained the names of five (5) Sextons sons of two brothers, three of these, all brothers, were lost in the war. These were brothers of Wm. C. Sexton, dead, who served as Clerk of Smyth County for about 50 years, and one of its most prominent citizens. There were also several others of both families enlisted in the Confederate service in various commands. Those of them who survive migrated west, and settled in Nebraska. Now of the great number of these names who lived in Smyth County seventy years ago only two bear the name of Sexton at Chatham Hill and none of the McDonalds.

I shall be satisfied if you are able to glean from what I have written any additional information to what you may already possess to complete a valuable and reliable history of Smyth County. Accept my thanks and congratulations on your success.

I am yours very truly,
T. C. Sexton.

P. S.: I was a medical student with Dr. Watson during your grandfather's Pastorate at Marion and knew him intimately. I wish to add, through the generosity of my grandfather, the pioneer, the land was donated and the first church built at Chatham Hill about 1820. Rebuilt 1859 largely through effort and aid of my father, John G. Sexton.

S.

In another letter, Dr. Sexton wrote:

I cannot give you the name of the father of Chatham Hill, which was the oldest Post Office and trading center for that region, nor am I able to give the date of its founding. Possibly my grandfather, Thomas Sexton, may have given the place its name as his land possessions extended to that point, and it is reasonable to suppose that it may have been named in honor of the Premiers of England who defended the American Colonies in their struggle for freedom. Olympia was a prewar P. O. secured by James Cox and others. He was appointed P. Master and kept the office at his residence. Ellendale and Nebo were established after the Civil War and why they were so named I do not know. Chatham Hill, a few years before the War, became a very active business point. An Iron Forge, a large Grist Mill, Carding Machine, Saw Mill, Boat yard, Wagon Shop, Blacksmith Shop, Cabinet making, two large general stores and a saloon. The Milling, Iron, and Woolen industries were operated by William Highley, The Boatbuilding by Pratt and Ferguson. The Merchants were L. & T. K. Sexton, and Snavely Brothers. John Lock was the cabinet maker. He was a son of Jacob Lock, a pioneer, and a miller by trade who operated the first mill then owned by Andrew Cox. The churches were Bethel at Chatham Hill, Zion near Olympia, and Long Hollow. Also a Mission church on the Ridge and a church on Cove Creek. Preachers were Noah C. Baldwin, Bapt., Robertson Gannaway and William Chrisman, Methodists. Jesrell Harmon operated a distilery on the road near Chatham Hill.

Capt. Grundy Buchanan tells us that it was named because so many people had a habit of congregating there and chatting about community affairs. Samuel Graham established the foundry and operated it. Jesrell Harmon kept the first store and it was the voting place in the early days. A still house was operated by Pickney A. Barker on the White Oak Branch. The Rev. Robt. Sheffey prayed both of these still houses out of existence. He asked the Lord to destroy

Harmon's by letting a tree fall on it which was done. An old dead tree struck by lightning fell on the still house, caught on fire and the whole thing burned up. Uncle Bob asked the Lord to destroy the still house on White Oak Branch and suggested that it might be an easy way to send a flood and wipe it out. The rains descended, the stream rose to heights never reached before, and when it subsided there was no still house.

Soon after the Civil War Dr. E. Blair Ward, originally from Tazewell, removed from the George Miles farm just west of Marion to Chatham Hill and practiced medicine there until he died.

John and Hugh Gwyn, brothers and natives of North Carolina, came to Chatham Hill after the war. Industrious, hardworking men of fine business abilities, they prospered. They added to their land holdings. John acquired farm after farm until at the time of his death he was the largest landholder in the Valley. Hugh removed from Chatham Hill to Marion in 1913 and died there in 1930. John M. Gwynn served in the Confederate army, emerging from the strife with rank of lieutenant. Before the War he had come to Graham's Forge in Wythe County where he worked for David Graham as foreman in the commissary of Mr. Graham's Iron works, later running a store at Max Meadows. While living at Max Meadows he married Miss Sally Crockett. He purchased some of the Richardson land near Chatham Hill and came to live on it in 1871. At the time of his death, Feb. 22, 1908, he was one of the wealthiest men in the county. His children were: Rush Crockett, who removed to Marion and built the beautiful home in Royal Oak addition where his widow now lives, and died March 6, 1927; Mary, who married Haynes L. Morgan and now lives on the old Aspenvale place near Seven Mile Ford; Myrtle, who married Robert M. Richardson and now lives in Marion; and Sally Cynthia, wife of Dr. E. A. Holmes, who died December 18, 1905.

Captain Charles Clark, whose sons are among the larger landholders of Rich Valley now, came to the neighborhood from Glade Spring before the War. Captain James Pratt and his brother, George Washington Pratt, notable men of the past generation, were natives of the section.

GROSECLOSE

Groseclose is one of the older villages of the county, named for the pioneer John Groseclose, founder of this family in Smyth.

There was a mill there called Groseclose's Mill when the county was formed. Above Groseclose at the present Wilson home is an old building now used as a carriage and farm storage house which was once the home of Jonathan Aker and a roadside inn of reputation. Andrew Jackson would make a point of stopping there on his trips through Smyth attracted by the excellent fare and also by the fine blooded horses that Mr. Aker kept. Old Hickory was a great lover of horseflesh and no doubt he and Jonathan Aker, who specialized in raising fine horses, found much in common. Jonathan Aker was one of the most progressive and successful farmers of his generation in Smyth.

NORTH HOLSTON

North Holston is a pretty village on the banks of the stream with that name, where nationally used products are manufactured from the gypsum that underlies so much of Rich Valley's fertile soil. I stopped my car in North Holston one summer's day in front of an attractive home with well-kept shaded lawn. Beside the lawn there is a shady clear mountain brook, and through the shade up the brook an inviting by-road leads off the main highway. Across the road is another beautiful home on a green and shaded knoll.

I called at this home. On the broad pleasant porch were reading tables and chairs, copies of the New York Times, some novels, some serious volumes, an old spinning wheel in one corner. A colored maid answered the bell. The lady whom I wished to see had gone to Bristol. I walked back to my car. There was some excitement. Two boys, according to report, had stumbled on a dead man high up on the mountain side. The coroner, the doctor, the deputy sheriff arrived. A crowd of men and boys gathered. I fell in with them. We went up the pleasantly shaded by-road for perhaps a mile. It got rougher and hotter and less shaded. Within two miles we left the car and walked. Crude bleak sticky cabins stuck about here on the scrawny mountain side, a mountain man or so slouching down the mountain with pails of berries to sell. Other mountain men joined the crowd, laughing. "They ain't no dead man up thar," they said. "Them boys lied." A woman came to the door of a bare cabin. She laughed. "You going to find the dead man? Them boys was playing a joke."

"Where are the boys?" asked the sheriff.

"Over there at Blank's," pointing across a hollow to a bleak shanty sticking to the mountain side. Around a rough path to the shanty. A swarm of women and children on the porch. A freckled-faced boy grinning and hiding behind his mammy. He was one of the culprits. The sheriff tried to scare him. He grinned.

"Where is the other boy?"

"In there under the bed, blubbering. Can't you hear him?"

From within the house came sounds of a scared child's sobs. Peering through a crack in the shanty, there he was crouching under the edge of the bed, a bedraggled little tad of twelve or fourteen, his arms around the neck of a mongrel bulldog cur, the dog growling and huddling close to him. The sheriff said he was going to take him to jail but he did not. His mother was in jail for immorality. His father was serving a twenty-year sentence in the penitentiary for stealing. Well the boys' joke had stirred up some excitement. And that little kid in the miserable charity of that sticky shack, under the bed, his arms about his dog, his parents in jail, and down at North Holston, the lovely homes of culture. Such are the contrasts of life in Smyth County.

North Holston was begun in 1907, on the old Pearson lands that had been Poston lands at first. The Pearson Plaster Bank had done business there for half a century, when the Southern Gypsum Company with Dr. F. A. Wilder in charge acquired the land and built its plant and town.

A writer of 1914 says:

It is seven years ago this new January that the writer came into this valley.

Where the hamlet of North Holston now stands were to be seen three houses, and a hole in the ground, where the shaft for the mine was being started. The three houses, which have been since remodeled and present a very different appearance, were the old Capt. Brown place, now occupied by Mr. and Mrs. R. W. Holmes; the Mitchell House, now the home of Mr. and Mrs. Birney Kefflinger, and the house next to the power house, where Mr. and Mrs. Lee Callihan now live. Across the creek, and not on the land of the Southern Gypsum Co., stood the old Dr. Watson place, now the home of Dr. Wilder. The tin roof flapped in the breeze, the porches sagged, paint had long ceased to be a known quantity, and it was altogether the most forlorn and dilapidated looking house in this vicinity. The beautiful maple trees in front and the fine old apple trees around the house, were all that gave the place any claim to its former respectability. It took a prophetic eye, indeed, to read into it the possibilities of an attractive home. Dr. Wilder bought the place and ten months later moved his family from Broadford to North Holston. Subsequently Mr. Ristine bought two and a half acres from the place, upon which to erect a cottage as a home for his bride. During this interim the construction work on the mill, power house, shaft and the work on the railroad and big trestles was pushed rapidly forward. The house built at this time for Mr. C. H. Wallinger, the first superintendent, is now occupied by Mr. E. T. Archer's family.

After seven years, one sees a hamlet of some thirty-five or more homes, housing some two hundred persons. There is a store, a post office and a school house. A church organization, a Sunday School, an Odd Fellows Lodge, a Neighborhood Club and a Picture Show furnish outlets for religious, philanthropic, and social activities.

Seven Mile Ford

Seven Mile Ford is a peculiar name for a town. Legends on car plates inform us that it is the only place with that name in the world. It is supposed to have originated from the fact that the ford of the river on William Campbell's land was seven miles from the ford near Arthur Campbell's fort at Royal Oak. The land around Seven Mile Ford from near the top of Preston Hill westward through Mr. Frank Sander's place was patented by Col. John Buchanan and transferred by him to his brother-in-law, Major Charles Campbell. About 1770, perhaps a year or two earlier, the widow of Charles Campbell, who died in 1767, moved out to this land with her son, William, and her four daughters. The son became famous as the hero of King's Mountain and Guilford Court House and the four daughters married and settled, as already told, in this county. Mrs. Campbell, who was Margaret Buchanan, lived to an advanced age and is buried in the notable Preston graveyard at Seven Mile Ford.

General William Campbell's daughter, Sarah, sole heiress of his estate, married General Francis Preston. Her daughter, Margaret, married Mr. John M. Preston, a distinguished citizen of Abingdon, and through her these lands were passed on to her sons, Capt. John M. Preston and Capt. Charles H. C. Preston.

Mr. John M. Preston, Sr., a business man of vision and enterprise handling both his wife's property and his own large estate inherited from his father developed these lands for farming and had certain buildings on them which he rented out. One was a log tavern. Another was a store run by Mr. Robert Beattie. He also built and operated a mill and the old stone mill dam on the creek testifies to the skill of the stone mason he employed. He built a large brick house which is now the Preston home. Family tradition says that Mrs. Preston wanted this house on her land built farther back from the river on a hill, and because her husband built it in the bottom she would never have anything to do with it. When Smyth County was formed Robert Beattie conducted a store in a log building just across the river from this house, and slightly below it.

The Campbell home was at Aspenvale below Seven Mile Ford. A stockade fort capable of housing four hundred people was built there in 1776. William Campbell's house stood on the hill about where the stone marker is. According to one story this old house was burned and a replica of it was built on this same site by Senator W. C. Preston and is the old house standing there now. Capt. Charles Preston, however, who inherited this part of the estate and built the beautiful home now occupied by Mrs. H. L. Morgan, told the author that this old house was standing while he was living. It had fallen into ruins and he had it cleared away, using the logs to build a hog pen. Captain Charlie, as he is affectionately called, was too good for his own material good. He helped everybody, even allowing himself to be imposed upon. Finding himself heavily involved he sold his beautiful home and ancestral estate to pay his debts, and removed to Eastern Virginia where he now lives with his son.

Mr. Haynes L. Morgan, a lawyer who had lived in Marion

and in Rich Valley near the foot of the mountain at Lyon's Gap, and who represented Smyth County in the State House of Delegates at one time, bought the property. Mr. Morgan's mother celebrated her one hundredth birthday on Feb. 24, 1932. His father was Vincent L. Morgan, sometime sheriff, and a prominent county man in his day. His great grandfather was Col. Haynes S. Morgan of Pittsylvania County of whom a friend has written me.

Colonel Haynes Morgan, who commanded troops on the Cherokee expedition, was an experienced soldier, having served through the French and Indian war in the 80th British Regiment, under Montague Wilmott, Esq. This regiment was raised in Virginia in 1758, and Morgan enlisted for six years, holding the office of Sergeant-Major. When the State Line Regiments were organized, in 1776, Colonel Morgan was appointed Lieutenant Colonel of the First Regiment. While these state regiments were the regular troops for the state raised in addition to the Continental Line, their services were not confined to the state, and several times they were sent beyond its boundaries. In June 1777 Lieutenant Colonel Morgan was promoted by the General Assembly, to be Colonel of the 1st Regiment, which was ordered north to join General Washington. The Colonel being a man of family and many business affairs, it was feared lest it might not be convenient for him to go so far from home. The Board questioned him and while the Colonel's answers were "full of Spirit and delivery" yet it was perceived that he would prefer a station in the state, and Colonel Bigson was appointed in his stead. In November of that year Colonel Morgan was placed in command of all the State Infantry.

While neither Colonel Haynes Morgan nor his son, Haynes, Jr., ever lived in Smyth County, the latter had two sons and three daughters to live in the county, namely, Vincent S. Morgan, who married Mary Jane Blessing, "Black" Morgan, who never married, Mary Morgan, who married Col. Joseph Thomas, Elizabeth Morgan, who married John Thomas, a brother to Joseph, (Joseph and John being sons of Thomas Thomas, the grandfather of Mrs. Mary Morgan) and Susanna Morgan who married Reese Thompson, the latter living in Burks Garden until his death when the family moved to Smyth, and afterwards in the 1870's to the West, except one daughter, Virginia who married George W. Buchanan of Rich Valley.

There is a probability that Col. Haynes Morgan went through what is now Smyth in 1759 or 1760 with the expedition under Colonel Byrd which was aimed against the Cherokees but missed its aim by disbanding after building a road to Kingsport, and a fort near that place.

Mr. W. N. McGhee, twice Sheriff of Smyth County, lives near Seven Mile Ford. He was born in the old Meek stone house in Washington County on Aug. 19, 1864. He says that when he was three months old the Yankees went by and left nothing to eat in that house but a barrel of molasses, which would be the work of Stoneman's raiders. His father was Joseph McGhee, who told him that he voted for "Marion" as the name of the new county seat, but unfortunately did not mention what other name or names were before the voters. This is interesting as showing that the name of the county seat was settled by popular vote, and is the only record of it that I know anything about. His father also told him that under the old property qualifications for voters if a man owned a horse he could vote, and that one fellow qualified by swearing that he owned a horse, which was in reality a shaving-horse on which carpenters shaved wood with draw knives. Mr. McGhee's grandfather, Thompson McGhee, came from Louisa County and landed on Staley's Creek just below the old Killinger place in 1799.

When the railroad was built through the Preston lands in 1856, Mr. John M. Preston gave the right of way in return for a contract awarding passes on the road to himself and his sons and their wives as long as they should live, and also stipulating that all trains should stop at Seven Mile Ford on demand. Mr. E. H. Copenhaver, who bought land from Captain John M. Preston and built his home on it said this stipulation had much to do with his locating there. The depot was burned in Stoneman's Raid and the present one was built in 1881.

Mr. F. P. Staley, grandfather of H. B. and D. D. Staley, of Marion, had a store at Seven Mile Ford until the seventies, in the building now occupied by Baldwin Rice. W. P. Bonham and F. Alexander succeeded Staley. Then Bonham and Dungan came in. Frank Kelly started in business working for the Union Supply Company and the Rices came up from Tennessee in the late nineties. Mr. Robert Gollehon had a good store there for many years.

When the railroad was first built the post office was put at Baker's Mill which was near the railroad bridge over the river between Seven Mile Ford and Chilhowie, and Mr. Staley opened a store near the crossing, in the house where Mrs. Lovelace now lives.

The Presbyterian Church was built in 1881 and the Methodist Church in 1909. Mr. George Tyler built his home in 1901. The house now occupied by John McGhee was built by Creed Carter, sold to J. W. Sheffey, then to James Pierce, to Mr. Hicks and to Mr. McGhee.

The old Preston house at Seven Mile Ford probably attracts as much attention from passers-by as any other on Lee Highway.

It is not a particularly old house and was not originally intended for a residence. It was built in 1842 as a tavern or stagecoach inn along the Wilderness Road and was converted into a residence by Captain John M. Preston, who took his bride to live there in 1864. Mrs. Preston and her daughter, Miss Nellie Preston, still make it their home and other daughters, the sons, and grandchildren of Captain and Mrs. Preston are frequent visitors. The house is very large,

VILLAGES AND COMMUNITIES 369

some twenty-four rooms, most of them very large rooms, with very thick walls, old silver, relics of historic value, and, until recently, more invaluable old documents than any other in Southwest Virginia and possibly in the state.

With a few selected exceptions, the last considerable batch of these old papers were sold to the Library of Congress. They include original letters written and signed by General William Campbell, Colonel Arthur Campbell, Colonel William Preston, George Washington, Thomas Jefferson, Patrick Henry, the Floyds, and many others from pioneer days down to the War between the States. There are among them the identical notices posted by tories threatening the life of General William Campbell. A letter from George Washington in his handwriting to Colonel William Preston and some letters in the handwriting and bearing the signatures of Jefferson and Monroe are kept back and remain in the old house for the time being, at least.

Large and imposing as this collection of original historical documents is, it is only a small fraction of what was once there. Professor Lyman C. Draper, of the Wisconsin Historical Society, visited the place years ago, when collecting his material for the documentary history of the western movement in national affairs. He found here a rich and rare treasure, and borrowed the greater number of the papers, promising, it is said by the owners, to have them copied and return them, but giving no receipt for them. He took them to Madison, Wisconsin, and they have never been returned. From them the Wisconsin Historical Society have published the volumes of Preston Papers, source material for a great deal of written history and story, and also a large part of the correspondence contained in two other volumes on *Dunmore's War and the Revolution*, edited by Reuben Gold Thwaites.

The house stands on a part of the General William Campbell lands, inherited from his father, Charles Campbell. General Campbell's daughter and sole heir married General Francis Preston, whose daughter married her cousin, John M. Preston, and left this property to her son, John M. Preston, Jr. She lived in Abingdon and her husband built this house on her land at Seven Mile Ford to replace an old log tavern.

Of this old log tavern, gruesome stories are told. It was on the wild and lonely wilderness road which emigrants to the western country were constantly passing, their money carried in money belts or saddle bags. Along here, too, droves of cattle, hogs, horses and mules were driven from the western counties, from Tennessee and from Kentucky to eastern markets and the owners came back with money instead of stock. Many a traveller with money about him is said to have stopped for lodging in that tavern, to have mysteriously disappeared in the night, and never to have been seen or heard of more. Servants and poor folk about the neighborhood whispered of stumbling on weird midnight grave diggings up certain wooded hollows where ghosts are reputed to walk until this day. Whatever truth may have been in these old tales of horror, it is certain that in 1892 a small cave was discovered not far away in which were found twenty-one skeletons. One was that of a woman with a child in her arms. A doctor examined them and declared they were bones of white men and their probable age corresponded with that of the old log tavern.

When the big brick house was built to replace the log one of gruesome repute it became one of the most commodious and noted public houses in Western Virginia. Soon after Captain Preston married and made his home there in 1864, Stoneman came through Southwest Virginia on his famous raid. His troops took possession of the premises. They hacked beef on the mahogany tables, stabled their horses in the halls and first floor rooms, and generally messed up the place.

From the close of the war until now, it has been a summer gathering place for a large family connection and when Captain and Mrs. Preston were in their prime and their children young ladies and gentlemen, it was habitually filled with guests even more numerous than the patrons of its tavern days, sometimes as many as fifty visitors being housed and fed at one time within its hospitable walls.

The old Preston graveyard is sacred and historic ground. Nowhere else in America, I daresay, is there another like it. A small country family burying ground where rest the mortal remains of men who served in all except one of the country's wars. There, too, are graves of women who were helps meet for these fighting patriots. It is located on a hill about three hundred yards off the national highway and one mile west of the village of Seven Mile Ford.

General William Campbell sleeps there under a horizontal marble slab. As lieutenant he fought in Dunmore's War at the Battle of Point Pleasant, a far-reaching victory profoundly affecting those subsequent events which brought all the north central west under the American flag. As captain and colonel he was a terror to tories in the earlier years of the Revolutionary War, and commanded at the pivotal Battle of King's Mountain, N. C., which turned the war in the South in favor of the patriots and led to final victory. As brigadier general he fought, until he died, with Lafayette in the campaign that issued in Cornwallis' surrender at Yorktown. Immediately in front of his grave under an exactly similar slab lie the remains of his wife, Elizabeth Henry, sister of Patrick Henry the fiery orator who kindled the flames of revolution. In her sphere and in another section of the state this great woman was as potent as her famous brother in moulding the character of the Virginia Commonwealth.

After General Campbell's death she married General William Russell, another officer of the Revolution, who, however, is not buried in this graveyard. William Campbell and Elizabeth Henry had two children, a son who died in childhood and a daughter, Sarah Buchanan Campbell, who became the wife of General Francis Preston. She is buried beside her father. She was the mother of General John S. Preston, of the Confederate Army, once a noted figure in the three states of Virginia, Mississippi, and South Carolina; and of Senator William Campbell Preston of South Carolina who was one of that brilliant coterie of great United States Senators of whom Daniel Webster was the most famous. He and Webster were warm friends. She was the mother-in-law of Rev. Robert J. Breckenridge of Kentucky, Governor Wade Hampton of South Carolina, Governor John B. Floyd of Virginia and Governor James McDowell of Virginia. Beside her grave is that of her husband, General Francis Preston. He was a member of Congress during Washington's second term when that body was assembling in Philadelphia. In the War of 1812 he served with the rank of colonel and afterwards was elected Major General of Virginia Militia.

The inscriptions on the horizontal monuments are of interest sufficient to warrant reciting them here:

Here lie the remains of Brigadier General William Campbell. He was born in the year 1745 and died in the service of his country in the year 1781 in the camp of General Lafayette near Richmond. By the unanimous election of his brother officers in command at King's Mountain. For his heroism and gallant conduct on that occasion The Congress of the United States voted to him and the officers and privates under his command the following resolutions: Resolved that Congress entertain a high sense of the spirit and military conduct of Colonel Campbell and the officers and privates of the militia under his command displayed in the action of October 7th in which a complete victory was obtained over superior numbers of the enemy advantageously posted on King's Mountain in the State of North Carolina and that this resolution be published by the commanding officers of the Southern Army in General Orders. At the head of his regiment he brought on the Battle of Guilford and was the last to quit the field. His zeal, talents, and courage were rewarded by high testimonials of his country's gratitude and have inscribed his name on the history of the Revolution. His bones were brought hither and this stone erected by the husband of his only daughter, Francis Preston.

Elizabeth Russell—born Henry. By a first marriage wife of General Will Campbell. By a second marriage wife of General Will Russell. A devoted and fervent member of the Methodist Church her life was passed in the love and practise of its doctrines. She died in March, 1825. Placed here by her grandson, Wm. C. Preston.

Among the Confederate soldiers buried here are Captain John M. Preston, G. W. Cochran, and Dr. H. K. Cochran. Just outside the stone wall which encloses the Preston family plot are the graves of three McCready brothers who were all killed in battle from 1861 to 1865.

The Mexican War veteran was Major James Bowen Thompson. The World War representative is Robert Rector, killed while on guard duty at a railroad bridge May 18, 1917.

There are other graves, two of which are so interesting that they must be mentioned. The monument over one bears this inscription: "Margaret Campell, born in Buchanan, Died in 1777. Erected by her great grandchildren."

The other reads: Master Burns. Erected by his scholars, T. L. and W. C. Preston in 1854.

Sugar Grove

Sugar Grove is a town of many and beautiful waters lying between the hills where three mountain brooks, Slemps Creek, Cress Creek, and Dickey's Creek come tumbling down into a bottom to mingle their waters with those of some half dozen bold, clear springs that bubble and gurgle out of the rocks and the soil to form the head of the South Fork of Holston. There is a fine grove of sugar maple trees at the lower edge of the village above the mouth of Dickey's Creek and another on the upper edge along the banks of Cress Creek, remnants of a once extensive forest of sugar trees. From these the village derives its name. In the old records the place is called the head springs of the South Fork of Holston and was one of the first places settled on Holston waters.

In 1751 Joseph and Esther Crockett living in the neighborhood of Greenville, in Augusta County, took up a survey of some four hundred and fifty acres there. They got a patent for it in 1753 and lived on it until the Indians began prosecuting the French and Indian War by burning cabins, killing and scalping everybody they could on Holston, and the white people all lit out for safety's sake. Joseph and Esther retreated to the eastern base of the Southwest Virginia plateau and selected another home site on another beautifully watered spot where they lived until Joseph died and Esther married again. This place is now called Crockett Springs and lies some six miles south of Shawsville.

When Indians temporarily ceased from troubling and white folks began coming again to Holston waters Joseph and Esther Crockett's sons, Walter, Hugh, and Joseph, all famous Revolutionary colonels, together with one Sayers, Esther's second husband, disposed of this head springs of the South Fork of Holston land and certain Jameses and Nelsons acquired it. These James and Nelson people came from eastern Virginia and brought a parcel of negro slaves with them, so that we have today on Cress Creek just above Sugar Grove one of the rather rare negro colonies of the mountains.

In the days when great herds of mules and horses were driven from the mountains to lowland markets the James

VILLAGES AND COMMUNITIES 375

farm with abundant water, feed, and pasturage was a spot the drivers would plan to reach at nightfall.

About a hundred years more or less after the Crockett colonels and their mother's husband sold this land the husband of a descendant of one of them bought a portion of it from a Nelson and her son, Robert Ward, lives there now. Being a squire who enjoys the confidence and affectionate esteem of folks he writes wills and transacts a mass of minor legal business for people in that valley. He has extensive farming and other interests, and he has done a deal of prospecting for metals in his time. He also hunts birds and other game and keeps fine pointer dogs. He gets a kick out of setting out trees, particularly balsam which is hard to make grow on land lower than mountain tops, and spruce. He is an authority on mountain evergreens. He has a sort of museum of ore specimens and a rare collection of old family and land papers so that genealogists and historical investigators have a way of coming to his home for information.

In 1804 a certain Frederick Slemp took up land on a mountain creek above Sugar Grove and the creek took his name and has kept it. Numerous Slemps descended from him live in and near the village now. One of his sons went to Lee County where he became the grandfather of C. Bascom Slemp.

A man named Jenkins Williams took up a corn right title on the South fork just below Sugar Grove and made there the first clearing in that valley after Joseph and Esther Crockett left. On that clearing the seventh generation of Williams is living now. The first of the line had an iron forge on the river which was the first forge on Holston. Tradition repeats a tale that cannon were made at this forge during the Revolution, but I suspect that the said cannon were the long heavy barrels of the backwoodsmen's muskets. Lead has been found around the abutments of the old forge and tradition says that frontiersmen used to come here to get lead which they would melt down and make into bullets.

The tale is told that back in the Balsam Mountain somewhere there is a spot where Wilburn Waters and other old-timers used to get native lead, chopping it out of the ground with an ax and without other process moulding it into bullets. If the tale be true, it is the only pocket or vein of native lead ever found in Southwest Virginia, all the other being a blend of ores. Frequent but unsuccessful search has been made for this lead.

Some years ago an educated Cherokee Indian from Oklahoma country came to Sugar Grove and spent many days wandering about in the mountains looking for lead deposits. He had some crude old maps inherited from his ancestors who lived in East Tennessee and would come to their ancient hunting grounds in Southwest Virginia. He said they used these maps to direct them to the source of supply of their bullet lead, and he was under the impression that they made bullets from lead secured by following these maps by simply moulding it into the desired size and shape. If he found any of it he kept its location to himself and has not come back.

Three James families came from Culpepper County to the neighborhood of what is now Sugar Grove prior to the Revolution and lived there until after the Civil War. Sometime, several years perhaps, after they came, a kinsman of theirs, named James, set out from Culpepper with his eighteen year old son to visit them. They did not arrive but the elder James' body was found in the woods and years afterwards a man named Ashby, who had known them in Culpepper, found the boy in company with some Chickasaw Indians at the mouth of the Ohio River and learned from him what had happened. The boy and his father were nearing the James settlement at the head of Holston when they were attacked by a party of Cherokee Indians. The father was killed and scalped. The boy was made prisoner. He was beaten severely. Then they piled heavy packs on his back and compelled him to carry them. When he would stumble and fall from exhaustion, they would prod him with sharp sticks and make him go on. They carried him to the Cherokee towns where he found a number of white prisoners. Among them an old man and a beautiful young girl from North Carolina. He was closely guarded but well treated in the Cherokee towns until a great pow-wow of many tribes assembled when it was decreed that the festivities should be enlivened by torturing and slowly burning to death at the stake young James, the old man, and the beautiful young girl. The three were bound to the stake and the preliminary torturing had actually begun when deliverance came unexpectedly to the young boy and the girl. The courage and beauty of the girl so appealed to a Creek brave that he paid the ranson price, rescued her from the stake and took her as his wife. And a comely Indian maiden, daughter of a Chickasaw chief, looking upon the handsome young James bound to the stake and stoically awaiting the torture, fell violently in love with him. She came up to him and patted his cheek crooning words that he could not understand and otherwise caressing him. He did not know what it all meant, but thought that she was either mocking his agony or else was expressing futile pity for him. She left him and sought out her father, a wealthy chief of the Chickasaw tribe. Young James was left standing at the stake unmolested and was grateful for this respite from torture. He saw the old Chickasaw and Cherokee, to whom he belonged, in conference and witnessed the sealing in Indian fashion of an Indian bargain between them. Then the Indian girl came back, cut the thongs that bound him, called him "pretty white boy," led him away to her wigwam, and gave him to understand that he was to become her husband. The third captive, the poor old man, was burned to death and in telling the story long afterwards, young James commented on his piercing agonizing shrieks.

Young James married the Chickasaw maiden and went to live at her home on the bluffs above the Mississippi where Memphis now stands. When found by the former friend of his father, he said that some time he would like to visit his relatives in Virginia, but he never expected to return to the white man's way of living, that he loved his Indian wife and his children, and that he was living happily with her people.

In 1776, John Griffitts, Sr., left the state of Pennsylvania and settled on the South Fork of the Holston River, in what is now Smyth County. He built a home on the exact site where Frank Griffitts now lives. His big log house was torn away and the house that now stands on this site was built in 1852. He reared a family of seven children. Later each of these sold their land interests to one John Griffitts, Jr., the only one remaining in Rye Valley. John, Jr., remained at the old homestead throughout his life time; married and reared a family of ten children, six boys and four girls, Martin the eldest son left home and settled near Fort Worth, Texas, where his descendants still live; William settled near Knoxville, Tennessee; John in North Carolina; Susan married a Kirk and lived in Grayson County; Betty Brown and her husband went to Washington state; Molly Norris to North Carolina; Matilda Richardson remained in Rye Valley and died while yet a young woman. Four of these sons were soldiers during the Civil War.

Granville, Henderson, and David remained in Rye Valley their sons still owning the original tract of land with the exception of a portion on the Northeast side of the river which was sold to the Williams by John, Jr., and now belongs to the Pughs.

In 1792 John Griffitts, Sr., surveyed and laid claim to 1650 acres of the Balsam Mountain timber land. This timber remained in the possession of the Griffitts for two generations. Was sold by John, Jr.'s grandsons after they reached maturity to the Douglas Land Company.

The family name was originally spelled "Griffith." Why or by whom it was changed is not known.

Just above Attoway, near the Marion and Rye Valley Railroad, is a spring known as the "Griffitts' Spring." It is so called because the Griffitts years ago would go there each autumn, camp, and hunt wild game.

CHAPTER XXI

LAUREL FARM

By Miriam Sheffey

IN THE files of the Register of the Land-Office at Richmond, Virginia, there may be found a government land grant from the Commonwealth of Virginia to James Heron, a merchant of Richmond. This grant is dated Dec. 14, 1795, and by its provisions the aforesaid James Heron acquired a title to an immense tract of government timberland in the mountains of western Virginia.

In the General Office at Richmond there may be found another document dated June 10, 1796, in which James Heron and his wife, Sarah, transferred this timber tract of eighty-seven thousand acres to George Douglas, Sr., of New York City. According to tradition James Heron, of Richmond, was deeply indebted to George Douglas, Sr., of New York, and this transfer was made in clearance of this obligation.

This tract with its various subdivisions lies mainly in the mountains of what is now known as southwestern Virginia, extending into three counties, Washington, Smyth, and Grayson, and crossing the border into North Carolina.

In 1846 a friendly suit was filed in the Washington County Court by the Douglas heirs for a division of this estate, and afterwards the Douglas Company was organized in New York City. The main object of this organization was the development of possible iron ore and other mineral deposits indicated in these mountains. The company expended a considerable amount of time, money, and labor in prospecting operations, but such veins as were disclosed were inadequate or else too elusive to justify further expenditure. In consequence the company ceased operations and disbanded.

For many years the virgin forest of which the Douglas realm was largely composed remained in a primeval state, wasting its charm upon the unappreciative mountaineers who sparsely inhabited it and the occasional camping parties hailing from "the settlements."

At infrequent intervals some member of the Douglas family would wander down from New York to Virginia and put up for a brief stay with "Uncle Saybird," the ancient mountain caretaker of the primitive log farmhouse. On such visits the Douglas representative spent the major portion of his time in the saddle, riding over his woodland domain. In those days the motor car was not much more than a vision and forest folk and city folk were separate entities. There must have been a peculiar fascination for the New York horseman in this novel White Top region with its long green vistas, dim and lovely, its singing streams, its superb heights, its steep trails bordered with giant fern and pastel-tinted laurel bloom, its wide silences, its almost illimitable views of countless mountain ranges, its primitive inhabitants. It was a land full of surprises. At every turn there was a new delight. Age cannot wither nor custom stale its infinite variety.

In his youth and before his marriage to the sister of Theodore Roosevelt, Douglas Robinson made rare pilgrimages, unattended, to White Top Mountain. His attitude toward the mountain folk was not one of aloofness. He made friends with them in their cabins and along the trails. Having a keen sense of humor, he enjoyed their primitive customs and childish simplicity. When he commented to Uncle Saybird on the lack of bathing facilities at the farmhouse the old man declared with scorn that thar wa'n't no manner o' sense in so much wawshin', nohow! Thar was a piece o' his back whar hadn'd seen watter for nigh on twenty years.

Sometimes nightfall would overtake young Mr. Robinson on his lonely rides and he would find himself many hours away from Uncle Saybird and the farmhouse. At such times he would stop at any mountain cabin whose firelight and smoke wreaths beckoned to him through the dusk. The mountain people are characteristically hospitable and he was welcome to "sich as they had." There was always room for him, too, no matter how small the home nor how big the family.

"Light, stranger!" the man of the house would call if he saw him approaching.

On a crisp frosty evening he stopped at a one-room cabin high up on the mountain side. A considerable portion of one wall of the little room was given over to the chimney and fireplace in which roared a great log fire. Around the "hairth" the family was grouped, the numerous pairs of eyes fixed avidly upon a large iron pot of Indian mush or "poor man's pudding," which hung from a crane in the chimney. This was supper, and when it was ready to serve with "long sweeten" poured over it, Mr. Robinson partook of it heartily. He had been riding all day. He was tired. He was cold. He was hungry. That cornmeal mush tasted mighty good.

After supper the mountain woman scraped the mush pot, rinsed it out well, filled it with water, and hung it on the crane again. Mr. Robinson went outdoors with his host to see about his horse, and when he reëntered the fire-lit cabin the mountain mother was bathing the family in the mush pot.

"May I have eggs for breakfast?" asked Mr. Robinson before turning in for the night. "And will you cook them in the shells, please?"

William P. Douglas Robinson, Theodore Douglas Robinson, and Monroe Douglas Robinson constituted the Douglas Land Company which was organized in New York in 1904 and which was a development of the Douglas Land Company of a much earlier period. The charter members of the Douglas Land Company were near kinsmen, William P. Douglas being the first cousin of Douglas Robinson's mother and the two younger members being the sons of Douglas Robinson. However, Douglas Robinson was the moving spirit of the enterprise, giving to it lavishly of his time and means before it was fairly launched as a business undertaking and after the company became actively engaged in timber development.

Elliott Roosevelt, the brother of Mrs. Robinson and father of Mrs. Franklin D. Roosevelt, wife of the present Governor of New York, was closely identified with the early development of the White Top property.

W. W. Hurt, a Virginian of marked executive ability, was appointed general manager of the company, and its accomplishments were due in a large measure to his efforts just as its disruption a few years ago was precipitated by his untimely death. For several years after taking over the affairs of the Douglas Land Company, Mr. Hurt and his family lived at Damascus, Washington County, Virginia, but later he moved his home and office headquarters to Marion, the county seat of Smyth.

Although timber disposal was the main object of the Douglas Land Company, it also prospected for mineral to a limited extent, under the direction of John Elliott, a cousin of Mrs. Corinne Roosevelt Robinson. Mr. Elliott came to Virginia as Douglas Robinson's representative and spent a winter at Mr. Hurt's house in Damascus. He manifested a warm interest in the welfare of the mountain people, declaring that the home mission field was of more importance than the foreign field and the needs more vital. At that time little had been done locally to elevate the status of the mountaineer and this dearth of moral, spiritual, and material advantages troubled Mr. Elliott.

However, a different order of affairs prevails at present.

Mission churches of all denominations have been established at various points throughout the mountain empire, training schools are less scattered and more accessible, community nurses are maintained by welfare organizations. There are also summer "moonlight schools" where the three R's are taught to the unlearned who are too old for admission into the regular public schools, or who are unable to attend in the daytime. If the mountaineer of Southwestern Virginia remains in heathen darkness now it is his own fault.

The Konnarock Training School for girls at Konnarock, southwestern Virginia, was founded by the Woman's Missionary Societies of the United Lutheran Church and in successful operation now, stands upon ground which was a part of the Douglas estate, the Douglas heirs having given to the enterprise one thousand dollars of the purchase price. In this school the mountain girls are skillfully trained along many lines, among them hygiene, sanitation, and every domestic art. The fame of the Konnarock school is widespread, but it has been brought into special prominence since the development of the Hoover Mountain School in Northern Virginia. According to reports in current newspapers the management and methods of President Hoover's school are being modeled after Konnarock.

The generosity of L. M. Hassinger, a Pennsylvanian and head of the Hassinger Lumber Company and his equally zealous wife, has aided conspicuously in bringing the Konnarock school to its present state of perfection. Mr. and Mrs. Hassinger were closely associated with Mr. and Mrs. Douglas Robinson in earlier welfare work in the mountains when the Konnarock School was only a dream. In fact, the Douglas Land Company was the first welfare organization in the White Top region, and its work was the entering wedge.

In addition to timber development Mr. Hurt directed his energies towards the establishment of various farming industries. Under his supervision enough land was cleared for the planting of a commercial orchard, several thousand apple trees being set out which grew and flourished, soon yielding a marketable harvest. He also organized a campaign for the conservation of fish and game within the Douglas boundaries. In many of his operations Mr. Hurt received valuable assistance from W. L. Umbarger of Chilhowie and Konnarock, Mr. Umbarger being especially helpful in establishing the proper boundary lines of the estate. Owing to the inaccuracies of earlier surveys a considerable amount of civil engineering was required. At Mr. Hurt's death Mr. Umbarger was made general manager of the estate, and since Mr. Umbarger's death a short time ago the property has been in the hands of H. P. Gills, of Marion, Virginia.

Under Mr. Hurt's direction graded roads adapted to motor travel were constructed through the mountains and valleys. A lovely highway leads direct to the homestead at "Laurel Farm," as the estate is called in deference to the wealth of rhododendron which decorates it. The farmhouse was remodeled outside and modernized within in order to accommodate more comfortably Mr. and Mrs. Robinson and their guests, but the logs and the old stone chimney were left and the house still retains much of its primitive picturesqueness.

In 1910, or a little later perhaps, the Douglas Land Company sold to the United States Government 28,000 acres of timberland for a Forest Reserve, which is laid out on the state and government forestry maps. Mr. Hurt also sold for the company quantities of standing timber to lumber companies located in Southwestern Virginia but operated by northern syndicates. In these contract sales Mr. Hurt retained the land and the young timber growth which in the course of time will develop into a marketable product, or perhaps be included in future government reserves. And as Mr. Hurt stated in 1916 at the Southern Forestry Congress in session at Asheville, N. C., an immense amount of fully-matured hardwood timber was left untouched on the mountain slopes.

One factor with which Mr. and Mrs. Robinson and Mr. Hurt had to contend in bringing their projects to fulfillment was the antagonistic attitude of the mountaineers who resented even an apparent infringement of their squatters' rights. Moreover, they cling tenaciously to their ancient beliefs and traditions, manners and customs. Anything which savors of an innovation incites them to rebellion. It did not take them long, however, to realize that the Douglas Land Company was not a selfish organization, and that its attitude towards the mountaineer was helpful and not harmful. As one old mountain mother said afterwards in speaking of the benefits which had occurred to them through the efforts of Mr. and Mrs. Robinson and Mr. Hurt:

The Douglas Land Company! How we used to jaw an' jaw an' jaw agin it! But we com to think it the greatest blessing in these parts!

In the published proceedings of the Southern Forestry Congress, 1916, Mr. Hurt is reported as saying during a discussion of the relations between the lumberman and the squatters:

Several years ago when I took charge of the Douglas estate adverse landowners and squatters had taken possession of certain portions of the property, and one man, at the point of a gun, had run the manager out. This I was told and afterwards found it to be true, and that manager never went back. Two or three years later I had more or less business in that section and coming into contact with this same man I gave him to understand that I was there to settle my company's business with him, and we had a settlement. Later I went to the man's house, he invited me in, and I had dinner

LAUREL FARM

with him. We discussed business matters and I arranged with him to do some work and look after some business for me, such as clearing land, renting property, etc.

If you protect your property in the right manner you will be respected for it. I do not mean to use a club on a man unnecessarily. I do not mean to go into a neighborhood and show no respect for that section. But if you go into a neighborhood and show the people that you are there to help them and that you want them to respect your premises and what you are doing, I believe that they will do it.

In working out a plan for the solution of the problems confronting the lumberman in dealing with the squatter Mr. Hurt advocated especially the employment of the mountaineer and his family by the lumberman at an adequate wage. This plan succeeded admirably.

While in operation the Douglas Land Company under the direction of Mr. and Mrs. Robinson and Mr. Hurt was active in many forms of community welfare, as stated above. The company maintained at its own expense a public school with excellent educational facilities including musical training. Mr. and Mrs. Robinson provided a community nurse, Miss Long, a Pennsylvanian, paying her a good salary, arranging for all her living expenses and nurse's equipment and furnishing a riding horse to carry her on her missions of mercy. Perhaps Miss Long was the greatest gift which the Robinsons bestowed upon the mountaineer. She was not merely a nurse to the folk of the mountain fastness. She was doctor, preacher, teacher, friend, comforter, companion, and adviser. She taught the mountain people better cooking methods, instructed them in sanitation and hygiene, showed them how to dress, how to be "mannerly."

Nothing daunted her. Through storm and darkness she rode on her way with a high courage, and the mountain people loved and honored her. With no doctor near she supervised the bringing of the mountain babies into the world, caring for both mother and child with the skill of an obstetrical specialist, overcoming the prejudice in favor of the old-fashioned mountain midwife. If she had done nothing else but officiate at the ceremonies of childbearing she would have been busy enough, for in the mountains there is no such thing as race suicide.

It was the custom of Mr. and Mrs. Robinson to spend the month of May each year at Laurel Farm. And that month they gave to the mountain folk. They entertained them with community parties and picnics which lasted all day long, Mr. and Mrs. Robinson personally arranging the amusement programs and providing an abundance of excellent food. At these mountain fiestas the attitude of the host and hostess was absolutely devoid of patronage. They mingled with their guests with a perfect friendliness which put the most timid ones at ease. They entered gaily into many of the games and contests, taking an active part in such diversions as basket ball, baseball, drop the handkerchief, and so on. There were sack races, potato races, hurdle jumping, public speakings, debates and prize essays on subjects pertaining especially to hygiene and sanitation. And there were cooking contests, too. In these contests prizes were awarded which were of Mrs. Robinson's providing. These prizes are still treasured by the recipients.

Mr. and Mrs. Robinson often brought distinguished guests with them to Laurel Farm where horseback riding and fishing were the chief modes of entertainment. Mrs. Robinson, herself, was an expert horsewoman and she and her horse, "Joe Wheeler," were frequently seen climbing the mountain trails or exploring the woodland valleys. These rides she describes in her poem, "The Trail to White Top," published by Charles Scribner's Sons. An extract is reprinted here by permission of both author and publisher:

"As we climb we see Elk Garden,
　　With its broad and grassy sweep,
And the crown of black old Balsam
　　Casting shadows long and deep.
But we mount forever higher
　　Where the wind plays like a lyre,
And the sunset's sudden fire falls on
　　Summits wild and steep.

"Here the delicate Spring beauty
　　Clambers up the mountainside,
And the windflower swaying gently,
　　Pristine as a pallid bride,
White Top's children shyly peeping
From the undergrowth where sleeping
Pine and fir their tryst are keeping,
　　Though we crush them as we ride.

"Now we scale the final hillock, and
　　Before our wondering eyes
Range on range of mountains rising
　　From the valley to the skies,
Far unto the dim horizon
Peak on peak the faint flush lies
And the young moon's shadow dies
　　On myriad purply mysteries."

Theodore Roosevelt, Jr., before his marriage and while his father was President, spent a week at Laurel Farm. Anxious to avoid reporters he traveled incognito. He left the train at Marion, Virginia, planning to cover the remainder of the journey by motor, hack, or horseback. It was soon noised abroad, however, that the President's son was domiciled at one of the Marion Hotels, and the streets were lined with townsfolk eager to catch a glimpse of him as he went on his way to White Top Mountain. But the townsfolk waited in vain. While they stood on weary feet craning their necks for a sight of the first son of a President who had ever come to "these parts," he had slipped through the hotel kitchen into an alley at the rear of the building and was on his way to Laurel Farm rejoicing in their discomfiture.

While at Laurel Farm Mr. Roosevelt attended a typical mountain coon hunt with baying hounds, kerosene lanterns, shotguns and all appurtenances. The shotguns are not used on the coon. They are only a picturesque part of the trimmings. Participating in a coon hunt, so it was reported, was the main object of young Roosevelt's visit.

There is a tradition that President Roosevelt also visited Laurel Farm, but it seems that this tradition has no foundation. It is true that President Roosevelt was deeply interested in his sister's mountain retreat and often planned to visit it, but presidential and other duties interfered.

In his speech before the Southern Forestry Congress, Mr. Hurt refers to President Roosevelt's advocacy of the conservation of our forests and states that Mr. and Mrs. Robinson, acting for Douglas Land Company which then owned fifty thousand acres of timberland, were anxious to carry out the President's ideas. The Douglas Land Company is no longer in active operation as a business enterprise, but the work which it has done stands as an everlasting memorial. Moreover, this quiescent phase is temporary. There is still a vast acreage of mature timber on its holdings, besides the new growth which will one day be ready for the lumberman's axe. The Douglas Land Company has gone for only a little while, perhaps. It may come back some day, changed in personnel but unchanged in faith and principle, and follow the old, old trails which its founders knew and loved.

INDEX

A

Abingdon Presbytery, 123
Adwolfe, 351
Agriculture, 170
Agricultural agents, 173
Aker, Jonathan, 361
Alexander, William, 182
Allen, Ferd, 252
American, The, 169
Anderson, Maj. Glenn, 266
———, J. L. C., 112
———, Jacob, 25
———, Charles E., 112
———, R. A., 111, 112, 164, 168
———, T. Marion, 167
———, Sherwood, 168
———, R. L., 169
Amsler, C. W., 190
———, L. A., 190
Anti-Mason Party, 104
Apperson, Dr. J. S., 180, 181, 277
Asbury, Bishop Francis, 122, 138, 140
Aston and Hull, 167
Aspenvale, 23, 58, 63, 138, 365
Atkins, Aunt Sukie, 145
——— Brothers, 188
———, Thompson, 124
———, Wm., 145
———, Joseph, 148, 188
———, W. J., 189
———, Z. T., 189
——— Lumber Co., 193
——— Tank, 350
Atwell, John, 243
Attoway, 351
Attoway Lutheran Church, 133
Augusta County, 76

B

Baldwin, N. C., 130
Bank of Marion, 307
Baptist Church, 128
Baptist Pastors, 129, 130, 131
Baryta, 179, 180
Battle of Marion, 249
Battle of Saltville, 245
Bear Creek Lutheran Church, 136
Bellamy, H. W., 131

Beattie, Alonzo, 283
———, C. W., 283
———, Robert, 80, 283, 365
Bethel Church, 122, 146, 356
Bird, P. E., 173
Bishop, Rev. Wm., 154
Black, Dr. Harvey, 240, 277, 313
Blackwell, C. P., 124, 128, 301
Blankenbeckler School House, 153
Blue Spring, 30, 140
Board of Public Works, 225, 277
Boatwright, F. W., 130
Bonham, A. F., 155
——— family, 293
———, H. L., 191
——— orchards, 294
———, Robert, 130
Boone, Daniel, 45, 49, 50
Botetourt County, 76
Bowen, Arthur, 26
———, Charles, 26
Brick making, 209, 289
Britton, Mrs. Wm., 126
Broadford, 7, 23, 172, 351
Broady, John, 63, 261
Brown, Edna, 124
———, H. B., 144
———, Mrs. Cynthia, 168
———, R. H., 167
Brownlow, Joseph, 145
———, Wm., 197, 329
Buchanan, B. F., 90, 111, 155, 168, 340
———, Col. John, 2, 4, 5, 340, 364
———, Capt. John, 28, 59, 60, 340
———, Dr. J. D., 155, 341
———, F. G., 155, 241, 245
———, G. W., 155
———, Jane, 286
———, John A., 155, 342
———, John L., 155
———, John P., 111
———, Mrs. Eleanor Sheffey, 124
———, P. C., 241, 340
———, Samuel, 226
———, W. M., 226
Buckeye Bottom, 28, 29
Buffalo Trail, 6, 9
Burns, Master, 153
Bushwhacking, 244

392 INDEX

Byars, Wm., 104
Byrd, Col. Wm., 219, 367
Byrd's Expedition, 9

C

Camp, 353
Campbell, Ann, (1), 22
———, Ann, (2), 23
———, Arthur, 17, 18, 26, 48, 49, 53, 58, 59, 101, 121, 151
———, Arthur, house, 298
———, children of David, 17
———, Charles, 4, 5, 23, 192, 335, 364
———, David, (1), 16
———, David, (2), 21
———, David, (3), 21, 102, 112
———, Elizabeth, 23
———, Capt. John, (1), 17, 121, 123
———, Capt. John, (2), 18, 24, 59
———, John, (3), 112
———, J. C., 124, 193, 229
———, James, 22
———, Margaret, (1), 17, 21, 121
———, Margaret, (2), 20, 23
———, Margaret, (3), 23
———, Martha, 22
———, Mary Hamilton, 16
———, Patrick, 23
———, Robert, 22, 23
———, Sarah, 22
———, Sarah B., 151
———, Wm., 45, 58, 59, 60, 102, 333, 364
Camp Meeting Ground, 287
Camp Meeting, 140
Candidates for Treasurer, 112
Capital punishment, 86
Carlock, Dr. L. L. H., 147
Carlock's Creek, 26
Cassell, Geo. E., 158
Caudill, O. V., 127
Caywood, Steven, 138
Cedar Bluff Baptist Church, 130
Cedar Run, 4
Cedar Grove Church, 134
Cedar Springs, 352
Centenary Methodist Church, 146
Census, 282
Chatham Hill, 353
Chatham Hill Presbyterian Church, 126
Charcoal Burners, 178
Cherokee Campaigns, 58
Cherokee Indian killed, 45
Chilhowie, 6, 172, 282
Chilhowie Horse Show, 290
Chilhowie Mayors, 295
Chilhowie Settlement, 121

Christian Church, 122, 149
Christian Pastors, 150
Christian, Wm., 58
Circuit Court, First, 84
Circuit Court Judges, 91
Circuit Clerks, 92
Cleghorn Valley, 8
Cobb Place, 23
Cole, A. P., 87, 166
———, Joseph, 180, 322
———, Lee, 173, 189
——— family, 325
Collins Brothers Dept. Store, 302, 309
Collins, Isaac, 298, 301
———, L. P., 93
Comer's Creek, 76, 173, 176, 193
Commission on County Seat, 78
Commissions on County Lines, 79
Commissioners of Accounts, 93
Commissioners of Revenue, 82, 93
Committee of Safety, 56
Commonwealth Attorney, 84
Confederate Companies, 237
Confederate Flag, 258
Copenhaver, B. E., 163
——— family, 322
———, Frederick, 157
———, Frank, 93
———, Dr. E. M., 93
———, Henry P., 124, 157, 173
———, John A., 127
———, John S., 93
———, Laura Scherer, 347
———, W. E., 260
———, W. H., 292, 293
———, Mrs. W. H., 153
Cotton Mill, 182
County Court, First Meeting, 83
County High Schools, 162
County Judges, 87
County Justices, 94
County Officers, 95, 100
County Representatives, 113
County School Board, 162
County School Superintendents, 162
County Seat organized, 80
Court days, 89
Courthouses built, 83
Court records saved, 254
Covered bridge, 252
Cox, A. L., 168
———, Rev. C. Brown, 161
———, James L., 81
Coyner, E. K., 171, 172, 299
Crab apple orchard, 3
Cripple Creek, 2, 30, 140, 229
Crockett, Esther, 30, 374

INDEX 393

—, Joseph, 30, 374
—, Jos. and others, 8
—, Madison, 300
Cronk, Mrs. Catherine Scherer, 136
Crow, Edward, 123
Culbert, W. F., 207, 208
—, D. C., 208
—, G. T., 208
Cullop, Frederick, 122, 133
Cullop House, 25, 133, 206
Cullop's Church, 133
Cumberland Gap, 5
Cummins, Charles, 121, 123
Currin Valley, 229

D

Davis Clinic, 278
Davis' Fancy, 24
Davis, James, 4
Davis Memorial Methodist Church, 147
Davis, Robert, 59, 353
Democratic Conventions, 109, 110
Denton's Chapel, 146
Depot Agents, 301
Desmond, Mrs. Henrietta, 158
Dickenson, B. L., 93, 313
—, Dr. S. W., 128
Dickinson, Maj. Ralph, 266
Douglas, Geo., 380
Douglas Land Co., 380, 383
Drake, Joseph, 26, 50, 283, 286
Dunkard Church, 122

E

Early Roads, 220
Ebbing Spring, 121, 123
Ebenezer Lutheran Church, 133
Edmondson, Wm., 26
Elizabeth Methodist Church, 140
Eller, June, 226, 293
—, Q. A., 291, 293
Ellis, E. P., 204
Emory and Henry College, 147, 230, 341
Ephratapha Brethren, 12
Episcopal Church, 122, 148
Episcopal Rectors, 149
Evans, Wm. E., 156, 157
Expedition of 1748, 5

F

Farmer, Wm., 158, 314
Fincastle Declaration, 56
Fincastle County, 58, 59, 76, 101
Fincastle Riflemen, 58
First Congressional Election, 104
First Congressional Election list of voters, 116 to 119
Flannagan, J. W., 345

Flat Boats, 174, 195, 227
Flournoy, T. S., 105
Floyd, Ben Rush, 109
—, Capt. John, 50, 284
—, Gov. John, 79, 284
—— Incident, 283
Fort Dickinson, 18
Fort Stanwix Treaty, 16
Francis family, 326
—, J. H., 168
—, Phillip, 107
—, W. P., 302, 319
Franklin, State of, 102
Frazier, Rev. J. Tyler, 124, 147
—, J. Tyler, Jr., 293
Fudge, Granville, H., 88
Fulton, Hugh, 173
—, John H., 104
—, Rev. Creed, 147
Furniture, 183

G

Gaddy House, 357
Game Wardens, 94
Gannaway, Robertson, 144, 145, 287
—, Wm., 145
Garden, Misses, 158
German Settlement, 131
Gilmore, J. H., 89, 149, 305
Glade Mountain Lumber Co., 189
Gordon, L. E., 258
Goodell, G. G., 112, 177, 181
—, R. M., 81
Goodpasture, Abraham, 123
Goodwin, Dr. Z. J. and S. B., 165
Goolsby, Robert, 237
Gooseberry Garden, 425
Graham, Samuel, 177, 356
Grand Jury, 84
Gregory, P. J., 166
Grey, John H., 126
Greenwood Methodist Church, 156
Greer, R. T., 304, 343
Greever, Hiram, 257
—, James, 258
—, Mrs. E. L., 258, 286
—, Phillip, 27, 77, 286
Greever's Switch, 288
Griffitts family, 378
Groseclose, 361
Groseclose, John, 25
—, Stephen, 243
Grosses Creek, 295
Guilford Courthouse, 59
Gwyn, R. C., 173
—, R. C., Jr., 173
—, John, 360

394 INDEX

——, Hugh, 360
Gwyn's Island, 60

H

Hale, Maurice, 30, 210
Haller, Mrs. Va., 124
Handle Works, 188
Harmon, Jesrell, 359
Harrod, Capt. John, 49
Hassinger Bros., 190
——, John H., 289
——, L. M., 384
Henderlite, G. W., 112, 113
Henderson, Dr. E. H., 278
Herald, The, 167
Heron, James, 380
Hobbs, Vincent, 150
Holiness Church, 122
Holston Mills, 129
—— River named, 1
——, Stephen, 1, 4, 5
—— Salt and Plaster Co., 198
—— Parish, 149
Home Guards, 237
Horne, J. W., 184
Horse traders, 91, 107
Hoyt, Dr. I. P., 165
Hubble, J. P., 156
Huff Lands, 3
Hull, Capt. D. D., 175, 251, 301
Hull family, 324
Hults, E. A., 199, 201
Humes, Wm., 78, 182, 298
Hungers Mother, 25
Hurt, W. W., 172, 383
Hutton, Frank, 128
——, I. W., 93

I

Indian raids, 50
Indian rangers, 53, 58, 59
Indian victims, 7
Iron forges, 179, 375
Iron foundries, 177, 359
Iron Mt. School, 137
Irons, John, 175

J

Jackson, Andrew, 80, 103, 361
——, Minter, 289
James family, 374, 376
Jones, Eugene, 167
——, G. W., 87, 301
——, W., 301
Juvenile Court, 93

K

Kelly, Frank, 162
——, John A., 88, 92
——, James A., 88
Kennedy, James W., 167
Kent, S. W., 81
——, H. L., 81, 343
Kentucky County, 59, 76
Killinger, Betty, 252
——, Geo., 122
——, Michael, 252
——, Peter, 127
——, Kenneth, 127, 135
——, J. P., 189, 298
Kilmackronan, 3
King, T. E., 127, 307
——, Dr. J. C., 277, 278
King's Mountain, 58
Konnarock Training School, 137, 384
Knight, E. L., 210
Know-Nothing Party, 105

L

Lane, Tidence, 120
——, Turner, 151
Laurel Spring Methodist Church, 146
Lawyers, 89
Lead deposits, 179, 376
Lee Highway, 6, 222, 226
Legislative candidates, 111
Lemmey, Samuel, 51
Liberty Academy, 155
Lincoln, A. T., 111, 157, 184, 187
——, C. C., 124, 187
——, C. C., Jr., 184
——, C. F., 185, 352
——, J. D., 184
——, W. L., 124, 184, 306
Liquor banned, 145
Lobdell Car Wheel Co., 177
Locust Cove, 28, 76
Logan, 50
Logan's Letter, 55
Long Island, Battle of, 58
Loyal Land Co., 5
Look and Lincoln, 184
Look family, 332
Look, N. L., 185, 351
Lumbering, 189
Lutheran Church, 131
Lutheran Pastors, 132, 133, 136

M

Madison, James, 104
——, Thos., 193, 336
Maiden, Rev. G. A., 147

INDEX

Magazine Spring, 24
Magisterial Districts, 84
Manganese, 179
Mann, Rev. L. S., 154
Marble, 180
Marion, 296
—— Academy, 157
—— Baptist Church, 130
—— bar, 316
—— barbers, 315
—— clothiers, 310
—— Charter, 318
—— Democrat, The, 167, 168
—— dairies, 315
—— drug stores, 311
—— doctors, 313
—— dentists, 314
—— Extract Co., 191
—— Foundry and Machine Works, 180
—— furniture stores, 312
—— groceries, 312
—— hardware, 311
—— harness makers, 315
—— Ice and Coal Company, 315
—— jewelers, 314
—— Junior College, 159, 301
—— Light and Power Co., 306
—— Lutheran Church, 133
—— Mayors, 319
—— Methodist Church, 144
—— News, 168
—— National Bank, 307
—— photographers, 310
—— postmasters, 319
—— real-estate agents, 316
—— Rye Valley R. R., 180, 181, 229
—— Visitor, 164
—— Water Works, 305
—— writers, 316
—— named, 78
Markets, 170, 173
Mathieson Alkali Works, 195, 196, 197, 198, 199, 267
Medical Society, 313
Meeks Spring, 77
Methodist Church, 137, 305
Middle Fork Baptist Church, 130
Middle Fork Valley, 2
Middle Valley Settlers, 26, 27
Miles, Rev. G. W., 144, 145, 168
——, G. W., Jr., 168, 229
——, Mattie Morgan, 230
——, Vincent M., 230
Miller, D. C., 88, 136, 157, 162
——, Phipps, 157
Mills, 173, 174, 176
Montgomery County, 76

Morgan, Mrs. Mary Blessing, 27
——, W. M., 104, 153
——, Mrs. H. L., 258
Moore, Andrew, 103
——, Dr. W. W., 124
Mt. Carmel Methodist Church, 145
Mt. Zion Church, 121, 133, 146
Music teacher, 152
Myers, Uncle Billy, 178

Mc

McCarty's Mill, 24
McClure, Samuel, 246
McCormack, Gilbert, 127
McDonald, J. V., 242
McGhee, W. N., 367
McKee, Dr. T. K., 290
McMahon, Edward, 125
McMullin, La Fayette, 106, 167
——, Mrs. Mary Wood, 108
McReynolds, Samuel, 123

N

Natural Bridge, 10
Neff, W. N., 293
Nelson family, 374
Nicks Creek, 122, 133
Nicks Creek Presbyterian Church, 127
Nitrogen Products Co., 267
N. & W. R. R., 229
North Holston, 24, 361

O

Olinger, Jonathan, 243

P

Pafford, J. R., 128
Palmer, Geo. W., 171, 195, 196, 288, 337
——, Rev. David, 154
Patriot, The, 166
Patton, Col. James, 1, 5, 6, 7, 282
Pendleton, James F., 80, 92
——, W. C., 11, 166, 169
——, Rev. Jos., 153
——, Lucinda, 153
——, A. G., 162, 165, 236
Perryville Chapel, 149
Peters, W. E., 231
Petition for County, 77
Plaster Banks, 171, 205
Pleasant Hill Lutheran Church, 133
Point Pleasant Campaign, 48, 50
Police patrol, 235
Polk-Clay Campaign, 104, 287
Pollard, Gov. John Garland, 345
Poole, Aunt Mary, 257
Poor, provision for, 82

INDEX

Poston, John C., 89
——, Richard, 24
Pratt, Washington, 244
Presbyterian Pastors, 124, 126
Preston, Capt. John M., 126, 258, 364
——, Mrs. John M., 126
——, Capt. Chas., 183
——, Gen. Francis, 103, 152, 193, 334
——, Robert, 23
——, Thos. L., 194, 336
——, Walter, 109
——, Col. Wm., 51, 53, 102, 287
——, Dr. R. J., 277, 313
——, W. C., 334, 365
—— House, 368
—— Graveyard, 371
—— Parish, 149
Primitive School, 151
Pruner, Walter, 301
Pruner, Madison, 302

Q

Quarries, 203, 206

R

Railroad meeting, 277
Readjusters, 105, 110
Readjusters convention, 111
Rector, Jas., 237
Red Cross, 267
Reith, W. A., 124
Rhodes, E. A., 184
Rhea, J. B., 305
Rice, A. C., 150
Ricks, Jas., 264
Richardson, W. L., 244
——, Geo. W., 88, 90, 156, 251
——, Jno. W., 113
——, Robt. A., 90, 111, 233
——, Robt. M., 29, 128, 156
——, Wm., 28, 29
Richardson's Chapel, 146
Rich Valley, 2, 51
—— Settlers, 30
—— Church, 125
—— Baptist Church, 129
Ristine, A. W., 206
Roanoke-Times Editorial, 348
Roberts, E. L., 81, 351
Roberts Family murdered, 53
Roberts' Mill, 146
Robinson, Douglas, 381
——, Mrs. Corinne R., 381
Roland's Creek, 1 22
Roosevelt, Theodore, 381, 390
——, Theodore, Jr., 389
——, Elliott, 383

Rosenbaum, Gen. Otho, 266
Rouse, C. B., 226
Royal Oak, 4, 16, 17, 24, 51, 103, 151
Royal Oak Church, 22, 63, 120, 123
Russell, Wm., 59, 101, 102, 130, 193, 335
——, Madam Elizabeth, 63, 138, 151, 261
Rye Valley, 2, 7
—— Settlers, 30

S

Saltville, 7, 192, 333
—— Doctors, 337
—— Mayors, 338
—— Methodist Church, 338
—— Presbyterian Church, 126
—— settlers, 336
Salt Works, 193, 194, 195
Salley, Peter, 10
Sanders, Marvin, 172
——, R. K., 204
——, James, 283
—— family, 289, 336
Scherer, Dr. J. J., 132
——, Dr. J. J., Jr., 136, 158
Scott Brothers, 312
——, John, 30
——, E. A., 92
Seaver, Geo., 302
——, M. M., 184
——, W. C., 161, 183
Seven Mile Ford, 3, 364
Seven Mile Ford Presbyterian Church, 126
Sexton, T. K., 122
——, Wm. C., 80, 81, 147
——, Legrand, 122
——, Mrs. Legrand, 237
——, John, 306
—— family, 354
——, D. T. C., 357
Shanklin, J. R., 4
Shannon, Chas., 339
Sheffey, Mrs. Eleanor, 123
——, Jas. W., 90, 106, 107, 165, 236, 240
——, Jno. P., Sr., 92, 165, 306
—— family, 326
——, Rev. Robt., 359
Shelton, F. B., 144
Shugart, Zachariah, 174, 298
——, Henry, 398
Sinclair, Charles, 3, 6
Sinclair's Bottom, 4
Sinclair's Bottom Church, 120, 129
Slemp, Frederick, 375
Smith, Maj. Geo., 262, 301

INDEX

Smyth, Alexander, 73–76
———, Rev. Adam, 73
——— County Fair, 171
——— Blues, 236
——— Home Guards, 242
——— County Telephone Co., 306
Snavely, John, 122
South Fork Settlers, 30
Southern Gypsum Co., 205, 363
Southwestern Turnpike, 224
Sparks, Jas. R., 205
Spiller, F. P., 298
———, W. H., 298
Spratt family, 345
Spratts Creek, 29
Sprinkle, O. C., 306, 311
Spruce Creek Presbyterian Church, 127
St. Jas. Lutheran Church, 135
St. Mathews Church, 133
St. Paul's Episcopal Church, 149
Staley, H. B., 176
———, H. B. Co., 174
———, W. S., 175, 288
Staley's Creek, 24, 78
Stalnaker, Samuel, 6, 7, 8
State Roads, 226
Stephenson, J. G., 168
———, J. W., 172
Stoneman's Raid, 246
Stuart, Henry C., 112, 337
———, W. A., 195, 196, 205, 337
———, John, 230, 337
———, Dale, 337
Sugar Grove, 8, 373
Sugar Grove Christian Church, 150
Sulphur Springs, 287
Survey Lists, 31 to 44

T

Tate, Dr. Thos., 23, 174, 351
———, Gen. Wm., 102, 352
———, Jas. D., 147
Tate's Chapel, 147
Taylor, John, 23
Taylor Campaign, 105
Teas, W. H., 191
Tevis, Mrs. Julia, 138
Thomas, Abijah, 125, 177, 180
——— Bridge, 3, 125, 181
———, Capt. Jas. M., 242
——— family, 326
———, J. E., 172, 176
———, Thomas, 78
———, Mrs. Freelove, 78
Thompson, Capt. Jas., 282

Thornton, J. L., 310
Tory Warfare, 26, 59, 63, 72, 73
Town House, 6, 7, 50, 80, 286, 288
Twombly, W. H., 168

U

Umbarger, W. L., 385
United Confederate Veterans, 237
University of Virginia, 230, 231, 341, 342

V

Vance Co., 291
Vance, Jas. L., 291, 293
Van Meter, Misses, 158
Venable, M. P., 167
———, R. J. and Bros., 166
Va. and Tenn. R. R., 227
Va. Southern R. R., 229
Va. Table Works, 184

W

Walker, Thos., 5
Walker's Creek Presbyterian Church, 29, 129
Ward, Dr. E. B., 360
———, Robert, 232, 375
Washington County, 101
Wassum, C. S., 309
Waters, Wilburn, 376
Watson, E. S., 237, 302
Weeping Willow Tree, 352
Weiler Dept. Store, 309
Whitehead, J. B., 182
———, Mrs. Jerome, 156
White Oak Branch School, 155
Wilder, F. A., 206, 363
Wilderness Road, 226, 368
Williams, Jenkins, 375
———, Robt., 172
Wilson, W. V., 302
Wise, John S., 105
World War Muster Roll, 105
Wood, Jas., 5
Woolen Mills, 182
Woolsey, Thos., 29, 129
Wright, Dr. Geo. A., 278, 282
———, John, 167
Wythe County, 76

Y

Yankee Raid, 241

Z

Zeta Tau Alpha Sorority, 351

www.ingramcontent.com/pod-product-compliance
Lightning Source LLC
Chambersburg PA
CBHW071941220426
43662CB00009B/947